SLOW TECHNOLOGY READER

WITH CONTRIBUTIONS BY

Paula Albuquerque
Kader Attia
Aïsta Bah
Scott Benesiinaabandan
Pacôme Béru
Cláudio Bueno
Derrais Carter
Raven Chacon
Joana Chicau
Guy Cools
Laura Coombs
Siobhán K. Cronin
Will Daddario
Edwidge Danticat
Thierno Dia
Mamadou Taslim Diallo
Henriette Essami-Khaullot
Silvia Federici
Mariana Fernández Mora
Ella Finer
Jem Finer
Mashinka Firunts Hakopian
Dakin Hart
Faïza Hirach
Candice Hopkins
Christine Hvidt
Carol R. Kallend
Theun Karelse
Danel Khojayeva
Suzanne Kite
Fran Kourouma
Jaron Lanier
Jason Edward Lewis
Pia Lindman
Gļeb(s) Maiboroda
Pierre Marchand
Michael Marder
Nanako Nakajima
Florence Okoye
Marina Orlova
Jogi Panghaal
Moisés Patrício
Rory Pilgrim
Elisabeth (elieli) Raymond
Milady Renoir
Oscar Santillán
Laurel Schwulst
Mindy Seu
Camila Sposati
Christel Stalpaert
Corey Stover
Melita Stover Janis
Foluke Taylor
Alberto Isifin Tchama
Ovidiu Țichindeleanu
Rolando Vázquez Melken
Evelyn Wan
Halidou Wuandaougo
Arkadi Zaides
Joanne Zerdy
Martín Zícari

SLOW TECHNOLOGY READER
A Tool for Shaping Divergent Futures

Carolyn F. Strauss (ed.)

Valiz, Amsterdam

How can my tomorrow be saved?
By the velocity of electronic time
*or by my desert caravan slowness?**
—Mahmoud Darwish

For Palestine

* Darwish, Mahmoud. *Mural*. Translated by John Berger and Rema Hammami. Verso, 2009.

CONTENTS

CONTENTS

CONTENTS

For Slow Technology

Carolyn F. Strauss

Look at us! We are still untired! Our hearts know no weariness because they are fed with fire, hatred, and speed! Does that amaze you? It should, because you can never remember having lived! Erect on the summit of the world, once again we hurl our defiance at the stars![1]
—Filippo Marinetti, 1909

Move slow and heal things.[2]
—Khadijah Abdurahman, 2023

1 The 'Manifesto of Futurism' was a passionate proclamation of the virtues of the machine world, the glory of war, and the dominance of man over Nature. Marinetti and his gang were by no means unique in staking their quest for modernity on such ideas, but they were perhaps the first to assign them a name that we now know so well: "speed." Strauss (2014), 82.

2 Abdurahman.

In the stillness of early morning, I sit down at my table to gather thoughts for this essay. The table is a modest, reliable object that came to me—or, rather, that I had the means to acquire—in part thanks to the wonders of technology. The lamp standing next to the table and the light it emits owe a debt to technology too. The gas and flint that light the flame on my stove, the carefully-curved edges of a small metal coffee pot that sits atop the flame, the precisely-ground grains I've just spooned into it, and even the spoon itself—all the result of hundreds, even thousands, of years of human technological development. Now I bring a ceramic cup to my lips, pulling the woven blanket more snugly around my waist as I conjure thoughts and translate them through the tips of my fingers into symbols, watching them appear, as if by magic, on the smooth surface of a screen, comfortably back-lit. In the next week or so, by another seeming stroke of magic, the resulting groupings of words will scatter into lots of tiny bits to travel across invisible networks, ping-ponging around the planet before reassembling (just across town), joining the other texts alongside which this one eventually will be typeset, printed, and bound. Soon thereafter, tucked within the solid matter of a book, these very words again will be sent out into the world, traveling more slowly this time across land and sea, until they finally come to nestle in hands like yours. There—here, at this very moment—they are being decoded yet again, this time by that ever-fascinating organ that is the human brain (yours), supported by the texture of the paper that's firing up the receptors in your fingertips, and mediated by an inky substance that's calibrated to meet both the surface of the page and your gaze that alights upon it.

For the last two decades, I have dedicated my life and work to ways of being Slow,[3] and more specifically to a field of inquiry and experimentation that I refer to as Slow research. The term is used not merely to denote a decelerated pace—literally slowing down—as a much-needed response to the dominant pace of contemporary life,[4] but also, much more broadly, as an encouragement to look at the world through an expanded spatial, relational, and temporal prism. It is an incitement to cultivating tools for sensing complexity, for tuning into more varied registers of pace and duration, for amplifying subtler voices or less visible positions, and for holding ourselves more accountable to the ecologies with which our lives and activities are entwined—both in space and across time. This is some of what unfolds at Slow Research Lab, a multidisciplinary research and curatorial platform that engages thinkers, artists, and activists from diverse backgrounds in multivalent encounters that take form as conversations, workshops, exhibitions, study experiences, and physical interventions (including books like this one). The platform aims to provide a generous and generative space for such encounters to take place, as well as for those involved to discover new dimensions of their own praxis.

3 At Slow Research Lab, we write 'Slow' with a capital S to denote the enlarged (and perpetually unfolding) meanings that the term holds for us.

4 Almost paradoxical is that slowing down often enables a clarity of mind that ultimately can catalyze the acceleration of one's projects: moments of epiphany that open new pathways.

I feel good about this work and the meaning it brings to my life and to others through its attempts to cultivate new horizons of thinking and creativity, and in doing so perhaps to enlarge the boundaries of human consciousness. Yet aspects of that work remain beholden to the dominant systems and structures it aims to resist, facilitated by a range of technologies that are their progeny—such as those tools and techniques required to complete the operations described in my opening paragraph here. I also am acutely aware that many of the technologies in question are far from neutral in how and by whom they came to be.[5] They are made possible in part by the dirty business of fossil fuels, at the expense of the biodiversity that helps our planet maintain its delicate balance. They exist thanks to processes of extraction that leave gaping holes in the ground and toxic sludge in their wake, inflicting damage on communities of life long after the activity has ceased and the prospectors have moved on. And, despite how intangible some of these processes may seem, they rely on continuously moving an enormous volume of materials around the planet on gas-guzzling vehicles that choke both air and sea with their putrid exhales, as well as on copious amounts of precious clean water to sustain the sprawling data centers that host the aforementioned ping-ponging. All of this is happening at a bewildering scale made possible by an accumulation of capital that was built on the backs of human slaves.

5 'Technologies result from a series of specific decisions made by particular groups of people in particular places at particular times for their own purposes. As such, technologies bear the imprint of the people and social context in which they developed.' Wajcman, 22.

Tracing this lineage, a direct link can be made from those horrible histories to the coffee in my pretty porcelain cup. I suspect that the clay to make the cup was procured through a process of permanently disrupting delicate layers of the earth's crust,[6] just as I am pretty sure that the blanket that warms my waist was woven by a machine the likes of which once displaced (and denigrated the dignity of) craftspeople for the sake of a more 'efficient'[7] supply of identical twin blankets. All of these thoughts are unfolding in a comfortable room in the capital city of a country that still would be a wetland were it not for feats of technical engineering underwritten by riches gained through colonial conquest—the same pot of money that eventually came to help pay for this book. And I would be remiss if I failed to acknowledge, in my use of terms like 'my' and 'acquire' in the first sentences of this text, the ease with which I employ a lexicon of possession (and dispossession) that are a legacy of those same forces.

6 Artist Lara Almarcegui details this process in her essay 'Clay Extraction Operation, Quarry Richaume Sud, Puyloubier,' a 'melancholic meditation on the irreversible transformation of rock and mountains.' Almarcegui, 41.

7 At Slow Research Lab, we often point out how terms like 'efficiency,' 'productivity,' and 'success' have been narrowly defined to fit the logics of capitalism. A Slower approach to those terms reveals possibilities for understanding (and using) them in more holistic ways.

All of the above is both humbling and troubling. And yet, on most days, I go on drinking coffee (the one currently in my cup is from Guatemala, 9000 km from where I sit), my 'smart' phone (made in China, using components from 43 countries) gets plugged into a wall socket every night, and at least once a year I knowingly fork over money to have one of the aforementioned gas-guzzlers (Boeing A320, operated by KLM courtesy of same pot of money) fly me halfway around the planet to spend time at my grandparents' cottage by the sea (in a place that, not all that long ago, was taken by force from the people who had subsisted there for upwards of 10,000 years).[8] In reflecting thus, I am confronted both by my incredible privilege(s) and by what writer Daisy Hildyard has called 'the second body': an 'uncanny global presence' distributed across a myriad of other bodies—near and far, both geographically and in time—with which my 'first' body (the one sitting here at my table) is inextricably intertwined.[9] We—that is, my body here and those extensions of my body out there—are bound up in an uneasy contract that includes and also is fulfilled by a wide range of technologies.

8 The place in question is on the fragile edge of a great continental shelf, its other edge giving way to an ocean that is host to a thickness of life we humans will never fully perceive. Long before it became famous for the 'information superhighway,' this area was part of what was known as the 'kelp highway,' a thriving ecological corridor hospitable to a range of species migrations and settlements.

9 'We might speak vaguely of global connections; of the emission and circulation of gases; of impacts. And yet, at some microscopic or intangible scale, bodies are breaking into one another. ... Your first body could be sitting alone in a church in the centre of Marseille, but your second body is floating above a pharmaceutical plant on the outskirts of the city, it is inside a freight container in the docks, and it is also thousands of miles away, on a flood plain in Bangladesh, in another man's lungs.' Hildyard, 16.

Meanwhile, even as I write this, not far down the road from my grandparents' home, the engines of the digital world are furiously churning. They've been at it for several decades, but there was a turning point of sorts when, in the early aughts, the motto 'Move fast and break things' was proudly taken up by both tech entrepreneurs and the investors who poured cash into their ventures. They justified their brazen embrace of speed and demolition—bearing a distinct echo of the hubris that had driven Filippo Marinetti and his Futurist comrades (the original 'tech bros') a century prior—with the exciting developments that it rapidly yielded. And in the tiny blip of planetary time that has passed since then, that very small subset of humanity has done an outsize job of making as well as breaking things. Unsurprisingly, the technological innovation born of that bold ethos[10] is celebrated with scant mention of the collateral damage—lives and livelihoods harmed, enormous stores of energy drained, mountains of waste—and the people involved rarely take responsibility (or are held accountable) for the residual effects that their choices inflict into the future. Instead, in the name of 'progress,' the high-tech industry minimizes their contributions to the steady and cumulative undermining of the Earth's complex and wondrous biosphere that makes all human life and activity possible. Its most sophisticated offspring are party to war, genocide, and epistemicide—the eradication of entire knowledge systems—perpetuating its shameful entwinement with the military-industrial complex. And with every advance it becomes better and better at surveilling and manipulating **us**—the ones it purports to be serving (and even saving). The whole thing is mad—and **maddening**—and yet here I am, composing this essay on one of the sleek commodities that has issued from all the madness.

10 While many lay blame on the particular individual who is said to have coined the phrase, such irresponsible whims of today's tech industry carry in their DNA the centuries-old playbook of colonial expansion, including insidious patterns of misogyny and anti-blackness that were baked into them. The same was true of Marinetti, whose manifesto explicitly cites 'contempt for women' and 'fighting … feminism.' Marinetti.

So where do I begin to tell the story of 'Slow technology'? Well, I have begun to do so here by exposing some of those fraught relationships, along with my feelings of culpability for going along with as much of it as I do, even as I know that it has not been mutually consented to by most of the others (human and other-than-human) involved. Approaching anything, including technology, through a Slow lens is not only to literally slow down the pace at which we engage with it, but also to cast a wider net, which includes taking stock (as I have begun to do here above) of the many ways that our bodies and our actions are caught up, embedded, implicated, and contaminated in space and also across time—and the role that technology plays in that entanglement. A Slow approach to technology also means interrogating who is included and who is missing, looking critically and reflexively at the limited range of bodies and subjectivities that have designed, built, and deployed many of the technologies that come to be used by all the rest of us—and equally to interrogate both the power structures they uphold and the market forces that reward them.[11] Importantly, that includes accounting for the ways that we ourselves may be complicit in or the beneficiaries of those forces, requiring us to look more closely at our own habits of using technology (of all sorts, not only the digital kind), or ways that a fascination with what the current lot can do may be blinding us to its odious underbelly. Our digital footprint[12] (as ephemeral as it may sound) is very much a part of the 'second body' described above, with every click and stream and voice command eating up non-renewable resources and polluting the Earth. If we don't wrestle with how our choices and behaviors are part of the problem, their effects will only become more pronounced. Making a commitment to do that reckoning is part of thinking through and with Slow technology. We practice Slowness together when we agree to witness each other in the discomfort of that process and when we consciously decide to seek other ways forward: joining to imagine the world(s) we want to live in, and committing to building tools and practicing techniques to get us there—a process that for some may begin by picking up a volume like this one.

11 Here I'm referring not only to recently emerging digital devices and artificial agents, but also to much earlier technologies that echo in the present: those of colonial conquest—ships built, maps used, languages imposed upon the oppressed—as well as those machines of the industrial revolution that fueled further expansion.

12 In his essay, 'A Foot in the Sludge,' Andreas Broeckmann evokes 'The romantic tableau of deceleration at the end of modernity is the (anthropomorphic) carbon footprint, which (atavistically) hails walking speed as the measure not of acceleration, but of survival in the 21st century.' Broeckmann, 72.

This book is an invitation—indeed a provocation—to consider a fuller spectrum of what technology is and can be, and to reach toward greater depths of awareness and more joyful and abundant realms of experience as we—you, me, us, humanity—collectively unfold our technological future. Many of the technologies it describes may not be as attention-grabbing as the latest fancy gadget or flying car—they are, after all, in less of a rush—but these are crucial sources of a special kind of sustenance that can help us to navigate the entangled realities of a planet in crisis. With them, and with this book, I hope you'll feel inspired to navigate forward more consciously and creatively, fueled by curiosity and conviction, in dialogue with positions that may be different from your own, and remaining open to whatever may follow, with trust and in the spirit of not-knowing: that ever-enticing, nebulous field of (Slow) possibility within and across which we all meet.

These pages are a reminder that, however tumultuous it all may feel, this particular chapter of human history has barely begun to be written. Let us proceed together, **Slow-ly**...

A Tool for Shaping Divergent Futures

By the end of the twentieth century, 'technology'[13] | had come to be synonymous with the digital: computers and modems, bulletin board systems and the world wide web. Today, a quarter of the way into the twenty-first, the techno-sphere is increasingly intertwined with the biological and the social, the geological and the atmospheric, reaching even the remotest corners of the planet and the most intimate layers of our lives. The scale of it is hard to fathom, even as it continues at an unprecedented pace, and the mix of excitement and anxiety it has aroused is well-founded. At the same time, it's important not to lose sight of how recent these developments are, and moreover of the fact that they are far from the sole markers of human technological prowess. Looked at through timescales of human civilization—let alone of the Earth—it is far too early in the temporal scope of things to accept the current state of affairs as the primary indicator of what technology can be or may deliver into the future. To do so would be to fall for another deception of the 'fast' world, which wants to convince us that its way of doing things is the only path forward.[14]

13 The word has its origins in the Greek word τέχνη (*tékhnē or techné*) meaning art, skill, or craft. Several contributors to this volume use this term instead of 'technology' to evoke associations beyond the digital.

14 This is an aspect of what Donna Haraway has long referred to as the 'god trick,' later differently nuanced by Édouard Glissant as 'continental thought.' Both refer to the realm of power structures that imagine themselves as encompassing the totality of the lived experience of the world. Haraway, 189; Glissant (2009), 45.

This book aims to offer a more wholesome perspective—and decisive glimmer of hope—on the potentials of the technological moment. It points to Slow forms of technology that nourish rather than diminish, that are vehicles of care rather than crassness, and that are animated by a more diverse assembly of 'intelligences' than those currently on offer in the digital realm. It imagines a future in which we have wrenched the reins of technological development from the hands of those who acted so recklessly, committing instead to building technology otherwise, to working toward more just and reparative outcomes, and to measuring 'success' not by metrics of capitalism but by measures of planetary wellbeing. It also paints a more diverse picture of emerging entities such as artificial intelligences: one in which they no longer mirror the limited thinking-knowing of the thin slice of humanity that drove their initial development, but rather have been trained on a spectrum of voices and embodiments, draw 'data' from a multiplicity of cultural and cosmological understandings,[15] and have come to model a fuller spectrum of relations. It posits a future in which we have scrapped the reductionist metaphors with which technology had been encoded as well as the limited vocabularies we used to describe it—insisting instead on technologies that speak more complex languages and give us more nuanced ways to read/write about the ecologies that sustain us and the worlds we share—urging us toward ever-deeper levels of awareness, accountability, and participation in the living world. Not least, this book encourages a view of technology that encompasses not only a wider range of human inventiveness, but also the ingenious ways of other species, and even of the Earth herself—imagining ways that we might learn from and with them, perhaps even (with the assistance of our digital friends)[16] to unlock previously inaccessible dimensions of planetary existence.

15 It's very important to say here that not all knowledge can easily be distilled into data. Elsewhere, contributor Jason Edward Lewis has pointed out the problem of running language that is deeply embedded in culture and landscape through simple machine translation processing. Just as important is to acknowledge that when it comes to preserving certain kinds of knowledge, 'data' needs to be cared for; the prospect that it would not be accorded that care by the tech powers-that-be is one of the reasons some cultures refuse to share it.

16 The prospect of digital tools supporting our evolution in such a way is an exhilarating prospect, but also one that is prone to the pitfalls of the fast world. For example, Neda Atanasoski and Kalindi Vora remind us that 'The claim that technologies can act as surrogates recapitulates histories of disappearance, erasure, and elimination necessary to maintain the liberal subject as the agent of historical progress.' Atanasoski and Vora, 8.

These are the broad strokes of 'Slow technology' that I've asked the contributors to this volume to help me fill in by bringing their divergent perspectives and modes of practice to bear on these issues. The majority of them are artists or are actively working in dialogue with creative fields. This is important because it means they already are intimately acquainted with the business of challenging prevailing systems of thought and behavior and, moreover, that they are unafraid to lean into uncertainties, welcoming into their thinking and practice that which is fuzzy or indeterminate. They are receptacles of what contributor Foluke Taylor calls 'unruly yet generative conceptions of being.'[17] Within these pages are dialogues between their ways of knowing, an encounter of impulses, a world—or many worlds—imagined differently. The contributors here ask us to join them in sensing into subtly networked ecologies of knowledge as they weave together different geographies and situated perspectives. They encourage us to tune into a fuller repertoire of possible speeds, to interrogate our ways through different cultural but also temporal frameworks, to stretch our awareness to meet other scales of space and time. They remind us that, beyond the digital, our lifeworlds are saturated by technologies of another order, some of which have been shaping human history for millennia: foundational tools, like the ones for leveraging fire and fiber that forever changed the game of human survival, but also social and spiritual infrastructures that scaffold our earthly existence, spectral presences that bridge us with other realities, techniques of repair and healing that reconstitute us and bind our communities. Their essays call for a more radical and inclusive approach, one in which a fuller spectrum of identities, histories, bodies, and epistemologies inform how we think about technology's past, present, and possible futures. Thus, while some of the essays here trace the development of human technologies already in existence, others embark on more poetic and speculative wanderings, reaching toward an expanded palette of possible expressions for the machine intelligences emerging in our midst. Some do that by summoning and centering the potent presences of those whose identities have been overlooked (or absent) from algorithmic systems, while others look to intelligences and 'technological' attributes beyond the human, proposing ways of collaborating with vibrant actors (like minerals) and companion species (like plants) to enhance our lives as terrestrial beings.

17 In her book *Unruly Therapeutic*, she writes of 'Unruly as a road: a not-yet road.' Taylor, 20.

Remarkably, throughout the varied contents here, an array of bodies are tangibly felt, reminding us that even in the realm of the digital, they—and we—are ever present. We encounter dancing bodies, celestial bodies, the body of the Earth. We are confronted by wasted bodies, ravaged landscapes, the bodies of our dead. Contributors call forth tools for emancipation and restitution, techniques for reclaiming corporeal agency and freedom of movement, for wresting our bodies back from the systems that seek to control and surveil them. Through their texts, we encounter bodies in joyful acts of resistance, as well as in states of rest and recuperation. We learn about unique sounds and vibrations that bodies carry (or can be trained to emit) to resonate with others—in fleeting, 'live' moments but also outside of the usual bounds of space and time. We encounter spectral bodies that echo in the present, sometimes asserting themselves in ways that are inconvenient to the status quo, as well as an array of other-than human forms and agencies: ones that prompt us to acknowledge not only their being-ness but also their computational powers. And then, of course, there are the bodies of machines themselves: reclaimed from the clutches of capitalism and reimagined as purveyors of healing and vessels of love.

Equally remarkable are the powerful threads of witnessing, care, and solidarity that run through the DNA of this book. Whether tracing technological developments of ancient times, the more recent history of cybernetics, or emergent potentials in evolutionary computing, in one way or another all of the contributions point to **who** shapes technology and the **possible relations** that might govern it. The examples they offer suggest a richness of representation and connection that often are absent in digital artifacts and systems. Several of the writings in this volume work to expose those missed opportunities, but more importantly, they turn it around: offering robust, life-affirming responses to technology's blind spots and willful omissions.[18] I like to think that they practice what feminist film scholar Barbara Zecchi evocatively refers to as 'filling (feeling) the archival void'[19]—a phrase coined by the happy accident of her difficulty pronouncing the word 'filling' with her Italian accent. With this phrase, Zecchi calls upon us to do the crucial work of addressing the gaps in archives, libraries, and historical records, to fill them in with missing data. At the same time, 'filling (feeling)' is an incitement to **feel into** what is missing, casting our imaginations (as well as our hearts) into those spaces: reaching toward the warmth of missing bodies, listening attentively and patiently for the soundings of those whose voices and stories have been suppressed or overlooked,[20] care-fully sensing our way into a more inclusive, radically affectionate[21] future. Through 'filling (feeling),' we begin to access more complex textures of (and relationship with) digital technology: conjuring alternative (Slow) futures in which a fuller cast of characters has infiltrated the old scripts, new coordinates are superimposed on the old maps, and the libraries of data from which digital systems formulate their view of the world have become annotated with a thick impasto of fresh impulses, thoughts, and experiences. As such, our technologies can become loci of what contributor Rolando Vázquez Melken elsewhere has called 'radical re-remembering,' described as 'a form of relating to time that can bring radical change ... not preserving the status quo of the dominant power, but healing ... safeguarding the possibility of continuing to exist and to create alternative worlds.'[22]

18 This is not the first book to call for dislodging science and technology from their positions of privilege, nor the first to do so in the name of Slowness: in *Another Science is Possible: A Manifesto for Slow Science*, Isabelle Stengers proposes scientific methods that embrace 'messiness' instead of trying to fit into neat categories of taxonomy or the rigidity of linear thought processes.

19 Zecchi.

20 Writer Amitav Ghosh reminds us that, 'As soon as you take the non-human seriously, the idea of history as a documentary record completely crumbles. You have to allow for views that do not produce records.' Ghosh.

21 'Radical affection ... is a fiercely defended and ever-evolving practice not only of holding and caring for, but moreover of liberating thoughts, bodies, communities, and creativity in ways that support all of us in rising up to meet the urgencies of our times.' Strauss (2021), 17.

22 Vázquez Melken, 51.

In all these ways, this book attempts to sketch some of the contours of what 'Slow technology' is and can be, providing examples through which to ground and orient oneself. Not delimiting boundaries or charting a specific path forward, but gesturing toward possible futures and pointing to some of the tools that can help bring them closer. Thus each of the contributions is conceived as a site both of knowledge transmission and of generosity from which other dimensions of knowing are able to unfurl. In his seminal work *Poetics of Relation*, philosopher Édouard Glissant encouraged us toward such generous spaces when he wrote, 'Relation identity does not think of a land as a territory from which to project toward other territories but as a place where one gives-on-and-with rather than grasps.'[23] This book is intended to operate in that way too, as a space of endless possibilities born in dialogue with you, the reader.

23 Glissant (1997), 144.

If it does the work that I hope it may, you'll both recognize yourself in its pages and also allow it to transport you beyond your own four walls and the comfortable realm of your knowns as the worlds it describes rub up against the boundaries of the one you inhabit. My hope too is that its contents may serve as a portal to as-yet-undiscovered textures of your inner world, tickling and prickling (Slow) intuitions, arousing new stirrings within. Above all, this volume wants your unique position and lived experiences to inform its scope: your imaginative capacities drawing lines between the contents here and the particular knowledge you hold, forming other constellations and generating new meanings. That's an important reason why the margin here is as wide as it is and intentionally left mostly blank. It is offered as a canvas for you to add your own thoughts and annotations, to read/write your own life into both the fabric of the book and our collective, Slow technological future.

As I draw these thoughts to a close, a new awareness is arising. An image of this book as a cryptographic labyrinth, laden with keys for unlocking a more expansive reality—or, more aptly, for accessing a multitude of possible realities. And with this image, the realization that you, the reader, hold some of the keys. That, through your encounter with its physical substance, its design, the ideas and energies it carries, another level in that process of decryption is reached. As you read, new worlds are opening up. A richer, deeper, Slower technological future draws near. It feels palpably within reach.

References

Abdurahman, Khadijah. 'The Rain.' *Logic(s)*. May 17, 2023. logicmag.io/supa-dupa-skies/the-rain/.

Almarcegui, Lara. 'Clay Extraction Operation, Quarry Richaume Sud, Puyloubier: A 33-meter Approach to the Underneath.' In *Slow Spatial Reader: Chronicles of Radical Affection*, edited by Carolyn F. Strauss. Valiz, 2021.

Atanasoski, Neda, and Kalindi Vora. *Surrogate Humanity: Race, Robots and the Politics of Technological Futures.* Duke University Press, 2019.

Broeckmann, Andreas. 'A Foot in the Sludge: Remarks on the 20th Century Culture of Speed.' In *Catch Me! Grasping Speed*. Kunsthaus Graz and Verlag der Buchhandlung Walther Konig, 2010.

Ghosh, Amitav. 'Writing the Ocean.' Conversation with Nishat Zaidi and Dilip Menon as part of the Ocean as Method webinar streamed live on February 2, 2021. Video, 1 hr., 36 min., 34 sec. youtube.com/watch?v=tQQF0O3KB4M.

Glissant, Édouard. *Poetics of Relation*. Translated by Betsy Wing. University of Michigan Press, 1997.

Glissant, Édouard. *Philosophie de la Relation: Poésie en* étendu. Gallimard, 2009.

Haraway, Donna. 'Situated Knowledges: The Science Question in Feminism and the Privilege of Partial Perspective.' In *Simians, Cyborgs and Women: The Reinvention of Nature*. Routledge, 1991.

Hildyard, Daisy. *The Second Body*. Fitzcarraldo Editions, 2018.

Marinetti, Filippo. 'Manifesto of Futurism.' *Le Figaro*, February 20, 1909. booksontrial.com/the-full-text-of-the-futurist-manifesto/.

Russell, Legacy. *Glitch Feminism: A Manifesto*. Verso Books, 2020.

Stengers, Isabelle. *Another Science is Possible: A Manifesto for Slow Science*. Translated by Stephen Muecke. Polity Press, 2018.

Strauss, Carolyn F. 'Speed.' In *Routledge Handbook of Fashion and Sustainability*, edited by Kate Fletcher and Mathilda Tham. Routledge, 2014.

Strauss, Carolyn F. 'Seeking Radical Affection.' In *Slow Spatial Reader: Chronicles of Radical Affection*, edited by Carolyn F. Strauss. Valiz, 2021.

Taylor, Foluke. *Unruly Therapeutic: Black Feminist Writings and Practices in Living Room*. WW Norton, 2023.

Vázquez Melken, Rolando. 'Healing as Re-membering.' In *Q: Meanderings in Worlds of Mourning*, edited by Sophie Krier. Field Essays. Onomatopee, 2022.

Wajcman, Judy. *Feminism Confronts Technology*. Pennsylvania State University Press, 1991.

Zecchi, Barbara. 'Filling (Feeling) the Archival Void.' *Feminist Media Histories* 9, no. 4 (2023): 14–27. doi.org/10.1525/fmh.2023.9.4.14.

THREADS OF SLOW INQUIRY

Slow research comprises diverse modes of theoretical and practical investigation to support the unfolding of more expansive (Slow) technological futures. This volume hones in on five threads of inquiry chosen by its editor to encourage alternative readings of the contents here, as well as to inform considerations of 'Slow technology' more generally. For each of the contributor texts, a unique combination of those threads appears as terms placed along the bottom of the page spread. These are by no means definitive framings of the individual essays, but rather are offered as possible prisms through which to view new facets of them. When used as a device for navigating the book, those terms along the bottom edge additionally begin to illuminate some of the common ground shared across the varied contributions. The pages that follow here provide insight into the five threads. For each of them, there is a short prose text introduction, as well as a selection of related key words or phrases sourced from the contributors' texts. Together they are an incitement to approaching the book's contents in a more dynamic, nonlinear way—nudging readers along divergent paths of discovery and serving as impetus to further imaginings.

Humans exist in webs of relationships. Our very survival is linked to a complex layering of planetary ecology that has taken billions of years to evolve. We are social-emotional beings: we need one another in rich and varied ways. This is a richness that is denied by the rigid infrastructures of the 'fast' world, which are organized hierarchically, broken into fragments, governed by strict rules and binaries, and assessed by metrics of profit rather than measures of true prosperity. The technologies born of them follow suit: adhering to languages and logics that aim to maximize 'efficiency' and minimize the possibility of anomaly, error, or unpredictability. By design, those structures (and the technologies that do their bidding) foreclose on free expression and discourage more complex forms of relating. Slow research processes do the opposite. They work to recuperate the fragments of a broken world and re-nest them within intricate spatial and temporal relationships. Those Slow-ly built infrastructures also are more horizontal and inclusive, designed to stimulate encounter and dynamic interplay between a diversity of perspectives and practices, mirroring the way living systems metabolize new connections and become resilient.

Across this book are examples of technologies old and new that are sources of support and sustenance: forms that are sturdy, but adaptable; frameworks that are reliable, yet not so rigid as to be unchangeable; infrastructures that are enduring because they have been designed by consensus and made stronger through practice. The essays along this thread invite us to consider not only physical tools and techniques that scaffold our lives but also social technologies of care and solidarity that, in the words of contributor Silvia Federici, 'reconstitute us and regenerate us.' These include ways we affirm one another through intimate postures of listening and witnessing, as well as the spaces of refuge and conviviality in which we attend to one another and hatch new creative projects. Several contributors here reflect about the scaffolding that is afforded by language, such as the words and grammars we share to decode each other's thoughts and describe the world we see around us—and the new ones we may need to invent for describing the world we **would like** to see. They include the stories we tell that bind us to place and hold us accountable to our communities, as well as practices of commoning that nurture feelings of belonging to something bigger than ourselves. Among them are ancestral intelligences like poems, songs, recipes, and rituals—those intergenerational technologies of knowledge transmission that have sustained our species from early human history up to the digital age. Not least, they include the webs we weave with other-than-humans—intimate interdependencies with flora and fauna, the Earth and her atmosphere, as well as the ones that we someday might weave with machines. The essays here trace lineages of knowledge and constellations of connection across timescales and geographies to point to a broad spectrum of Slow technologies that fortify our existence—ones that have earned our trust, enliven the imagination, and carry a promise of more just and joyful futures.

abundance

accompaniment

afterlives

a Good Way

aide-mémoire

a mix of before and beyond
ancestors

asking for help

attending

belonging

bound by love

bridge between worlds

care-taking
ceremony

collective practices

comfort
commemoration
common world

connective tissue

corporeal powers

cosmos and microcosmos
courage

dialogue with the world
different histories

dignity

dreaming with
duration

earthy and ancient

entangled lineages

ethical care
everyday beacons

extended circle of relations

faith

fecundity

feeling of home

fluid constellations

furious love

gathered around

gentleness
gestures of care

gift of attention

holding space

hospitality

human and nonhuman elders

imaginary matrices

inheritance
inner states

intentionality
intergenerational space

intimacy
intuitions

kindness

kinship

language

learning trails

lineages

lived experience

love of the world

membranes
memory

minimal, slow forms
momentary comfort

mourning

multiplicity

natural cycles

natural limits

nested links
networks

not-knowing

others vibrate along

pattern recognition

planting seeds

powers of protection

proportionality
protocols

reciprocity

refuge

relationality

resonance

respite

rhizomes
rituals

sensing
sensuality

shared language(s)
sharing affections

silent learnings
simple pleasures

slow-made medicine

solidarity

songlines

spaces of visibility
space-times of coexistence

speaking with

spells

spiritual forests within

story

sympathetic relations

telluric force

tenderness

theater of human connections

the tools we make

the weave of reality
thinking with
third space

thriving above and below

trust

unknown wiring

unseen forces

vastness of perspective

warm data

welcoming
what came before

witnessing

As the power and ubiquity of the digital grows, and as artificial agents steadily infiltrate our lives, we are called upon to remember and gather around the many other, equally potent—if less visible—agents that accompany us through this earthly life: forces of nature and of the supernatural, apparitions from the past that echo in the present, envoys from beyond the veil. These, too, are a kind of technology, their enigmatic presences serving as devices that sharpen the intuition and keep our values in check. Several contributors to this volume carve out space for those otherworldly entities to (re-)assert their centrality in our life stories—sometimes proffering guidance and protection, while at other moments lending their boundlessness to bolster our capacities for meeting the turmoil of the contemporary moment. Some of the essays here, spanning diverse cultural traditions and cosmologies, invoke other-than-human beings who are the central protagonists in sacred and ancestral practices, enforcing protocols and keeping us in alignment, stoking the fires of memory and igniting sparks of creativity. Others call forth more slippery and less predictable beings: shadowy shapeshifters that lurk outside the borders of dominant systems and ways of knowing, or that dazzle in the dark folds of histories from which they have been excluded, playfully taunting the taxon and, as curator Legacy Russell says, 'refusing to perform the score.'

Through their accounts, the contributors here also begin to locate certain 'ghosts in the machine'—those haunting presences that trouble digital culture and its logics, that threaten to destabilize algorithms, and murmur inconvenient truths about the slow violence of the industries fueling our digital habits. Drawing inspiration from filmmaker and political theorist Trinh T. Minh-ha's 'inappropriate/d other'—that liminal presence who is inappropriate and also cannot be appropriated—this thread running through the book challenges prevailing narratives of the machine, re-locating the sensuous body in the digital realm and resurrecting spectres of early feminist technoscience such as the cyborg. They convene within these pages not only to keep us company, but also to awaken invisible strands of knowledge held latent inside each of us—spectres that shimmer within. Together with the myriad of others inhabiting this book, they offer glimpses of what anthropologist Marisol de la Cadena has called 'the complex we'—a rich and unruly heterotopia of collective possibility.

accompaniment
accumulation of energy
active elements

afterlives

a grandiose choir

a life of its own

ambiguity

ancestors

ancient and vibrant

beyond the boundary
Black note-making
blurring

bridge between worlds

cognitive spring(s)

consciousness

contingency

decentralized
declaration

differently abled
digital hum

disorderliness

divergence

dysfunctional pride

embodiments

energetic events

entanglement
errancy

extending the range of the ‘who’
extraterrestrial

forensics

furious love

ghosts

glitch

haunting presence

hidden between

holographic aunties

immaterial worlds

incompatible truths

inner vitality
inscrutable tools
instability

intimacy

inverting the agent
invisibility

ir/rational
irrepressibility

liminal space

membranes

messiness

monster(s)

mystery

new lifeforms and beings

objects as subjects

other-than-brain

point of view of the Earth

possible history

powers of protection

provocation

reading omens

refusal

residue
resilience

secrets

sentience

shadows
shapeshifting

side-effects

signals

situated at the border
slippage

somewhere away from our attention

spatial secrets

spirits

that which cannot be grasped

the right to remain undefined

transgression

underlying potential

unknown wiring

unseen forces
unsettled definitions

warnings

whispers

Our planet is a symphony of rhythms: interwoven expressions of human and non-human with varying metabolisms, velocities of movement, and sequences of exchange. Across this book is a wide variety of soundings and silences, pacings and intensities, stillnesses and flows. These include the steady cycles of the natural world and the circadian rhythms that undergird our daily lives, but also the ones that we generate as we move through space and interact with others. In this volume, rhythm also pertains to the cadences of how we show up for one another and take care of ourselves: unhurried states of attention, the uneven pace of teaching and (un)learning, the beats of belonging.

Contributors here take us beyond the predominant space and time metrics with which contemporary life (including the digital) is encoded by amplifying alternatives, such as the wise ways of older bodies and the wanderings of divergent minds. Their writings point to enduring patterns rooted in particularities of place, family, community, and culture, while also prizing spontaneous surges of desire and creativity, errantry, and unpredictable movement. Readers are encouraged to attune to the rising and falling of language of the essays here, as well as to the instances of poetry, song, and musicality that are central to several of them. Such contributions call us to imagine circulations of breath, the textures of vocal chants, and the soundings of musical instruments, and also the variable rhythms of improvisation: that form of making-doing that is in dialogue, always in motion, generative, evolving, open to the unknown. Alongside these, the tempos and timestamps of an array of non-human agents make themselves known, urging us to align with their rhythmic ways of being. Contributors evoke the subtle unfurling of plant beings and the hum of their attendant rhizomes, the staccato starts and stops of seismic activity, and the slow unfolding of geological time. They invite us to stretch the imagination to follow the clicks and melodies of whales along their migrations, and just as intently to tune into the speed of electronic networks, the thrum of automation, and the half-lives of toxic waste. Not least, this volume welcomes the diverse personal rhythms of readers as they encounter the substance of this book—each individual with their own pace and ways of navigating it—as well as the new rhythms of dialogue that may be generated as they (after Katherine McKittrick et al) 'think across and with tracts of knowledge.'

Consciously orienting toward a diverse repertoire of rhythms, such as those found in this book, simultaneously helps us to better recognize those paces of our lives (including our interactions with technology) that are rushed, involuntary, or the result of decisions made by somebody else. This is a first, vital step toward recuperating agency and imagining the rhythmic potentials of our digital future. The contents here are an incitement to ditch the monotony of the metronome and play in the folds of time, trusting in processes of gestation—that is, right timing—and embracing the mysteries of the non-beat.

contemplation

continuous correspondence

conviviality

gathered around

afterlives

getting lost

a Good Way

gift of attention

dance of relationality

grieving-healing
groundlessness

aligning with the cosmos

heartbreak

anchoring in wonder

differently abled
digital hum
dignity

an idea about how to be

hospitality

a praxis of being

arts of ripening

divergence
doing medicine
dreaming

imbalance

attunement

duration
dwelling in time

being present
belonging

infusion process

emergence

enactments
energetic events

breathing

errancy
ethical care

intuitive imagination

calmness
care-taking

inward process

circulation of struggles

co-creation
coexistence

joy

kinetic landscapes

collectivity

fecundity

flow

lasting yet fragile

communal states

fluid temporalities

liminal space

forgiveness

listening for alternatives
listening to the body

meeting place of ontologies
melodies

metabolisms
minimal, slow forms

moving within

natural cycles

never hurried

not a contest

ongoing experiments

others vibrate along

patience

performing the self

play
pluriversal times
poetry

postures

precarity

protocols

pulse

refuge
refusal

remembering
repair

resistance
resonance
respiration

rest

return
revelry

rituals

saying no

self-discovery

sentipensar

singular-plural

slow attention

slow processes of learning

sovereignty

spontaneity

stillness

temperatures of process
tenderness
tension
textures of contact

time traveling together

trust

unhurried

very slight

waiting

weaving together
welcoming

witnessing

RHYTHM

Recalibration is a course correction. An adjustment when we notice aspects of our existence and of the world we inhabit that are out of whack. At times, this can be achieved through a subtle shift in awareness, a minor fix akin to (in digital terms) a 'software update.' At others, a more elaborate 'system upgrade' is needed to make space in our lives for new dimensions of knowledge and the expanded capacities that go hand-in-hand with them. There are times, however, when neither of those is enough, because we have come to understand that the 'operating system' underneath it all is deeply flawed—and in need of a radical overhaul.

This thread running through the book compels us to look honestly and reflexively at our habits of mind and body, interrogating the assumptions and value systems upon which they rest, as well as the larger structures of which they are a part. And, when necessary, to commit to making a change. In that sense, recalibration is a matter both of consciously reclaiming personal time and pace and also of setting the collective along a better path. It asks that we cultivate methods to meaningfully counter the speed of contemporary life, and equally is a call for restitution and reparation—a reckoning with and making good on the injustices of the past. Among the essays here, recalibration refers to other modes of repair too, with several of them here exploring technologies—from plant medicines and ancestral presences to algorithmic systems—as purveyors of individual, collective, and also planetary healing. Their slate of remedies include prescriptions of rest for exhausted bodies, tools for restoring connections with living systems and tending to the wounds we have inflicted upon the Earth, and techniques of partnering beyond the human (including with machines) to nurture new paradigms of collective well-being. In this volume are strategies for disrupting discriminatory encodings of technological systems, as well as lessons in the arts of cutting, splicing, annotating, and 'glitching' to facilitate more complex and inclusive tellings of history. The writings here also speculate about possible recalibrations of tempo and temporality in the digital realm, proposing interactions that unfold at more diverse registers of speed and across longer (multigenerational and more-than-human) spans of time. They propose protocols for training machine intelligences on 'data' from a wide variety of sources, while also scrutinizing—and, when necessary, taking steps to revise—the logics they follow and the languages with which they are built. Toward that end, in this book are innovative approaches to scoring, choreographing, and coding with and for non-Western knowledge systems and non-normative positions to broaden the parameters of emerging digital spaces, as well as contributions that urge us to take up analog tools—like the ones some readers may use to mark up these pages—to write our own perspectives into the record.

Not least, several essays here evoke technologies of mourning as powerful catalysts to recalibrating our lives and reimagining the future. They point to techniques for metabolizing sorrow—whether in response to loss of human life or in the face of climate catastrophe—that can enable new qualities of being to emerge. This is a process that some psychologists refer to as 'positive disintegration,' which the late ecophilosopher Joanna Macy says occurs at every major inflection point in human history and is an essential step toward birthing new realities. 'However uncomfortable,' she explains, 'our "going to pieces" can open us up to new perceptions, new data, and new responses.' It is toward such a recalibration of our ways of thinking-sensing-knowing-relating that Slow research strives. This book offers a bold palette of technologies to help get us there.

accepting the unknown

adaptation

against the clock

a Good Way

alchemy

aligning with the cosmos

arranging

attunement

balance between worlds

beyond the boundary

breaking

bringing subtlety into

chanting down
circling back

co-becoming

collective practices

commemoration

composting

continuous correspondence

deceleration

declaration

de-instrumentalization

disrupting cartographies
dissolving hierarchies

dysfunctional pride

emptied from the inside

energetic reparations

errancy

evolving social bonds
expanding the liveable realm

fluid constellations

forensics
forgetting
forgiveness

generative movement

getting dissolved

giving space

healing
heartbreak

imperfection

infusion process

integration

intervening

invention
inverting the agent

leaps of time

listening for alternatives

losing learned time

making room

messiness

mourning

natural feelings
natural limits
negotiation

new vocabularies
night vision

offerings

pluriversal times

possibility of inclusion

praise

pretensions drop away
promise of rebirth
proportionality

pushing through toward life

radical gift-giving

recombinations
recovering complexity

refusal
reinvention

relinquishing agency

repair

resistance

responsiveness

restoring flow
retelling

ruptures

saying no

self-discovery

shaping a shared understanding

shift in attention

singular-plural

slowing down the workflow
slow-made medicine

space in the body

speaking with

starting over

storying ourselves

teaching flaws

threading together

transgression

unlearning
unpredictable movement

vastness of perspective

warm data

It is believed that humans can only perceive the tiniest fraction of all that is going on in the world around us, that we are steeped in a field of energy and information that our human instruments lack the capacity to grasp. Acknowledging this can be a relief at a time when those aspects of which we **are** aware feel increasingly precarious. Ours is an era in which uncertainty and restlessness abound, with digital technologies contributing to the discord: aiding and abetting the harm to ecosystems and social fabrics alike as they fuel evermore-rampant consumption, undermine respectful discourse, and unsettle truth. We must not look away from those things—indeed, it is crucial to our very survival that we take them on—but nor should we ignore the potencies that lie latent in the spaces and paces that exist beyond what we can perceive. Rather than descending into despair and burrowing further into our echo chambers, we must find ways to meaningfully open ourselves to the chaos and contradictions of the present moment—loosening our grip on what we purport to know and instead seeking out the unfamiliar and unrehearsed as thresholds to new realms of creativity and connection.

This thread running through the book is inspired by philosopher Édouard Glissant's 'poetics of trembling' or 'trembling thinking'—a way of moving through and resonating with the unpredictability of the world, where people with diverse identities meet not at fixed points of understanding but rather in and as 'whirlwinds of encounter.' For Glissant, trembling links people together not by the knowledge systems they mutually conform to, but rather by the space of the unknown and the unknowable that they share. Several of the contributors here take up that mantle, embracing ambiguity, leaning into that which cannot readily be seen or known, trusting what lies beyond. Destabilizing notions of 'authority,' their essays leverage the palpable tensions of the obscure and indeterminate as ground on which to build alternative forms of technology. They reach out tenderly toward the mysteries of the natural world in search of new algorithms to enliven our computational systems. They tap into cross-currents of historical and energetic events, inviting us to immerse in those charged spaces to feel for possible expressions of artificial agents.

They vigorously reject cartographies of exclusion in favor of 'deep mappings' and ever-unfolding fields of multiplicity through which alternative futures come into view. Those contributions—and this book as a whole—urge us to move beyond guarantees of certitude or stability and instead to join them in braiding knowledge and jumping timelines, gathering up technologies both ancient and (still-) emerging to access new dimensions of existence—even as we come to accept how much of it will forever be beyond our reach.

In this book, trembling also is a call to turn inward. To wade into the waters of the unknown that lie within, anchoring ourselves there as the waves and tremors of a wild, wonderful, troubled world roll over and through us. Glissant reminds us that 'we can no longer influence the world according to plans we've drawn up in advance.' The contents of this volume reach powerfully into the future through that lens.

against white noise

a language we don't know

ambiguity
a mix of before and beyond

anti-taxonomic

a step beyond

Black note-making

boundlessness

bridging opacities

complexity

consciousness

contingency

continuous seeking

cosmic acts of creation

curiosity

deeply unknown

de-materialization

different histories

digital hum

emergence

entanglement
errancy

evolutionary robots

exponential love

fantasy

feeling free

fracture

generative movement

glitch

groundlessness

hovering just beyond the edge
of understanding

immaterial worlds

impermanence

inscrutable tools
instability

irrepressibility

joy

leaps of time

looking for alternative worlds

magical thinking

messiness

momentary freedom

morphologically boundless

multiplicity
mystery

new vocabularies

not-knowing

other futures

paradox

planting seeds

poetry

possibility of liberation

radical gift-giving

re-enchantment

refusal

relinquishing agency

revelry

seeking

shifting time and scale

signalling an otherwise

spatial secrets

species horizons
speculation

spiritual forests within
spontaneity

techné for a new reality
telluric force

tension

the edge of chaos
the right to remain undefined

the un-structurable

thresholds of comfort

time portals

uncontrollable

unknowable

unsettled definitions

warm chaos

what might arrive

References

De la Cadena, Marisol. 'An Invitation to Live Together: Making the "Complex We".' *Environmental Humanities* 11, no. 2 (2019): 477-484. doi.org/10.1215/22011919-7754589.

Glissant, Édouard and Hans Ulrich Obrist/Institut du Tout-Monde. *The Archipelago Conversations*. Translated by Emma Ramadan. Common Era Inc., 2021.

Macy, Joanna. *World As Lover, World as Self: Courage for Global Justice and Ecological Renewal*. Parallax Press, 2007.

McKittrick, Katherine, Frances H. O'Shaughnessy, and Kendall Witaszek. 'Rhythm, or On Sylvia Wynter's Science of the Word.' *American Quarterly* 70, no. 4 (2018): 867-874. dx.doi.org/10.1353/aq.2018.0069.

Minh-ha, Trinh T. 'Introduction', '*Discourse* 8: *She, the Inappropriate/d Other*, no. Fall-Winter (1986-87) jstor.org/stable/i40165811.

Russell, Legacy. *Glitch Feminism: A Manifesto*. Verso Books, 2020.

RHYTHM RECALIBRATION TREMBLING

slow attention
space in the body
dance of relationality
yin and yang
natural cycles
aligning with the cosmos
energetic reparations
pluriversal times
meditation
contemplation
grieving
dreaming
looking for alternative
worlds
sentipensar
time traveling together
a praxis of being
against the clock

Restoration, Rest, and Respite

A Decolonial Praxis Against Capitalist Time

Evelyn Wan

Technology ties us to capitalist time. Clocks tell us when to head into the office, and calendars send us alerts for meetings. Ever-faster microchips are invented to cut down computation time, and so-called efficiency is hailed as one of the most important driving forces behind an ever-growing list of ride-hailing, food delivery, and so-called productivity apps.[1] At the same time, social media apps vie for our eyeballs and monetize our attention, stealing time away from ourselves. Health and wellness apps use data tracking to help keep us healthy and fit. But what really happens is that we reroute our senses of wellbeing from somatic awareness to informational streams on heart rate and step count to ascertain how we feel in our skin. Digital technologies that function on this logic encapsulates the dualism between mind and body, a long-standing hierarchy of knowledge brought on by Western modernity.

1 At the time of this writing, Uber has reached over 10,000 cities worldwide from car rides to e-bike rentals to food delivery, and its Asian-counterpart Grab calls itself the 'Everyday Everything platform' that covers food, groceries, package delivery, rides, e-payment, and even hotels.

Digital technologies are time technologies. As media scholar Wolfgang Ernst suggests, 'the power of clocks has migrated into the computer itself'.[2] Not only are computers intricate clocking machines that produce internal rhythms of processing that are completely removed from human perception, they also function to compress and accelerate time, automating tasks and predicting outcomes at superhuman speeds. Computational logic emphasizes rationality, and the rhythms of computation steadily perform the capitalist values of speed and efficiency. —

tempos of
technoscientific progress
p.257

2 Ernst, 181.

More importantly, digital technologies, like earlier time technologies, form a series of abstractions that remove us from our innate connection with nature. In the background, the Earth spins on, in an intricate dance of relationality with the sun and the moon and other planets, as natural beings enter and exit cycles of growth, repair, decay, and rebirth. There are sunrises and sunsets, time to wake, and time to sleep. And there are seasons—seasons to sow, to harvest, to let fields fallow and rest. But like casinos that trick customers with artificial daylight, calendars and clocks give us man-made references to time to latch on to. These references replace other potentialities of time consciousness, ones that align with natural cycles and the cosmos. As we socialize into this 'universal' clock and calendar time scheme, we lose sense of what time it truly is on the planet as well as our innate senses of time dictated by the body's rhythm. This effect is exacerbated by digital technologies—we stumble around in our built environments, our circadian rhythm disrupted by the exposure to lamps and screens, our awareness lured away from our bodies towards our gadgets. We scroll on our social media feeds, our attention spans reduced to the length of a TikTok dance, and we are prompted to pay to skip through twelve seconds of YouTube advertisements. Clocks and digital technologies form mediated senses of time, whose synthetic rhythms and durations replace time sensibilities tied to our bodies, as well as our immersion in nature and its cycles.

listening to languages and rhythms of the natural world p.211

As I landed on these conclusions at the completion of my PhD project on time, technology and biopower, I found myself yearning to break free from capitalist and digital time. I challenged myself to figure out ways to decouple my consciousness from capitalist technologically-mediated time, even if I could only manage for fleeting moments. This essay encapsulates my personal reflections on these attempts, and how in returning to myself, mind, body, and spirit, I attempt to carve out decolonial spaces of being in time that allows for restoration, rest, and respite from capitalist time.

searching for renewal and balance p.125

From One World Time to Ancestral Times

What time is it? The answer cannot be limited to the carefully kept Universal Time Standard, where the clocks and computer networks synchronized to it dominate our beings. This set of time belongs to the series of objectifications and standardizations that characterize the edifice of modern Western civilization. Clock time forms the infrastructure of Western modernity, one that was implemented and introduced to natives and to colored bodies in colonizing missions around the world. In Arturo Escobar's terms, clock time and technologized time is the time of colonialist one-worldism. To learn to decouple from One World Clock Time means that we begin a journey of decolonizing time itself, and to release it from the Western dualism of culture over nature, and to look for alternative worlds. —

journey of unlearning p.417

Escobar proposes to look to ancestral knowledges and traditions in this search for alternative worlds. He emphasizes the practice of sentipensar, used by activists in Latin America, 'a way of knowing that does not separate thinking from feeling, reason from emotion, knowledge from caring.'[3] Sentipensar in Spanish means to feel (sentir) and to think (pensar), a holistic approach that foregrounds embodied knowledges over the Western epistemological ideals of disembodied objectivity. In feeling-thinking new modalities of time consciousness, I turn towards my body and my cultural roots, to learn anew the wisdoms embedded in knowledge from bygone times. I embrace the need to move beyond Eurocentric conventions of science into a praxis of being.

3 Escobar, xxxv.

My first attempt was to break from the hegemony of the Gregorian calendar, a calendar tied to the sun, by returning to the traditional Chinese lunisolar calendars. Having grown up in Hong Kong, I am used to lunisolar calendars[4] where the moon is of equal importance. I always know when the moon peaks and wanes, and on the little rectangles of the calendar I mark my bleeding days as a menstruating cisgendered woman.

4 Funnily enough, complimentary lunisolar calendars are often handed out every lunar new year by banks and insurance companies in Hong Kong, a reminder that we are never far from the capitalist control of time.

In Chinese cosmology, the sun and the moon represent day and night, yang and yin, masculine and feminine energies. The moon cycle is seen to be tied with the female menstrual cycle, as they both last around twenty-eight to twenty-nine days. My Chinese herbal doctor chides me if my menstrual cycle deviates from this duration, as it is a sign that I have not been taking care of my body. Initially my desire to reconnect with the lunar calendar was only cognitive, but soon it became clear that there was no mind/body separation here if I were to take the inclusion of the yin energy of the moon seriously. The moon cycle has an extra layer of meaning for my reproductive rhythms, and I felt inclined to attend more closely to it. As the months went by, my cycle became synchronized to the moon cycle—bleeding when the moon is full and round, and ovulating when the skies are dark. Any deviation brings a reminder for self-care and contemplation, a clear signal that my body is out-of-sync with nature.

Another piece of crucial information found on the Chinese lunisolar calendar concerns seasonality. The Chinese calendar marks the transition moments for twenty-four seasons, known as solar terms in English, which is a much more intricate system than the four seasons in the Western world. Each term poetically names the weather and botanical conditions associated with that time of the year, at intervals of fifteen to sixteen days. For example, after the lunar new year marks the commence of spring, rainwater falls, then the insects awaken, and afterwards we reach spring equinox. Each solar term is further divided into three phases called pentads. At spring equinox, first the dark birds arrive, then thunder sounds, and then lightning begins. Dark birds refer to swallows that make their northward migration, thunder and lightning mark the onset of spring storms. The third pentad also refers to lightening, the prevalence of sunlight and the lengthening of daytime. Even though the lunisolar calendar is printed and designed much like its Gregorian counterpart, its content provides me a different way of telling time. It reminds me of our ecological interdependency with animals and insects, as well as with the cycles of growth and harvest of crops that are celebrated in traditional festivals.

In carving out space against One World Time through my ancestral knowledge, I recognized the seamless connection between this type of calendar technology and nature. I began to use my calendar less as a way to arrange my meetings and order my social life and more as a tool to access the natural rhythms that I could observe outside. From Gregorian calendars to digital Google calendars, the monotonous calendar grids decouple users from the reality of gradual fluctuations of seasons that a lunisolar calendar affords. If one follows Chinese seasonality closely, a new pentad is marked every five to six days. Rather than the repetition of Week 1 through to Week 52, one could follow the ebbs and flows of biological life cycles captured, re-centering oneself as a subject embedded in the ecological lifeworld. This is in contrast to a capitalist subject whose labor and productivity are extracted in the repeated rhythm of five-day work weeks all year round. As the independent podcast Upstream slogan goes, 'You don't hate Mondays. You hate capitalism.'

For the Body, Against the Clock

My first attempt aims at addressing the duality of culture over nature in the coloniality of knowledge represented by calendar technologies. My second step at decoupling from capitalist time connects to the somatic knowledges of the body that are also written off by Western episteme. My attempt was to go against the clock, or I should say, to opt for the sanctity of my body instead. — Between work and rest, I asked myself to frequently choose rest, as inspired by the work of Afro-Latinx artists Navild Acosta and Sosa in *Black Power Naps* (2018–) in the US who propose that beyond economic reparations, energetic reparations in the form of rest and sleep are necessary. They suggest abolishing all structures that benefit from the lack of sleep of people of color, migrant folk, and Indigenous folk, as their work, sleeplessness, and anxiety feed the production-based culture of capitalism.

the body as a ground of resistance p.207

As a formerly colonized body, I wondered how these proposals of redress stemming from the US connect to the histories of colonial violence in Asia. This opened the possibility to investigate the kinds of collective trauma that characterize

Hong Kong as a city that prides itself on speed and efficiency and promotes itself to tourists as a city that never sleeps.

Growing up as a teenager, I was chronically sleep-deprived. Schoolwork was demanding and the performance pressure for university entrance exams was high. Sleep took a backseat to the pursuit of success. At university, I studied in a prestigious double-degree program, where competition was fierce, and I often studied late into the night in a 24-hour library. Sleep was for the weak. After graduation, working as a freelancer in the arts, I juggled seven to eight jobs to make ends meet. In a city as unaffordable as Hong Kong, the culture of overwork transcends social classes. A tax accountant is as likely to work overtime as the security guard who moonlights as a cleaner. The prevailing belief is that success is achieved through relentless hard work, reflecting the deeply ingrained grind culture where one's worth is tied to financial success.

I have never questioned how this came to be, nor how this was intertwined with Hong Kong's colonial history. After all, the East Asian work ethic proved to be advantageous in my relocation to the Netherlands: during graduate school, I gained a reputation for being fast and reliable. But now, in deciding to work against myself and my own speeds, I gave myself the space to process where this ethic stemmed from and the potential damage it was bringing to my body.

It wasn't until I encountered Tricia Hersey's manifesto *Rest is Resistance* (2022) that I began to connect the dots. Hersey writes about ancestral trauma of violence and theft experienced by black Americans enslaved on plantations and the legacy of exhaustion. She calls slavery 'an experimentation in how to push a human body to a machine-level pace for centuries led by white people',[5] reiterating that capitalism was built from slavery and plantation labor. She encourages readers to grieve and meditate on this, so that healing could begin. — To rest is to reclaim the power of our bodies away from the systems that want to capture our labor and attention. To rest is to dream.

grieving-healing journey p.137

5 Hersey, 35.

Hersey's book became a permanent fixture on my nightstand. In meditation, I began to recognize that I, too, come from a legacy of labor and exhaustion. My ancestors were not slaves, but they were coolies, indentured laborers used throughout the British colonies to replace slaves when slavery was abolished. The coolies toiled on plantations, in mines, and in large infrastructural projects for the colonizers. As Asian American scholar Lisa Lowe traces in *The Intimacies of Four Continents* (2015), the British colonial governors conceived of their Asian colonial subjects, especially the Chinese, as a 'plentiful, tractable form of labor that could alternately oppose, replace, or supplement slavery.'[6] We were the easy backup, another less-than-human population ready to be shipped across continents in droves, torn apart from families, in the cruel optimism of finding better futures elsewhere. Through Lowe and through Hersey, I was able to align the struggles against the legacies of slavery and indentured labor that cut across ethnic and racial lines, and the shared trauma of having been turned into soulless labor machines. — Black slaves and Chinese coolies underwent different but connected forms of colonial violence where their white masters remained top of the racial hierarchy. Liberation from this world order requires collective resistance, activism in another form.

giving body to the system p.193

6 Lowe, 8.

To Hersey, rest is resistance because it challenges 'the lie that our worth is tied to the grind of capitalism and the lie of white supremacy.'[7] In contemplation, I began to hear my mother's voice reminding me to work on my English but never on my Chinese—the advice of a colonial subject who has internalized the supremacy of the colonizer's tongue; I hear my university classmates discussing how to make money fast, and how to retire by 40—and in the absence of their real dreams, I recognize how time as well as their bodies have been stolen by the misplaced significance of the capitalist rat race.

7 Hersey, 40.

As descendants of coolies, as the pre-programmed laborers of capitalist and colonialist infrastructure, we must retreat into our bodies and learn to rest. Rest is physical, psychological, and spiritual—body, mind, spirit. It is a 'lifelong deprogramming'[8] that requires our collective investment against colonialist structures, clock time, and capitalist time. In committing to this work, I find myself reconnecting to parts of my being in ways I never imagined. The little voice in my head that once pushed me to work harder has softened, and instead reminds me to sleep, to dream, and to be creative. To smell the flowers, to gaze at the moon, and to observe the stars.

8 Ibid., 81.

Concluding Thoughts: On Inhabiting Pluriversal Times

In *Pluriversal Politics* (2020), Arturo Escobar asks, 'What practices of resubjectivation are needed for actively and effectively desiring nonpatriarchal, noncapitalist, and deeply relational modes of being, knowing, and doing?'[9] Important as this question is, we must first recuperate time from capitalist extraction to even build a foundation for resubjectivation, for when we are tired our bodies belong more to the labor systems that exhaust them than to ourselves.

9 Escobar, xii.

dissolving hierarchies p.76

Resubjectivation is a deeply personal durational process that requires slow attention and space in the body for reflection and dreams. Resubjectivation also requires collectivity, such that your story might inspire mine, and my tactics could become yours, and together, we share a new temporality that is social and community-driven — and we create an alternative to the capitalist lifeworld. For it takes collective resistance to divest from the colonialist Western modernity that still governs the world, and the clocks, schedules, work rhythms, and technologies that hold this world order together. For pluriversal times to flourish, we need to lean into the communal times of social organization, collective healing, communal eating, dancing, so as to restore joy in our bodies. In collectivity, we listen to the wisdom of our ancestors, and we time travel together against the linear progressiveness of One World Time. We gain more agency in opening ourselves to the potentials of new time sensibilities, to kinship, to relationality, to beyond-human natural cycles, and to new political alliances.

This personal experiment of decoupling from capitalist time has opened my spirit to sentipensar, to feel my way through my ancestors' teachings, and to decolonize my own ways of knowing that are built entirely through scientific methods from the Western episteme. My knowledge of time and technology is no longer filtered only through the language of rationality, but it opens up the sensuous, emotional side of me that had to grieve and heal from colonial violence.

My job as a digital scholar is to remain critical towards the technologies of today. I do not want technologies of time that compress time and accelerate life, nor do I want technologies that extract from colored bodies in capitalist labor. I desire technologies that would open me to the depths and sensuality of time, to help me reconnect with natural planetary rhythms such that I too could realign with cycles of growth, repair, decay, and rebirth of my organic body... —

re-enchantment p.213

Next time, when someone asks you 'What time is it?', I hope you will have an answer untethered from One World Clock Time.

Is the moon waning; are the monsoons rolling in? Are the ground squirrels preparing to hibernate; are the warblers ready for their first songs of spring? Is it time to dance, to protest, to occupy the streets, to find community, and to demand for new ways to be?

The time is now. The time is plural. The time is yours.

References

Ernst, Wolfgang. *Chronopoetics: The Temporal Being and Operativity of Technological Media*. Rowman & Littlefield International, 2016.

Escobar, Arturo. *Pluriversal Politics: The Real and the Possible*. Duke University Press, 2020.

Hersey, Tricia. *Rest Is Resistance: A Manifesto*. Little, Brown Spark, 2022.

Lowe, Lisa. *The Intimacies of Four Continents*. Duke University Press, 2015.

rituals
invention
hospitality
comfort
simple pleasures
unhurried rhythm
new vocabularies
dissolving hierarchies
evolving social bonds
shaping a shared understanding
theater of human connections
feeling of home
third space

Chai Stall

Where Fire Brews Tea, Words Flow, and Communities Are Born

Jogi Panghaal

Mornings have always carried a promise—stepping out into the world for my first cup of tea. It is a ritual that stirs not only the senses but the whole being, pulling me out of bed and into the unhurried rhythm of whichever city I am in. It feels as though I wake the city even as it awakens me.

Tea stalls are where the city gathers to truly wake up. These modest spaces—often little more than a weathered cart or a makeshift counter on the pavement—are the beating heart of morning life. In winter, a small crowd huddles closer to the warmth of the fire, seeking both comfort and *chai*. The fire tells its own story. In the cities, it's often replaced by the rules of safety and efficiency of gas burners, but in smaller towns and villages, the glow of wood or coal persists, crackling with the echoes of an older, slower world.

At the center of it all is a brass pan, poised above the flames, holding the beginnings of a new day. Within its gleaming embrace, the alchemy of tea unfolds. The tea-making itself becomes a performative act of a naturally evolved choreography. Ramesh, the artist behind the counter and by now my friend, works with a rhythm that feels timeless. The metallic sounds of the ladle spoon scraping against the pan are unmistakable, as he expertly manages the boiling brew while engaging with his customers. He smiles, acknowledging our presence on yet another morning, even as his hands are busy extracting fresh ginger into the brass pan. The milk concoction dances with energy, reaching several lows and highs of cooking as it nears a boil. Just as it threatens to spill over, Ramesh catches a small bit in his ladle spoon, drops it in his left palm to taste. He is satisfied with his balance of flavors. For this chai artisan, continuity of taste is the name of his 'brand' game. His customers associate him with 'that' taste. If they crave for another taste, they need to go to another artisan. To fuss over taste is what keeps his identity alive among his customers, keeping them hooked to his stall.

Lowering the flame, he picks up the pan with a special handle and carefully strains the tea through a fine piece of muslin, folded into a makeshift sieve, and pours it into a serving kettle. A whisper of excitement ripples through the waiting customers as the aroma of ginger-laden tea fills the air, alerting even passers-by to stop and join the melee of the hopefuls to catch that fresh steaming cup.

Now begins the ritual of serving. With practiced precision Ramesh pours tea from the spout of his kettle into a variety of vessels. Some customers bring their own mugs, eager to savor a more generous helping. Others receive their tea in glasses, promptly washed and reused by his attentive assistant. For the traditionalists, tea is poured into saucers, where they sip noisily, enjoying every slurp as the hot liquid revives their spirits. Each serving method carries its own charm, reflecting the diverse ways people embrace this morning wake-up call.

As regulars, we often claim our spots on makeshift seats crafted from wooden logs of fallen trees or recycled metal drums, new avatars of past lives as ghee containers. The tea stall becomes a microcosm of the city, a space where lives intersect and conversations bloom. — Some customers dive into the morning papers, fully absorbed in the day's news, while others speak unfamiliar languages, their voices blending into the hum of the street. For a few fleeting moments, the tea stall transforms into a lively theater of human connections, its sounds and sights forming the tapestry of life.

exuberance of blossoming p.388

As the serving kettle empties, Ramesh is already brewing the next batch, this time catering to those who prefer their tea unsweetened. Yet the majority still favors it sweet, often with a touch of excess. The second round comes quickly, as conversation flows and the energy of the morning settles into a familiar rhythm.

The city has awakened and now its stories are ready to unfold.

The Role of Fire in Early Social Spaces

The domestication of fire marked a profound moment in our evolutionary journey. A key insight was that fire, though seemingly uncontrollable, could be tamed if fed a measured amount of fuel. Through this finding, fire became a collaborator, a partner in our experiments with food making and heating, and also, as some anthropologists believe, the first tool that turned a group of individuals into a community. — Fire created the first true social spaces as early humans gathered

tools for conviviality p.191

around it to cook, eat, and protect themselves from predators. It thus provided a central focus for early human settlements, enabling communal spaces where people would meet, share food, and socialize.

In such ways, fire played a foundational role in shaping early human culture and social structures. It was much more than a means of survival—it became an emblem of human ingenuity, collaboration, and community making. While in many cultures across the globe fire also became symbolic, representing purification, creation, and transformation.

In India, where I live, fire has long held deep spiritual significance. From ancient rituals to modern religious ceremonies, fire, or *agni*, is seen as a purifying and transformative element. It is central to rituals such as marriages, where the sacred fire witnesses the vows of the couple; birth, where fire across a threshold ensures that anyone entering to see the newly born baby and the mother goes through fire's purifying role; and funerals, where the body is offered to the flames in the belief that it will facilitate the soul's passage to the afterlife. These rituals demonstrate how fire is not only a practical tool but also a force that connects the physical and spiritual realms. — This connection between fire, spirituality, and community is a thread that runs through Indian culture, manifesting in both the domestic hearth and later in public spaces like tea stalls.

a bridge between worlds
p.162

Transition from Fire to the Hearth

The act of arranging three stones or bricks to support a vessel while pushing fire underneath may well represent one of the first major developments in human domesticity. Over time, this basic setup evolved into a more refined set of techniques: with more varied vessels and cuisines, and with other sources of fuel allowing fire or heat to be controlled for different culinary needs. The invention of tools like the 'lighter,' made from striking stones or bamboo to create sparks, meant that fire could be lit at will, further embedding it in day-to-day being and living together.

A place with these three stones became the focal point for daily life, and gradually, a shelter was built around it. This space we now call home, a place centered on the hearth, where fire cooked the food that nourished us. Here, particularly through the work of women, food, stories, and practices intertwined. Women were the inventors of recipes and shared experiences of ingredients that gave form to the dishes we know today, including *chai*, the special fragrant tea that is a staple of the Indian diet.

As humans honed the domestication of fire, the transition from open fires to enclosed hearths marked a significant cultural and technological shift. In India, the early hearths consisting of three stones or bricks developed into the traditional *chulha* (clay stove), which was widely used in rural areas and remains a symbol of domesticity to this day. The chulha was typically located in the courtyard or kitchen of the home, where families would gather to cook meals and smoke would escape into the skies. The hearth thus became the heart of the home, a place where food and warmth converged.

This evolution of the hearth led to more structured family and community living. As homes expanded to accommodate the hearth, the architectural design of shelters also evolved. In rural India, mud houses were designed with courtyards that contained the chulha, allowing for both cooking and communal living in an open, airy environment. In urban settings, homes were built with enclosed kitchens, making the hearth an integral part of the domestic architecture. This shift from outdoor fires to indoor hearths represented a major advancement in human technology, as it allowed for more permanent and stable living conditions.

Birthplace of Conviviality

The hearth soon became not only a practical feature of the home but also a space where social and cultural life was nurtured. Much more than just a cooking place, the hearth was a gathering point, a place where families, elders, children, and extended kin connected. Those repeated acts of gathering around the fire were key moments for communication, and new words and language began to emerge more regularly, expanding as people exchanged notes, experiences, and instructions. — Fire was perhaps the original social network and

find-invent (a) shared language p.366

continues to act to this day as an *adda* space, a place where conversation is born over cups of tea. A vibrant democracy's first building block.

Those fertile sites of social exchange naturally gave way to storytelling, an essential aspect of human culture. In ancient times, storytelling was a communal activity, with families and neighbors gathering around the fire to share tales of fears, gods, ancestors, and local legends. Oral traditions were central to the transmission of knowledge, history, and values in pre-literate societies. In India, epic tales like the *Mahabharata* and *Ramayana* were passed down through generations via oral storytelling, often around the communal hearth and expressed in performance forms such as dance, theater, or singing. The stories served not only as entertainment but also as moral and cultural lessons that shaped the collective identity of the community. —

collective story-telling as a way of existing p.371

This tradition of storytelling eventually migrated to public spaces like tea stalls, which became modern hubs for connecting people across generations and geographies. Much like the ancient hearths, they are spaces where stories flow freely. As my own tale that opens this essay attests, these are places where strangers become acquaintances, and acquaintances become friends, all over a simple cup of tea.

The Hearth: From Home to Public Space

In India, among the cooked dishes that emerged through the use of fire, tea is the one that became truly iconic—a beverage that bridged domestic life and the emerging opportunities in the public sphere. Unlike meals, tea is a 'secular' drink, more global in its recognition, even though each geography adds its own interpretation and thus taste to it. It's also an edible item that does not have a prescribed time or appetite for it. It's a 24-hour item.

As highways and cities opened up, strangers, drivers, and passengers sought tea to refresh themselves along the way, to feel at home even if it was another person's home. Women took their domestic skills into this public domain, transforming the hearth into professional places like *ketalee* (born of kettle) and *dhabas* (popular roadside restaurants serving basic food), and even into chains of tea franchises. Thus tea became not only a product but also a space for conversation. The hearth had stepped outside the home, taking with it the memories and traditions of warmth, hospitality, and social exchange.

Thus the spread of tea stalls marked the beginning of a new social fabric—one built on the values of meeting, sharing, empathizing, and cooperating with strangers and people from diverse trades. These interactions opened up new possibilities for businesses, education, and the future. Still today, in tea stalls across India, people from all walks of life gather to discuss everything from politics to local gossip, engaging in conversations that reflect the diversity and complexity of Indian society.

With the rise of cities came the migration of millions of people from rural areas, expanding the significance of the tea stall. As migrants settled into India's rapidly growing urban centers, they brought with them the culinary traditions, stories, and social practices of their native villages. Tea stalls became the place where rural migrants could find familiarity in an unfamiliar landscape.

Tea stalls, in this sense, became (and still are) the public hearth, a space where more complex communities were forged and able to flourish. Conflicts are addressed, new realities encountered, new matrimonial alliances proposed, and new vocabularies embraced. Time spent in these spaces is the glue holding together evolving social bonds, enabling conversations that shape our shared understanding of the world. —

binding agent(s) p.446

Technology: The Transformative Force Behind Public Hearths

If fire was humanity's first technology, then what followed were innovations that redefined how we live, work, and interact. The public hearth, centered around the modern tea stall, owes much of its evolution to advancements in technology. From the introduction of clay stoves and vessels to more sophisticated heating systems, technology has played a role in making these spaces functional and sustainable.

With industrialization, technology transformed even the humble tea stall. The introduction of new cooking tools, such as the primus stove and later the widespread use of LPG (liquefied petroleum gas), allowed tea stalls to scale their operations. No longer dependent on firewood, these stalls could operate more efficiently, serving larger numbers of customers with faster turnaround in smokeless environments.

Rural and remote areas host tea stalls that still use wood as fuel. Cow dung cakes are another frequently used fuel mode. Invented by women, these cakes are made from animal dung, particularly from cows and buffaloes. Cakes are crafted by hand, dried in the sun, and then used in chulhas, the traditional stove.

Electricity added a whole new dimension. The once-primitive tea stalls transformed into hubs of modern technology. Electric kettles, powered stoves, and refrigeration allowed for more sophisticated setups, where perishable goods could now be stored and fresh food could be prepared throughout the day. Tea stalls, once bound by the limitations of fire, became 24-hour operations. Some even expanded their offerings beyond tea, serving a variety of snacks, meals, and drinks to cater to their growing clientele.

More recently, digital innovations such as e-payments have further revolutionized tea stalls. Customers can pay for their tea with the tap of a smartphone. This technological shift has made tea stalls more efficient and accessible, enabling them to remain competitive in a rapidly digitizing economy, while sparing tea sellers the headache of managing cash and keeping a stock of loose coins for change.

The Mobile Kitchen: How Mechanized Transport Shaped Tea Stalls

Transportation technology has also played a crucial role in the growth of tea stalls. The rise of mechanized transport—trains, buses, and automobiles—created a new class of traveler, one who needed quick, accessible food options while on the move. Tea stalls became a natural fit, providing travelers with a convenient place to rest, refuel, and enjoy a cup of tea and a snack before plunging back into the acts of survival in a city.

Railways, in particular, transformed tea stalls into vital social spaces. Railway stations across India became synonymous with the ubiquitous chaiwallah, whose cries of 'Chai! Chai!' are now an indelible part of the Indian travel experience. As people waited for trains, tea stalls became places of social interaction, where strangers exchanged stories, discussed politics, and formed temporary communities.

Many of the younger lot of entrepreneurs prototyped solutions to carry large tea containers by hand into moving trains while managing to keep tea warm with a red hot charcoal stove under the bottom of these containers. In a sense, these sellers would bless a passenger train compartment with the qualities of a hearth, so that conversations never stop and connections continue to be forged among the traveling public. —

stirred up by rituals p.122

Availability of tea in moving trains has eased the boredom and aches of passengers in long journeys that can last three to four days in our vast country.

Mechanized transport also allowed for the mass transportation of goods. Where once tea stalls were limited by the availability of local ingredients, now they could source products from distant regions, adding new items to their menus. From freshly baked bread to exotic spices, technology expanded the culinary possibilities for tea stalls, making them more diverse and inclusive.

Women: The Original Technologists of the Tea Stall Revolution

Women have always played a central role in the evolution of tea stalls, both as entrepreneurs and cultural stewards. In the early days, they brought in materials and know-how from their domestic spheres to the public domain, setting up stalls that were extensions of the home, providing nourishment and hospitality to strangers much in the same way the hearth had done for families. —

technologies of collective care p.118

As India's infrastructure developed and travel became more frequent, women entrepreneurs were among the first to recognize the wider business potential of tea stalls serving travelers. They set up roadside *dhabas* and stalls, offering tea and affordable meals to truck drivers, laborers, and tourists. In doing so, they helped shape India's evolving culinary landscape, introducing regional flavors and dishes to a wider audience.

Despite the central role women played in establishing and operating these spaces, the economic success of tea stalls eventually led to a shift in ownership. As they became more profitable, men gradually took over their operation, sidelining the women who had originally built and run them. This marked a significant historical injustice, as women, who had long been the keepers of the hearth, were pushed to the margins in the very spaces they had created.

Shifts like these mirror broader patterns of gender inequality in India's informal economy, where women's labor is often undervalued or appropriated by men. Efforts are being made now to reclaim these spaces for women through state-sponsored programs that offer financial and logistical support to women entrepreneurs, helping them regain control of the businesses they once dominated. These efforts reflect a growing recognition of the need to address gender imbalances.

More recently, as the new formal economy grows without creating any additional jobs, it falls on vast armies of educated youngsters to find ways to support themselves. For many of them, tea stalls have become an easy but competitive option to start a new livelihood—a scenario that poses new challenges to ensuring more inclusive opportunities for women in public spaces.

The Global Village: How Tea Stalls Reflect 'Glocalization'

In today's interconnected world, tea stalls are more than just places to grab a cup of chai—they are symbols of the global village. With the proliferation of mobile technology, wifi, and digital payment systems, tea stalls are no longer isolated roadside stops; they are nodes in a vast, interconnected network. As Marshall McLuhan famously said, 'The medium is the message,' and in this case, tea stalls are more than places to drink—they are sites of global connection. While locals sip chai and exchange stories, others might be engaging in global conversations, attending virtual meetings, or making digital transactions via their smartphones. Technology has turned these once simple spaces into key nodes in the global village. A traveler in a tea stall in Mumbai could be engaging in a

WhatsApp conversation with someone in London, paying for their chai via a mobile wallet, and sharing their experience on social media—all in real-time.

This blending of the local and the global has transformed tea stalls into spaces where people can engage with the world while staying rooted in their own local culture. — Becoming glocal! The traditional clay cups might sit alongside modern disposable ones, and conversations in local dialects mix with global discussions about technology, politics, and culture. These tea stalls, once simple, utilitarian spaces, have become vibrant centers of exchange, where the global village is experienced over a cup of tea. In this way, the traditional hearth has transformed into a modern digital hub. And a charging point.

respecting rich and productive differences p.311

Sustaining and Growing Community

At their core, tea stalls are places that foster community. They bring people together, whether they are local residents, travelers, or digital nomads. Over a cup of tea, conversations flow—about politics, sports, family, and business. Tea stalls offer a unique kind of social space where hierarchies dissolve, and people from all walks of life can engage in meaningful exchanges. The modest tea stall has, in many ways, become a new 'third space,' offering an alternative to home and work where people can connect, relax, and reflect.

In rural areas, tea stalls remain critical to sustaining the local economy and social fabric. These stalls provide a meeting point where farmers, laborers, and villagers can discuss local issues, share news, and maintain a sense of community. In urban centers, tea stalls have adapted to the fast pace of city life but continue to offer a respite from the hustle and bustle, a place where one can slow down and engage in face-to-face interaction in an increasingly digital world.

As cities experience an unprecedented influx of job-seeking migrants, tea stalls act as their new gateways. They are thresholds through which newcomers enter and begin to acclimate to the city, just as the traditional hearth once provided families with nourishment and cultural grounding. For many migrants, tea stalls provide much more than just a place to eat and drink; they are spaces of adaptation and resilience.

Over a shared cup of tea, migrants exchange tips on how to navigate the complexities of urban life, from finding work to securing housing, from a small loan to borrowing money. The tea stall offers a sanctuary of familiarity, offering a sense of a new emerging community in the chaos of the city.

In all these ways, tea stalls could perhaps safely be considered hearths around which past, present and future gather. Just as the simple arrangement of three stones over a fire once nurtured families by providing warmth, nourishment, and a space for storytelling, tea stalls continue to play a similar role in a completely new context. They offer sustenance, but more importantly, they provide a space where people from diverse origins and points of view can connect, share ideas, and form communities.

The Future of Tea Stalls: Balancing Tradition and Modernity

As India continues to urbanize and modernize, tea stalls are poised to play an even more significant role in shaping the country's social and cultural landscape. On the one hand, they will continue to serve as vital spaces for the invention of new words and languages, of traditions of hospitality, and thus of new community making. On the other, they will increasingly incorporate technology, sustainability, and global influences to stay relevant in the 'present moment' in a rapidly changing world. Modernity also has played a significant role in the evolution of tea stalls. Younger patrons have encouraged tea stall owners to experiment with their menus, introducing fusion dishes that blend regional flavors with global culinary trends. In cities like Bengaluru and Pune, some tea stalls have adopted a more contemporary aesthetic, blending traditional Indian chai culture with modern, minimalist design elements. These 'hipster' tea stalls attract a younger demographic, offering creative menu options such as flavored teas, artisanal snacks, and fusion dishes that combine local ingredients with international influences. The infusion of youth culture into these spaces has transformed tea stalls into hybrid places of experimentation and cultural exchange, where tradition and innovation coexist harmoniously.

Simultaneously there is a growing movement to make tea stalls more environmentally resilient. With increasing awareness of climate change, as reflected in unseasonal rains and water shortages, along with concerns about plastic pollution and environmental degradation, tea stalls across India are adopting eco-friendly practices to reduce their environmental impact. Once reliant on plastic cups and disposable cutlery, many stalls are now embracing more sustainable alternatives. The revival of ancient clay cups (*kulhads*), which are biodegradable and impart a rustic flavor to tea, has seen a resurgence, particularly in rural areas. Glass containers are back, and after a wash, they are fresh again.

In urban centers, some tea stalls are transitioning to zero-waste practices not only to reduce waste but also to position themselves as leaders in the movement toward sustainable, eco-conscious living. This focus on sustainability reflects a broader cultural shift, where tea stalls are not just places of consumption but sites of ethical and responsible practices. As such, they serve as a dynamic model for how ancient local practices and global trends can align in one actionable whole. — The hearth is once again reasserting its community-building role.

leaps of time p.176

In the future, tea stalls may perhaps emerge as urgent spaces that encourage new conversations and relationships between rural and urban, between oral traditions and reading traditions, between high-tech and high-touch systems, and between localism and globalism. Hopefully, more of these spaces will be mediated by young women, who would thus continue to build upon their pioneering role in shaping the hearth—a role widely celebrated but not as widely acknowledged.

The Eternal Flame of Connection

The journey that brought us to this point was initiated and nurtured by women from the earliest days. The domestication of fire, the making of meals, and the emergence of the hearth as a social and familial space were all foundational steps. These hearths also gave rise to words and languages—first in oral form, then written, and now in digital forms that seamlessly bridge the gap between past and present. This mirrors a migration of ideas and innovations that continue to shape the world today.

The evolution of tea stalls in India is a reflection of the country's 'tryst with destiny'[1]—one of resilience, innovation, and the ability to balance the old with the new. From their humble beginnings as roadside stalls to their modern incarnations as tech-savvy hubs, tea stalls remain deeply embedded in the fabric of Indian society. They continue to evolve, adapting to technological advancements and global influences while preserving the core values of hospitality, warmth, and connection.

[1] 'Tryst with Destiny' was the title of a speech by Jawaharlal Nehru, the first Prime Minister of India, delivered on August 14, 1947, the eve of Indian independence from British colonial rule.

In a world that is increasingly fast-paced and digital, tea stalls stand as symbols of both continuity and change where the flame of traditional timelines burns alongside the sparks of modernity. — They remind us that, no matter how much technology changes our lives, there will always be a place for the simple pleasure and meaning in sharing a cup of tea, a story, and a moment of connection.

a mix of before and beyond p.363

impermanence
ambiguity
the edge of chaos
a step beyond
comfort
breath
pulse
irrepressibility
transcending abstractions
bringing subtlety into
  consciousness
aesthetic interiority
multilayered joy
hovering just beyond the
  edge of understanding
pretensions drop away
not a contest

What My Musical Instruments Have Taught Me

Jaron Lanier

It started after my mother died. She was a concentration camp survivor—a prodigy concert pianist in Vienna who was taken when she was only a girl. She taught me the piano by holding her hands over mine, bending my fingers into arches above the keys. When I was just a boy, she died in a car accident. Afterward, I was both boundlessly angry and attached to the piano. I played it with extreme force, sometimes bleeding onto the keys. I still feel her hands when I play. I feel them even more when I'm learning a new instrument.

As I write this, on a laptop in my kitchen, I can see at least a hundred instruments around me. There's a Baroque guitar; some Colombian *gaita* flutes; a French musical saw; a *shourangiz* (a Persian instrument resembling a traditional poet's lute); an Array *mbira* (a giant chromatic thumb piano, made in San Diego); a Turkish clarinet; and a Chinese *guqin*. A reproduction of an ancient Celtic harp sits near some giant penny whistles, a tar frame drum, a Roman *sistrum*, a long-neck banjo, and some *duduks* from Armenia. (Duduks are the haunting reed instruments used in movie soundtracks to convey xeno-profundity.) There are many more instruments in other rooms of the house, and I've learned to play them all. I've become a compulsive explorer of new instruments and the ways they make me feel.

I keep a small *oud* in the kitchen, and sometimes, between e-mails, I improvise with it. Ouds resemble lutes, which in turn resemble guitars. But where a guitar has a flat back, an oud has a domelike form that presses backward against the belly or chest. This makes playing one a tender experience. You must find just the right way to hold it, constraining your shoulders, moving mainly the smaller muscles below the elbows. Holding an oud is a little like holding a baby. While cradling an infant, I feel pretensions drop away: here is the only future we truly have—a sacred moment. — Playing the oud, I am exposed. The instrument is confessional to me.

kairological time
p.249

But that's not how all players experience their ouds. The most famous oud player of the twentieth century was probably the Syrian-Egyptian superstar Farid al-Atrash, who was both a respected classical musician of the highest order and a pop-culture figure and movie star. (Imagine a cross between

Jascha Heifetz and Elvis Presley.) His playing was often crowd-pleasing, extroverted, and muscular. I have an oud similar to one Atrash played; it was created by a member of Syria's multigenerational Nahat family, whose instruments are often described as the Stradivariuses of the oud world. In the nineteen-forties, my Nahat was savaged by a notorious Brooklyn dealer who tried to claim it as his own by covering the original label and marquetry. Later, an Armenian American luthier tried to remake it as an Armenian instrument, with disastrous results. After I bought the oud out of the attic of a player who had given up on it, two remarkable luthiers restored it, and the oud started to speak in a way that possessed me. Listeners notice—they ask, 'What is that thing?'

Nahat ouds can be especially big. My arms have to travel more in order to move up and down the longer neck; the muscles around my shoulders become engaged, as they do when I'm playing the guitar. Moving this way, I become aware of the world beyond the small instrument I'm swaddling; I start to play more for others than for myself. The cello also makes me feel this way. You have to use your shoulders—your whole back—to play a cello. But cellos summon a different set of feelings. Playing one, you're still bound up in a slightly awkward way, bent around a vibrating entity—not a baby, not a lover, but maybe a large dog.

The *khaen*, from Laos and northeastern Thailand, is the instrument I play the most in public. It's a mouth organ—something like a giant harmonica, but with an earthy, ancient tone. Tall bamboo tubes jut both upward and downward from a teak vessel, angling into a spire which seems to emerge, unicorn-like, from the forehead of the performer. I first encountered one as a teenager, in the nineteen-seventies, during a time when I was exploring Chinese music clubs in San Francisco. These were frequented mainly by older people, and often situated in the basements of faded apartment buildings. The khaen isn't Chinese, but I noticed one resting against a wall in a club and asked if I could try it. As soon as I picked up the khaen I became a rhythmic musician, driving a hard beat with double- and triple-tonguing patterns. The old men applauded when I finished. 'Take it,' a woman holding an *erhu* said.

Later, I learned that my instant style was completely unrelated to what goes on in Laos. It emerged, I think, from how the khaen works with one's breathing. On a harmonica, as on many instruments, the note changes when you switch between inhaling and exhaling—but on a khaen, one can breathe both in and out without changing pitch. Breathing is motion, and so the khaen and its cousins from Asia, such as the Chinese *sheng*, are liberating to play. I've been lucky enough to play khaen with many great musicians—with Jon Batiste and the Stay Human band on *The Late Show with Stephen Colbert*, for instance, and with Ornette Coleman. When I played the khaen with George Clinton and P-Funk, Clinton stood facing me, leaning in until we were just inches apart; he widened his eyes to make the channel between our beings as high-bandwidth as possible, breathing ferociously to transmit the groove he was improvising. — It was the most physically demanding performance of my life.

energetic umbilical cord
p.130

If playing the khaen turns me into an extroverted athlete, then the *xiao*—which is held vertically, like a clarinet or an oboe—invites me to explore internal dramas. This isn't just a mind-set but a physical sensation: while playing xiao I feel a rolling movement in the air just behind my upper front teeth, and a second area of resonance in my chest, and I seem to move these reservoirs of air around as I use the instrument. I'm not the only one to have this kind of sensation: singers often say that they experience air in this way, and flute teachers I've known have talked about 'blue' or 'yellow' air flows. I've had long conversations with wind players about how we seem to be painting the flow of air inside our bodies. I have to suspend my skepticism when this sort of talk starts—I don't think we're really doing what we describe, but I do think we're describing something real. It's possible to shape tone by adjusting the mouth, tongue, lips, jaw, throat, and chest. When I find my tone, I even feel the presence of a structure in the air between my lips and the flute—a tumbling, ineffable caterpillar, rolling rapidly on its long axis. The caterpillar collaborates with me, sometimes helping, sometimes pushing back, and by interacting with it I can explore a world of tone.

Did the xiao players of the past perceive invisible caterpillars like mine? Maybe they did. Xiaos have come in many shapes and sizes over the centuries, but, judging by the illustrations that have been preserved, they've all been recognizably xiao. On the other hand, there are many ways to play a flute. Perhaps xiao notes used to end in elegant calligraphic rises; maybe the breath was emphasized so that the sound of the flute seemed continuous with nature; or possibly ancient xiao tones were lustrous and technical, with perfect stability. Perhaps the sound that xiao players sought was deceptively transparent but filled with little features, or maybe they were show-offs, playing high, fast, and loud. These descriptions fit contemporary flute-playing styles, and it seems possible that historical styles resembled them—or not.

In recent years, a heightened spirit of experimentation in xiao-building has developed. Most of the experiments have to do with the shape of the blowing edge—the place where one edge of a flute's tube has been thinned, forming a tiny ridge that's positioned against the bottom lip to receive the breath. At the blowing edge, the air alternately flows more to the inside or the outside of the flute. This oscillation radiates as sound. Flutists of all cultures are vulnerable to debilitating fascinations with the tiniest design choices in blowing edges and the nearby interiors of their flutes. In Taiwan, a small cult has arisen around the idea of combining an outside cut in the form of a letter 'U,' which is typical of some schools of xiao design, with an inside form that's more like a 'V.' Debates about the new cut run rampant in online forums.

After reading some of them, I finally ordered a flute with the new cut. (That I could do this so effortlessly made me feel momentarily better about how the Internet has turned out so far.) When I played my U/V xiao for the first time, I made the futile blowing sound familiar to beginning flutists. Eventually, though, I managed a few weird, false notes. I was surprised but also delighted. Some of my favorite moments in musical life come when I can't yet play an instrument. It's in the fleeting period of playing without skill that you can hear sounds beyond imagination. — Eventually, I cajoled the caterpillar and found a tone I love, solid yet translucent. When that

momentary freedom p.344

happens, the challenge is remembering how to make those fascinating, false notes. One mustn't lose one's childhood.

I'm a computer scientist by profession, and I started travelling to Japan at the beginning of the nineteen-eighties, when I was developing the first virtual-reality headsets and searching for business partners and technical components. I was surprised to find few young people there interested in traditional Japanese music. Precious and playable antique instruments like the *shakuhachi*, a traditional bamboo flute, could be bought at flea markets for less than the price of breakfast—and they were being snapped up not by Japanese students but by young Westerners who worshipped the remaining teachers. Meanwhile, interest in European classical music, which was declining in the West, was growing in Japan. I met many Japanese musicians who found Mozart as appealing as the Beatles, and who played violin and piano along with rock and roll. In Western countries, the social institutions that kept classical music alive—conservatories, instrument builders, teachers, contests—were being sustained by an influx of stunning musicians from Asia. A kind of cultural trade was taking place.

My experiences studying music in Japan were often astonishing. I chased down a teacher who claimed to be the holder of an ancient Buddhist shakuhachi tradition that had been suppressed by the mainstream musical world; his lessons were fused with a tea ceremony. I met another teacher who would only accept a student who could walk into the forest and choose a stalk of bamboo that, when it was cut down, would turn out to be in tune as a flute. (He gave me only one chance to get it right, and I failed.) In one of the main shakuhachi 'lodges' in Tokyo, I came across a culture of male-dominated locker-room talk, in which some styles of playing were approved as sufficiently macho while others were denigrated as 'gay.' Much of what I encountered startled me—it didn't reflect what I'd read in books back in America about the shakuhachi.

Music operates on a plane separate from literature, and a lot of information about it isn't written down. Most of the world's compositions were never notated, and what was written down is often minimal; although scores do exist for very old Chinese music—some of the oldest are for the noble *guqin*, a kind of zither—they amount to mnemonic devices, lists of strokes and playing positions. The earliest European scores are similar, with lists of notes. What we now call 'early music' is largely a modern stylistic invention. I tend to learn the rudiments of my instruments and then develop my own style; I'm an eternal amateur. But I console myself by noting that there are very few musical conservatories structured enough to preserve musical styles over long periods of time. We can study how Bach's music might have sounded, or how the shakuhachi was actually played, but we can never really know. What would it have sounded like to be at court in ancient Egypt, Persia, India, China, Greece, Mesopotamia? The truth has been lost to time.

The exquisite skills involved in making instruments can seem to hover just beyond the edge of scientific understanding, and can easily be lost when war, plague, and famine break the chains linking masters and apprentices. And yet the traditions of a lost musical culture can sometimes be revived. Modern instrument makers can copy preserved examples of old instruments, or even work from illustrations. In the case of the xiao, much was lost through the centuries, and then again in the Cultural Revolution—but xiaos are small and easy to hide. Some musicians are said to have buried them in secret locations, in hopes of escaping Mao Zedong's attempts to engineer culture from scratch. This complex history means that, today, there are contrasting contemporary approaches to playing the xiao. Some players see learning and performing with the instrument as a spiritual quest to reconnect with the past; others play what sounds to me like a Hollywood composer's idea of Chinese music from the early twentieth century—a musical genre that's aged surprisingly well. There's no verifiably authentic way to play such an ancient instrument.

the vibration of matter
in relation to time
p.200

As a technologist, my work has often focussed on the creation of interactive devices, such as head-mounted displays and haptic gloves. It's sobering for me to compare the instruments

I've played with the devices that Silicon Valley has made. I've never had an experience with any digital device that comes at all close to those I've had with even mediocre acoustic musical instruments. What's the use of ushering in a new era dominated by digital technology if the objects that that era creates are inferior to pre-digital ones?

For decades, researchers have been attempting to model acoustic instruments with software. Simulated saxophones and violins can sound impressive but only within an artificially constrained frame. Listen to one note at a time and the synthetic instruments sound good. Connect the notes together and the illusion fails. This may be because the experience of interacting creatively with such models is sterile, vacant, and ridiculous. One is usually clicking on little dots on a screen, or pushing buttons, or—in the very best case—adjusting variables with physical knobs and sliders. From a commercial point of view, this doesn't make simulated instruments useless; embedded in the mix, splashed with reverb and other effects, they sound just fine. But physical instruments channel the unrepeatable process of interaction, — a quality lost with modern production technology.

a process of continuous seeking p.111

Human senses have evolved to the point that we can occasionally react to the universe down to the quantum limit; our retinas can register single photons, and our ability to sense something teased between fingertips is profound. But that is not what makes instruments different from digital-music models. It isn't a contest about numbers. The deeper difference is that computer models are made of abstractions—letters, pixels, files—while acoustic instruments are made of material. The wood in an oud or a violin reflects an old forest, the bodies who played it, and many other things, but in an intrinsic, organic way, transcending abstractions. Physicality got a bad rap in the past. It used to be that the physical was contrasted with the spiritual. But now that we have information technologies, we can see that materiality is mystical. — A digital object can be described, while an acoustic one always remains a step beyond us.

inner qualities of matter p.297

Today, tech companies promise to create algorithms that can analyze old music to create new music. But music is ambiguous: is it mostly a product to be produced and enjoyed, or is the creation of it the most important thing? If it's the former, then being able to automate the production of music is at least a coherent idea, whether or not it is a good one. But, if it's the latter, then pulling music creation away from people undermines the whole point. I often work with students who want to build algorithms that make music. I ask them, Do you mean you want to design algorithms that are like instruments, and which people can use to make new music, or do you just want an A.I. to make music for you? For those students who want to have optimal music made for them, I have to ask, Would you want robots to have sex for you so you don't have to? I mean, what is life for?

Much of the music we enjoy today makes use of audio loops, by means of which a note can be repeated with absolute precision. Because of my work with computers, I had early access to looping tools, and I was able to play around with loops earlier than most musicians. At first, the techniques didn't speak to me; music is about change, I thought, while loops are about artificially preventing change. When so-called minimalist composers—Philip Glass, Terry Riley—ask musicians to play the same phrases repeatedly, what emerges from this technique isn't repetition but an exquisite awareness of change: — using a traditional, physical instrument, each repetition reflects your breath, your pulse, the weather, the audience, the light, bringing subtlety into consciousness. My understanding of loops shifted when hip-hop appeared. Here was a genre that was often angry, often a protest—the use of loops could evoke the strictures a rapper raged against. Some musicians now make their loops a little blurry, as if to suggest impermanence. For many people, of course, loops have become so commonplace that it's hard to perceive them as a contrast to anything else.

generative
space of making
p.416

In my own musical life, I prize the edge of chaos; that which cannot be repeated. I usually don't record myself when I play alone; I don't want to trick myself into a false mentality that lives outside of time, as if we weren't time's prisoners. I want to send music out into the universe, not into a computer's memory. As crazy as it is to learn to play a multitude of instruments, my madness is the opposite of the loop. I'm often asked if I've learned all these instruments in order to make a sample library, or if I'd be willing to have someone come to the house to make such a library. Though I offer positivity from afar to musicians who like samples, I am travelling in a different direction.

If you work with virtual reality, you end up wondering what reality is in the first place. Over the years, I've toyed with one possible definition of reality: it's the thing that can't be perfectly simulated, because it can't be measured to completion. Digital information can be perfectly measured, because that is its very definition. This makes it unreal. But reality is irrepressible.

I sometimes dwell on these ideas when I play the piano. A piano is essentially a row of keys, plus some pedals. Once a key has been depressed, a mechanism sends a felt hammer flying toward a string, which is not in direct contact with the key. In theory, this means that a piano played without the damping pedal ought to be abstract, like an electronic keyboard. The only information the hammer seems to convey from a key to a string is a single number—velocity. That's also how much information a key press communicates in an electronic keyboard. And yet the experience of playing an acoustic piano, and of listening to one, is that more is being conveyed. When pianists trade off on the same instrument, they perform with individual touches and sounds. Pianos are somewhat abstract devices that have transcended abstraction.

My fondest hope for computing is that digital devices will become as much like pianos as possible. But the subtlest qualities of analog instruments are hard to study, in part because the controls necessary to make studies rigorous risk obscuring important elements of musical experience. There have been many studies comparing old and new violins, for instance, or flutes made of different metals, in which a player is hidden behind a screen and listeners are asked to identify which instrument is being played. The problem with this approach is that the difference between a good instrument and a great one could inhere in the player's experience, rather than in the external sound. If an instrument inspires a musician, then the music will be more meaningful, even if listeners can't distinguish the sound of one instrument from another. Music is an interior art before it becomes exterior.

For me, the piano has an interior aspect. The piano is one of the few instruments that's bigger than you. Playing it, you are the baby: strike as much as you like, it remains the same. After my mother died, I became obsessed with fast arpeggios, and I zoomed between the extremes of the keyboard; I was also drawn toward the American-Mexican composer Conlon Nancarrow, who wrote superhuman piano music for player pianos, using hand-punched player-piano rolls. When I was a teen-ager, I often hitchhiked from New Mexico to visit him in Mexico City. I was determined to play as fast as the pianos automated by Conlon; his machines, in their unreality, were a flight from human frailty and trauma. I emulated them by challenging them in my own piano playing. In my fury, the piano became a chunk of reality to obliterate, though quixotically. You can caress a piano or attack it, be loud or soft, become proficient or not, make as much beauty as you can or flail in chaos—the instrument will most likely endure beyond you.

Decades have passed since that time. Today, I love to have musicians over to my house, where we can combine different instruments to see what happens. The joy that transpires when things go well is multilayered. There is the pleasure of connection with other people, and there is also the happiness of finding a new little corner of aesthetic interiority together. Music can conjure a new flow, a new pattern, a new flavor, between and inside people. — And playing sufficiently obscure instruments forces a different approach to music. How can you be competitive about raw skill, or get into some other macho trap, when the task at hand is so esoteric? Who is to judge the winner in a contest that must invent itself over and over? When music made collaboratively with other musicians goes right, I feel a budding, rising warmth and comfort. Is this my mother smiling on me? Or maybe it's me, smiling on her.

welcoming us on the inside and the outside p.387

This text was first published July 22, 2023 in The New Yorker.

f(r)iction
curiosity
making room
aide-mémoire
intervening
errancy
messiness
chanting down
storying ourselves
signaling an otherwise
resistance
respiration
furious love
pushing through
  toward life
Black note-making

A Note from The Annotator (when the Reading Kills You)

Foluke Taylor

As I read, I annotate. Annotation is a habit of relation—the relation between me and books and papers in which each of us is indelibly marked by our encounter. My school teachers would have disapproved, but given that many, or even most of them, are no longer living—inhabitants now of an ancestral realm—I imagine they have access to a bigger picture and can be more relaxed. I trust they appreciate that annotation is a necessary and generative practice; a practice of curiosity and desire; a meeting of the need, as I walk with a text, to slow down and engage it in conversation. Much of my own writing—as those familiar with *Unruly Therapeutic* will likely know—begins here in the seedbed margins of annotation. This note from The Annotator began with an *R*—a single letter added in parentheses to the title of a journal article written by another therapist that frustrated me greatly. Without annotation, a textual conversation was impossible mainly because of the strong sense I had as I read, that the text was either trying to kill me or worse, had been written from and in a world in which I was already dead. The **'Fictional Frame'**—the title of the piece—became, with this initial annotation, the **F(R)ictional Frame**. To be able to name the f(R)iction, as a first, life-giving perforation of the article's stifling failures of address, — brought relief. After that, the annotations flowed—a furious spill of resistance and refusal that eventually became this; an account of the encounter between fiction and f(R)iction and/or between **The Framer** (the article and its author) and **The Annotator** who attempts—via a series of notes—an act of intertextual resuscitation.

a veil is lifted
p.453

Resistance

'...all *stories are built on three fundamental blocks*'

The Fictional Framer declares it and so it must be true and yet the Annotator's pen—alert to the '**all**' of '*all stories*'—is raised. In the Annotator's world, *all* is a word with the power to enact erasure in the most casual ways. *All* becomes a technology for distortion—the process by which a very specific gaze appears so much wider to itself than it is, thereby coming to imagine itself universal. *All* as a vehicle for a gigantic, world-bending fisheye lens that enables the gaze that sees itself as *All* the gazes and the only gaze. From here, it assumes (of course) that it is authorized to voice, and make declarations, for us all. The Annotator feels their breath being taken away. Is their alert warranted? Does the word 'all' **always** signal this kind of trouble? The Annotator does not know how to answer this, so they offer what they do know—that this '*all*' is a feature in the routines through which Black life has been, and is, habitually disappeared. They know that stories that **don't** take the form of *all* the stories in The Framer's declaration are not mentioned or even hinted at here in this text. The nonconforming stories are not included in this *all*. — The knowledges and ways of being they hold and carry are not included in this *all*. Given that the stories, knowledges, and ways of being are not here for The Framer to think with as he expounds on storytelling therapeutics, The Annotator—who is also a writer and *therapist[1] working with creative writing—has trouble taking him seriously.

the question of whose histories are told p.155

[1] The asterisk, following the work of Christina Sharpe, *In the Wake* (2016), functions before the word therapist here as both wildcard and placeholder.

The Annotator, drawing from Elleza Kelley's review of Christina Sharpe's *Ordinary Notes* writes,

> 'Formal errancy has always offered writers a way to conjoin theory and method in the study of black life.'[2]

[2] Kelley.

These notes on form and errancy offer recognition; are another way of saying **do not despair**. The notes are reminders that as much as The Framer misses us, we know ourselves outside of his description. — Our living is excess to his *All* and its attendant categories, genres, and sanctioned narrative forms.

the right to opacity p.239

The Framer continues with his ignor(e)ance and expands on the *'all stories'* statement to state that it is *'...as true for therapeutic stories as it is for blockbuster movies.'*

The Annotator reads this claim on truth, underlines *'blockbuster,'* and adds a question mark. This makes space for various doubts and curiosities, calling—as some annotations do—for further research. It turns out that the term 'blockbuster' was popularized in the 1940s—originating from blockbuster bombs which were so-called because of the power they had to destroy. A single bomb could take out an entire city block. The Annotator does not dispute *blockbuster* as a signifier of wide impact but does have to take time to consider how bombs become movies become **therapeutic stories**. How can they be left to inhabit the same sentence, unremarked and unexamined? It seems to The Annotator that much like the bombs after which they were named, the impact of blockbuster movies is not necessarily therapeutic; not *all* good, and certainly not good for *All* of us. The Annotator adds a reference to a debate in 1965 at Cambridge University in which James Baldwin was a participant. With Baldwin's name now in the margin, The Annotator listens again to the recording of that debate. Baldwin describes a scene using the second person pronoun, You. It feels like an invitation to time travel.

> 'You, he says, are a child watching Westerns. You are
> rooting for Gary Cooper as he kills off the Indians.
> You are shocked to discover that the Indians are You.'[3]

[3] See teachrock.org/video/james-baldwin-on-gary-cooper/. For Baldwin's full debate, see Baldwin, 14:04–38:00.

The Annotator recognizes the watching and the shock discovery. The Annotator knows that moment; knows they are the *You* invited to remember; knows the power of the blockbuster and the extent of its impact on a life.

The Annotator wonders if The Framer would be one of the people who downplay and fictionalize the impacts they cannot contend with—who insist that the harm cannot be **real** because the movie is **not real**. Surely though, given that this article centers on the power of storytelling and stories as agents of therapeutic change, The Framer would not attempt to reach for this defense? The Annotator thinks (hopes) that they can agree—now that they are in the conversation and have made space to register R for **resistance** —that the power of fiction to help cannot be assumed, and is certainly not aided by ignoring its shadow, the power to destroy. This power takes many forms; towards the destruction of a child's sense of reality; towards the imposition of a devastating set of epistemic conditions that consolidate the ontological hierarchy of whiteness. Other destructions and impositions, taking other forms, are annotated elsewhere;[4] references for another day. For now, The Annotator's proposition to The Framer is that fiction's potency lies in the tension between **made-up-ness** (the ways in which it is not real) and **making-up-ness** (the ways in which it creates what then becomes real). This tension, as one of many complexities of being, is not unliveable. It is the splitting—the attempt to deny or escape the f(R)iction—that becomes deadly and needs to be resisted. To be resisted, it must first be re-appeared and remembered. The Annotator's R offered as a gift—an *aide-mémoire* meaning **remember to resist**.

4 Taylor. (Including a brief telling of a story told in 1493 by Pope Alexander VI, drawing on Sylvia Wynter's 1995 essay, 'The Pope Must Have Been Drunk.') See also Wynter.

The notes for this section include Dionne Brand—a writer whose words are in every room of The Annotator's personal resistance arsenal. The selected quote—on the subject of movies—is from the poem *Nomenclature for the Time Being*,

> 'They had the temerity to sell me movies and portfolios and terabytes of their lousy activities and I bought them, and it punished me to hear their awful news of their victories over me that made me laugh and love them as they insisted.'[5]

5 Brand (2022).

Refusal

The Framer says that stories *'...convey lessons about how to survive in a sometimes, dangerous world'*.

Here, the note from The Annotator is a question of **who**. Whose survival is it that is being described? The Annotator also tries to imagine what it might be to conceive of the world as only *sometimes* dangerous; to not have to contend with, or live the fact of imminent and immanent death[6] that surrounds Black life? With this fact missing, the statement about the stories can only be **refused**—refused because something vital has been left out. By vital, The Annotator means life-giving, for example stories we share with our children—often against the counsel of our hearts—about the other children we have lost to a dangerous world. 'The Talk' is one name for these stories—ones that describe what we know, and what we **need to know**, about the folk who have been choked and shot, and strip-searched in school,[7] and restrained to death?[8] 'The Talk' speaks of danger and of how dangerous it would be to not talk about the danger that is everywhere. Fiction is incomplete without the f(R)iction, which is to say it is not credible; not liveable. The R here is for **refusal.** — Also for **respiration**, which is to say that The Annotator, because they know the reading hurts, wishes you to **breathe**.

taking our body
out of the line of fire
p.210

6 Sharpe.

7 See theguardian.com/uk-news/2022/jun/15/child-q-four-met-police-officers-facing-investigation-over-strip-search.

8 I recently visited the exhibition 'Souls Inquest' at 198 Contemporary Arts and Learning and was reminded that, while navigating their own grief, there are people committed to showing us how to care-fully remember (and refuse to forget) lives lost to state violence.

According to The Framer, when we engage with a story *'...we share in a collective experience that takes us beyond our own lives...'*.

The Annotator refuses the Framer's version of sharing. They do not wish to pick holes, but The Framer will absolutely need to be more specific about what is and is not shared. The *'we'* in the claim of collective experience will need to be discussed—even more urgently now that The Framer has gone on to repeat it with added enthusiasm *'Suddenly'* he writes, *'we're part of that novel, that movie, with all the drama and thrills those narratives might bring!'* The exclamation mark arrives as annotation—is present in The Framer's text only as a vibrational frequency. The Annotator feels it; registers the attempt—via a fronted adverbial—to generate collective excitement. They understand that it **is possible sometimes**—from one's unmentioned, unrecognized, marginal space—to suspend disbelief; One can, as Dionne Brand's quote suggests, *buy* (into) these movies and *laugh* and *love*. Questions remain however, about the *we* who are imagined to be sharing in an experience. The shared ground is disaggregated—strewn with what for some is drama and thrill, but for others dispossession and death. With so many monuments sitting atop of so many unmarked graves, the ground is seismic. The Annotator notes a *'we'* long collapsed.

> '*We* is an aggregate already disaggregated ... *we* is a doing already undoing'[9]

9 Brand (2021).

The Annotator **refuses** the falsely aggregated *we*—Ana-Maurine Lara's 'assumptive we'[10]—and makes Black notes instead. Black note-making as a practice of speaking from a **We** already disaggregated. — Black note-making meaning adding bell hooks to the conversation and *talking back*,[11] and insisting on polyvocality and our polyexistence which, in the words of Lata Mani, has

Declaration p.255

> '[d]iversity as its nature, relationality its grammar.'[12]

10 Lara.

11 hooks.

12 Mani.

We are relation; A declaration of **We** that does not rely on erasure or murder. Though The Annotator recognizes that inhabiting this relational **We**—fractured as it is with race and gender and other forms of socially produced difference—often requires acrobatics not entirely compatible with life-full-ness. Included here is a reference to the peculiar skill of double consciousness[13]—the ability forged through having to take note of oneself through the gaze of others alongside one's own. This capacity, though fired by and forged in racism—born of terror and the need to survive it—is nonetheless a relational skill. The Annotator wonders about double consciousness as a potentially useful acquisition for The Framer. The annotation—a challenge to expand awareness by looking back at himself through a Black woman's eyes—is quickly struck out. The Annotator's work is already too much. There is no energy to spare for The Framer's education. An overwrite; **Refuse this labor**. An addendum; *Rest as Resistance*. The Annotator can hear Tricia Hersey calling from down in the footnotes, telling them to **go lay down.**[14]

13 Dubois.

14 Hersey.

Resuscitation

The Framer turns to the historical, which causes The Annotator to put the text down and take a moment to **chant down**. Later, when **simmered down** sufficiently to be able to read the sentence again, they return. Another *we*, this time a 'one' who *'...yearns to know "what it was like" to experience certain historic events.'* Which of these historic events does The Framer imagine that *we*—the ones who have been declared by his forebears to *have* no history—are yearning to experience? The Annotator notes a book title, *Silencing the Past*.[15] This note is here to remind us to consider how power influences the creation and recording of this thing called **history**. The Annotator is thinking with Saidiya Hartman and Christina Sharpe and sitting in the vicinities of Black feminisms. From this location, they do not agree that slavery and/or colonization can be claimed to be *historical or past events*. There is simply too much evidence of continuous unfolding—of afterlives[16] and wakes[17] being lived.

15 Trouillot.

16 Hartman (1997).

17 Sharpe.

There is a note from NourbeSe Philip reading *'their history, my memory'*. It refers to Philip's essay[18] on the historical monument known as Leopold's Gate. The gate, which stands in Wales, not far from the Gladstone's Library where Philip was in residence, is a tourist attraction. The gate commemorates Leopold because he is (presumably) judged to be a figure for whom a historical record is justified. As the tour guide references **the history**, Philip remembers **the terror**. She remembers the people in Congo who lost lives and limbs and loves in the brutal invasion and occupation that Leopold oversaw. *Their history, my memory*, she writes. The Annotator's memory is also filled with terrors; with ships, holds, plantations, and imprisonment; with a continuum. The Annotator notes the yearnings that are not nostalgic and do not map towards a time called past or a thing called history; the yearnings of the ones with memory more than history who already know *what it was like* because it still is. The Annotator knows what it is like to have to continually resurrect themselves in spaces that would deny them life. Their notes are acts of furious love inserted into a text and trying to move it closer to what it says it aims for but fails to do—offer writing as a therapeutic. The Annotator notes a past that can neither be yearned for in, nor amputated from, the present. The best we can do, in The Annotator's assessment, is to attend to what then is saying now and story ourselves in the direction of marronage; freedom; and *how can I live*?[19]

18 Philip (2018).

19 Hartman (2019).

> *'There is something about stories and storytelling that expands our awareness and gets us through life in one piece. They explain the unexplainable, calm fears, and make us feel safer.'*

The Annotator underlines, but does not excise, this assertion from The Framer. There is perhaps, something in this statement—though *safety* and the promise of *getting through life in one piece* lie beyond the reach of The Annotator's credibility. There is simply too much unsafety around for such a statement to be swallowed whole; too many people who do not get through intact who deserve our respect. *Zong!*[20] | is the annotation. This is the title of an account of not getting through life in one piece—a narrative poem that is both heartbreaking and stunning. The Annotator would, if they could, put this text on every curriculum. They would like more people than currently do to remember between 130 and 150 African people on the slave ship Zong who were murdered by their captors—thrown into the ocean by the crew who feared supplies were running short. The writer—NourbeSe Philip—knows that this is a story that must be told and can only be told with care. It requires painstaking work amongst the fragments of lives and the lack of regard for those lives. She writes of exhumation—the act of retrieving bodies from earth—and not finding a corresponding word for retrieving bodies from underwater. How to return dignity to those left to be forgotten in a **liquid grave**? The Annotator understands that in the (colonial) English language they have available to them, the words to tell Black life will have to be continually (re)made. — They appreciate *exaqua*—the word that Philip alights on—and the ways that the poem performs this act of returning bodies from underwater. Fashioned from words used to record a legal case (Gregson v. Gilbert) brought against the ships' insurers, the poem is arranged on its page to leave space between and around each word. In this way, Philip creates space for breath and possibilities for breathing.[21] | The Annotator asks The Framer to respect the intention here, which could never be to *explain the unexplainable* (what terrible injury would be done in the attempt?) but rather to tell the story **that cannot be told** while taking care to not murder the dead all over again. This is, The Annotator points out, writing in life-giving mode; something like resuscitation. No, writing does not provide a ticket to *getting through life in one piece*. It can perhaps be part of the living and breathing that makes space for the drowned and undrowned.[22] | Writing can perhaps (because the past is not past, and the event not historical) create space in which we do not look away from, and are able to stay with, the ongoing drowning.[23] | The Annotator is curious to know what The Framer is making of the annotations. Does he see

developing a shared language and formulating a collective request p.226

exaqua enacted here; notes pushing into and breaking through his suffocating frame, surfacing toward life?

20 | Philip (2008).

21 | To anyone interested in writing in life-giving modes, I would highly recommend reading the chapter titled 'Notanda' toward the end of Zong! in which Philip reflects on the process of writing, with care, over time and *telling the story that cannot be told*.

22 | Gumbs.

23 | I write this aware of the many lives being lost currently in ocean crossings to Europe, and in the same week that anything up to 700 people have drowned in Greek waters as authorities looked on, aware of the risks, and failed to act. See theguardian.com/commentisfree/2023/jun/20/the-guardian-view-on-danger-at-sea-looking-out-for-all-those-in-peril.

The Framer's article begins with his own story of resuscitation. In his account this is facilitated by a therapist who offers a writing exercise. The Framer is asked to first divide a piece of paper into six sections and then to write or draw in each section to produce what is described as *'a complete, self-contained narrative'*. The Annotator chooses not to try out this activity. The proposition that the story should be *self-contained* and follow a *'classic three-act structure'* seems to them to have room only for a figure who has the privilege of imagining themselves to be individual. The activity seems to have this figure at its center. The figure is self-possessed and possessing, economically independent, and somehow detached from their social surround. The figure is someone self-contained and therefore unaffected by the bigger stories that structure this social surround. The figure finds the fictional frame capacious enough for their living; The Annotator does not. The frame is sealed in an airlessness created by what it misses—by the missing address; the missing blockbuster destructions of reality; the missing imminent and immanent death; the missing danger; the missing Talks; the history that misses the memory. Hence, while the fiction that the frame invites might follow a linear path—introduction, inciting incident, rising tension, crisis, and climax/denouement —the f(R)iction cannot live here. The f(R)iction is invited to absent itself; to melt away; to remain below the abyssal line;[24] to become an **Other** story that only the Others would need to care about.

24
Santos.

The Annotator cares—enough to add the notes that make the f(R)iction visible. Now that the **race** and **resistance** and **refusal** has been returned, the text looks a little messy. In The Annotator's world, messiness is essence. This is what it looks like to break (out of) the fictional frame that refuses (to see) you. This mess is commitment. The practice of annotation is a commitment to **resisting** a colonial lexicon that crushes and disappears Black life despite that lexicon being saturated with the deadly fiction of *race*[25] that it wanted to make real. The Annotator is not attached to tidiness. Their intention is to intervene in persistent care-less-ness; to make room for the knowing, beauty, and joy of Black life. — They recognize ink in the margins (however messy) as inhalation; as the sketching of tiny airways through dead, deadening, and deadly textual zones; and ultimately as a way to survive being **Black while reading**. This is important because The Annotator (like The Framer) believes in writing and stories and in the therapeutics they make possible. They hope, as they send the annotations out into the world, to signal an otherwise; in the direction of other ways to read that make other spaces to read, and write, and **live** in.

multiplicity
p.292

25
Spillers.

This text was first published on the Unruly Therapeutic Substack *as 'A Note from the Annotator' on June 24, 2023.*

References

Baldwin, James. 'Has the American Dream Been Achieved at the Expense of the American Negro'. Debate featuring James Baldwin and William F. Buckley at the Cambridge Union, Cambridge, England, February 18, 1965. Video, 58 min., 57 sec. Posted August 16, 2013. youtube.com/watch?v=VOCZOHQ7fCE.

Brand, Dionne. 'What We Saw. What We Made. When We Emerge.' Lecture given at the Kitty Lundy Memorial Lecture at York University, Toronto, Canada, March 11, 2021.

Brand, Dionne. *Nomenclature*. Duke University Press, 2022.

Dubois, W. E. B. *The Souls of Black Folk*. A. C. McClurg and Co., 1903. gutenberg.org/cache/epub/408/pg408-images.html.

Gumbs, Alexis Pauline. *Undrowned: Black Feminist Lessons from Marine Mammals*. AK Press, 2020.

Hartman, Saidiya. *Scenes of Subjection*. Oxford University Press, 1997.

Hartman, Saidiya. *Wayward Lives, Beautiful Experiments: Intimate Histories of Social Upheaval*. W. W. Norton & Company, 2019.

Hersey, Tricia. *Rest is Resistance: A Manifesto*. Little, Brown Spark, 2022.

hooks, bell. 'Talking Back.' *Discourse* 8 (1986): 123–128. jstor.org/stable/44000276.

Kelley, Elleza. 'Ordinary Allurements: Christina Sharpe's Reading Lessons.' *The Yale Review*, June 12, 2023. yalereview.org/article/elleza-kelley-ordinary-allurements.

Lara, Ana-Maurine. *Queer Freedom: Black Sovereignty*. SUNY Press, 2021.

Mani, Lata. *Myriad Intimacies*. Duke University Press, 2022.

Philip, M. NourbeSe. *Zong!* Wesleyan University Press, 2008.

Philip, M. NourbeSe. 'The Declension of History in the Key of If.' In *Letters to The Future: Black Women/Radical Writing*, edited by Erica Hunt and Dawn Lundy Martin. Kore Press, 2018.

Santos, Boaventura de Sousa. *The End of the Cognitive Empire: The Coming of Age of Epistemologies of the South*. Duke University Press, 2018.

Sharpe, Christina. *In the Wake: On Blackness and Being*. Duke University Press, 2016.

Spillers, Hortense J. *Black, White and in Color: Essays on American Literature and Culture*. The University of Chicago Press, 2003.

Taylor, Foluke. *Unruly Therapeutic: Black Feminist Writings and Practices in Living Room*. W. W. Norton & Company, 2023.

Trouillot, Michel-Rolf. *Silencing the Past: Power and the Production of History*. Beacon Press, 1995.

Wynter, Sylvia. 'The Pope Must Have Been Drunk, The King of Castille a Madman: Culture as Actuality, and the Caribbean Rethinking Modernity.' In *The Reordering of Culture: Latin America, the Caribbean and Canada: In the Hood*, edited by Alvina Ruprecht and Cecilia Taiana. Carleton University Press, 1995. trueleappress.files.wordpress.com/2020/04/wynter-the-pope-must-have-been-drunk.pdf.

RHYTHM RECALIBRATION TREMBLING

body
breath
witnessing
negotiation
micro and macro
point of view of the Earth
relinquishing agency
(de)instrumentalization
inverting the agent
accepting the unknown
fantasy
complexity
provocation
objects as subjects
accumulation of energy
magical thinking
lived experience
continuous seeking

Phonosophia's Bodies

Camila Sposati

From a physiological point of view, the eye has two types of cells that transmit the information the brain uses to create images: cones and rods.

Cones are convex. They are the brain's gaze, which analyzes and names.

Rods are concave. They are irrational. They are linked to sensation rather than memory or form.

At the same time, from a sensorial point of view, the gaze never works alone; the ear sees, the nose tastes, and the eyes touch. This paradoxical movement is that of sense itself. This dynamic makes it possible for us to be affected by one another.

A certain kind of nomadism arises from the crossing between the senses. The unstable terrain between them invokes a state of continuous invention, one that would not be possible if the geography were fixed and smooth. In our body, it is possible to make micro-predictions of what will happen at a given moment, but it happens in a controlled way. When there is an invasion, we have to reformulate and create new methods.

In my artistic work, I have explored the passage between worlds in scales and meanings. Since 2015, that exploration has been manifested through the creation of musical instruments that I call Phonosophia instruments. The creation of an instrument invokes questions. What can you do with an instrument? Do you play it, or does the instrument perhaps play you? Who touches and who is touched?[1] These are also intrinsic questions for the observer's gaze: an eye that also listens and imagines. —

horizons of intelligibility
p.196

[1] In English, German, and even French, when it comes to a musical instrument, we say that we 'play' the instrument. In Portuguese and Spanish, on the other hand, we say that we 'touch' an instrument. This reverses the sensory understanding of the relationship between the player and the instrument.

The concept of Phonosophia instruments emerged during the construction of the *Earth Anatomical Theater* (2014), my contribution to the Bahia Biennial. I modeled the project on the Anatomical Theater of Padua, a particular sixteenth-century architecture for witnessing the dissection of the human body. My project in Bahia was a steep, conical architecture dug into the body of the earth at a site that, during the same historical period as the anatomical theaters, was being 'discovered' for the first time. In my project, the architecture informs the body of the Earth. My intention for the *Earth Anatomical Theater* was that the conical shape descending into the crust of the Earth could serve as an eye, engaging the Earth as a witness of what had happened there, and also as a device for the amplification of sound coming from the planet outwards. —

a body that is involved with the world p.194

This work was an 'equivocal'[2] reading and adaptation of the classic Italian theater of observation: rather than directing the gaze towards a dead body in the center, its architecture, partly subterranean and roughly finished with sandbags, drew attention to the earthen wall. I wanted to show the point of view of the Earth in relation to the violence of extraction and the exploitation of humans at this location—a place that was pivotal to the early stages of Brazilian colonialism and slavery.[3]

[2] Concept of Eduardo Viveiros de Castro in *Tipití: Journal of the Society for the Anthropology of Lowland South America*. The essay was presented as the keynote address at the meetings of the Society for the Anthropology of Lowland South America (SALSA), held at Florida International University, Miami, January 17–18, 2004. Viveiros de Castro.

[3] The island of Itaparica was the place where enslaved Africans were brought after the trans-Atlantic crossing and before they were sent to the mainland to be sold. This place carries vestiges of the ultimate asymmetrical relations of power and exploitation that enabled colonialism to flourish.

When I asked the *Earth Anatomical Theater*: what is there to dissect? the work answers: unofficial histories of those from the sixteenth century who could not have a voice and whose biographies were not recorded in high colonial times. As I dug into the ground, it unleashed energy and made sounds. — All

life-giving perforation p.93

of these converged and found form in tubular shapes that are also the Earth's internal organs. Just like humans, the Earth has its body, its eyes, and its ears.

With the subterranean theater, as with the other instruments born of it, I propose a view of the body, the Earth, and history in cross-section: an understanding that simultaneously traverses and collapses scales, geographies, and time. When the vertical section cut is turned ninety degrees to instead be viewed in plan, the cross-section becomes a crossroads: a meeting place of past, present, and future that transform each other. This intersection generates movement—of spinning, rotating, and inside out—and a feeling of vertigo. It is an anachronic, paradoxical condition that demands not only a shift in understanding, but also a different awareness of one's own body and of the 'self' that can be both individual and collective. —

expanding beyond borders
p.444

Phonosophia instruments are breath instruments. The instruments evoke and provoke a meeting place where the body of the player and that of the instrument make a relation to earth as material and to Earth, the planet. To date there have been six generations of the instruments.[4] Each generation is in some way built upon a tripartite foundation: the structure and function of internal organs (anatomy and physiology), breath instruments as actors (theater), and clay/earth (the Earth).[5]

4 I use the word 'generation' because they are charged with similarities. The term does not refer to progress but rather to different preoccupations of the context and time. It also makes clear that the instrument is a being and not only an object.

5 With the early generations of instruments, I was interested in having oppositional scales: Earth capital E, earth small e, the relation of the organ of the Earth and at the same time the material earth. Clay is not merely representational, it embraces the complexity of scales and relations.

That most of the instruments are made of clay is crucial to me. The use of clay is a very ancient practice. Shaping clay is intimate: the heat and humidity of my hand affect the clay which can easily break at any point in the process, whether it is wet, dry, or baked. To avoid this, it is necessary to understand each stage. How fully the material is expressed depends on my knowledge of both it and the shape I wish to draw it into. The twists and folds have limitations—the quality of the clay matters, as does the temperature of the kiln. As a maker, I let the material take the lead. The more closely I work with it, the closer I get to hearing its sound. — In the making, the object as subject is revealed: the initiating subject—the maker—retains intentionality but must relinquish agency (that is, control).

tactile resonance
within the body
p.405

In Phonosophia, the player of the instrument also needs to accept something unknown as valuable. To approach an instrument that you do not know how to play and have no tutorial to access requires a degree of fantasy.[6] From ancient Greece to modernity, musical instruments have been understood as having varying functions, whether in service to the individual or the whole society. By contrast, Phonosophia instruments are a medium to find out more about oneself — and in doing so they lose their capacity for instrumentalization. In actively seeking to de-instrumentalize the instrument, Phonosophia transforms function and execution into a potential for the accumulation of energy and power. The instruments are both object and subject—each position continuously informing the other.

bringing subtlety
into consciousness
p.88

6 I adopted the name Phonosophia from Athanasius Kircher, a seventeenth-century polymath who was preoccupied with the musical anatomy of the body, the ear, and the voice, not only of humans but also animals. In *Acoustics Today: A Publication of the Acoustical Society of America*, acoustician Lamberto Tronchin explains that, 'Kircher's works express a typical Baroque vision of the "marvellous world" [and] reveal a strong alliance between science and magic' that were central to European science at that time—applied equally in explorations of the inner body as in expropriation of lands around the world. Tronchin, 11.

None of the Phonosophia breath instruments have keys or finger stops, so for all of them only one tone may be played in each tube. But making sound is not their main function.

Rather, it is the relation of the player with the instrument; in other words, how much the instrument can tell the player(s) about themselves, and make them listen. By its nature, the process is one of continuous seeking. Through the interaction with the instrument, breath becomes a practice of political, cultural, and spiritual negotiation.[7] The intensity of the activator's breath produces rhythm and volume in the sound, bringing it into relation with their lived experience and thoughts.[8] Thus, it's possible to create a sound with Phonosophia instruments that is not only sound.

7 Here I draw from Stephen P. Hugh-Jones in *Tipití: Journal of the Society for the Anthropology of Lowland South America* 16. Hugh-Jones.

8 I use the word 'activate' to describe the relationship with the instrument, because the word 'performance' places the performer in the central role. In Phonosophia, the objects are of equal importance. There is no protagonist.

I consider the *Earth Anatomical Theater* itself to be the first generation of Phonosophia instruments. The second generation (2015), produced in Brazil, marked a shift in scale to accommodate a human player. With those instruments, I was interested in listening/saying/voicing. In the third generation (2018), produced in the Netherlands, a colored glaze on the ceramics features as sound notes. In the fourth generation (2019), the subjectivity of the instruments became more dominant, with metal mouthpieces that allowed the body of the instrument to vibrate. The fifth generation (2021) was developed during a two-month residency in the northeast part of Brazil where a group of fourteen people produced instruments departing directly from their own body parts. For the most recent, sixth generation (2022), the instruments were produced not from clay but with natural rubber material called balata, originating in the Brazilian Amazon area.[9]

9 Composed of a liquid extracted from the inside of a tree in the rainforest, the Balata instrument (2023) responds to the violence of latex and rubber production that catered to international industrialists until the second half of the nineteenth century—a violent history of extraction that has left holes, if not gaps, in the tranquility of the rainforest. For this reason, the fifth generation of my instruments, in the shape of insects, leaves or even shells, have blade-like mouthpieces. In refusing to be touched or played, they resist extinction.

Here are some characteristics of their body/ies:

Trumpet Livre (2015) is a trumpet without valves that therefore can only play one tone. The ends of the instrument, a mouth and three or more ears, are joined by a tubular shape that embodies 'gravity.' In physics, gravity is the force by which a planet or other body draws an object toward its center. In the case of Phonosophia instruments, it is a universal constant in the interaction between mouth and mouth or mouth and ear—also because we know that the inner part of the ear, the organ of balance, is responsible for gravitational equilibrium. What interests me here is the relationship of scale between the body (human, in this case) and the planet. Each Phonosophia instrument is understood as a component of the body. In this generation, the color of the clay referred to the color of the skin and at the same time to internal organs, which for all humans are the same color. In all generations of the instruments, their shapes—containing mouths and ears—provoke vital questions on what can happen between the domains of saying and listening, or the other way round?

Tumbum Liber (2018) is made up of an ear, a mouth, and gravity. Here too, I call the tumbum—a hollow structure in the central part that connects the ends of the instrument—'gravity' because it is involved in a complex game of micro and macro relationships between the earth and Earth. Gravity is what makes all beings united to the macro and at the same time to the inner domains (micro). In these tubes of the instrument, what has been said or heard is processed and given new meaning. — Their purpose is to unite, not polarize. Playing this instrument well involves a movement of internalization, a continuous recalibration of how air moves inside and outside the body,[10] demanding the sensory nomadism of the receiver.

inward process that ripens p.416

10 My instruments claim the reversibility that is central to Marília Librandi's writing on listening. She explains that, on the one hand, 'hearing' means to understand the meaning of the message, to understand what is being said by means of the intellect. On the other hand, 'listening' denotes intense and special concentration on that which is received in terms of bodily resonance, paying attention above all to the intonation, the timbres, the noises, and the silences. Librandi, 30.

Solua (2019) is an instrument from the fourth generation. The name is a palindrome of the Greek instrument *aulos*, and it is named as such because it inverts both the form and the position of the agent. Whereas the aulos is a double reed flute for one player, *Solua* is a single form with three mouthpieces that up to three people can play. Three breaths join in relationship as the conjoined agent of the instrument. By inverting the Greek instrument, I recast the dimension of the pipes and how the people who participate act in relation to the instrument and to one another. A negotiation opens between the players' bodies, the relationship between who they are playing for and when. And the third layer is the macro meaning of this event: What does it mean to play together in different bodies?

Solua depends on the intensity and timing of the breath to generate a note. This requires each player to think about their own breathing, and at the same time pay attention to the person next to them without having eye contact. The concentration of breath, sound, and vibration opposes a focus on sight, accentuating the value of embodied experience and multisensory perception. As one person intensifies more and another less, the field of air negotiation is narrow. If a player pushes too much air, the intensity can return back to them, and creates a situation where they do not allow others to play together. The negotiation is subtle and very close, with each player bringing their own unique rhythm and breath to vibrate the body of the instrument. — Together they join to form one body.

sympathetic reverberation
p.262

In a way, aulos and *Solua* are the same breath instrument, but inverted. By performing an inversion, the instrument is no longer an object, nor just a subject, it is a cross-section of different realities. For a prelude to the exhibition 'Breath Pieces (part 1)' at ifa Stuttgart in 2023—the event Digging for Samples in the Theatre of the Long Now: A Subterranean Experiment—we drilled three points in the ground (about 3 meters deep and 8 centimeters in diameter) and adapted the mouthpieces to the holes, reproducing the instrument in the ground. This is not merely a scaling up of the instrument, *Solua* (2023), it is an inversion that requests one to understand the relations between humans, layers of the Earth, and the cosmic. It reflects my fascination for dissection, stratification, and subterranean spaces, emphasizing the importance of geological time and intricacy. The inversion here implies a transformation of the agent, the possibility of multiple scales, and therefore of vision.

SPECTRES

References

Hugh-Jones, Stephen P. 'Thinking Through Tubes: Flowing H/air and Synaesthesia.' *Tipití: Journal of the Society for the Anthropology of Lowland South America* 16, no. 2, art. 2 (2019): 20–46. doi.org/10.70845/2572-3626.1275.

Librandi, Marília. *Writing By Ear: Clarice Lispector and the Aural Novel*. University of Toronto Press, 2018.

Tronchin, Lamberto. 'Athanasius Kircher's Phonurgia Nova: The Marvelous World of Sound During the 17th Century.' *Acoustics Today: A Publication of the Acoustical Society of America* 5, no. 1 (2009): 8–15. doi.org/10.1121/1.3120723.

Viveiros de Castro, Eduardo. 'Perspectival Anthropology and the Method of Controlled Equivocation.' *Tipití: Journal of the Society for the Anthropology of Lowland South America* 2, no. 1, art. 1 (2004). doi.org/10.70845/2572-3626.1010.

fracture
trust
starting over
care
collectivity
precarity
silent learnings
invisible paths
mystery
ancestors
telluric force
spiritual forests within
sharing affections
minimal, slow forms
balance between worlds
space-times of
  coexistence
the promise of rebirth

Èṣù and the Living Earth
The Heart at the Crossroads of Existence

Cláudio Bueno and Moisés Patrício

When we face an existential dilemma, such as the loss of something or someone dear to us, the heart and the Earth show us how to go on living. Like the separation of tectonic plates, the end of a relationship causes deep tremors. However, just as the Earth regenerates, we must find new ways to walk. Èṣù, the guardian of the crossroads, teaches us that every rupture can open up a new path instead of being an obstacle or a place of no way out. Through these fractures, we learn to deal with pain, failure, and starting over.

This text is part of a dialogue between the visual artist and *babalorixá* Moisés Patrício, who lives in Sao Paulo, and the visual artist and educator Cláudio Bueno, who lives between São Paulo and California (a place affected by significant earthquakes and geographical fault lines). At the time of this writing, Bueno was going through a significant breakup after sixteen years of living with his partner. Aware of the inevitable sufferings that come with such ruptures, he looks to the ancestral knowledge of the *terreiros de candomblé* for other social technologies that can help us understand, feel, and navigate through these significant transformations and renewals of life. Technologies that enable paths toward freedom, joy, and connection with the Earth and all beings, visible and invisible. —

ontological joy
p.389

It is becoming increasingly necessary to think about different times and spaces for living together where collective life can flourish healthily and sustainably, even if they are invariably affected by, and impossible to isolate from, the conflicts, hegemonic ways of living, institutional power, and world violence. Ancestral knowledge, such as that of Candomblé[1] and Indigenous cultures in this territory, offers ways forward that contrast with hegemonic Western solutions, proposing more harmonious ways of living based on mutual respect, caring for the environment, and valuing communitarian life. This knowledge is not just a tool but a philosophy of living and a cosmovision that integrates the spiritual, social, emotional, and the whole Earth.

[1] Candomblé is a religion of the African diaspora that developed in Brazil during the nineteenth century.

Access to such knowledge should also not be seen as something exclusive to black and Indigenous peoples but as an available social technology that predates the periods of slavery and colonization and has been developing repertoires to deal with these threats to life perpetuated to this day. Old forests, such as the Amazonian rainforest in Brazil or the redwood forests in the United States, which have existed for thousands of years, may provide some answers, too. —

the lessons of a forest p.147

This knowledge clarifies how damaging and precarious modern and contemporary major technological infrastructures can be. Infrastructures that control access to water, information, electricity, mobility, and many forms of living in urban environments today. And when these infrastructures fail, so do we. Modern technocratic, rational design and the rigidity of its grids are incompatible with the natural movements of the Earth.

There is a certain pleasure in imagining the possible fragility of the big techs of Silicon Valley—one of the largest economies in the world, exploiting lands all over the world—sitting on countless geographical faults, collapsing in the face of an unpredictable response from the Earth itself. And we will have to live with this haunting and mystery, given the impossibility of human intervention or any geoengineering to paralyze or reverse geological processes, such as the movement of a tectonic plate or the melting of a glacier.

When the Earth shakes so severely that we are forced to live in an environment without infrastructures—when cell phones no longer work, the water no longer comes from the taps, and it's not even treated, and the lights don't come on, the roads are broken, and all planes stop—we will need to reactivate elementary social technologies of collective care among all beings, against modern forms of systemic isolation. What are these minimal, slow forms that reorganize themselves in line with the immensity of the Earth's movements? — Ways of moving, feeding, celebrating, and caring for ourselves. Some peoples, more than others, faced with systemic inequalities, have been living for a long time in this fracture produced by modernity (as Malcom Ferdinand tells us in *Decolonial Ecology*, 2019), or on a damaged and ruined planet, as anthropologist

urgency in what unfolds slowly p.373

Anna Tsing says in *Arts of Living on a Damaged Planet*, 2017 and *The Mushroom at the End of the World: On the Possibility of Life in Capitalist Ruins*, 2021. To live in the world today is invariably to live on the fault line.

The paths offered by social technologies such as Candomblé are based on the belief that the answers to regenerating the planet as we find it today may come not only from major political and technological changes but also from a radical transformation of the sensitive, spiritual, and cosmological fields that suggest ways of interacting with the Earth that also go through the heart. —

rebalancing emotional and energetic bodies p.130

Therefore, in this article, approaching a healing process from a breakup in a relationship is also a way of reflecting on broader healing processes that are intertwined with the forms of life on Earth, individually and collectively. Care and healing cease to be an isolated responsibility and become a collective act where the well-being of one reflects the well-being of all.

Healing, therefore, is a process that takes place in layers: **collectively**, when we allow ourselves to live in communities (of those we live among, of ancestors, human and non-human species), sharing knowledge and affections; and **individually**, when we immerse ourselves in our challenges and learnings, turning deep within while being sustained by the support network around us. In this interaction, we find ways to heal and grow together in new spaces and times of coexistence, where life is celebrated and ritualized in its totality and interdependence. Approaches found in the so-called Global South reaffirm these ancestral practices as essential for a future where social and spiritual ties are strengthened, providing a lasting balance between the individual, the community, and the environment.

Candomblé as a Basis for Thinking and Living on this Planet

Candomblé offers us a profound and integrative way of interacting with our realities. Unlike Western views that tend to separate body and spirit, nature and the human being, Candomblé proposes a connected existence where everything is part of a continuous cycle. This ancestral religion teaches us that life is communal with nature and the *orixá*.[2] These forces represent natural elements and aspects of life like fertility, wisdom, time, and justice.

2 Orixás are deities in the Afro-Brazilian religious tradition of Candomblé, as well as in other African diasporic religions like Santería and Vodou. They are believed to represent natural forces and human experiences, each embodying specific attributes, powers, and domains. To name some of the main ones: Oxalá, Exu, Ogum, Oxóssi, Xangô, Oxum, Iemanjá and Iansã.

In Candomblé, life is anchored in the understanding that we are part of the Earth and the universe, and that our actions, choices, and rituals influence and are influenced by greater forces. This perception that everything is interconnected generates a deep respect for ancestors, the environment, and each other. The ritualistic practice of Candomblé reminds us that existence takes place not only on the material plane but also on the spiritual one, and that the balance between these worlds is fundamental for a fulfilling life.

To see the world from the Candomblé cosmovision means understanding that we are not alone on our journey; every step and every decision is part of a larger context, guided by the orixás and ancestral energy. The crossroads of life, represented by Èṣù, show us that there are always choices and paths—and that the freedom we exercise also brings responsibility. The crossroads is a pedagogy:[3] a way of learning and deciding from life's multiple possibilities and mysteries.

ancestors' voices
p.161

3 Rufino.

Candomblé is a socio-environmental technology offering an ecological, relational, and spiritual perspective of living. It teaches us that life is not linear but cyclical, and that ruptures, failures, and new beginnings are part of existence. The orixás worship reminds us that to live is, above all, to be in tune with the universe, learning from the Earth and all the natural elements and cycles.. It is a way of resisting the logic of exploitation and disconnection that dominates the contemporary world, proposing a return to the sacred, care, and community instead.

In this sense, Candomblé offers a powerful key to thinking *with* the world, not as something to be dominated but as something to be experienced, cared for, and celebrated. It is an eternal dance of creation and re-creation, where each being has its role and importance in the balance of the cosmos.

The religious part of the *terreiro* is actually the smallest one. The *terreiro* known as a sacred and communitarian space where the orixás are worshipped by the community, and above all, a philosophy of life, a way of being in the world, and its complexity. What may seem precarious to many—such as walking barefoot on the ground, washing clothes in the river, or carrying out simple, everyday activities—is actually an opportunity to be in direct connection with life. It is a deep sense of presence in the world, of resistance to the systemic isolation and attention economy imposed by the modern world. —

sanctuary of familiarity
p.77

How many times have we pulled away from the land, and stopped feeling the texture of the ground? How many times have we missed the chance to connect with other beings around us? When was the last time you talked to a plant? And, more importantly, how did that moment resonate with you? What information did it bring you? Each such interaction is a form of silent and profound learning, a connection slowly being stolen from us by a system that alienates bodies and spirits.

The body, which used to be an instrument of connection and presence, has become a place of guilt and shame. By neglecting these essential connections, we lose the opportunity to nourish ourselves with wisdom. In the *terreiro*, what many see as simple or outdated is actually an experience that is deeply connected with nature, with the sacred, and with one's own being. Spiritual practice is reflected in every daily act, where life is celebrated and felt in its fullness.

Earth and Spiritual Geography

The word 'Terra' (Earth), which comes from the Latin *terra*, carries with it the idea of soil, territory, and ground. However, it goes beyond the physical and also encompasses the invisible and sacred. In the context of Candomblé and other Afro-Brazilian and Indigenous traditions, the land is not just the ground we walk on. It is also a place of memory, ancestry, and vital energy. It involves the spaces where physical and spiritual life meet. Each element of the Earth, be it a mountain, a river, or a forest, is charged with invisible meanings and is closely linked to the orixás and the ancestors.

Rituals performed on the land evoke a deep connection with the cycle of life and death, with the telluric force that sustains existence. Thus, this geographical approach teaches us that our space is not an empty void but is charged with power and meaning. — It is the meeting point between the visible and invisible forces, stirred up by rituals, revealing a sacred dance between these worlds.

spectral infrastructure p.233

Heart and Spiritual Forests

The heart, commonly associated with being the vital organ of emotions, can be seen as the center of spiritual life, where it meets the emotional and the physical. In this context, the heart can also be a metaphor for an inner sacred territory, an intimate forest where ancestral memories and energies coexist and intertwine.

Like a physical forest, it is home to life, mystery, and regeneration. 'Spiritual forests' are symbolic spaces for wisdom and renewal. In Yoruba mythology and many other traditions, forests are places of power where the spirit can reconnect with nature and the ancestors. Under this perspective, the heart is where our emotions and experiences are transformed into wisdom, ruptures become seeds of new growth, and the cycle of life and death is reflected in deep introspection and regeneration.

Earth, Heart, and the Spiritual

When we think of the Earth as something beyond the physical and of the heart as more than just an organ, we realize that both are directly connected to our relationship with the spiritual world. 'Spiritual geography' reveals that the space we inhabit, whether physical territory or the heart's inner space, is filled with meanings. The 'spiritual forests' within us are the places where we meet our deepest essence and the vital energy that connects the human being to the cosmos.

Candomblé teaches us that the heart is a place of crossing, an internal crossroads, — just as the Earth is a vast landscape of sacred meanings. Earth and the heart harbor transformative forces that help us understand life in its multiple dimensions, always in constant movement and continuity, like nature.

spectral infrastructure
p.233

The words 'Earth' and 'heart' and the beauty of how one carries the other can offer an expanded view of our relationship with the physical and intangible worlds.

Laroyê Èsù, Èsù Elégbára, Òrun n yé!

(Hail Exu, Lord of the Crossroads, the Heaven is clear!)

'Èṣù killed a bird yesterday with the stone he threw today.'
—Yoruba saying with a counter-intuitive meaning,
as it inverts the cause-and-effect relationship.

Orixá Èṣù is the principle of all movement, the basis that sustains the dialogue between worlds, between life and death, between the past and the present. By saluting Èṣù, we recognize that moving, communicating, and learning from/with the Earth, from what is telluric and spiritual, is needed. Energy is in the Earth, and so it is in us. Èṣù teaches us that everything is interconnected, that every rupture and failure is a continuity. To break is also to begin again.

In the pedagogy of **failure** or **fault** (these words are the same in Portuguese, written as *falha*), we also live and learn from our mistakes. The world is made up of failures/faults/fault lines, and we shouldn't fear them but rather understand them as part of the life cycle. Èṣù reminds us that there is always a new choice and path to follow. The freedom he offers us lies in the power to decide and, simultaneously, the duty to bear the responsibility for those decisions. Looking at the heart, which pulses incessantly, and the Earth, which moves constantly, we understand that we are not separated from the surrounding environment.

The orixás teaches us that after the catastrophe comes healing. — The Earth regenerates, as do our hearts. Death is not the end but a continuity in another reality. Èṣù, with his wisdom, shows us that to live is to be in constant movement and that life's crossroads are opportunities for reflection, decision, and transformation. That's why, even in the face of failure and the end, life always finds a way to continue.

slow stitching together of a new sense of self p.134

> *Igbésẹ̀ Èṣù, ṣí àwọn ọ̀nà, kí a lè rí àwọn ọna tuntun sí iwájú*
> (With the footsteps of Èṣù, we open the paths to see new routes ahead.)

This philosophy, based on the communion between body, Earth, and spirit, is reflected in how we deal with love and loss. How can we reorient our lives after a major rupture? Just as the Earth moves on after an earthquake, we must also learn to release this energy and move on. As a social technology, the orixás worship teaches us to live in harmony with nature and others, allowing us to find healing and meaning in the connections we can build.

In Èṣù, we find the strength to break and the wisdom to rebuild.

To Break is also to Continue

This is a profound concept that, in the context of Candomblé and life, reminds us that every break is not an end but a transformation. This new beginning is part of the natural cycle of existence. In the Western world, we are often taught to fear a breakup, to see it as a failure or a definitive loss. However, looking at nature and the universe from a Candomblé perspective, we understand that everything constantly moves and transforms, and every fracture carries the seed of something new.

When something breaks, be it a relationship, a project, or a life structure, the immediate impulse can be to resist change.

But Candomblé teaches us to seek the continuity hidden within the rupture. Like tectonic plates that move apart or tense up and cause earthquakes, what breaks through the surface creates new forms of life and territories. The rupture can generate pain, but it also opens up space for regeneration, for the birth of new possibilities and cycles.

Èṣù, the orixá of crossroads, reminds us that every break implies a new choice. When we break, we open up paths, even if they are initially invisible, and we are called upon to decide how to move forward. Continuity lies in this movement, in this ability to reconfigure life based on what has been broken. Breaking is an act of creative transformation, and continuing is the acceptance that life, in its essence, is fluid, never stagnant. It's a dance between destruction and creation, where every end is the beginning of something new.

Furthermore, the concept of rupture as continuity is deeply linked to the cycle of life and death, which is so present in Candomblé. Death is not the absolute end but a transition to another form of existence. In the same way, in every small death or rupture that might occur in everyday life—the end of a cycle, the end of a phase, the separation of a part of us—there is the promise of rebirth, of a fresh start. Continuity lies in accepting that breaking is part of the vital dynamic and allowing new forms to manifest by letting go of what has been broken.

On an individual and social level, 'to break is also to continue' challenges us to see crises and collapses as opportunities for change, growth, and invention. When something breaks, it is an invitation to rethink, reframe, and recreate. — Rather than trying to preserve what can no longer be sustained, this vision encourages us to embrace change and trust that there is a new path to follow. Therefore, breaking up is an act of courage, of accepting impermanence, and it is also an act of continuity. Life, in its essence, does not stop. It transforms, flows, and takes us in new directions, always searching for renewal and balance.

thinking anew
p.311

Finally, what happens after a disaster? Life must find forms to go on.

Beginning, Middle, Beginning again

According to *quilombola* intellectual Antônio Bispo dos Santos, there is no end. It's always beginning, middle, and beginning again. — With the collective strength of the knowledge of the *terreiros*, of the hearts at crossroads, of the Earth, of masters like Moisés Patrício, and of Èṣù (the divinity of communications and paths), we are invited to ritualize failures and faults as a path, to trust in paths as mysteries, trusting in every choice made, without knowing where they will lead us.

endlessly regenerating p.360

This text was written as a form of healing, provoked by the editor Carolyn F. Strauss, who had a dream saying to Bueno, 'You know, such a breakup is also like an earthquake.' It has been generated through a profound and careful dialogue between the authors, involving cooking, eating, sharing ideas, ritualizing, and sleeping when needed.

References

Rufino, Luiz. *Pedagogia das Encruzilhadas*. Mórula Editorial, 2019.

Wikipedia. 'Candomblé.' Accessed October, 2024. en.wikipedia.org/wiki/Candomblé.

patience
shift in attention
giving space
restoring flow
grieving-healing
others vibrate along
ritual
rest
infusion process
somber choreography
alchemy
intuition
connective tissue
slow-made medicine
weaving together
gathered around

The Slow Techniques of Mourning and Gardening

Guy Cools, Will Daddario, and Joanne Zerdy

> *All technical objects are pharmacological, in other words, are both remedy and poison, curative when used with moderation and destructive when used with excess.*[1]
> — Lysiane Lamantowicz

1 Lamantowicz, 81.

The first time I (Guy) experienced a demonstration by Greek traditional lamenters, the *moirológhista*, I was particularly impressed by the quality and depth of their performance technique. We were with an interdisciplinary group of European artists in Monodendri, one of the Zagori villages in Epirus in the North of Greece, close to the Albanian border. There we participated in the first edition of the Summer University organized by the National Theatre of Greece, curated by Eleni Varapoulou, with a research workshop, 'Rites of separation and union as a source of contemporary performance practice.' We had invited some local lamenters to join the workshop and share their traditional knowledge with us and the participants. When they gave a first demonstration of their craft, we were all blown away. Within seconds of having started their demonstration, the whole audience, which consisted mainly of young performing arts practitioners, were in tears, myself included. As there was no real experience of loss, the embodied release was solely triggered by the somatic and vibrational quality of their vocal technique. Mourning was performed and grief was liquefied in tears. At the end of their demonstration, they snapped out of the communal state they had created for themselves and their audience and were able to continue to converse with us lightly and jokingly. How did they do this? As so often in my life, the not-knowing triggered my curiosity and set me on a journey of trying to understand. This eventually led to the publication of *Performing Mourning. Laments in Contemporary Art* (2021).

Around the same time that I discovered the *moirológhia*, I had started a yoga practice with my first yoga teacher, Eric Gomes, in Belgium. Through Eric's guidance, I started to understand and practice yoga as an ancient bodily technique that teaches us to become conscious of the different bodies that we are, and how they are interconnected. The word 'yoga' is etymologically related to the word 'yoke,' the bridge that connects two oxen and allows them to work together. In yoga philosophy, the individual doesn't have just one body but many, interrelated ones: the physical, the mental, the emotional, the energetic, the spiritual, and so on. If one body is active, the others vibrate along. Different techniques—such as hatha yoga, which practices the physical body; meditation, which works with the mental body; or nada yoga, which focuses on voice and sound vibration—have been developed and passed on to make us conscious of how these bodies are interrelated and how we can influence one body by working on and with another. — Practicing the physical body, we can quiet the mind and rebalance the emotional and energetic bodies. While meditation can have a beneficial impact on our physical health, as proven in the research of Jon Kabat-Zinn, among others.

movement of enjoining p.200

What is true for the multi-layered nature of one body is also true for how that body is interconnected with other bodies, human and non-human, as well as with the larger environment. The mood of my partner or son influences my own mood and energy. A toxic work environment can have serious consequences on your health. Our cats and the trees in my garden act as pharmakons that rebalance my energy house.

Since *Performing Mourning* was published, my thinking on the techniques of mourning, the laments in particular, has further evolved. We create an energetic umbilical cord with people (but also with animals, places, or objects) that we have been closely connected with over a longer period of time. When this umbilical cord is cut as a result of a separation or more tragic loss, our own energetic household becomes short-circuited and we have to learn how to restore its flow. This is why it is useful to 'perform' our mourning in rituals guided by experienced practitioners and supported by techniques such as the laments. Like any pharmakon, the laments have to be used with moderation. A good lament maintains a balance between loss of control in order to release the emotions and the control of the musical form, which holds the space to do so.

In *What a Body Can Do* (2015), Ben Spatz discusses how embodied techniques such as yoga and most acting or dancing techniques are valuable branches of human knowledge alongside the sciences and humanities.[2] He also gives examples of how particular techniques 'transform the morphology of the physical body.'[3] In a similar way, the technique of lament or other artistic forms of 'performing mourning' allow the morphology of grief to transform. It doesn't disappear, but it becomes liquid again; that is, the energetic short circuit is deblocked and there is an energy flow again, — albeit an altered one.

new patterns
p.332

2 Spatz, 219.

3 Ibid., 56.

Parallel to this new understanding of the underlying reasons to perform mourning, I also started to become aware of its equally important flipside: the importance of longer periods of inactivity and rest during which the body reintegrates its energy flows without conscious interference. Again, it was my yoga teacher Eric Gomes who made me aware of this. He would teach the asanas of the hatha yoga, inviting us to have pauses between each asana (posture). Ideally each pause would have the same length as the preceding asana, since in the pause the body would make the necessary adjustments to continue to deepen the practice. Consciousness happens in the non-beat, the non-activity.

What is true for shorter time cycles is also true for longer ones, such as the seasons. I have recently moved back to Montreal, Canada, where I have become the custodian of a very special garden. Applying the first principle of permaculture,[4] during the first year of living with it I have been merely observing the garden during the different seasons, without interfering. The garden has a huge variety of trees: eastern hemlock, Japanese and yew maple, apple and gingko, red spruce and katsura, honeysuckle and hawthorn, beech and a majestic dawn redwood. I have been observing how they create and shed their canopies of leaves at different times, giving each other space and support to do so. In the Canadian winter, this layer of leaves is covered with a thick pack of snow and ice most of the time, allowing the earth underneath to regenerate by composting the decaying leaves.

4 Permaculture is a design practice, originally developed in agriculture by Bill Mollison and David Holgrem. Its contribution is to offer, in twelve principles, partitions of work applicable to all fields of human activity.

It is the start of a new long-term investigation, which I have given the title of *Winter Garden*, inspired by the reflections of the South-Korean philosopher Byung-Chul Han:

> 'Inactivity has a logic of its own, its own language, temporality, architecture, magnificence—even its own magic. It is not a weakness or defect but rather an intensity, which is, however, neither seen nor acknowledged in our active and performance-driven society.'[5]

5 Han (2024), 1.

With the Swiss choreographer Gregory Stauffer, I have started to research how we can apply the principles of permaculture to creative processes and how the process of soil aggradation can inspire ways to regenerate our human bodies. The *Winter Garden* is both a concrete environment and a metaphor for a space-time where processes of mourning and creative processes can meet and support each other. The first part of the new research is to visit existing gardens that have already been created to do so. Finlay's Garden is one of them.(...)

energetic reparations p.61

I (Will) am sitting on my couch, immersed in a world of activity. An email arrives. It's from Guy. How nice. What does it say? It says he's writing something on slowness, on slow technology (What's that?), and he'd like Joanne and me to collaborate. First thought: we're probably already collaborating. I ponder how that might be so. Here, 'to ponder' fills my mind alongside 'to gather.' I gather. What all gathers 'round'? What all has already gathered around? What kinds of slow have gathered? Is 'gathering' a technology? A technology of the serendipitous? The τέχνη of all who are patient?

the gift of human attention p.372

Slow gathers first but appears in my mind as sloe. Slow sloe. I think of gin. But what is sloe? Turns out: *Prunus spinosa*. Well, the fruit of *Prunus spinosa*, 'globose' and 'astringent' fruit. Some call the whole plant blackthorn. For its thorns. For its dark bark. And oh, look, the wood has been used traditionally to make walking sticks. I'm on a walk—'the mind at three miles an hour,' as Rebecca Solnit says.[6] Slow. Sloe.

6 Solnit, 14.

Here comes hawthorn. They resemble each other, hawthorn and blackthorn, as both are members of the *Rosaceae* family. Note: hawthorn leaves are lobed, and blackthorn have thorns with lateral buds. But the hawthorn has a special place in my heart because it reminds me of Wild Hawthorn Press, the means through which Scottish poet and gardener Ian Hamilton Finlay propagated his concrete poetry and unique chapbooks. Finlay's most impressive work is Little Sparta, his sprawling art garden in the Pentland Hills of Scotland. Little 'Sparta' because he intended his work to be a thorn in the side of the art scene in Edinburgh, the 'Athens' of the north. Wild Hawthorn is, then, appropriate: beautiful, but watch out. There are thorns in there.

We named our first child Finlay, after the poet and gardener. His death, our child's, though also the poet's, has spurred the emergence of many creative practices in the last decade, one of which is Joanne's project Finlay's Garden (more on which below). On my body, Finlay (both of them) and hawthorn gather in the form of an extensive tattoo along my left shoulder and down the upper part of my left arm. It depicts a hawthorn branch attended by loose gingko leaves. Joanne is the hawthorn and I am the gingko. I carry a little bit of Finlay's Garden on me. I carry a bit of Finlay in me, too. His ashes are embedded in the ink that spells out 'make tiny changes to Earth' on my right forearm. Tattooing is itself slow technology, a rite of passage, a method of mourning and memorializing the dead, and a ritual that translates physical pain into bodily transformation.[7]

[7] Daddario.

Back to *Prunus spinosa*. Spinoza: 'A people who live near hawthorn' (or maybe blackthorn, hard to tell).[8] The philosopher gathers round. He tells us, in Proposition XXV of Part 5 of *Ethics*: 'The highest endeavor of the mind, and the highest virtue is to understand things by intuition.'[9] In other words, the aim is to apprehend at a glance the way in which all that gathers round is a mode of the primary Substance. Gathering around and on and in me: Slow, sloe, blackthorn, hawthorn,

[8] In other words, the word is derived from *espino*, meaning 'hawthorn.'

[9] Spinoza. Propositions 21–34.

Wild Hawthorn Press, Ian Hamilton Finlay, our Finlay, gingko, tattoo, Spinoza, intuition. I am this arrangement (and more), akin to the many interrelated bodies of which Guy wrote. In this state, I enter Finlay's Garden.

...

Time slowed. People's movements grew less frantic. Voices grew quiet. I (Joanne) was encouraged to slow down my breathing. What motivated the deliberate extensions of time that I felt and the somber choreography manifested by those of us assembled in this hospital room in central Illinois, United States? My first child—our to-be-named son Finlay—had died suddenly and inexplicably during childbirth. Too shocked and terrified to cry or speak, I held my breath.

The days and weeks and months that followed Finlay's departure that June a decade ago remain, on the one hand, clearly etched in my memory. Effortlessly, I return in my mind to our home, our neighborhood sidewalks, my slow bicycle rides to a gentle yoga class several blocks away. On the other hand, though, recalling on which part of which day I mourned in a particular way is challenging. Slowness absolutely orchestrated my days—as I woke to the dreaded remembering that Finlay was physically absent; as Will and I cried and fell silent; as I wrote, read, and stared off; and as I reluctantly ate food delivered by colleagues and neighbors. And as I gardened. Each of these activities provided a kind of sustenance for the slow physical healing of my confused, postpartum body and the even slower stitching together of a new sense of self forced to come to terms with our son's death in my present and future life.

A rose had bloomed in the wee backyard garden that accompanied our cozy rental home. It happened while we were in the hospital. (Apparently, the house's previous long-term resident had been quite a gardener before her own death.) The morning after a painful first night at home with its empty nursery and our empty arms was resolutely grey. A deep cloud cover refused us sight of the sun overhead. That was fine with me. And yet, somehow, as if the gods had reluctantly agreed to displaying the narrowest of sunbeams through the clouds, a spotlight shone on a yellow rose. This illumination appeared almost immediately after my mother asked for a sign that Finlay was OK. And there was the sign: the beam of light on the perfect flower. In that moment I realized that we were in Finlay's Garden.

I planted an upcycled slate roof tile—our Finlay's Garden sign—beside the yellow rosebush. It oversaw my often solitary and sometimes collaborative-with-Will work of tending the young plants whose seeds I'd sown while pregnant with our child. As Will and I cleared some of the overgrown vines and trimmed Holly and Pine tree branches that had been left unattended since the previous gardener had departed, the garden grew. To fill my too quiet, and too slow days, I followed my impulse to study herbalism, organic gardening, and permaculture design. As others have noted,[10] the principles and methodologies of permaculture would do well applied to our social environments. Knowing how loss and death irrevocably impact social dynamics, it seems vital to expand permaculture into the realms of grief and mourning to the social landscape of loss. If we take the permaculture design practice of zoning, for example, we create a visual representation of the different parts of our 'home' and how they intersect and interact with one another. In the outer zone, we find the wild edges of grief and similar tumultuous affective states. Closest to the heart, in Zone 00, we find the body, perhaps the collective body. How do we harmonize the inner with the outer? How can we let grief in so that it intermingles with social institutions, practices, and behaviors, — rather than trying to keep grief at bay 'out there' somewhere, as if it wasn't already sending energetic waves through each and every person?

finding ways to heal and grow together p.119

10 Macnamara.

Deepening my connection to the more-than-human world felt essential to my grieving and mourning processes. I said Goodbye to an academic teaching career and Hello to an independent research study in grief. I read Kierkegaard's essays and Stonehouse's poems in Finlay's Garden. I sobbed there too. I began living in and through this world as a grieving parent.

Intuitively, I made tea blends from herbs that I grew and others I had purchased, and gave them to friends (some of whom are also grieving parents). One suggested I sell them and reach more people. After relocating from Illinois to North Carolina and giving birth to our second son, Phalen, I began a two-year Herbal Immersion course with the Chestnut School of Herbal Medicine. As our family moved from a house to an apartment, Finlay's Garden morphed into an indoor sunroom: Finlay's Garden 2.0. And its third iteration took shape as my wee online apothecary. The ancient technology of plant medicine infused my days.

A talented graphic designer friend created my logo with the hawthorn bud as inspiration. The hawthorn, you see, is very old medicine for grief. Kin to the rose—and the apple, pear, cherry, plum, and so on—hawthorn berries are cherished for their cardiovascular benefits. They nurture our hearts. The leaves and flowers, light and floral tasting, can uplift our spirits.[11] Hawthorn features in three of the herbal products that I craft in small batches. Heart Tea incorporates hawthorn and linden, rose and hibiscus. I make Heart Honey by infusing the bees' sweet gift with rose petals and hawthorn berries. And my Grief Bitters coalesce from hawthorn berries, dandelion root, mimosa bark, and orange peel soaking in apple brandy.

11 For more on hawthorn's medical properties, see Groves, 153–160; Wood, 211–217.

Significantly, slowness dictates the infusion process as my honeys and bitters sit in Finlay's Garden 2.0 infusing for at least four weeks and usually closer to eight. Gently warmed by the Western sun and tipped over and over again—by myself, Will, or Finlay's younger brothers, Phalen and Ren—the medicine comes together. Alchemy takes place. Before I strain the honey or bitters, I light incense and circle our kitchen, inviting Finlay's energy to guide me to make the best medicine I can that day.

sacredness in preparation p.169

This is slow-made medicine crafted in small batches after many slow days passed studying plants and navigating my grieving-healing journey. And I hope that it fosters in those who taste it a gentle sweetness and a kind invitation to metabolize their grief in whatever ways, and at whatever pace, they need that day.

...

We have not yet mentioned mushrooms, but they are surely there. There is no winter garden, hawthorn, or blackthorn without the fungal mycelial network that weaves them all together underground. Any agricultural or botanical permaculture project would need to consider the mycelial connective tissue that, while invisible to the eye, plays a crucial life-supporting role in many ecosystems. Likewise, any social permaculture project would need to consider the fine weave of interconnective tissue that entangles human beings. — Just as we can think of permaculture as a combination of care and design that works *with* ecological systems rather than imposing desires *on* those systems, social permaculture combines care and design to tend to existing practices of interpersonal repair, growth, and empowerment in order to create a more harmonious global society. To accomplish the former, we must understand how elements of an ecosystem interconnect, and fungus is an excellent teacher of that kind of understanding. To accomplish the latter, we must acknowledge the forces that unite people no matter how far flung they might be. Grief is an excellent teacher of this acknowledgement. It isn't analogous to the mycelium-like fine weave of connection in the natural environment; rather, grief is one force that lays bare the weave of social entanglement. Grief and mushrooms turn out to be transsystemic relatives that, once seen as such, teach us how to connect and how we (humans and nature) are always already connected.

an invisible map where we are all joined together p.177

To that point, we see the grief work of this piece of writing as a testimony to the grief that runs through human and more-than-human practices and domains. Grief is not something unique to people. More than that, the full transformative power of grief may only become knowable once we recognize how individual grief, social grief, and planetary grief inform one another. To conclude by returning to where this piece of writing started, we can invite Greek lamentation singing back into the picture. In the Greek tradition of the *moirológhia*, the role of the leading voice, the *koriféa*, is passed on from one person to the next in 'a polyphony of pain.'[12] In a similar way, we have written this short essay, weaving our voices and experiences together. The slow technologies that become sensible through our weave of voices include vocal lamentations, yoga, gardening, tattooing, and plant medicine. And the purpose of acknowledging these technologies and tapping into our shared polyphony of pain is to help others recognize how sustainable grief practices reveal deeper and deeper connections not just between people but between all things. — The connections may always already exist, like the unseen mycelia beneath our feet, but feeling and participating consciously with them requires a shift in attention that grief is particularly suited to instigate.

the weave of reality
p.204

12 Seremetakis, 106–107.

References

Cools, Guy. *Performing Mourning: Laments in Contemporary Art*. Valiz, 2021.

Daddario, Will. 'Careful Pain: Tattooing as Grief Work.' *Still Standing Magazine*. February 26, 2020. stillstandingmag.com/2020/02/26/careful-pain-tattooing-as-grief-work/.

Groves, Maria Noel. *Body into Balance: An Herbal Guide to Holistic Self-Care*. Storey Publishing, 2016.

Han, Byung-Chul. *Un voyage dans les jardins: Éloge de la terre*. Translated by Olivier Manoni. Actes Sud Editions, 2023.

Han, Byung-Chul. *Vita contemplativa: In Praise of Inactivity*. Translated by Daniel Steuer. Polity Press, 2024.

Kabat-Zinn, Jon. *Coming to Our Senses*. Hyperion, 2005.

Lamantowicz, Lysiane. 'Alone and Connected.' In *The Architecture of Loneliness: Reflections on Displacement and Welcoming*, edited by Mieke Bal. Valiz, 2024.

Macnamara, Looby. *People & Permaculture: Caring and Designing for Ourselves, Each Other and the Planet*. Permanent Publications, 2012.

Seremetakis, Nadia C. *The Last Word: Women, Death, and Divination in Inner Mani*. University of Chicago Press, 1991.

Solnit, Rebecca. *Wanderlust: A History of Walking*. Penguin Books, 2000.

Spatz, Ben. *What a Body Can Do*. Routledge, 2015.

Spinoza, Benedictus de. 'Part V: Of the Power of the Intellect, or On Human Liberty.' In *Ethics*. Translated by E. M. Curley. Penguin Books, 1994.

Wood, Matthew. *The Earthwise Herbal, Volume 1: A Complete Guide to Old World Medicinal Plants*. North Atlantic Books, 2008.

vectors
intuitions
species horizons
dreaming with
situated
embodied
tender
unknowable
extending the range
of the 'who'
kinships
rhizomes
kinetic landscapes
meditative interiors
groundlessness
anchoring in wonder
co-becoming
emergence

Every Point a Center

Siobhán K. Cronin

fluid — any substance that under ordinary pressure and temperature conditions can sustain shearing stresses without deforming continuously as long as stresses are applied.

evolutionary computing — a subfield of artificial intelligence that studies algorithms of global optimization inspired by biological evolution.

proprioception — the sense of self movement, force and body position.

The sea is a body that can be intuited only through the poetic.[1]
—Karin Ingersoll

[1] Ingersoll, 183.

I was 12 years old when I first heard whale song. My grandparents had taken me and my family to the aquarium in their town, and as we were leaving I heard a call emanating from a wooden display box in the gift shop. I had never heard anything like it. The sonority presented to my young mind a horizon of expression I didn't even know existed. It was whale song. Humpback whale. I had saved up money to buy something special on our trip, so I followed the sound to a little cassette, purchased it and played it on my Walkman the entire flight home. I remember imagining that we, the passengers on the airplane, were riding on the back of the whale I was hearing as clouds became kelp forests and schools of fish. The experience was thrilling and planted a seed of wonder that germinated over the years as my interest in evolutionary computing and interspecies exchange developed.

We find ourselves in a contemporary moment thick with curiosity of other intelligences, including artificial intelligence. This article is situated in the space between my practice exploring embodied intelligence of non-human species, which I have been engaged in as a movement artist since 2008, and my work as a software engineer conducting independent research on evolutionary computing. My personal interests lie in understanding what human technology advancements are possible when we extend our purview of inspiration beyond human heritage.

When we encounter other intelligences, including those that exceed ours in some dimension, we may not have the facility to comprehend their significance. This is a concept I first began to grapple with in conversations with Dr. Ellen Winner in my undergraduate research days. Her work with colleagues at Harvard Project Zero on multiple intelligences introduced me to the challenge in both identifying forms of intelligence but also appraising their relative adaptation significance. When it comes to whales, much like the terrains of our imagination regarding artificial general intelligence, the realm of their abilities may simply be beyond the comprehensible. — So where do we begin? This is where I believe both kinetic empathy and evolutionary computing can be of service.

requiring a different imaginary matrix p.300

Strategies for navigating complex solution spaces in evolutionary computing have referenced everything from honeybee swarms to ant colonies for inspiration. I find this research to be a bright light in the history of AI as it opens a robust curiosity beyond our species. A central branch of this area of research originated with Kennedy and Eberhart's introduction of particle swarm optimization.[2] While decades have passed since then, particle swarm optimization remains a lively research arena to explore collective behavior structures and the many ways they adapt and change. Some core concepts include algorithms that articulate what of the collective's knowledge can be known and leveraged by the individual at any given moment—and under what conditions that knowledge should be overwritten by more preferable information gathered at the local or individual level. Determining where individual agents are in a model in relation to one another and how and what they communicate is the backbone of systems research on how information propagates through a system, and particle swarm optimization algorithms offer useful mechanics for analysis of such systems.

2| Kennedy and Eberhart.

Evolutionary computing, including the modeling of whale intelligence, facilitates access to a peak of technological advancement from another species whose methods—whether spatial orientation or some other fitness objective—have been honed across generations and geographies beyond our own. I believe that the world of whale navigation and song, studied collectivity, has the potential to inspire a bouquet of fascinating new algorithms: yielding a portfolio of possibilities that stand to expand the horizons of computer science.

So how does one discover a new evolutionary algorithm? Access to that knowledge begins with situating ourselves in contexts where we can listen deeply and observe from a place of genuine desire to understand and honor other forms of intelligence. —

a deep sense of presence in the world p.121

In the span of their lifetimes, a whale may travel up to tens of thousands of kilometers, covering vast regions of the world's oceans, often in a social context. The gray whale, for instance, has been known to navigate over 19,000 kilometers in a single round-trip migration. To know what's around them, whales make sounds and analyze the returning reverberations those sounds make off everything they encounter. While the whale auditory cortex, like that of humans, is responsible for processing those reverberations, it is their melon, a special organ used for refining the clicks they use to echolocate, that has helped whales become such masterful cartographers. The melon itself is a fatty structure in the forehead that helps whales focus the sounds they create into a beam they use to sweep their surrounds like a sonic flashlight. The series of clicks whales emit, called 'trains,' vary by species and context and provide information of varying detail. How all the returning sound bouncing off of everything is integrated into a mental map is still not fully known, but it is clear this process aids in whales' ability to get around and avoid danger. The ocean is always changing. How are migrations successfully completed in such a context of continuous change?

I see a future in which we deepen the connection between marine life researchers and evolutionary computing researchers to advance algorithm development in real time as fresh insights into whale perception, cognition, and collective behavior develop—and as we continue to learn about how climate change is affecting the world's oceans. Such algorithms could form a living handbook on the state of what humans understand of how whale species explore survival fitness in our shared biome, with the volume evolving as our understanding grows. An album of whale technological advancement honed across generations and geographies, born of survival necessity yet codified and cataloged through human care.[3, 4, 5] I have long hoped that something like this could emerge within our open science community; a practice of creating more open archives of our research as a sign that we are moving past institutional sequestering of knowledge. And doing so not only for the utility of these algorithms in developing system optimization strategies for our own species, but also for demonstrating empathy for others.

3 Whitehead.

4 Potter and De Jong, 249–257.

5 Whitehead and Rendell.

Human beings are holobionts. We exist as an interspecies agreement. It seems that when we regard one another as humans we are regarding something far more categorically tidy than the 10x bacteria to human cell ratio we actually are. How might one go about developing an identification as an interspecies self in a broader interspecies world? What shifts happen when we take as much interest in the experiential realities, dreams, and hopes of other species as we do in our own species horizons? Dreaming with—not just dreaming of—other species. Unlike cosmologies created within knowledge born of human minds, the cognitive life of whales—they too holobionts—is so empirically other than human that it represents the possibility of concept formation on earth that is truly alien to our own. Perhaps venturing into such waters of the unknown would relieve humans of some of the claustrophobic exceptionalism that at times can laden our conversations on planetary thriving. We are living here with other species, and they are developing and evolving practices of adaptation to climate change alongside us. Yes, there is competition for survival fitness, and much has been said about that. But we can also hold one another in webs of mutual care, concern, and action.

scope of intelligences on Earth p.296

hovering just beyond the edge of scientific understanding p.86

In 2008 I began to explore these ideas in earnest as I embarked upon creating a performance archive of the morphology and movement patterns of plants and animals that I call the *Somatic Natural History Archive*. The work began in the high desert of northern New Mexico, far from the Pacific coast where I now live. I had reached an inflection point in my creative life as a dancer and found myself occupying a groundlessness I have often experienced before a conceptual shift. My lineage of dance training included dialogues with choreographers JoAnna Mendl Shaw, Jennifer Monson and Deborah Hay who helped me see the possibility of apprenticeship with other species, — and the power of asking questions as a means to excite and prime perception, with varying degrees of comfort in how or if they are answered.[6]

expanding the physical imagination p.345

6 See Somatic Natural History Archive: youtube.com/dancingecologist.

The clearest way I could think to begin was to start dancing outside and learn how other creatures move, either of their own volition or in response to forces of wind, gravity, water, and interaction. The work began with so many naive assumptions that I can now extend grace to as I look back at the younger me. I remember not knowing where to put my attention. I would feel I had to either stay incredibly still or move in very clear ways that would proclaim my presence. I found I would gravitate to specific organisms as my focal points, like seeking out a friendly face in the crowd at a party. I would catch the movement of a bird and follow it until it slipped from view. Or I would trace the outline of a curling fern with my eyes and imagine where in my body I could feel such tenderness. Before long I realized there was only so much mapping I could do onto my physical form, so I began making gestures that inscribed bodies I could never fully occupy. Perhaps I would trace a wing. Or maybe a long tail draping over a rock. I would search inside myself for the points where I would originate movement in those bodies, and for brief moments I could feel a kinship with forms quite divergent from my own.

As committed as I was to this process, I discovered that my map of the kinematics of living creatures remained coarsely drawn. I wanted higher fidelity in my understanding of how these other creatures actually moved about their world. So I slowed my system down even further to see whether I could inspire my human cells to the pace of the organisms I was spending time with. There were shifts and dropping-ins at different intervals. Like the letting go of feeling a human-level connection in favor of other more bioprocess exchange bonding. — I imagined: if I lay here without moving long enough, these creatures will redistribute my bio resource. I meditated: I breathe out the thing you need. The lessons of a forest.

sharing a new temporality p.64

While developing this work, I attended a three-months residency at the Santa Fe Arts Institute, which supports the creative practice of interdisciplinary artists. During that time, I had encounters with many more plants and animals, among whom my dearest collaborators were the aspen trees of the Santa Fe National Forest. Aspen stands are single organisms. They can live up to 80,000 years (recorded as the oldest organism on the planet) with as many as 47,000 individual trees existing in a stand. As a species extending back to the Pleistocene epoch, when you stand among a stand of aspens you perceive a many that is in fact a one that has been around for quite some time. —

singular-plural p.391

This was the first time I worked with a species whose experience of space so greatly differed from my own. While aspen trees do not migrate like whales, they do transmit information via their shared rhizome. I would go every day and sit long enough to feel my sensorium extend in some measure towards theirs, attempting to comprehend how acres of what appeared to be separate organisms were in fact a single clonal colony.

The aim of my 'Somatic Natural History Archive' was not to wiggle around mimicking other creatures, but to seek out understandings that might prime more mutually beneficial, interconnected webs of multi-species thriving. One of the things I'm now able to see is how this extended contemplation of the life histories of non-humans extended the range of the 'who' I am dancing this life with. The practice shifted my focus away from my individual self to a more complex relational dynamics of the broader kinetic biomass. The aim has not been to silence myself or erase my humanness, which seems impossible, but to create space to investigate being-ness beyond the human. Imagination does not supplant the need to bolster my knowledge with empirical research, but it does compel me to explore outside the realm of my knowns.

After working with dozens of plant and animal species on land for the Somatic Natural History Archive, a day came when I turned to the ocean. I was in San Diego, a coastal city on the edge of the Pacific. I waded into the surf and immediately could feel many forces at play on my body at once. The pattern of waves looked like a steady advance, yet in the water I could feel crosscurrents and undertows as articulations of larger kinetic landscapes shaping and reshaping me as I was bobbed, propelled, and overtaken. I began tracing the vectors of movement I was experiencing in the same way I had moved with plants and birds and land animals, only now I could yield my volition to an environmental material that would move me further still, even while at rest.

I continued my research out of the water, which brought me to Alexis Pauline Gumbs, whose *Undrowned* (2020) offers sweeping gestures of scientific fascination, emotional intimacy and marine wonder, as well as to Karin Amimoto Ingersoll, whose generous invitations in *Waves of Knowing: A Seascape Epistemology* (2016) compose diaphanous interlocking layers of understanding of ocean as place.[7, 8] I found myself postulating the possibility of a mobile kinetic-sonic sense of place orientated along a whale migration. How is place defined, remembered, and referenced in whale culture in the absence of the kind of static niche formation we experience on land? Humans spend their kinetic development relating to the reality of gravity pulling our bodies to earth, providing the necessary dynamics for bone and tendon development. And as human dancers we learn ways to use the kinetics of release and falling as propulsion for our movements. Yet whales can plummet hundreds of feet into darkness and mounting water pressure with grace and ease. — Might the kinetics of water

a being reveling
in its power to be
p.389

itself—with its vocabularies of hydro propulsion, current, temperature, pressure, salinity— offer organizing principles of meaning? What somatic intelligences can only be born in the water?[9]

7 Gumbs.

8 Ingersoll.

9 Writing of fish, Andy Clark and David Chalmers offered, 'The extraordinary efficiency of the fish as a swimming device is partly due, it now seems, to an evolved capacity to couple its swimming behaviors to the pools of external kinetic energy found as swirls, eddies, and vortices in its watery environment. The fish and surrounding vortices together constitute a unified and remarkably efficient swimming machine.'

As I contemplate these ideas while moving through daily life, I sometimes find myself looking at the ground beneath my feet and imagining a vast expanse opening below me. These moments of imagination help me feel connected to the physical realities of whales in the present moment, and they also lead me to imagine the rich datasets of movement and modes of communication that might be observed in whales over many years. If we were to map their expressive movement and collective navigation strategies over time and then retract to the core topologies of their movements, what would we find? How would this further enrich understanding of how individuals and groups of agents explore novel situations? How might it influence human behavior in areas such as group coordination, orientation, consensus building, and collective navigation of the unknown?

body as a compass p.208

It appears we are on the verge of having meaningful conversations with whales. What advances will we make as we come to understand the spatiotemporal context of whale life? How might we imbue these conversations from the onset with a deep chord of care? What would it look like to lead with empathy as we embark on those interspecies dialogues?

It's one thing to cast hope into the great beyond that things will get better, and it's another thing to join with others poetically and pragmatically in addressing the state of our earth and the lives of the creatures living upon it. For me, the energy needed to do this work season over season requires a commitment to improving the quality of living conditions for water life as much as for land life, shifting the orientation to an identification with the realities of the entire biomass. — A full spectrum seeing of clouds becoming clouds becoming oceans to again form clouds. A fluid presence cast in hues of awe and kindness, with whales contributing their living cathedral of perception of our earth's oceans.

learning to care for the world p.440

References

Clark, Andy. *Supersizing the Mind*. Oxford University Press, 2008.

Gumbs, Alexis Pauline. *Undrowned*. AK Press, 2020.

Ingersoll, Karin Amimoto. *Waves of Knowing: A Seascape Epistemology*. Duke University Press, 2016

Kennedy, James, and Russell Eberhart. 'Particle Swarm Optimization.' In *Proceedings of ICNN'95: International Conference on Neural Networks*. Perth, WA, Australia, 1995, 1942–48. dx.doi.org/10.1109/ICNN.1995.488968.

Potter, M. A., and K. A. De Jong. 'A Cooperative Coevolutionary Approach to Function Optimization.' In *The Third Parallel Problem Solving from Nature*. Springer-Verlag, 1994.

Whitehead, Hal. 'Consensus Movements by Groups of Sperm Whales.' *Marine Mammal Science* 32, no. 4 (2016): 1402–15. doi.org/10.1111/mms.12338.

Whitehead, Hal, and Luke Rendell. *The Cultural Lives of Whales and Dolphins*. The University of Chicago Press, 2015.

entanglement
fecundity
transgression
remembrance
lineages
meeting place of
  ontologies
underlying potential
hidden between
innovation
beyond the cliché

The Africanist Cyborg

Florence Okoye

What does it mean to say that we are all cyborgs? Implicit in this statement is an understanding of what some might describe as humanity's innate dependence on technology. Homo Sapiens have always used technologies, both material (e.g., from flint knives to computers) and immaterial (e.g., from taboos to complex legal systems) to supplement the individual human being. As per Albert Cherns's socio-technical framework of technology, in the same way that artefacts and their usage reveal the mechanics of everyday life and deeply held cultural understandings, the techniques used to create technology convey the metaphysical framework of the society they were made to serve.[1]

1
Cherns.

Why does this matter? It matters when it comes to the digital, given that the socio-cultural context from which our current paradigm emerged seems to make digital technologies more prone to the ur-fascist modernist narratives that bolster its sense of exceptionalism. It matters because this concept of technology **can** critique and **should** eliminate the blithe normalizations of kyriarchy, for example as seen in the implicit ableism where the cyborg depicts what is—from an abled perspective—a 'ruined' humanity that requires technology to exist on an equal footing in the world they inhabit;[2] the anti-collectivism that worships the stolen glory of capital and denies agency and resources of the commons. It matters because in a time of avoidant rhetoric regarding the so-called 'black box' of contemporary tech, we still need to figure out a means of accountability. —

choices for
the benefit of life
p.199

2
Okoye (2014).

In his essay 'Electronic Networks and Subjectivity,' Steven D. Brown interprets technology as the practice 'which reveals things for what they are.'[3] Once this revelatory act is complete, the technological object can then become either a 'supreme danger' or a 'saving power,' to quote Sean Sutherlin, 'depending on whether humans are able to maintain objectivity in their relation to technology.'[4] Technology involves the meeting of imagination and nature, enabling humans to reify a view of the world, to bring out an ontology of environment and thus 'assure an objectificatory function.'[5] As such, whether in the form of the plantation system and its underlying logic of genocide,[6] assistive technologies that express what is considered valuable about a body in a capitalist paradigm,[7] or digital infrastructure that both reinforces gender binaries (such as Wordnet) and exacerbates inherent bigotries,[8] technology reveals ontologies and idealizations of our humanities where the ideals may be dreams or nightmares conjured up from social, cultural, ritualistic, or economic paradigms.

3 Brown, 157.

4 Sutherlin, 6.

5 Pérez, 48.

6 Okoye (2020).

7 Turner; Okoye (2014).

8 Bolukbasi et al.; Zhao et al.; Benjamin.

'not exclusively human affairs' p.295

In the pre-colonial Africanist philosophy of technology, the cyborg is entangled, 'a meeting place between ontologies of the environment and ontologies of the body'. — This is exemplified by the explicit mingling of humanity and machine reflected in the reproductive symbolism associated with metallurgical processes. One finds 'representations of the furnace as the womb of a fecund woman who gives birth to an iron child' and 'a panoply of associated symbolism such as ... blow pipes as phalluses, bellows as testicles and slag as birth placenta.'[9] This adoptive model of technology that is seen in cultures ranging from the Fipa people of Tanzania, to the Hausa of Northern Nigeria/Southern Niger,[10] is perhaps due to the lack of a socially destabilizing experience at the scale of the European industrial revolution marked by the growth of extreme poverty and widening divisions between the classes.[11] This is not to suggest that the development of technology did not change or restructure African societies. For example, there is evidence of such a shift in the creation and enforcement of blacksmith endogamous, almost 'caste'-like, groups such as the *numuw* in the Mande nation. Nonetheless, the anxieties were of a different order to those elsewhere by Luddite and Romantic alike.

9 Schmidt.

10 Iles.

11 Sutherlin.

At this point it's worth mentioning just how ancient and widespread the technological lineage of pre-colonial Africa is. If we focus on iron working alone, where African methods pre-date the Eurasian by some distance, we have the Bassar region in Central Togo where iron smelting is considered to date back to 200–400 BC[12] to the Nok culture centered around Jos, Bauchi, Daima, Kano and Zaria, where archaeologists have dated iron working to about 500 BC.[13] Iron was produced and used around the Kanji dam in what is now the Niger State of Nigeria, around the 2nd century BC and there are older sites, reaching back to the middle of the second millennium BC[14] such as at Obobogo, Cameroon, that have been dated to 950 BC ± 100 and 1675 BC ± 165.[15]

12 Eichhorn and Robion-Brunner.

13 Onipede.

14 De Maret and Thiry.

15 De Maret.

Evidence for an organized and thriving technological culture can also be found in colonial sources that report specialized 'iron villages' where inhabitants devoted their time to mining and smelting iron which would then be exported to neighboring towns and villages, some of whom would have had their own production specialty. One German arriving in Banjeli in 1885, compared the noise and heat from the metropolis of furnaces to the industry in his native town of Ruhr. By 1895 the number of working furnaces was estimated to be in the hundreds, the scale of the industry leading to a high degree of regional specialization where individual villages specialized in the various stages and different kinds of metallurgical processes.

The blacksmiths of South Eastern Nkwerre (a town forty kilometers North-East of Owerre, the capital of Imo State, Nigeria) were famed throughout Igboland for their expertise, and made ironmongery on a large scale for the local populace. Their ability to absorb foreign technologies was particularly demonstrated in their production of *egbe cham* or flint guns from the middle of the seventeenth century. By the late nineteenth century, these had evolved into canons of varying complexity, from the *mkponala* (a small cannon) to the *egbe-ndu*, which was of more technically challenging design.

The scale of technological culture, the widespread trade of iron goods and methods,[16] as well as the frequent—although not necessarily universal—parent-child conception of relations between humanity and technology, suggests a panethnic philosophy of technology able to accommodate the cyborg as much as it demonstrates humanity-as-cyborg.

16 Eichhorn and Robion-Brunner.

How does this impact the depiction of humans interacting with a now birthed technology? In the histories of Mali, we see a figure similar to the archetypal cyborg of science fiction in the great King of Mande oral history: Sunjata, crippled from birth and born of a disabled mother.[17] Much like the cyborgian superhero of comic book lore, here is a character who 'resists the consequences of boundary transgression'[18] by overcoming the difficulties of nascent assistive technologies and conflicts with an ableist society to become a great military leader. In one version originating from Gambia, we are told that when he was of age to start walking, the leader of the Griots were told to 'forge iron that he might rise up.'[19] The inspiration for these calipers is revealed when the storyteller informs us that such ironwork was available for those who break their legs,[20] a small insight revealing so much about the development and use of contemporary technology by disabled and abled alike.

17 Rutledge.

18 Heggs, 185.

19 Suso and Kanute, 61.

20 Miles.

There is much to consider about what Sunjata the cyborg—and the socio-technical context he arose in—can tell us, whether from the perspective of 'class' analysis, which can give insight into the question of whose histories are told, — or who interacts with which technologies and to what extent. Sunjata, with the privileges of royalty and under the social pressure to fulfil his role as a warrior, would have had greater access to any technologies that would have enabled him to do so. As is generally the case, surely the imperatives of a society would also dictate the opportunities for technological innovation.

Who is missing?
p.318

One notable aspect is the role of the technologist in his society. The smith (particularly in his contemporary Mande culture) is a figure of immense spiritual and cultural power, and yet also one whose structural power was specifically curtailed, for example ensuring no smith, no matter their power over nature, could ever become kings.[21] This pattern, wherein a society might have the smith—the technologist—in a highly valued yet stringently circumscribed role, caste or class is another example that frequently appears across various African contexts. Their role—be it as economic powerhouse or transgressive co-creator (in many ways typified by the blacksmiths who in certain cultural contexts were at times desexualized, forbidden from sexual intercourse during the smelting proces)[22]—in reifying humanity-as-cyborg is intimately connected with the ways that traditional Africanist political theories and social mechanisms balance between that which *remembers* the past and that which *innovates* for the future. — An example of this concept of balance from Mande philosophy are the notions of *Badenya*—forces that emphasize social cohesion and stability—and *Fadenya*—which refers to forces of 'social stress and disquiet.'[23] Other cultures will have philosophies tied to the material realities of their environment, from the collective pragmatism of the Yoruba *Imo*[24] to the pan-Bantu concept of *Ubuntu*.

conjuring a space
for intervention
p.258

21 McNaughton (2011).

22 Goucher and Herbert.

23 McNaughton (2012).

24 Bekele et al.

setting into vibration relationships and dimensions p. 264

As such the African cyborg is to be found amongst the ashes of the old blacksmiths' forge, hidden between the stanzas of the ritual songs honoring the ancestral technologists and inventors[25] sung to coax the underlying potential of the metal ore to reveal itself — as it is smelted and forged. And for us, beyond the cliché of science fiction, cyborgs are thus not only portents, signifiers of an existential battle played out between man and gods, within the natures of the individual human; rather, they should be taken as our inherent state, a revelation of the monism that makes up humanity, not an exceptional development. In this way they reveal tensions (not contradictions) of our existence offering mechanisms for how we can continually re-create better ways of being, cocooned as we are both among one another and between Earth and the heavens.

25 Goucher and Herbert, 44.

An earlier version of this article was published in the journal Disability and the Global South *1, no. 1 (2014): 64–84.*

References

Bekele, Teklu Abate, Samuel Amponsah, and Ibrahim M. Karkouti. 'African Philosophy for Successful Integration of Technology in Higher Education.' In *British Journal of Educational Technology* 54, no. 6 (2023): 1520–38. doi.org/10.1111/bjet.13364.

Benjamin, Ruha. *Race After Technology: Abolitionist Tools for the New Jim Code*. Polity Press, 2019.

Bolukbasi, Toga, Kai-Wei Chang, James Zou, Venkatesh Saligrama, and Adam Kalai. 'Man is to Computer Programmer as Woman is to Homemaker? Debiasing Word Embeddings.' In *NIPS'16: Proceedings of the 30th International Conference on Neural Information Processing Systems*, Barcelona, Spain, December 5, 2016, 4356–64. doi.org/10.48550/arXiv.1607.06520.

Brown, Steven D. 'Electronic Networks and Subjectivity.' In *Cyberpsychology*, edited by Ángel J. Gordo-López and Ian Parker. Macmillan Press Ltd., 1999.

Cherns, Albert. 'The Principles of Sociotechnical Design.' In *Human Relations* 29, no. 8 (1976): 783–92. doi.org/10.1177/001872677602900806.

De Maret, Pierre 'Recent Archaeological Research and Dates from Central Africa.' In *The Journal of African History* 26 (1985): 2–3 March 1985.

De Maret, Pierre and Genevieve Thiry, 'How Old is the Iron Age in Central Africa?' In *The Culture and Technology of African Iron Production*, edited by Peter R. Schmidt. University Press of Florida, 1996.

Doering, E. von. 'Reiseberichte von Premier Lieutenant v. Doering aus den Jahren 1893 bis 1895.' In Vol. 8, *Mittheilungen von Forschungsreisenden und Gelehrten aus den deutschen Schutzgebieten: mit Benutzung amtlicher Quellen*, edited by Freiherr von Danckelman. Berlin, 1895. archive.org/details/mittheilungenvon08unse/mode/2up?q=v.+doering.

Eichhorn, Barbara, and Caroline Robion-Brunner. 'Wood Exploitation in a Major Pre-Colonial West African Iron Production Centre (Bassar, Togo).' In *Quaternary International* 458 (2017): 158–77. doi.org/10.1016/j.quaint.2017.08.073.

Goucher, Candice L., and Eugenia W. Herbert. 'The Blooms of Banjeli: Technology and Gender in West African Iron Making.' In *The Culture and Technology of African Iron Production*, edited by Peter R. Schmidt. University Press of Florida, 1996.

Heggs, Dan. 'Cyberpsychology and Cyborgs.' In *Cyberpsychology*, edited by Ángel J. Gordo-López and Ian Parker. Macmillan Press Ltd., 1999.

Holl, Augustin F. C. 'Early West African Metallurgies: New Data and Old Orthodoxy.' In *Journal of World Prehistory 22 (2009): 415–38. doi.org/10.1007/s10963-009-9030-6.*

Iles, Louise. 'Gender in African Metallurgy.' In *Oxford Research Encyclopedia of Anthropology*, edited by Mark Aldenderfer. Oxford University Press, 2020.

McNaughton, Patrick R. 'The Smiths in Sunjata: What Epics and Oral Traditions Suggest About West African History.' In *Mande Studies* 13 (2011): 1–19. doi.org/10.2979/mnd.2011.a873570.

McNaughton, Patrick R. 'Nyamakalaw: The Mande Bards and Blacksmiths.' *Word & Image* 3, no. 3 (1987): 271–88. doi.org/10.1080/02666286.1987.10435385.

Miles, M. (2001). 'Deafness and Blindness, Disability and Inclusion in West African Tradition and Modernity: Review of Books and Materials' [Online]. *Disability World*. Available at: disabilityworld.org/03-04_01/resources/bookreviews.shtml [Accessed 15 February 2013].

Okoye, Florence. 'Does Africa Dream of Androids?' *Disability and the Global South* 1, no. 1 (2014): 64–84. dgsjournal.org/wp-content/uploads/2012/06/dgs-01-01-05.pdf.

Okoye, Florence. 'Caliban at the Boiler.' Second keynote address at the Beyond Borders: Empires, Bodies, Science Fictions online conference hosted by the London Science-Fiction Research Community, September 10–12, 2020. Video, 30 min., 32 sec. Posted October 28, 2020. youtube.com/watch?v=6Ou0VhIeUmc].

Onipede, Kayode Joseph. 'Technology Development in Nigeria: The Nigerian Machine Tools Industry Experience.' *Journal of Economics* 1(2) (2010):85–90

Osuala, Uzoma S. 'Colonialism and the Disintegration of Indigenous Technology in Igboland: A Case Study of Blacksmithing in Nkwerre.' *Historical Research Letter* 3 (2012): 11–19. iiste.org/Journals/index.php/HRL/article/download/2488/2510.

Pérez, Carlos Soldevilla. 'Vertiginous Technology: Towards a Psychoanalytic Genealogy of Technique.' In *Cyberpsychology*, edited by Ángel J. Gordo-López and Ian Parker. Macmillan Press Ltd., 1999.

Rutledge, Gregory E. *The Epic Trickster in American Literature: From Sunjata to So(u)l*. Routledge Studies in Twentieth-Century Literature. Routledge, 2013.

Schmidt, Peter. R. 'Reconfiguring the Barongo: Reproductive Symbolism and Reproduction Among a Work Association of Iron Smelters.' In *The Culture and Technology of African Iron Production*, edited by Peter R. Schmidt. University Press of Florida, 1996.

Suso, Bamba and Banna Kanute. *Sunjata: Gambian Versions of the Mande Epic*, edited by Graham Furniss and Lucy Durán. Translated by Bakari Sidibe and Gordon Innes. Penguin, 1999.

Sutherlin, S. (2012). 'The Cyborg as a Crisis Figure in Science Fiction Cinema.' Presentation also given at 2015 Research, Art, Writing symposium hosted by the School of Arts and Humanities of University of Texas at Dallas. utdgsa.wordpress.com/.

Turner, Bryan S. 'Social Fluids: Metaphors and Meanings of Society.' *Body & Society* 9, no. 1 (2003). doi.org/10.1177/1357034X030091001.

Zhao, Jieyu, Tianlu Wang, Mark Yatskar, Vicente Ordonez, and Kai-Wei Chang. 'Men Also Like Shopping: Reducing Gender Bias Amplification using Corpus-level Constraints.' In *Proceedings of the 2017 Conference on Empirical Methods in Natural Language Processing*, Copenhagen, Denmark, September, 2017. doi.org/10.18653/v1/d17-1323.

unseen forces
ancient rhythms
humming
weaving
witnessing
never hurried
refuge
comfort
protection
welcoming
planting seeds
powers of protection
whispers of lineage
bridge between worlds
bound by love

Zhety Apa Chronicles

Danel Khojayeva

The term Zhety Apa *originates from the Turkic concept, meaning family tree. Traditionally, Turkic cultures document male generations in Shezire, known as* Zhety Ata, *or 'the seven grandfathers' (*ata*—grandfather;* apa*—grandmother/sister/an older female relative). This practice not only serves as a way to transmit collective and historical memory but also as an alternative to the social capital structures. Initially, both male and female names were included, but as Central Asian culture became increasingly masculinized, female names were gradually excluded, leaving only the male lineage.*

Chilltans (from Persian: '40 people, 40 saints') are mythical, non-binary entities in Central Asian cultures, without corporeal form. These beings exist not only in memories but also within objects, landscapes, prayers and rituals, functioning as a form of 'spiritual technology' that guides, protects, and harmonizes the world. ▬ *This concept draws partial inspiration from the DAVRA Research Collective contribution to documenta fifteen, which provided international audiences with insights into the culture of women in Central Asia.*

balance of the cosmos
p.121

Chilltans can take any form—be it a human, animal, household object, or element of nature. They embody protection, blessing, and balance. Across these seven texts, I explore the lives of seven generations of female ancestors, each embodying the spirit of Chilltans—offering strength, harmony, and spiritual nourishment. While Chilltans transcend gender, I view them through the lens of these women who, though often hidden from historical records, preserved the spiritual essence of their communities.

Oynaxon

Oynaxon's presence was known throughout the *mahallah*, though she moved like a whisper in the wind. She was the healer, the woman who carried the knowledge of the earth deep in her bones. Her hands, calloused from years of gathering plants and mixing salves, could cure fevers and soothe the spirit. But it wasn't just her touch that worked wonders—it was the deep bond she shared with the natural world. Every herb she picked, every root she unearthed, every flame she kindled seemed to carry with it the echoes of her ancestors' voices.

At dawn, she often rose with the first light of the sun, her feet guiding her to the steppe where Adraspan grew. The plant, revered in these lands for its powers of protection and cleansing, was a gift from the earth itself. Its scent was sharp, and when burned it filled the air with a pungent smoke that had the power to ward off evil and restore balance. Oynaxon's fingers, steady and sure, would gather the dried adraspan, ensuring it was collected after flowering when the round seed pods formed along the stems.

On this particular morning Oynaxon prepared for a ritual of purification. Her granddaughter had fallen ill, and Oynaxon knew it was time to call upon the ancestors. She gathered the adraspan, careful not to break the stems, and made her way to the sacred spot, where her grandmother had once taught her the rituals of fire and smoke.

Oynaxon waved the smoke over her granddaughter, who lay quietly on a woven mat, her feverish body shimmering in the morning light. 'Adraspan will cleanse you,' Oynaxon whispered, her hands hovering over the girl's brow. As the fire began to die down, her granddaughter stirred, the fever already breaking. Oynaxon smiled, knowing that the ritual had worked, knowing that the Chilltan had spoken.

The sun climbed higher into the sky, but Oynaxon remained, her hands brushing over the ground where the fire had burned, feeling the pulse of life beneath the earth. She was a healer, yes, but more than that—she was a bridge between worlds, between the living and the spirits that moved unseen through the land. — And as long as the Adraspan grew in the steppes, as long as its smoke filled the air, she knew that the Chilltan would be there, guiding her, protecting her, as it had done for all the women before her.

meeting point between visible and invisible forces p.122

Railya

At ten years old, Railya saw her for the first time—a gray silhouette, sitting on the *korpe* beside her mother, wrapping her in an almost tangible embrace. Her mother wept quietly, not wanting her children to see the tears. The night before, Railya's father had said goodbye in a way that felt final. His voice had been soft, subdued; his eyes glistened, and his hands clutched them tightly, like roots holding them close to the earth. Two years later, she encountered the gray figure again. This time, she noticed a womanly shape, but when she turned, she saw her father's eyes in the figure's face. At that moment, she felt sharp, tiny knots tightening in her belly, spreading across her back, sinking downwards—a faint whisper of lineage, like a thousand women's voices echoing from deep within. —

spiritual geography
p.122

As Railya grew, the silhouette transformed. When she left the mahallah where she was born, the figure began to carry the scent of home—of earth and grass, of the bustling bazaar. Each time Railya longed for the life she had left behind, for her mother who remained alone, she would see the figure in the corner, as constant as the land itself.

Years later, after her mother's passing, the figure softened, and Railya began to notice dark hair cascading from under its hood, shining with the gentle waves of her mother's. At night, when the figure settled beside her, she almost felt her mother's fingers combing through her own hair, soothing and comforting her, bringing the bittersweet warmth of memory.

When her husband left her world, Railya saw the figure shift once again—her form now carried a slight, thin body, strong hands that had once held their daughters. By then, she understood that this silent visitor was bound to her not by cruelty, but by love. She felt her presence as a patchwork of everyone she had lost, each part familiar, each feature shifting with her grief. — And when she finally asked: 'Why have you stayed with me for so long?'

holographic aunties
p.312

The figure looked back at her, eyes like her father's, hair like her mother's, hands like her husband's. 'You have always welcomed me', she replied in a voice as soft as a lullaby. 'And I am all that you carry. I am here because I am a part of you.'

Railya closed her eyes and let the ache settle into a familiar comfort. She felt the shadow's hand, warm and steady, resting over hers. They sat together in the dimming light, both knowing they were bound by the stories of those who had come before. She was not an enemy but a reminder of the love and strength she carried.

Kharinissa

At five years old, on nights when the moon brightly lit up the house, Kharinissa would sneak to her mother's jewelry box. Its wooden walls were carved with delicate round sun-like symbols and the thick wooden handle was adorned with heavy metal plates that jingled treacherously at any attempt to open the box. Glancing around cautiously, she would grip the lid and lift it toward the heavens. A quiet clanging echoed through the house. She froze, hearing her heart pound loudly. Everything was silent. Her small hands reached for the gold, silver, coral, and pearl adornments.

Just a little more, and she would have felt the pleasant coolness in her hands, but a stern voice came from the room: '*Kharinissa, oynama*!' ('Kharinissa, don't play!') As time went on, she opened the box less and less, even after her mother passed it on to her during the matchmaking ceremony. On her wedding day, her head and temples were adorned with silver jewelry from that box. Thin metal plates, almond-shaped, hung from her forehead, reminiscent of the soft gleam of moonlight in that childhood room.

A sudden clang of a falling metal object snapped her out of her memories. She flinched, noticing a crooked, blackened spoon on the floor. She was no longer 5 or 20; over time, her hands had grown rough from labor, and the thrill of her mother's jewelry had been dulled by the weight of a hard life.

'Хариниса, Үйге Кайту керек', ('Kharinissa, we need to go home) came a woman's voice from another room. 'Д-домой пораа', ('Home... It's time to go home) the woman repeated.

She grimaced and instinctively touched her temples, where only the phantoms of the jewels remained. Now, standing in the cold office, Kharinissa tightly clutched her wooden jewelry box. She knew she had to give it up to get a job in the cafeteria and feed her seven children. Her fingers dug greedily into the wood carvings, wanting to memorize these patterns forever, to imprint them in herself and pass them on to her daughters through touch. The heavy door opened before her. Uncertainty and trembling gave way to strength as she silently crossed the threshold and stopped two steps from the large desk covered in white sheets of paper. Without hesitation, she thrust the jewelry box forward.

The man in uniform reached into the contents, now forever tainted. He slowly recited her name, and information about her family, parents, and children. After each word, he lifted his broad eyes to her, trying to gauge if she understood. She nodded but said nothing, even though she knew his language. — Her children, grandchildren, and great-grandchildren would speak it, forgetting the words flowing in their blood. She knew this for certain, which is why she refrained from speaking it for as long as possible, trying to prolong the existence of her ancestors' language within herself.

sprouts of resistance
p.234

When they came, she knew they would take everything: the house, the Quran, the chest with the shroud, the language, and the memory. The elders said it would pass. At night, they cautiously buried the family gold in the gardens. They believed their children would return to their homes and live as before in a few years, but that never happened.

'It's time,' the voice of the senior cafeteria worker brought her back to the bright, tiled room. 'For the children,' the woman quietly said again, turning away so as not to see Kharinissa carefully transferring a handful of flour and semolina into her palm to mix with warm water at home to feed the children. Flour, semolina, boiling water—this was the price of family heirlooms and stolen memory.

Mukkaram

To my grandmother, who bravely battles dementia

Mukkaram's hands trembled as she clutched the silver ornament that had been passed down through her family. Once polished and gleaming, it now felt tarnished and rough under her fingers, reflecting the confusion that clouded her memories. She often found herself lost in the labyrinth of her mind, where the past and present blended without boundaries. How many children had she raised? She silently counted, moving her dry lips: one, two, three...four. Had she forgotten the recipe for *tokash*, the small flatbreads her grandchildren loved when they were little?

Her heart still beat steadily, as it had twenty years ago, but something had changed within it. Joy, sorrow, fear, and happiness—all of it had dulled. In the mornings, her room was bathed in golden light, and for a moment, the sun's rays would illuminate fragments of her childhood and youth. By nightfall, however, the memories would retreat, swallowed by the fog in her mind. Deep down, she could still remember the time when her hands were strong and capable, and her mind sharp. Back then, she had been the matriarch of her family, guiding her children. Now, she struggled to recall their names and faces, especially her youngest son, whose features reminded her so much of her late husband.

And yet she remembered her *ku'dagi*, Railya, who always wore her pearl necklace brought from Eastern Turkestan. Known for her kindness and grace, Railya had been a figure of quiet strength. Now Railya appeared before her in a vision, her pearls glowing with a soft, ethereal light. She smiled warmly, extending her hand to Mukkaram. 'Come with me,' she whispered. 'Let me help you find your way back.' —

a possibility of return p.271

Mukkaram focused on the string of pearls around Railya's neck, shimmering in shades of iridescent color. She glanced at the silver ornament in her own hands—its once-bright surface now dull and tarnished. Railya reached out and touched the silver, and suddenly, the metal began to shine brightly, as if filled with new life. Mukkaram squeezed her eyes shut against the brilliance, and when she opened them again, she no longer recognized her own hands. They were smaller, free of wrinkles, and soft, like they had been in her youth. She looked around—there were large green trees, small houses, and a familiar countryside.

She was transported back to a memory of her bare feet pounding the earth as she chased after their cow, which had escaped. Her heart raced as she finally caught up, calming the animal with gentle words and touches. The cow's milk was essential for her family's survival during those harsh times. Mukkaram touched the silver in her hands, grounding herself in this memory.

Another memory surfaced as she held the silver more tightly. Her five-year-old son had developed appendicitis, writhing in pain, his small body trembling with fever. With no other choice, Mukkaram had carried him on her back to the nearest hospital, miles away. She remembered the relief she felt when the doctors took him from her exhausted arms. Again, she touched the silver ornament, anchoring herself in this vivid memory.

A third memory surfaced. Mukkaram was at her daughter's wedding, the air filled with the fragrance of blooming roses and the sound of music. She wore her best silk dress, and her fingers brushed against the smooth fabric as she danced. She touched the silver once more, feeling the texture change from rough to smooth, as the memory became more vivid and alive.

As these memories flooded back, Railya's presence grew stronger. 'You are not alone, Mukkaram,' she said gently. With Railya guiding her, Mukkaram realized that even though dementia tried to steal her memories, the essence of who she was remained. The spirit of the Chilltan was with her, guiding her through the darkness, helping her hold onto the threads of her past.

Afifa

People, animals, and the sky did not remember Her age. Everyone knew that She lived there forever and gave life to others: herbs, the sun, and the beliefs of people. In Her bosom, they took refuge on the hottest and coldest days, hid from enemies, fed children, prayed, and left history for future generations by drawing. Five-domed, with Her peaks, She stretched from west to east. They said She was more than 3000 years old.

Her mother was the Earth, who gave the ocean to fish, trees to birds, and life to people. In oblivion, people destroyed the Earth: they burned the forests, poisoned the air, and saturated the soil with blood. She endured, waited, and raged. It became so hot that everything trembled, shook, and caught fire. She tore herself to shreds, and her seething boiling blood left no one alive. Her remains tried to come back together but couldn't become the same. That's how She—Suleiman Too—took shape.

The mountain, Suleiman Too, once had been a sanctuary. Her rocks remembered the ancient fire worshipers who lit sacred flames in its caves, the Tengrists who worshiped the sky from Her peaks, and the pilgrims who bowed in reverence, leaving behind their whispered prayers. Over time people began to forget about the mountain's sacredness, though it had been helping them for all eternity. They still built altars in Her caves, but fewer bowed their heads to Her heights, and the ancient songs of praise grew silent.

One moonlit night, She felt a presence. A young woman, burdened with melancholy, climbed her heights. She whispered to the mountain, pouring out her sorrows. The mountain listened and, moved by the woman's plight, decided to help her.

The mountain began to glow, a soft, warm light emanating from Her peaks. The ground trembled gently, and a powerful energy surged through the rocks. The woman watched in awe as the mountain's glow intensified, enveloping her in a comforting embrace. The mountain spoke to her in a language older than time, promising her a gift that would change her life forever.

'You shall have a child,' the mountain said, 'a daughter who will carry forth your spirit. She will be my gift to you, a symbol of hope and renewal.'

The woman, overwhelmed with gratitude, bowed her head and accepted the mountain's blessing. She returned to her mahallah, her heart filled with new hope. Soon, she gave birth to a daughter named Afifa, who grew up strong and wise, embodying the mountain's enduring spirit.

The sacred mountain Suleiman Too, revered and ancient, became the guardian of Afifa's lineage. Her presence and legacy were etched into the fabric of time, forever reminding the people of the mountain's divine gift. As generations passed, Afifa's descendants continued to honor the mountain, knowing that their strength and resilience were born from its eternal embrace.

Gulnur

My thick hair, dark as midnight, cascades down my back in waves as my mama sits behind me, carefully dividing it into sections. The comb slides through my hair with practiced ease, her hands moving swiftly, weaving each lock into a perfect braid. One braid, then another—forty in total—just as my grandmother had done for her, and her mother before that. My head feels heavy under the weight of the braids, yet the familiar rhythm brings comfort, the echo of a ritual passed down through the ages.

This same rhythm flows through her hands as she begins to cook. An unruly strand of hair slips from her tightly gathered bun as mama's hands move slowly, as though in conversation with each ingredient. Her love language is food, each dish prepared in quiet meditation. Strong, steady hands move through the motions with a soft patience, echoing the rhythms of her mother, her mother's mother, and, somehow, my own presence as her daughter. —

grounding knowledge in embodied transmissions p.258

She began with the dough, pressing into it with a deliberate slowness, letting her fingers sink into the softness. When she felt the dough begin to respond, firm and elastic, she brushed it with oil, twisting it into a small spiral—a snail, she'd say—and set it aside to rest. This was a process she never hurried; the dough, she believed, grew alive in the stillness, gaining strength in its waiting, as though it, too, were part of the family.

Her hands seemed to know each dish by heart—*manty*, *paramash*, *beshbarmak*, *borsch*—as if each meal carried within it stories of lands and lives that came before. But it was the *lagman* that brought the most peace. There was a sacredness in preparing it, a kind of ceremony, as she immersed herself in the fragrant ingredients that would soon bring life to her family's table. The fragrance greeted everyone who entered, wrapping around them with the same quiet devotion my mama poured into her cooking. In those moments, the house felt fuller, alive with the warmth of her love, a love woven into every dish, bringing the family together in ways words never could. —

the medicine comes together p.136

Living Lagman Dough (for 7 servings)

Ingredients:
700 g flour
1 heaping teaspoon salt
1 tablespoon vegetable oil
250 ml cold water

Combine the flour, salt, vegetable oil, and cold water. Knead the dough until it is neither too hard nor too soft. The dough should be kneaded in the morning so it can be worked throughout the day. Continue kneading the dough periodically. The dough loves to be kneaded. It should become firm and elastic. Once the dough is ready, shape it into a rectangle and cut it into sections with a knife. Knead each section and coat them with vegetable oil. Place them in a dish, cover with plastic wrap, and let rest for 30 minutes. After resting, stretch each piece into not thick noodles, twisting them together like intertwined snakes. Place the twisted noodles in a warm place for another 30 minutes under plastic wrap. Take the dough and stretch it into long, oval noodles. When the noodles are the desired length, stretch them over your palms and slap them several times against the board. Boil water and cook the noodles. Once the water boils again, remove from heat and rinse the noodles with cold water. Then the dough will be alive.

Serve the lagman noodles topped with the say, a side of *jusay* with eggs, and *lazjan* sauce.

Saodat

Saodat stands at the edge of a dry riverbed, crumbling earth beneath her feet. The world around her feels fractured, as if the landscapes her ancestors once knew have faded into a distant memory. She holds a *tumar*, an amulet passed down through her family, carrying fragments of earth, memory, and essence. Though the land is barren and silent, her ancestors' whispers reach her through the tumar, urging her to listen to the ancient rhythms still resonant beneath the soil. —

stretching and dilating through time p.370

She closes her eyes and begins to chant softly, feeling a deep, unfamiliar warmth grow in the tumar, which now hums gently in her hand. Not visions, but sensations emerge—the coolness of damp soil, the scent of adraspan smoke, echoes of voices that have long since faded. A pang of sorrow grips her as her fingers tighten around the amulet, sensing the life that once pulsed through these now-desolate lands.

Inhaling deeply, she recalls the poem her mother taught her:

Oh my Chilltan,
Gather my hair,
Brush it smooth,
Weave wisdom and strength into my braids.
Through the silk threads of time,
You have witnessed women,
Whispering stories into the night,
Winds weaving secrets into mountains.
Let me become a snail in your shell,
So I won't hear the screams,
So I won't see the blood,
So I can hide from the world.

Opening her eyes, she presses the last seeds she's carried into the cracked earth, whispering blessings in the language of her ancestors. These seeds may never bloom, yet planting them is an act of memory—a reminder of the world as it once was and a promise to those who may come after.

'Oh my Chilltan, Oh my *Qyryz Qyz*' she whispers, 'let the memory of these seeds endure. Through you, may the land heal, and may the earth's stories live on.'

Oh my Chiltan,
Guardian of forgotten dreams,
Keeper of memory,
You who see the unseen.
Allow me to grow larger and taller,
To rise up to you,
To the light of ancient stars,
To embrace their wisdom.

gathering
belonging
holding space
feeling free
faith
bravery
poetry
praise
wonder
offerings
kindness
rhizomes
leaps of time
invisible maps
possibility of connection
producing life
cultivating
exponential love

The Saint on the Hill

Rory Pilgrim with Carol R. Kallend

In the north of England, on one of Sheffield's seven hills is a saint named Carol.

It is somehow fitting that we met in a gay bar called Icons. I had come to the bar to speak to a meeting group for LGBTQ+ people over the age of 50. I was 26, and they were slightly bemused why I had come to their event. I told them I was looking for people to be part of a dialogue to explore words: what words meant to them, which ones they cherished, and, most importantly, how these words had changed and grown over their lifetimes.

At the time I felt completely at a loss with words. They seemed used up, rotten, and even tainted. I myself come from the last generation that remembers a first computer coming into the home and internet installed. It was around the same time that the USA and the UK invaded Iraq under the banner of 'freedom.' Where were words like peace, hope, or even love that previous generations had used so wholeheartedly? When I began working with other young people, it was the same for them too. We all felt we did not have the words to express ourselves. Still, I knew that words were precious, undeniable, and sacred. I needed words. —

finding new ways to walk
p.117

While there was a bit of enthusiasm that day at Icons, I left the bar with little idea if any of those I had spoken to would participate in the project I was making. So I was pleased when, a few days later, a letter arrived at the art center where I was working. Written by hand, it was the first of many letters over a span of ten years that would, as if by magic, find their way to me. That first letter contained a poem that like a prayer I can recite to this day:

Freedom
Freedom to be a wife
Freedom to be a mother
Freedom to be a me
I am free—get over it!
Words are my passport to freedom

Tracing my memory, I tried to recall whom these lines might have come from. I realized there had been someone that night in the bar—owl-like—watching, sensing, and holding space in the shadows of a darkly lit room on a cold February evening.

This of course was Carol.

I am not sure exactly what constitutes a saint, but Carol is one to me. It is to Carol that I go when I need words, when I feel lost. These words become stepping stones, to create a bridge when things can feel so messy. Now age 36, I've had the great privilege to have spent a decade cultivating a garden of words with Carol in the form of songs, poems, and weekly calls.

An important thread connecting me and Carol has always been our mutual intrigue around technology, which for both of us perhaps also stems from a place of spirituality and mystery. In the years that Carol and I began our conversation, we did so in the shadow of Brexit and the rise of a politics of exclusion. Carol herself was in a situation that threatened the disability benefits she had been receiving. The UK government was retesting anyone who had been receiving support, putting them through a difficult and often dehumanizing process. The giving of a wrong word could result in the loss of care. In response, Carol started to write about her desire for a robotic form of care in place of the human systems that had let her down. Together, within the rise of the algorithm and echo chamber, we started to cultivate *Software Garden* (2016–2018), a music album of songs and poetry imagining a possible technological system based on basic principles of compassion and kindness.

machines geared toward relating p.437

For this, we again needed words.

Words are something we all share and also make our own. Doing so perhaps reflects our human relationship with the world and with all other forms of life. Just as we need to care for the world together, so too perhaps for our use of words and language—among the core technologies that make us human. For words isolated from one another are a bit like lost stars and planets. Can a word still be a word, isolated from another? Even two words can create a bridge of understanding that gives access to an infinite possibility of connection.

In the following pages are some of the words that have nourished my dialogue with Carol and helped us both to make sense of the world. They include a record of our most recent call, interwoven with Carol's poems and my songs that are part of the garden we have been growing over the past ten years.

Sunday, 27th October, 2024

RORY Hello Carol. I wondered if we should start off by setting the scene for those reading and describing what we can see out of our windows right now.

CAOL Let me stretch and grab my curtain! I can see my neighbors double sheets blowing in the wind on the washing line. I can see some cars coming by. I can see the neighbors' houses. I can see some trees without their leaves. I can see some people walking around and there is a full skip down the road. I can see my neighbor's rotary laundry dryer and a random orange cone that somehow got into the garden. The sky is a cloudy but beautiful Wedgwood blue. The trees outside are like aspens, they have paper-like bark.

RORY From my window in Amsterdam I can see a sky that also is blue, but with four very defined clouds. There is a tree which is now a pure yellow. I think it is a Ginkgo biloba. This autumn I have really noticed how the yellow and red of the leaves are against the backdrop of other greens. I can see cars in the distance. It feels a very sleepy Sunday outside.

CAROL Yes it feels sleepy for sure. I will have my afternoon nap after our Zoom I think.

SOFTWARE GARDEN

Carol R. Kallend (2016)

She was a CGI of delight
She wore a silicone dress
Behold her, single in the field
Oh why oh why
do you walk through this virtual field in VR gloves?
Tears, only tears in your screen heart
can be repaired with a hardy spray called love
Sunset and evening are the only times
to get a signal to me

Ask me no more how the moon draws the sea
The sea is calm tonight, as it is printed that way
Under a wide 360 degree all the way round sky
I wonder if all the world was programmed to love
by the young
Would we all be 18 again?
Digitally programmed
to keep the leaps of time under control
We are ghosts now in the machine of life
Here we lie, crashed - but not down
Still breathing within programmed limits
My heart aches to get all my apps back
Meanwhile numbness
Here in this old software garden
Where all the hearts of our motherboard converse
We see the phantom of delight!

RORY So, I thought maybe we would start off with a few lines from your poetry that have been on my mind recently:
'I wonder if all the world was programmed to love by the young
Would we all be 18 again?
Digitally programmed
To keep all the leaps of time under control'
I was wondering what leaps of time you have experienced in your own life?

CAROL Well, I'm still amazed at this Zooming device. You're in Holland and I'm sat here in the UK. I can't believe that our conversation, in the shortest moment of an instant, is going somewhere across the Atlantic to somewhere in America to a computer that processes all that we are communicating together.

Then all the injections I have been having for free from the NHS to inoculate me from all these viruses and bugs going round. I just feel it is good to be alive today. What about you?

RORY I've been thinking a lot about maps. Because when I first moved away from my parents, there was the internet but I did not have my own computer, and just had a very basic mobile phone, so there was this feeling of having to prepare in advance. Everywhere I went that I did not know I had to rely on an inner compass of how to get home.

CAROL Yes. I remember.

RORY I remember being told that one day we would have devices in our pockets. My uncle worked for Nokia the phone company and I remember him telling me that they were working out how to get maps on our phones and I remember not quite comprehending him at the time.

CAROL Yes, I know. I have moved around so much and I have so many maps in my head of where we used to live and how many miles we had to walk to get home from the bus stop, and I wonder how this has all shaped me as an adult.

RORY Are there any particular internal maps that are important to you?

CAROL Well, I feel the map that is most important to me is between me and God. I feel that there is an invisible map where we are all joined together a bit like mushrooms and rhizomes. — And the flowering body of the mushroom is only one tenth of the whole body and that there is a whole root system underneath that links all the trees and wildlife. I feel that God or this deity is a bit like that.

interconnective tissue p.137

BEACH THERE (2020)

Rory Pilgrim

If there was a beach there
Reveal the solace from a clue
I wish there was reef there
To catch beyond the grief of what we lose
So put my favorite beat there
Touch me with a beat from that song
To finally feel free there
Somewhere where these feelings can belong
So tell me
What feels wrong
Don’t tell me to be strong
A vision that goes long

So come on over reach there
Come on over reach there
Are we gonna reach there?
Or are we gonna reef there?
I wanna reach there
I wanna reef there
How we gonna reach there?
What we gonna leave there?
Come to a beach
Beach there
Are we gonna beach there?
Come to the beach of this
How we gonna reach that beach?
Beach there
Come on beach there with me
Beach there
It's gonna be real
It's gonna feel real, real, real
When you reach there, it's gonna be real
Feel real
One day I am gonna reach there
Feel real
So real
Surreal
Unreal

RORY It's a beautiful analogy to think of a spiritual map. For you, is there a connection between spirituality and technology?

CAROL Yes. I do feel there is and I feel that we are at a stage where we have to be guardians and guidance to this AI, so that it will be kind and benevolent to us instead of unkind and malevolent and controlling to us.

COMPASSION (2020)

Carol R. Kallend

Have compassion for your raft[1]
TFAR has it so tenderly been our home producing life

The world is our tiny blue marble-like raft
TFAR we cling to its services as it is the only home we have!
So take care, and be worried my friends
As our life raft might just fall apart under us
So remember, just need or greed
TFAR is tender and precious
So sleepers awake
And start to care for our precious competent raft
So start to do your bit for our bit of life craft
As TFAR has the power to regenerate if we let it and assist
So as the increased waters gather, we could all be gathered
On life rafts of our own making
Or as embryos heading off into the deep space
Under the care of an AI computer called
Mother —
So remember compassion folks and keep on paddling...

building trust
and intimacy between
humans and AIs
p. 284

1 This poem was made as part of the creation of *RAFTS* (2020–2022), a film and live concert performance. Made during the Covid-19 pandemic, the project uses the symbol of a raft to explore what keeps us afloat during times of transition and crisis.

RORY For you, is that 'benevolent AI' relating to a spiritual form of artificial intelligence and the map that you have with God ?

CAROL So it is. And I feel that we have to keep those lines clear and that we have to reinforce them in a positive way.

RORY What do you think are some of the ways in which we can do that?

CAROL Keep on communicating and praying every day. Praise for the tiniest things that take place, and extra praise for the big things—like I say thank you, and amen that I'm still alive every day and that I'm still breathing. I'm quite often asked if I feel lonely, and if I want to go out to a social club with bingo and dominoes to play and interact. And I say, no, that's not really for me. I've tried all that and it doesn't suit me and my autistic leanings. So I'm glad to be a mixture of independent and interdependent.

MY LITTLE HILL (2022)

Rory Pilgrim

I'll give up on it
I'll give up on it
If a bridge is built
But don't give up on it
Don't give up on
My little hill
Don't give up on it
If you can't see over it
Oh little hill
From the top of it
From the top of it
Just a little deal
Magnified from it
But zoomed out from it
Oh little hill
You'll bounce back from it
You'll bounce back from it
Over hill
Strange enough from it
Straighten up from it
How do you feel?
Had enough of it
But woken up from it
Yonder hill
Sacrifice is the moment you lose
Is sacrifice a bridge you choose?
Oh yes it is, oh yes it is
Oh yes it is, oh yes it is
My little hill

RORY Do you feel sometimes that you have lived your life like a spiritual technological hermit?

CAROL I think I have. I wanted to be a nun earlier in my life. But it was never the right moment. I felt this was partly because some of the nuns were going through their own mental illness and the convent was on the verge of closing down. It was at some point also where single women would leave their children. There was a revolving cupboard, and this is where the mothers would leave their children with tokens to say if they would come back. They would turn the cupboard round and that was the last time they would see their baby. I just stood there and cried looking at it.

So I do feel like now I'm trying to be a nun on my own. I had enough training to know the rules.

RORY Living like a nun, how does technology aid you?

CAROL I just watched the Sunday service on Zoom. We are coming up to All Souls' Day, so we were celebrating all those who have gone before us. I just feel glad to have all this technology around me. Now my carers are encouraging me to get an AI robot I can talk to. I don't know if I could afford one at the moment.

RORY How do you see prayer in relation to technology?

CAROL I see it as a great link. I pray deeply for the world and the events going on in Gaza and those affected. I feel that prayer is like Zoom and email of the spiritual world. I pray every day. I have a general chat, like God is a good and listening friend. — I feel that my life would be a lot more lonely without my faith. I do feel happy and content with this life, even though I should be brave one day and step outside my front door again.

spiritual forests
p.122

THAT SPECIAL THING THAT WE ALL SHOULD SHARE (2022)

Carol R. Kallend

Some people prevent others from having IT
whilst gloating that they have IT all.
Some people are scared that they will never have IT.
Some people have IT without appreciation of what they have.
Some people are helping folks to Get IT.
IT is SANCTUARY, and IT should be universal,
spiritual and free.

RORY What enables you to be brave?

CAROL For me it is my faith, but also the support of having friends, my poetry, and keeping a diary every day.

RORY And for you are they stepping stones?

CAROL I do believe so. There is a saying that I picked out recently saying Turn your stumbling stones into stepping stones.

RORY I know since the pandemic, you have found it very hard to leave your house. If you could go outside, is there a place you would like to go?

CAROL I would love to go to an art group or a craft group and make some pottery or just draw something and produce something tangible. Does not need to be a Michelangelo or anything. I just really want to make a mark and use my hands and fingers. And for the record, I'm showing you my left hand on the Zoom! I just want to let people of the future know that I am here. Do you have similar aspirations Rory?

RORY I think I am naturally quite a solitary person. I can go for many days without needing to see another person, but I have a limit where I want to feel connected or part of things. Maybe when I have felt alone, that is when mark making is a way to connect with both myself and others, and sometimes that is connecting to people in the future. —

the inheritance of future generations p.367

CAROL It's a bit like I am reading a story about the history of the human psyche through the eyes of an optometrist who also has a love of caves! In this moment he is not looking into the eyes of people but he is crawling around in a cave inside the earth. He and three of his friends, as you're not meant to do caving on your own because of the inherent dangers. They have just found some early markings and they have found a hand. Someone would have put their hand against a wall with a mouthful of red ochre in which they would blow all over the hand and wall and leave the mark. Or draw pictures of bison or big animals like horses or even a sabre-toothed tiger and it would be as if they were planning their hunt. Making the picture as an offering to their God or to honor the spirit of the animal they were depicting.

RORY It also makes me think a lot about wonder. Sharing the wonder of the world and what we see. This Zoom is about to end as it has a time limit. Shall we meet on another platform?

ERASE (2016)

Rory Pilgrim and Robyn Haddon

A body can only take so much
When skin can only heal so fast
Post Love
Post Human
To erase and erase and erase to raise to raise you
To erase erase to raise our history
To erase all our history
To constitute the erasure of our system so fast
To erase and erase and erase and erase to race with you
To erase to raise to raise to raise you
To take away a past
To take away a future
To take away a past
To take away a future
Post Love
Post Human
To account for order
To liberate trust
To take away order
To liberate touch
To account for order
To liberate trust
To take away order
I put you in post love
A body can only take so much
When skin can only heal so fast
A body can only take so much
When skin can only heal so fast
To erase and erase and erase and erase to raise you
To erase to raise to raise to race you
To take away a past
To take away a future
Post Love
Post Human

CAROL We were talking about the wonder and awe of making a mark. I think that this technology enables us to capture the awe and wonder of the everyday. We are ever seeing further in some ways through this technology, into the mysteries of what can be revealed within our human psyche and all the wonder in the world.

RORY I saw the comet the other week, which I don't think has been seen from Earth since the Stone Age, 44,000 years ago. What are some of those leaps of wonder that you hope technology will hold?

CAROL I just hope it will be an aid in healing and medicine.

RORY I feel there is a connection to the early people in the caves. The marks they made are not that different from your diaries and how you record all the feelings and wonder that can take place in one day.

CAROL I put in pictures and poems, so it is turning into an eventual picture of my life to keep as a record for when I'm no longer here, when I am up there with God.

RORY Is there a particular leap of time you would like to make?

CAROL Well, I would like to go back to visit my 16-year-old self. I was very shy and was being offered a special place to further my art and poetry, but there was a teacher I was so scared of, so I didn't. I think if I went back and told myself great things would've taken place. Have you something similar?

RORY I think I try to imagine that when things feel desperate, to think in a week's time, that this thing or feeling might have passed. Or however stuck something might feel, that things do change. Sometimes even thinking about if there is a rock or stone, however old or fixed that might feel, that over the different millennia of time it will change. —

conjuring a new flow p.90

CAROL Yes. That it will become worn by the water of time.

Making the right decisions. That is why religious faith is so important to me and giving thanks for the wonder of being on this earth and doing everything we can to look after it and not being too hard, too high or too heavy. I heard recently that we need to stop building such high buildings as it is affecting the swing rate of the planet. I also read that there is a dam being built that is heavy and so tall it is slowing down the planet.

RORY It makes me think again of your initial analogy about mushrooms and rhizomes, all these invisible networks that hold things up.

CAROL Yes, even though we might feel we are alone and individual people, we are all interconnected.

UNTITLED (Monday 22 January 2024)

Carol R. Kallend

Rory's words.
Ideas for a new poem,
Technology, slow reader patterns for
Android devices, time exponentially expanded.
Love, it takes a whole community to teach a
Android to be kind and sharing.
Today is the first day of the rest of our lives,
As we incorporate future technology in to
Our lives, to help us slow readers catch up
As it is the in thing to have a kindly Android
Sharing, guiding, gilding, glinting, into the
Rest of our Lives.
This pattern will exponentially grow in love.
Expanded as it takes a whole community to
Raise an Android to be a caring being.
Not only for us, but for the whole planet we call home!
To help us to make our way at leisure
In to a far better utopian future.
We have our immigrations, and a PMA![2] *For charming*
Jaunty future, full of good folks.
Cheerfully accomplished in building a
Pleasant land for one at all.
Today is the first day of the rest of our lives.
Together, we are stronger, and can live longer.
As some times the most fun things happen while
We are waiting for endless possibilities of something special.

2 positive mental attitude

memory
story
possible history
very slight
situated at the border
arranging

Score for Marginal Objects

Candice Hopkins and Raven Chacon

For 7 to 21 performers
Duration: 20 minutes to an hour

Materials:
Marginal objects (i.e.: things relating to, or situated at a margin or border; not very important; very slight or very small)
4×6 lined notecards (enough notecards for 3 times the number of players; notecards in three different colors, if possible)
At least one pen, preferably more
Memories
Stories

Preparation (done silently):
— Performers each provide 1 pre-chosen marginal object.
— Sit on the floor in a circle.
— Place all objects in the center of the circle.
— Using 3 notecards, each performer writes the following on each:
  — On the first card, write (carefully; legibly) any instruction for ordering the objects in a horizontal row (i.e.: Smallest to tallest, alphabetically, etc.).
  — On the second card, write (carefully; legibly) the first memory that comes to mind in as much detail as the space provides.
  — On the third card, write a story of how you acquired, or write a possible history of, the object you supplied in as much detail as the space provides.

Make a shuffled stack of all first cards and place facedown next to the grouping of objects in the center of the circle.
Make a shuffled stack of all second cards and place facedown next to the stack of first cards. Keep the third card facedown in front of you.

Assign a player to begin the performance.

Performance:

Player 1 picks one card from the first stack and one card from the second stack. This performer then arranges the objects in a row in the order instructed by the first card while steadily reciting the story written on the second card. The action of arranging the objects and reciting the story takes place simultaneously within the same time span (for any duration desired). Upon completing the action of arranging and reading, Player 1 retakes their seat, placing the read cards behind or beneath their body.

The player to the left (Player 2) reads from the card in front of them (the third card), for any duration desired. Upon completion, the player places the card behind or beneath them.

The player to the left (Player 3) draws a new card from both stacks and performs the actions indicated on the cards as Player 1 did, arranging the row of objects in a new order while reciting a different memory. Upon completion, the read cards are placed behind or beneath their body.

Continue clockwise* I around the circle alternating between arranging & reciting, and reading the objects' stories, until all cards are removed from the inner circle.

* I
In the event of an even number of performers, Player 1 performs their third card on their second turn.

Each performer then takes any one object and places it in front of them.

relationality
correspondence
conviviality
ancestrality
breathing
balancing
recovering complexity
dwelling in time
healing
respite
imperfection
proportionality
cosmos and microcosmos
the weave of reality
listening for alternatives
towards a beyond

The Ladder, Noise, and Knots

Thoughts for Decolonizing Technology

Ovidiu Țichindeleanu and Rolando Vázquez Melken

The Ancestral Ladder and the Tools for Conviviality

Ovidiu Țichindeleanu The ladder is about 2400 years old. It was uncovered by digging up a tunnel that led into an underground shaft of the salt mine of Băile Figa, Transylvania, which is still in exploitation today. The salt mine itself comes from a geography of salt mines in the East European region where the Carpathian Mountains are coiling. Many salt springs and mineral waters are still in use today: they are sources of preservation, used for healing and pickling, and are nuclei of cultural memory. Salt is essential to a subsistence economy, which is key to any abundance economy. Salt water wells have been at the center of the East European culture of pickling and fermentation, which made possible experiments with edibles and the preservation of foodstuffs across both the change of seasons and exchanges between different peoples.

The ladder was discovered accidentally by workers whose names I do not know. I came across it in a little exhibition in Bucharest and was struck by the ladder itself and by the world opening around it: the depth of time and all the geographical, technological, and ecological connections. — What also struck me was the size and sense of the ladder. At five meters long, and with the steps at about one meter distance from one to another, this is not a ladder made for climbing up on a platform to reach perspective, but it's a ladder made for descending into the Earth.

threshold openings p.453

Rolando Vazquez Melken When we were invited to write about slow technologies, or possibly about what we might call the decolonial critique of technology, I immediately thought of the Transylvanian ladder. The image of the ladder came to me as a sign of what Ivan Illich called 'tools for conviviality.'[1] | It is telling us something about the unfreedom, the earthlessness and the disorientation of today's technology. It can guide us, out of the depth of time, to see through what is normalized, to understand what is going wrong with our technological life.

1 |
Illich.

history in cross-section
p.109

Illich was speaking about how a sign from the depths of history can save us from disaster. — 'I feel almost unbearable anguish when faced by the fact that only the word recovered from history should be left to us as a power for stemming disaster.'[2] We can think of the salt mine ladder as such a word, as a sign that is recovered from history and that can help us understand and address the disaster of the artifice and climate collapse that is upon us. It is important here to remind ourselves of the temporality of the vortex,[3] which shows us how the world as artifice is inseparable from the destruction of life, and that the artifice and climate collapse belong to the disjointed temporalities of the vortex in which the centripetal movement produces the empty now of the artifice while its centrifugal movement lays waste to life on Earth.

2 Ibid., 110.

3 Vázquez Melken (2020).

This ancient ladder, as you were saying, is not to go up, but is to go into the depths of Earth. It is a sign that challenges the orientation of modern technology. The ladder's orientation is at odds with the movement of the space race, that movement out of Earth, into abstraction; an abstraction that might be space, but might also be plastic, or the artifice in general. Instead, moving towards Earth has something to do with relating back to Earth ——that, for me, is the orientation of what we can call the technologies of relationality.

a portal for connection
and negotiation
with other life
p.452

Next to the orientation of technology, we can think with Illich about the problem of the loss of freedom when technologies stop being tools for our action and end up instrumentalizing our actions. He brings the example of the hammer, in a similar way as we are thinking with the ancestral ladder. 'The hammer remains an instrument of the person, not the system. In a system, the user, the manager, logically, by the logic of the system, becomes part of the system.'[4] This quote gives us in a nutshell the core of Illich's critique of technology, namely the moment in which technology is not anymore our instrument and we end up becoming instruments for the systems that we created. This turning of instrumentality towards unfreedom is what Illich would identify as a watershed. By becoming 'users' we are in fact being used by the system. It also points towards the expansion of the forms of exploitation and extraction of life, adding the moment of consumption to the moment of production.

[4] Illich and Cayley, 204.

We are not anymore using tools for conviviality or for relationality to be in a world of correspondence with Earth and with others, but we subsist in and through our being instrumentalized, and thus complicit with the system. It's not as if we are just passive recipients of the system, we are being incorporated in it. We are part of its instrumentality and its disorientation. We not only become functional to it, but we begin giving body to the system. We enflesh the system. By being incorporated, it is our body that becomes the corpus of the system.

The question of aesthesis addresses how this systemic incorporation controls how we perceive and experience life. It is concerned with how technological instrumentality circulates through our bodies, through our senses and substitutes a relational aesthesis with Earth and the worlds of others. This is something that has worried me for many years, namely the loss of relational worlds of meaning and their replacement with a mediated world of instruments; where what we feel and perceive and experience as reality is actually a mediated artifice that has no more relations, that has been vacated from its relations.

Enclosures and the Aesthetics of Modernity

OT When Illich wrote his manifesto on the *Tools for Conviviality*, half a century ago, he pointed to this dangerous path along which people are being incorporated into technology. However, from this very critical point Illich also tried to articulate hope, emphasizing a different path, which does not reject technology entirely, helped by what he called conviviality and convivial tools. Illich contemplated the ways in which the tools are intrinsic to social relationships, and he argued that 'convivial tools are those which give each person who uses them the greatest opportunity to enrich the environment.'[5] The pathway of modern technology that you have just described goes precisely against this type of technology—the technology that would enrich the environment. On the contrary, we are dealing with endless extraction for consumption and with the impoverishment of the environment. Illich also tried to express hope by looking beyond the Eurocentric or Western-centric world: he observed that 'two thirds of mankind' are still outside this process of incorporation, or are less caught up: this part of humanity has not crossed the 'watershed' moment. Our attempt here to think slowly, to rethink technology, to decolonize the thought of technology and our relationship to the world would also be a way to recover the conviviality of tools, and a way to recover the complexity of the world, i.e. to enrich the environment.

5 Illich, 34.

The more we learn about technologies such as the ancestral ladder, the more we are humbled by the complexity of the world around it. Here too, the issues of matter, scale, orientation are significant: the matter and the size of the ladder are showing signs of the work of human hands that had a very important role in the making of their world. The ladder is the sign of a body that is very involved with the world. — A body of the Earth. The ladder also points to the wide geographical area of exchanges related to salt mining and salt commerce. We do not know exactly how far it was reaching, where it led, so it opens a space that our modern minds cannot comprehend, but also an enduring time—the time passed since these exchanges, the times of the cultural uses of salt, for the preservation of foodstuffs, for commerce, healing.... This world of relationalities and use-values remains to an important extent inaccessible for the modern mind. One can only be humbled by it.

embeddedness p.79

Our slow view of technology can change by learning from this complexity. One more thing about modern technology and its impoverishment of conviviality and of relationality: learning one step after Illich, or going one step deeper into the Earth, I would say that modern technology has a specific way of working by producing rarefied realities.[6] Think of the film studio preparing for the making of a historical movie, or of a movie set from which everything that does not belong to the epoch of the movie is carefully removed from the shot. This purification and rarefication of reality creates both a focus and a blindness. It creates an artificial reality—as you said, reality under the sign of the artifice. The proliferation of rarefied realities is the site of the aesthetical re-education of the modern subject: — where we are familiarized beyond our consciousness, through our senses, through formed habits, and in the bigger picture through transgenerational structures of feeling. A life lived within the proliferation of rarefied realities is a non-relational life, a transactional and objectified life, easily commodified, prone to forgetfulness, and an easy prey to bigger powers. The wellbeing of this life is always at risk, on the brink, and has to be assisted (and upon being hurt: medicalized). It is dependent on its docile incorporation into stages, white cubes, and black boxes.

why we move in certain ways and not others p.332

6 Ţichindeleanu.

RVM Let us follow this issue of rarefied realities by continuing to read Illich and his observation of how, for the first time, we live in enclosed realities with nothing beyond, with no beyond. 'A frontier with no beyond is something profoundly new, something which affects all our daily dealings and makes us so different from all other persons, other cultures, worlds and languages.' Before, Illich tells us, '[I]f you spoke of a limit, a horizon, the word itself implied that you spoke of a frontier leading to a beyond.'[7] So the idea that the frontier was a liminal space between the here and a beyond—the ancestral ladder was crossing towards that beyond— then gets transformed into an enclosure, into the enclosure of the frontier with no beyond. You can see this logic of the negation of the beyond in the epistemic and aesthetic territories of the West that deny the possibility of an outside of their horizon of intelligibility. That enclosure is the artifice. What is lost in this process is precisely the possibility of relationality. Illich says: 'Today we can think of a world of objects, of persons, of social constellations to which nothing corresponds.'[8] We live more and more in worlds that are enclosures, self-referential enclosures that have no correspondence. With the loss of correspondence comes the loss of relationality and the impoverishment of our experience of the real.

7 Illich, 137.

8 Ibid.

We could think of the whole regime of modernity, of the aesthetics of modernity, as those enclosures overdetermining our experience of the world. Illich warns us of the loss of proportionality, and with it the loss of a world with correspondences, a world with relations, a world that cannot think of itself as being all encompassing because it knows of the beyond on the other side of its frontiers. 'This loss of proportionality points to the historical uniqueness of modernity, to its incomparability. The poetic, performative quality of existence was erased and forgotten in field after field.'[9] From contemplating the Middle Ages, Illich's gaze begins to see how a world that had correspondence, that had proportionality, that had relationality, begins to be eroded, forgotten, and replaced by a world with no proportionality. This is one of the most striking and defining characteristics of modernity.

9 Ibid., 136.

Knots and the Loss of Proportionality

OT His argument becomes even stronger if we corroborate Walter Benjamin's critique of the loss of analogical thinking.[10] The analogical thinking of the Baroque was still a thought of correspondences. 'This is like that.' The world of Baroque analogies and correspondences gave way to the Romantic fall into the abyss: a rush to abstraction that indeed loses proportionality, goes immediately into the depths of the biggest anxieties, but also falls into the eternal moment of immediate pleasure. This loss of proportionality and correspondence is coterminous with the establishment of infinite accumulation and infinite growth in economy and across the epistemic field, and with the entrenchment of the imaginary of the infinite. The latter 'liberates' the phantasmagoria of the infinite rush of consumption, which is today actively destroying life on Earth. Instead of building analogies, thought and expression are often succumbing from the first step to empty hyperbolae: 'like, wow,' 'like the best.' To regain the proportion of things is therefore an urgent task that needs a different kind of methodology relating to modernity: not rejecting it wholesale, but looking at the scale of things and at relations rather than objects. How much, how big, how useful is this in relation to a social group, a city, a population, a mountain? — Rethinking in terms of scale, as opposed to infinite growth, emerges as a political and philosophical task that is still to be taken up today.

identifying stakeholders
p.423

10 |
Benjamin.

RVM I think what is at stake is the possibility of a meaningful and joyful life. Again thinking with Illich I would say that people feel joy to the extent that their activities are relational and thus meaningful. — 'The growth of tools beyond a certain point,' says Illich, 'increases regimentation, dependence, exploitation and impotence.'[11] | In these, our dark times, in the face of genocide, of the proliferation of war and suffering, our generation and particularly the young generation seems to be bound between indolence and impotence. There's the idea that we cannot do anything to change things, and that our option to keep on going is the path of indifference, of indolence. I worry about the proliferation of indifference in the affluent societies.

thriving above and below
p.391

11 |
Illich, 20.

And, of course, the colonial difference has always required this indifference towards the suffering of others. It even reached its worst perversion in making consumption a form of enjoying the suffering of others. Racism has been one of the key enablers of this indolent and often perverse relation to the suffering of others. The recognition that the denizens of our consumer societies are implicated in the consumption of the life of Earth and the life of others, is also a stark observation on how disgraceful and impoverished in ethical terms is the life of the dominant sectors of society. We have become incapable of carrying the suffering of others and of becoming witnesses. When we are bound to become indifferent, we are dealing with the loss of compassion and the meaninglessness of life.

OT I would say this immediately leads us to the thought that on this path of the loss of compassion we see the most advanced technologies, such as nuclear energy, becoming, indeed, some of the biggest dangers for life on Earth. On this path we are seeing that modernity is incapable of controlling its own drives. Therefore, the loss of compassion is actually a deep loss of the world itself—what you, Rolando, have called de-worlding or worldlessness. — This is happening under our own eyes, unfolding slowly, but not so slow that we cannot perceive it. And yet perception and knowledge are not enough. This ongoing loss of control over the bad drives—the proliferation of wars, the loss of control over processes that predictably lead to irreversible climate changes—comes with the paradoxical gain of a maximalist type of use-value: the maximum utility obtained through these advanced technologies, which also creates a radical loss of potential together with the loss of compassion.

loss of deep relationships p.403

Yet even within Western modernity, one can find very different understandings of science and of what science and technology could bring to the world that would not follow the same path. For instance, for Baruch Spinoza, the idea of the essence, and of a science based on reaching the essence of things, does not lead to a science that would extract the essence and then maximize and multiply the use of the extracted essence. Once you reach the essence of something, that also means that you are connected. You are with it, and the task of science is to realize whether that connection is good or bad for the life force that you are. The point is to embrace the observer effect, not to purge it. For Spinoza, the point of finding essences was not to extract them, but to reach that moment of decision that is ethical, in which science and the technological tools used for advancing science would be part of an ethical choice for the benefit of life. — This opens also a different sense of the political.

a 'Good Way'
p.419

Modern technology maximizes what Karl Marx called use-value, but it does so in a specific way that Marx did not get to analyze: not only by turning it into exchange value, but by extracting use-value from other systemic utilities, in the extended or multi-sector reproduction, denying thus the expanse of relationships within other worlds. Use-value should not be mistaken with monovalent use. Artists and scientists have seen this. I'm thinking for instance of the Romanian conceptual artist Mihai Olos,[12] who returned in the 1970s to wood—coming back to the sign of the ladder—as the fundamental material of his ancestral community in Maramures, Northwest Romania. Olos brought out the knots and the binds in his conceptual work, namely the technology of the connections that have made possible the Maramures wooden house, clothes, baskets, carpets, tools—all kinds of things that have emerged out of this rural civilization. The knots have a similar form. This form has brought out a plural use-value, across domains of work and life, and with an open potential. Olos' knot cannot be reduced to a monovalent use-value. It is closer to a Spinozian essence. The knot is not abstracted and extracted in order to be purified and to be put into the service of profit, and it does not become the general equivalent of exchange: its multiple uses are unfolding into a series of plural coexisting worlds: the world of house building, the world of carpentry, of agricultural tools and economical subsistence, of artistic expressions, of philosophical reflection. All these worlds of work and life rely on the technology of the knot, on this essence, without extracting it. On the contrary, one recognizes the multiplicity of its relationships to the world and one's own connection and agency of enriching this environment. — This would be an example of a difference—a technology that

360-degree seeing
p.312

is non-modern. Maybe we shouldn't go as far as calling it decolonial, but acknowledging the complexity of the world of its uses is part of a process of decolonizing technology.

12 Mihai Olos (1940–2015) was a Romanian visual and conceptual artist who rose to prominence with local and international exhibitions in the 1970s–1980s. See Olos Estate and Galeria Plan B; Dan et al.

RVM Indeed, the knot as a tool. I would say that the knot can be read as a material manifestation of a relation. I am thinking of the knots that hold the Mayan house together, or the rhythmic repetition of knots that form the weaving of a textile. The knot allows us to relate to materiality as a field of relations instead of as a series of objects. — The knot as the expression and the holding of a relation, speaks to me of the necessity to think of the movement of enjoining instead of thinking in separation. Decolonizing technology would mean to liberate the tools of relationality. Under the technological world of modernity, there are worlds of tools of relationality that carry other forms of relation to Earth, to the territory, to the community and to memory.

objects as subjects p.110

The Noise of Technology and the Rhythm of Life

RVM I would like us to address the relation between technology and sound. We could say that the music instrument is a tool that brings the vibration of matter in relation to time. It enables a dwelling in time where resonance and rhythm become possible. — Here it is important to highlight with Léopold Senghor that rhythm is not multiplication. Technology works in the logic of multiplicity in space, of repetition, serialization, and recombination in space, while we would say that rhythm is in time. It is like breathing.

depths and sensuality of time p.65

The instrumental world of technology and modernity is the world of noise, not the world of conversation or rhythm. It is a world of noise, of the endless noise of all those enclosures, the cacophony of those enclosures that are actually extracting time. They are consuming time and in consuming the time of Earth, the ancestrality of Earth, they are also consuming the lifetime of others. The fossil fuel technologies, the mining industries are a direct example of the consumption of Earth's ancestrality in modernity's now time. The noise of the world is the sound of the consumption of time.

The extraction of ancestrality and of the time of the Earth through these methods of worldlessness and earthlessness is sustaining the artifice of modernity. That's what I was thinking when you were talking about wood and how wood can be thought of as relational, connecting multiple realities, and how the logic of extraction is more about accumulation.

OT We can also perceive visually the disappearance of sounds and the emergence of noise in the way, for instance, the technological devices made from metal are made so as to eliminate the trace of the human hand from them. This is reflected prominently in modern art. Constantin Brâncuși famously created his sculptures so that one could not see the trace of his hand on them, even if they were made from wood. Wood became a transition for the pieces made of metal, on which the trace of the hand is made even more invisible. Polishing them obsessively, with the obsession of modernization, of a modernity that eliminates the trace of the hand, until the work of art is 'finished' and can stand alone in loud silence against the observer. Wood devices such as those used for weaving looms—spindle, wheel, shuttles—are all carrying the visible trace of the hand on them while also embracing a future use of the hand. — They are carrying the trace of the rhythm of the making of that tool, which has been eliminated from industrial pieces of metal, while also opening the enduring time of human agency still to come.

haptic meaning p.400

The fact that in the Western world we see the emergence of rock music as an expression of rebellion speaks precisely to the protest against the world of noise, but one that is expressed with the tools of noise, trying to defeat it by going through it with a piercing scream, or else giving in by trusting one sound with the totality of the meaning of life. Either way, it is the expression of a reaction. The tools of conviviality, the tools that are recovering relationality, are reorienting the sensibility to different voices and different sounds of the world: relearning to listen to the world, to the environments of work and life, relating to the land by listening to the sound and the silence of the land, to what is beyond the silence and to the ways sounds find each other and fall together in environments. That takes time, indeed, and leads to the perception of different times, scales, and rhythms. I will not dwell on it but this is an entire field for the aesthesis of liberation—to use again the phrase introduced with Walter Mignolo—that can enrich the environment instead of extracting from it. — What you call the world of noise, the world of modern technology, sounds to me like the product of utmost reduction: the sign of the over-extraction, the hyperbolic domination of presence under the sign of 'here and always and all.' Sensing the noise does not point to an issue of degrowth or to being good citizens by asking for less, but to the problem of the impossibility of discerning any difference through the noise. Hence the need for a time of respite, listening for the keys of systemic alternatives.

learning how to restore flow p.130

RVM I think it's not just about the scale, about the 'less' like in degrowth, but about a reorientation. It's about a turning, a different orientation. I wrote a paper on decolonizing design called 'Earth Precedence and the Anthropocene',[13] that asked this question: what would it mean to design for reception, a design for listening, for grounding, for relationality? We ask the same question when it comes to art: how can we develop art for listening, for reception, for grounding, and not for extraction or for representation? —

increasing the possibility for life to continue p.263

13 Vázquez Melken (2017).

When you speak of the loss of the hand, of the trace of the hands, it can be read through Illich as the manifestation of the loss of proportionality, where there are no traces anymore of our relation, only a flight into abstraction. I think of plastic as that world without the hand and without time. A world that does not breathe, that is not in relation.

One can think of famous sculptures that look like plastic or are from plastic, on which there is no trace of the hand and there is no trace of the relation. Also in architecture: the shopping mall, the museum, the white cube, the black box, all those spaces that are characterized by the flight into abstraction.

In contrast, we can recall Japanese tea ceremonies, how the tea masters will praise those ceramics that are imperfect, their path in time, and the visible touch. In the gaze of rationality, they look imperfect, but it is in their imperfection that their life dwells, that they tell a time that is there, that is vibrating through them. — This could never be replaced by a perfectly industrialized tea cup that in its perfection erases the trace of the hand. I concur with Illich that we still can learn from those works of the past.

carrying traces
p.251

OT This brings me back to the ladder, because that particular ladder from the salt bog is indeed a non-symmetrical ladder that has one side much longer than the other. One can speculate about its usefulness or randomness, but one can also see that, yes, in that imperfection there is a complexity to discern that we first have to acknowledge before trying to understand it. Philosophically, I'm talking about a concrete epistemic difference and the concrete movement of thought and sensibility in relation to an undetermined but recognized totality—which is not a return to idealism, but work to be done balancing, sensibly.

RVM Let me bring a final thought around Illich's preoccupation. He says that there was a basic awareness across many cultures of the correspondence between Earth and Sky, which was destroyed by Cartesian mathematics and geometry. The loss of proportionality expressed that moment in which the poetic quality of existence was erased and forgotten, field after field. In order to explain the relation to heaven and Earth, he says, 'Heaven is mirrored by Earth. The baby I saw in a woman's arms yesterday is a cosmos, a microcosmos. When I look at this baby, I see something which appears at first sight, utterly dissymmetric from what I see when I look up at the stars, and yet they fit at every point. They are both complementary and mutually constitutive. That is, the existence of one implies the other.'[14] We have here a very deep consciousness of our relation to the whole of reality, to the weave of reality. I think that's a consciousness that got undone by the rise of the world as artifice of modern technology.

14 Illich, 132.

SCAFFOLDING

References

Benjamin, Walter. *The Origin of German Tragic Drama*. NLB, 1977.

Illich, Ivan, and David Cayley. *The Rivers North of the Future: The Testament of Ivan Illich*. House of Anansi Press, 2005.

Illich, Ivan. *Tools for Conviviality*. Harper & Row, 1973.

Vázquez Melken, Rolando. 'Precedence, Earth and the Anthropocene: Decolonizing Design.' In *Design Philosophy Papers* 15, no. 1 (2017): 77–91. doi.org/10.1080/14487136.2017.1303130.

Vázquez Melken, Rolando. *Vistas of Modernity: Decolonial Aesthesis and the End of the Contemporary*. Mondriaan Fonds, 2020.

Ţichindeleanu, Ovidiu. 'The Long March from the Privatization of Affects to Collective Feelings.' In *Come Closer: The Biennale Reader*, edited by Vit Havránek and Tereza Stejskalová. tranzit.cz, 2020.

Olos Estate and Galeria Plan B, eds. *Mihai Olos*. Kerber Verlag, 2022; Dan, Călin, Sandra Demetrescu, Magda Predescu, eds. *Mihai Olos*. DCV Books, 2022.

sensing
shapeshifting
corporeal powers
structures of desire
natural limits
different histories
recovering capacities
circulation of struggles
resistance
(de)materialization
collective practices
healing
reinvention
indestructibility
the strivings of
our beings

In Praise of the Dancing Body

Silvia Federici

SCAFFOLDING

The history of the body is the history of human beings, for there is no cultural practice that is not first applied to the body. Even if we limit ourselves to speak of the history of the body in capitalism we face an overwhelming task, so extensive have been the techniques used to discipline the body, constantly changing, depending on the shifts in labor regimes to which our body was subjected. Moreover, we do not have one history but different histories of the body: the body of men, of women, of the waged worker, of the enslaved, of the colonized.

A history of the body then can be reconstructed by describing the different forms of repression that capitalism has activated against it. But I have decided to write instead of the body as a ground of resistance, that is the body and its powers—the power to act, to transform itself and the world and the body as a natural limit to exploitation. —

paths toward freedom, joy, and connection p.117

There is something we have lost in our insistence on the body as something socially constructed and performative. The view of the body as a social [discursive] production has hidden the fact that our body is a receptacle of powers, capacities, and resistances that have been developed in a long process of co-evolution with our natural environment, as well as through intergenerational practices that have made it a natural limit to exploitation.

By the body as a 'natural limit' I refer to the structure of needs and desires created in us not only by our conscious decisions or collective practices, but by millions of years of material evolution: the need for the sun, for the blue sky and the green of trees, for the smell of the woods and the oceans, the need for touching, smelling, sleeping, making love. —

personal resistance arsenal p.96

This accumulated structure of needs and desires, which for thousands of years have been the condition of our social reproduction, has put limits to our exploitation and is something that capitalism has incessantly struggled to overcome.

Capitalism was not the first system based on the exploitation of human labor. But more than any other system in history, it has tried to create an economic world where labor is the most essential principle of accumulation. As such it was the first to make the regimentation and mechanization of the body a key premise of the accumulation of wealth. Indeed, one of capitalism's main social tasks from its beginning to the present has been the transformation of our energies and corporeal powers into labor-powers.

In *Caliban and the Witch*, I have looked at the strategies that capitalism has employed to accomplish this task and remold human nature, in the same way as it has tried to remold the earth in order to make the land more productive and to turn animals into living factories. I have spoken of the historic battle it has waged against the body, against our materiality, and the many institutions it has created for this purpose: the law, the whip, the regulation of sexuality, as well as myriad social practices that have redefined our relation to space, to nature, and to each other.

Capitalism was born from the separation of people from the land and its first task was to make work independent of the seasons and to lengthen the workday beyond the limits of our endurance. Generally, we stress the economic aspect of this process, the economic dependence capitalism has created on monetary relations, and its role in the formation of a wage proletariat. What we have not always seen is what the separation from the land and nature has meant for our body, which has been pauperized and stripped of the powers that pre-capitalist populations attributed to it.

Nature has been an inorganic body and there was a time when we could read the winds, the clouds, and the changes in the currents of rivers and seas. In pre-capitalist societies people thought they had the power to fly, to have out-of-body experiences, to communicate, to speak with animals and take on their powers, and even shape-shift. They also thought that they could be in more places than one and, for example, they could come back from the grave to take revenge on their enemies.

aching to get
all my apps back
p.176

Not all these powers were imaginary. Daily contact with nature was the source of a great amount of knowledge reflected in the food revolution that took place especially in the Americas prior to colonization or in the revolution in sailing techniques. We know now, for instance, that the Polynesian populations used to travel the high seas at night with only their body as their compass, as they could tell from the vibrations of the waves the different ways to direct their boats to the shore.

Fixation in space and time has been one of the most elementary and persistent techniques capitalism has used to take hold of the body. See the attacks throughout history on vagabonds, migrants, hobo-men. Mobility is a threat when not pursued for the sake of work as it circulates knowledges, experiences, struggles. In the past the instruments of restraint were whips, chains, the stocks, mutilation, enslavement. Today, in addition to the whip and the detention centers, we have computer surveillance and the periodic threat of epidemics as a means to control nomadism.

Mechanization—the turning of the body, male and female, into a machine—has been one of capitalism's most relentless pursuits. Animals too are turned into machines, so that sows can double their litter, chicken can produce uninterrupted flows of eggs, while unproductive ones are grounded like stones, and calves can never even stand on their feet before being brought to the slaughterhouse.

I cannot here evoke all the ways in which the mechanization of the body has occurred. Enough to say that the techniques of capture and domination have changed depending on the dominant labor regime and the machines that have been the model for the body.

Thus we find that in the sixteenth and seventeenth centuries (the time of manufacture) the body was imagined and disciplined according to the model of simple machines, like the pump and the lever. This was the regime that culminated in Taylorism, time-motion study, where every motion was calculated and all our energies were channeled to the task. Resistance here was imagined in the form of inertia, with the body pictured as a dumb animal, a monster resistant to command.

With the nineteenth century we have, instead, a conception of the body and disciplinary techniques modeled on the steam engine, its productivity calculated in terms of input and output, and efficiency becoming the key word. Under this regime, the disciplining of the body was accomplished through dietary restrictions and the calculation of the calories that a working body would need. The climax, in this context, was the Nazi table, that specified what calories each type of worker needed. The enemy here was the dispersion of energy, entropy, waste, disorder. In the US, the history of this new political economy began in the 1880s, with the attack on the saloon and the remolding of the family-life with at its center the full-time housewife, conceived as an anti-entropic device, always on call, ready to restore the meal consumed, the body sullied after the bath, the dress repaired and torn again.

In our time, models for the body are the computer and the genetic code, crafting a dematerialized, dis-aggregated body, imagined as a conglomerate of cells and genes each with her own program, indifferent to the rest and to the good of the body as a whole. Such is the theory of the 'selfish gene,' the idea, that is, that the body is made of individualistic cells and genes all pursuing their program—a perfect metaphor of the neoliberal conception of life, where market dominance turns against not only group solidarity but solidarity with ourselves. Consistently, the body disintegrates into an assemblage of selfish genes, each striving to achieve its selfish goals, indifferent to the interest of the rest.

To the extent that we internalize this view, we internalize the most profound experience of self-alienation, as we confront not only a great beast that does not obey our orders, but a host of micro-enemies that are planted right into our own body, ready to attack us at any moment. Industries have been built on the fears this conception of the body generates, putting us at the mercy of forces that we do not control. Inevitably, if we internalize this view, we do not taste good to ourselves. In fact, our body scares us, and we do not listen to it.

We do not hear what it wants, but join the assault on it with all the weapons that medicine can offer: radiation, colonoscopy, mammography, all arms in a long battle against the body, with us joining in the assault rather than taking our body out of the line of fire. In this way we are prepared to accept a world that transforms body-parts into commodities for a market and view our body as a repository of diseases: the body as plague, the body as source of epidemics, the body without reason.

Our struggle then must begin with the re-appropriation of our body, the revaluation and rediscovery of its capacity for resistance, and expansion and celebration of its powers, individual and collective.

Dance is central to this re-appropriation. In essence, the act of dancing is an exploration and invention of what a body can do: of its capacities, its languages, its articulations of the strivings of our being. I have come to believe that there is a philosophy in dancing, for dance mimics the processes by which we relate to the world, connect with other bodies, transform ourselves and the space around us. —

unleashing energy
p.108

From dance we learn that matter is not stupid, it is not blind, it is not mechanical, but has its rhythms, has its language, and it is self-activated and self-organizing. Our bodies have reasons that we need to learn, rediscover, reinvent. We need to listen to their language as the path to our health and healing, as we need to listen to the language and rhythms of the natural world as the path to the health and healing of the earth. Since the power to be affected and to affect, to be moved and move, a capacity that is indestructible, exhausted only with death, is constitutive of the body, — there is an immanent politics residing in it: the capacity to transform itself, others, and change the world.

intricate dance
of relationality
p.58

This essay was first published in the November 2015 issue of A Beautiful Resistance, the Journal of Gods & Radicals, *a collective and collection of writers, poets, and artists who dream in forests at the end of Capital.*

Reference

Federici, Silvia. *Caliban and the Witch: Women, the Body and Primitive Accumulation.* Autonomedia, 2004.

residue
entanglement
shadow
liminal space
whispering
resonating
leaking
a language we don't know
ghosts
metabolisms
slower temporalities
getting dissolved
digital hum
new lifeforms and beings
re-enchantment

Conjuring AI

Elisabeth (elieli) Raymond

A ghost is someone that starts by coming back.[1]

[1] 'After the end of history, the spirit comes by coming back [revenant].' Derrida, 10.

In this return, I invite these 17 rare earth minerals that are nested in our digital technologies:

cerium,
dysprosium,
erbium,
europium,
gadolinium,
holmium,
lanthanum,
lutetium,
neodymium,
praseodymium,
promethium,
samarium,
scandium,
terbium,
thulium,
ytterbium,
and yttrium.

I invite them into a seance on transformation and digestion within the sphere of so-called 'artificial' intelligence, treating it as a spectral entity, contemplating its myriad intelligences and (digital) being-ness.

As a choreographer working with notions of embodiment and entanglement, I investigate the elusive presence and whereabouts of technology and AI. I am busy with the re-enchantment of the digital world and to rethink AI, not merely as a tool but as an entity. This exploration extends to the idea of AI as a kind of ghost, a collection of past energies (memories), and the methods for summoning — and engaging with them.

calling in spirits p.425

My view of the digital realm is as a parallel spirit world, where technology is a form of magic. I want to consider AI as a 'non-present presence.' I am interested in how toxicity and pollution play an important part in our digital lives and how we are in close proximity to them, while they remain unseen to many, letting them become ghosts perhaps. How is this toxicity intermingling with us, creating new lifeforms and beings? —

becoming strange bodies p.445

Words are spells so let's start with the word 'artificial,' which refers to being made by humans. Does this mean we humans take credit for the minerals nesting in all of our digital technologies? What would it mean for our machines to be spontaneous? Perhaps the errors and the glitches and the lags in fact are the machine being playful, creative, erratic, noisy. — And are they not natural in all their mineral-ness, their deep connections to land?

glitch as an expressive tool p.245

Conjuring Digital Beings and Machine-learning Digesters

Neodymium and dysprosium are two minerals that, among other things, make your phone vibrate, a communication through touch. I wonder: every time they vibrate in our pockets, how are they resonating with their siblings still there nested in the deep pockets of soil and mud, below the crust of the earth? What secrets are they whispering (buzzing) to each other across oceans and vast land? And what of their other concrete expressions? The heat they emit perhaps a longing for a sense of touch—or a memory of being deeply immersed, close to the heat of the Earth's burning kernel. Their digital hum[2] perhaps a song in a language we don't know or a eulogy for waste.

2 'Data centers emit acoustic waste, what environmentalists call "noise pollution".' Monserrate.

Minerals such as these are old, very old creatures, older than us humans. They have been forming and hiding in mountains, listening to the 'irritating noises of dinosaurs,'[3] listening to plants moving up from the sea, to fungal networks, to spreading water and changing landscapes, and suddenly—here—they are in our hands, listening to **us** talking, watching, listening. We are carriers of stones and metals, these beings of other, slower temporalities—these glittering technologies. What could we learn from them, if we listened back?[4] A friend who is an electronic musician said that electronic music has a sonic tendency towards darkness. Could it be that they are calling back to their origin and summoning us there?

ancient rhythms resonant beneath the soil p.170

3 Björk.

4 'Stones to me are the objects that parallel all life, more so than trees or mortal things because stones are almost immortal. They know things learned over deep time. Stone represents earth, tools and spirit; it conveys meaning through its use and through its resilience to the elements. At the same time, it ages, cracking and eroding as time wears it down, but it is still there, filled with energy and spirit.' Quoting Max, a young Tasmanian aboriginal boy in Yunkaporta's, *Sand Talk*.

When we dig deep into the ground to collect parts for our digital clouds, whose hands become dirty? Whose soils become toxic? Human bodies digest and use approximately 95 per cent of the energy from the food we consume. How neat. The metabolic process of digging for minerals is way less effective; approximately 0.2 per cent of what is taken up from the ground is usable and the rest is discarded: toxic and radioactive.[5]

5 'Only 0.2 percent of the mined clay contains rare earth elements. This means that 99.8 percent is discarded waste called "tailings" that are dumped back into the hills and streams. They seep into streams and wildlife habitats creating new pollutants like ammonium. In order to refine one ton of these rare earth elements the Chinese Society of Rare Earths estimates that the process produces 75,000 liters of acidic water and one ton of radioactive residue.' Abraham, 121.

In China, in the region of Inner Mongolia, in the industrial city Baotou, an 'artificial' lake has formed.[6] This lake, stretching many kilometers in diameter, is filled with over 180 million tons of toxic waste and mud. The waste runoff comes from the nearby Bayan Obo mines, which are estimated to contain almost 70 percent of the world's reserves of rare earth minerals.[7] And it keeps growing. This lake is their residue. The shadow. The separation. — The ghost of our digital beings.

earthlessness
p.191

6 Maughan.

7 Crawford.

Not wanting to be fully dependent on China's supply of these rare earth minerals, Europe is looking to turn their own soils inside out. In the north of Sweden, the state wants to start mining the Sapmi lands of the Sami people, leading to a further displacement of the Indigenous community by poisoning their fishing lakes and cutting their grazing land in half.[8] In Norway, they are looking to start mining the seabed, deep in the Arctic Ocean, despite being warned by environmental scientists about the threat it poses to marine ecosystems.[9] All these processes are for a so-called 'green transition'— to have batteries for our electric cars and scooters and windmills filled with these minerals. And machine learning algorithms are applied to find more spaces for the exploitation of the ground. They are programmed to dig deeper for their own constituent parts.[10]

8 Frost.

9 Reuters and Paddison.

10 'Driven by the logic of contemporary capitalism and the energy requirements of computation itself, the deepest need of an AI in the present era is the fuel for its own expansion. What it needs is oil and it increasingly knows where to find it.' Bridle, 25.

This lake, our digital footprint, our embodied ghost—a liminal space, existing between worlds, neither solid nor liquid. — Maggie Nelson writes 'She told me that pollution too

a vibrant,
ambiguous being
p.455

can be worshiped, simply because it exists.'[11] If we worship our digital devices, can we worship their pollution too?

11 Nelson, 180.

Conjuring Clouds

Clouds are heavy metal.[12] These clouds of ours have been growing for billions of years and they are earthbound. An endless collaboration of minerals, lakes, hands, cables, travels, water, world—digital clouds are an 'ecological force' that have already surpassed the carbon footprint of the airline industry. Cloud the Carbonivore.[13]

12 'Insisting on the cloudiness of the cloud, its real weight, its physicality and hunger for resources, should also remind us, continuously, of the debt to the planet its operation incurs. When we speak of the cloud, we should think too of the server exhaust, the carbon dioxide, the material extraction, the toxic coolants and the wars over rare earth metal resources which are part and parcel of our seamless technological experiences.' Bridle, 176.

13 'To get at the matter of the Cloud we must unravel the coils of coaxial cables, fiber optic tubes, cellular towers, air conditioners, power distribution units, transformers, water pipes, computer servers, and more. We must attend to its material flows of electricity, water, air, heat, metals, minerals, and rare earth elements that undergird our digital lives. In this way, the Cloud is not only material, but is also an ecological force. The cloud is material: on the environmental impacts of computation and data storage.' Monserrate.

Technologies exteriorize our memories,[14] all saved and uploaded to the (digital) cloud. Can we experience the present without uploading it? Or wanting to? Creating a digital ghost body of our traces online, a companion of algorithms that knows your innermost desires of what shoes you want and what music you like, holding you in a perpetual loop of fictitious necessities. Perhaps the dream of having your mind uploaded to the cloud is a dream of getting dissolved back into the earth again, — becoming mineral.

death cycle(s) p.426

14 'Technology is now standing in for memory, consciousness and experience, feeding it back to us in the form of an uncanny affect. Technologies exteriorize our memories (in the form of a database or archive) offering us "tertiary memory" (a secondary or nonlived memory) and image-consciousness (a consciousness that does not derive from embodied perception).' Ravetto-Biagioli, 14.

What if we meet our digital companions not as beings in service of us, but rather existing in another time and space? Traveling between worlds[15] and temporalities. The embodiments of these creature-companions are so incredibly complex and entangled—stretching among vast lands, but also local, right here. A non-present presence. A ghost is someone that starts by coming back. When we converse with a machine-learning algorithm, aren't we actually always talking with a ghost? A machine that has metabolized parts of some culture from the past, spitting it back out in present moments. Ghosts come to us in clouds and fog. They exist between worlds.

15 See Lugones's beautiful text.

Enter the Ghost

Let me whisper into you, oh stone of wisdom.[16] Take my secrets and carry some of my burden. We—as in you and me—are in relation with the lake of Baotou. This black lake filled with mud, toxins, ectoplasm. Growing, soon to be escaping the borders of China, falling over landscapes, eating everything in its way, seeping into our skin, leaking into the pores of our waters, like in the horror film *The Blob*,[17] ...for which blobs know of borders anyway?

16 'Computers themselves are one of the words spoken by stones. And in turn, they speak like stones.' See Bridle, 188.

17 Russell; Yeaworth.

For now, we are in this lake together.

References

Abraham, David S. *The Elements of Power: Gadgets, Guns and the Struggle for a Sustainable Future in the Rare Metal Age*. Yale University Press, 2017.

Björk.'The Modern Things.' Track no. 3 on *Post*. One Little Indian Records, 1995.

Bridle, James. *Ways of Being*. Penguin Books, 2023.

Crawford, Kate. *Atlas of AI*. Yale University Press, 2021.

Derrida, Jacques. *Specters of Marx*. Routledge, 1994.

Frost, Rosie. 'Mining Europe's Biggest Rare Earth Deposit Could Make Life "Impossible" for Sámi Communities.' *Euronews*, February 11, 2023. euronews.com/green/2023/02/11/mining-europes-biggest-rare-earth-deposit-could-make-life-impossible-for-sami-communities.

Lugones, María. 'Playfulness, "World"-Travelling, and Loving Perception.' *Hypatia* 2, no. 2 (1987): 3–19. doi.org/10.1111/j.1527-2001.1987.tb01062.x.

Maughan, Tim. 'The Dystopian Lake Filled by the World's Tech Lust.' *BBC*, April 2, 2015. bbc.com/future/article/20150402-the-worst-place-on-earth.

Monserrate, Steven Gonzalez. 'The Cloud Is Material: On the Environmental Impacts of Computation and Data Storage.' In *MIT Case Studies in Social and Ethical Responsibilities of Computing*, no. Winter (2022). doi.org/10.21428/2c646de5.031d4553.

Nelson, Maggie. *Bluets*. Jonathan Cape, 2017.

Ravetto-Biagioli, Kriss. 'The Digital Uncanny and Ghost Effects.' In *Screen* 57, no. 1 (2016): 1–20. doi.org/10.1093/screen/hjw002.

Reuters, and Laura Paddison. 'Norway Discovers Huge Trove of Metals, Minerals and Rare Earths on Its Seabed.' *CNN*, January 30, 2023. edition.cnn.com/2023/01/30/business/norway-minerals-seabed-deep-sea-mining-climate-intl/index.html.

Russel, Chuck, dir. *The Blob*. TriStar Pictures, 1988.

Yeaworth, Irvin S. Jr., dir. *The Blob*. Paramount Pictures, 1958.

Yunkaporta, Tyson. *Sand Talk*. Harper Collins, 2020.

dignity
commemoration
forensics
gestures of care
(in)visibility
warm data
shared language(s)
common world
seeds
solidarities
fertility
belonging
proclamation
inheritance
collectivity
haunting presence
against white noise
speaking with

Beyond the List

Ecologies of Mourning and Resistance to Fortress Europe's Border Violence

Aïsta Bah, Pacôme Béru, Thierno Dia, Mamadou Taslim Diallo, Henriette Essami-Khaullot, Faïza Hirach, Fran Kourouma, Pierre Marchand, Milady Renoir, Christel Stalpaert, Alberto Isifin Tchama, Halidou Wuandaougo, Arkadi Zaides, and Martín Zícari

AISTA BAH, PACOME BERU, THIERNO DIA, MAMADOU TASLIM DIALLO, HENRIETTE ESSAMI-KHAULLOT, FAÏZA HIRACH, FRAN KOUROUMA, PIERRE MARCHAND, MILADY RENOIR, CHRISTEL STALPAERT, ALBERTO ISIFIN TCHAMA, HALIDOU WUANDAOUGO, ARKADI ZAIDES, AND MARTÍN ZÍCARI

This text takes the form of a reflection as a hyphen between institutions, disciplines, and experts, referencing ideas, actions, and gestures considered by numerous companions involved in mourning, honoring the dignity of those who have died or disappeared during their migrations. — These include:

circulating knowledges p.209

1) the ongoing performance project *Necropolis*, initiated in 2018 by choreographer Arkadi Zaides, which investigates the politics of death, migration, and border violence by constructing a performative archive of those who have lost their lives while attempting to cross the European borders. The project traces the impact of migration policies, making visible the often-erased histories of the deceased.
2) numerous works of art and discursive strategies developed as part of La Voix des Sans Papiers (Voice of the Undocumented) in Brussels, a self-organized collective with the intention to rebuild a political movement around the issue of undocumented immigrants, to inform, raise awareness, mobilize, and fight for a dignified life. As well as some members of Le Comité des Femmes Sans-Papiers, formed by undocumented women from different backgrounds, both with and without papers, looking to share their struggles, experiences, and knowledge. La Voix des Sans Papiers (VSP) is represented by Aïsta Bah, Halidou Wuandaougo, Thierno Dia, Mamadou Taslim Diallo, Modou Ndiaye and Alberto Isifin Tchama. Le Comité des Femmes Sans-Papiers is represented by Leticia Assemien, Henriette Essami-Khaullot, Bintou Toure.
3) the *Necropolis United*[1] research project, with Christel Stalpaert as Principal Investigator, and *Atelier Cartographique* (represented by Pacôme Béru, Pierre Marchand), Milady Renoir as a close neighbor, and *UNITED for Intercultural Action* (Geert Ates) as third parties. Martín Zícari, appointed post-doctoral researcher and research coordinator on the project, and Fran Kourouma, a member of the project's scientific committee.

[1] The Research Foundation Flanders (FWO) has financed the underlying research project *Necropolis United: integrated data-platform of dead and missing migrants in Europe* (2022–2026), hosted by Ghent University.

Together, we offer our intertwined reflections on the expansion of choreographic gestures of care within ecologies of mourning. It is important to emphasize that, in alignment with VSP's work, we do not view death and disappearance as the sole fatal consequences of European border policies. Rather, we also consider the liminal state of migrants who, due to various administrative and bureaucratic classifications (refugee, asylum seeker, undocumented), find their lives in their destination countries completely stalled, forced to endure extreme precarity. In response, VSP proposes the concepts of *petite-mort* (small death) and *mort-vivant* (living death) to describe this condition.

I

All (human) life is life.
It is true that one life comes into existence before another life,
But a life is not 'older,' more respectable than another life,
Just as one life is not superior to another life.
...
All life being life,
Any harm done to a life requires reparation.
Therefore,
Let no one attack his neighbor gratuitously,
Let no one harm his neighbor,
Let no one martyr his fellow man.
...
Let each one watch over his neighbor,
Let everyone revere their parents,
Let everyone educate their children as they should,
Let everyone 'maintain,' provide for the needs
of the members of their family.
...
Because any country, any land which would see
men disappear from its surface
Would immediately become nostalgic.
People of old tell us:
'Man as an individual
Made of bone and flesh,
Of marrow and nerves,

Skin covered with hair,
Feeds on food and drinks;
But his 'soul,' his spirit lives on three things:
Seeing who he wants to see
Saying what he wants to say
And doing what he wants to do;
If even one of these things were to be lacking
in the human soul,
It would suffer
And would surely wither.'

Consequently (...):
Everyone now has their own person,
Everyone is free to act,
Everyone now has the fruits of their labor.

This is the oath of the Manden[2]
To the ears of the whole world.

[2] Mandé: an ancestral kingdom of West Africa, a stronghold of resistance against slavery and colonization, and a space for the imagination of transformative prophecies. According to the griot Babou Condé, the name Mandén would mean 'child of the manatee.' In the French language, *Mandé* refers to someone who is summoned, notified, or ordered to come. *Mander* is synonymous with calling or summoning.

The Charter of Mandé[3] resonates in the Semira Adamu room at the building in Brussels occupied by La Voix des Sans Papiers (VSP) at the start of 2025. There, news of new shipwrecks and other pushbacks reaches the participants of *Necropolis United* who share an easter cake and coffee while connecting the words of the Sages who advocate dignity and response.

insisting on polyvocality and our polyexistence p.98

3 The Manden Charter dates back to the early thirteenth century and is considered one of the oldest known declarations of human rights in the world. It was conceived (without foreign influence) during the completion of the Mali Empire under Sundiata Keita. This charter is addressed to the 'twelve parts of the world,' and thus, according to its authors, it carries a universal purpose. It consists of seven statements, each serving as the heading of an article in the charter, which is also known by other names, such as *Donsolu Kalikan* (The Hunters' Oath), *Dunya Makilikan* (Admonition to the World), or more commonly *Manden Kalikan* (The Mandé Oath).

II

The *Necropolis United* project[4] seeks to explore how virtual space can become a site for commemoration, mourning, and action. It aims to develop software—an information system—that is democratic. With the rise of techno-fascism within countries across Europe, challenging concepts and values such as democracy, we can also name this information system as non-extractive.

urgent spaces p.78

4 The *Necropolis* United project brings together members of various migrant-led initiatives and civil, as well as human rights organizations in meetings called Multi-Lingual Encounter (ME), to refer to the multiplicity of working methodologies, languages, and discourses involved. Organizations include Comité des Femmes Sans-Papiers, La Voix des Sans Papiers de Bruxelles, Getting the Voice Out, Agir pour la Paix, Abolish Frontex, Collectif les Morts de la Rue, IWW Belgium, Santé en lutte, Réseau Salariat, as well as artists, researchers and members of the Brussels-based cooperative of cartographic practices Atelier Cartographique. ME are organized in different Brussels cultural organizations such as Globe Aroma, Pianofabriek, Maison de la Paix, La Loge and the occupation of La Voix de Sans Papiers Fritz Toussaint.

Pacôme resists defining our work in negative terms—by what is not (in this case, extractive)—and instead proposes the concept of an information system that is self-organized. Taslim suggests that we focus on redefining what we mean by **democratic**, bringing new significance to the term. Faïza frames it under the concept of **co-responsibility**. Through all these perspectives, we aim to create an information system that is described and conceptualized by those who will use it—both contributors and end users—in a direct and non-hierarchical relationship with those responsible for its technical development.

We believe that such an effort is a necessary foundation for designing a technological infrastructure that deals with deaths and disappearances through migration. Why? Because violence at the borders is a continuation of colonial violence, driven by an imperialist and supremacist agenda. — Technocratic violence, facilitated by multinational corporations, is part of a long-standing fascist cybernetic project—one in which companies such as Google, Amazon, and Microsoft are deeply implicated. To prevent marginalized bodies from being subjected to cybernetic, colonial, and border violence, we shift our approach: rather than speaking **about**, we prioritize speaking **with**.

naming the f(R)iction p.93

The methodology for designing and producing the system involves bringing together a group or community united by a common cause, prior to any software writing. Workshops are organized to allow stakeholders to collectively define the issues, objectives, uses, target audience, and aesthetic of the forthcoming information system.

Each participant's contributions are recognized as equally valuable, with respect given to expertise rooted in lived experiences, as well as professional, political, cultural, or social knowledge. The term 'work' is intentionally used to describe those contributions, emphasizing the importance of active engagement and fair remuneration for all participants.

This collective work establishes a distinct economic approach and timeline, fundamentally opposed to the production methods typically used in the software creation industry. The focus shifts from optimizing technical production flows to prioritizing relational quality and collective co-creation. —

slowing down
the workflow
p.251

This shift repositions technically proficient individuals, who must put their skills at the service of the common cause, as well as future users, who must actively participate in defining their technical needs.

The attempt to create democratic software writing places questions of social and collective organization at the center of the software design process, reinforcing the long-term effort to develop a shared language and formulate a collective request. —

threading together
what we know and are
still learning
p.314

III

In her book *Our Grateful Dead*, Vinciane Despret suggests that, to be treated properly and with respect, the dead must be situated. They need to be given a place where they can guide, inspire, haunt, or demand care. Without a proper place or recognition, they remain in a kind of limbo, unable to 'complete' their purpose, whether that purpose is to be remembered, mourned, honored, or integrated into the ongoing lives of the living.[5] This means establishing an ecology of mourning: a space made for them, where they can manifest their ways of being and where their effects can be felt by those who remain.

5| Despret, 9.

Despret frames this care for the dead as an ecological issue. She examines and creates the conditions in which the dead can exist, asking, 'What makes a dead person able to carry on? What is a dead person holding on to? What are the right conditions to make the dead enabled? What kinds of trials strengthen them, and what kinds put them in danger? What are they in need of? What do they ask for? What do they make other beings capable of? What makes for a good milieu for them and for those who have taken on the responsibility for their accomplishment?' For Despret, these questions 'stand apart from [those] that mainstream science typically focuses on,' instead addressing 'the needs that have to be respected in the continual creation of an association.'

IV

Taslim, spokesperson for La Voix de Sans Papiers, adds:
Don't wait until I'm dead...
Faïza replies:
to greet me...
Fran completes:
to bring me back to life
Thierno, also a spokesperson for VSP, bounces back:
to offer me heaven and earth beyond my lifetime
And then Aïsta and Halidou, Modou, Milady, ask themselves who can restore, define or confiscate the DIGNITY of others, and who holds it, and who loses it?

The group listens and VSP recounts their Odyssey:[6]
Once upon a time, there was an Elsewhere, not so far,
founded before, stretching from yesterday to today.
A land of births, of horizons,
a breath of dreams and ambitions.
Journey. Crossing. Danger. Epic.
By plane, through tunnels, by train, by boat,
conquered lands never subjugated,
in bags and in cargo holds,
seeds of ideals and illusion.
Collision. Landing. Shipwreck. Arrival.
A polluted breeding ground, a disappointing environment,
which ferments with precarity and hypocrisy.
A swamp of state violence
Quicksands of suspicion,
winds of criminalization,
The breath of discrimination,
storms disrupting the breath, forming a giant hurricane:
Western mythification

6 See ep.cfsasbl.be/vsp-l-odyssee-des-sans-papiers.

V

The shipwreck that occurred on October 3, 2013 off the coast of Lampedusa could mark the beginning of the so-called refugee crisis—or rather the 'crisis for refugees,' as Gurminder K. Bhambra more precisely calls it,[7] to dispel any doubt about who is truly suffering.[8] Following the shipwreck, Italian Prime Minister Enrico Letta granted Italian citizenship to the 372 individuals who lost their lives in the disaster. At the same time, the 155 people rescued from the same ship were placed in a detention center without any rights.

7 Bhambra.

8 The term 'migration crisis' has been used in political and media agendas since the early 2000s. More than a migration crisis, it is, in Europe, a crisis of reception. Furthermore, the term 'crisis' is problematic, because it gives the impression of an unexpected, unmanageable phenomenon. This framing helps justify the reinforcement of external border controls. It benefits numerous actors involved in 'crisis management,' both public and private. We suggest avoiding the use of the word 'crisis.' Moreover, a whole semantic framework has developed in media and political discourses to create a distorted image of migratory movements as being overwhelming: flows, waves, tsunamis, etc. We propose refraining from using such terms that liken migration to liquids, as they are dehumanizing. Instead, we prefer terms like movements or displacement.

We wish to expose the imperialist nature of what is called citizenship: Ariella Aïsha Azoulay refers to it as 'the institution of citizenship as a set of rights against and at the expense of others.'[9] What is omitted in these imperialist narratives of citizenship 'proclaiming the progress of citizens' rights,' she argues, 'is the violence involved in defining citizenship as a constitutive element of belonging to the state rather than a shared trait among co-citizens concerned with a common world.'[9] One can only belong to the state if one has the proper documents to present. This divides people into those who have the correct documents and those who do not, all in the name of progress. Imperial citizenship, Azoulay asserts, 'condemns different people who share a world to not ontologically or politically coincide within it.'[9]

9 Azoulay, 16, 39, 16.

With Azoulay, we propose unlearning this type of imperial citizenship and instead proclaiming co-citizenship. Co-citizenship is an ongoing, ever-evolving composition of a common world; it is a set of assumptions and practices shared by different people as companions who oppose imperialism, colonialism, and racial capitalism.

VI

UNITED List of Refugee Deaths is a database documenting the deaths of people who have perished on migration routes towards Europe. This database was created and is maintained by UNITED for Intercultural Action, a European network fighting against nationalism, racism, and fascism, supported by more than 550 organizations across 48 European countries. 'Fatal Policies of Fortress Europe' is a related, ongoing campaign of the UNITED network that examines the consequences of the European Union's restrictive border policies. It is assembled row by row, each record a death or a group of related deaths. The information is broken down into six columns: the date of the reported death(s), the number of bodies found in that case (ranging from one to as many as 1,100 in the deadliest incident reported), the deceased's name, gender, and age, their region of origin (if known), the cause of death (such as drowning, suicide, police violence, or lack of access to medical care), and the source(s) that reported the case. Between 1993 and 2024, 60,620 deaths have been recorded in the UNITED list. 99 percent of the victims are mentioned as N.N., which stands for *Nomen Nescio*, Latin for 'I do not know the name.' Thousands more have never been reported.

Necropolis, the stage performance by choreographer Arkadi Zaides, takes the UNITED List of Refugee Deaths as its starting point. It seeks to transcend the two-dimensional, flattened nature of the list itself, turning it into a warm body of data.[10] | In the context of this artistic project, the team has developed a ritual that involves searching for and geolocating the graves of the deceased, thereby giving them a physical and geographic presence beyond the abstraction of the list. Through this process, *Necropolis* transforms the list of the dead and disappeared into a narrative of remembrance and recognition, challenging the audience to engage with the victims of border violence who are structurally rendered invisible. — Another aim of the project is raising awareness about the lack of proper forensic investigation needed in order to determine the identities of the victims.

connected existence p.119

10

Mariam Ghani's concept of 'warm data' refers to the complex interplay of personal, historical, and cultural contexts that surround and give depth to information. Unlike 'cold' data, which is often stripped of context and presented as raw, objective, and neutral, warm data acknowledges the human elements that shape and influence it—stories, emotions, and power structures. Ghani explores how this layered, textured understanding of data can bring a more holistic perspective to archives, histories, and narratives. By focusing on warm data, she challenges the detachment often associated with traditional archival practices, emphasizing the need to account for the subjective and relational dynamics that imbue data with meaning and life. This concept encourages the use of archives and records not just as repositories of facts, but as spaces where memory, identity, and connection can be actively engaged and interrogated. Ghani and Ganesh.

In the first part of the performance, the audience is guided by two performers and a disembodied voice through a virtual map on Google Earth, where all the localized graves are marked. Beginning with the theater space, Google Earth zooms out to reveal the graves of people who died on migration routes, showing those buried nearby as well as farther away. In the second part of the performance, a sculpture resembling human body parts is examined by the two performers on stage. This act ritualizes a forensic procedure—one that many victims at Europe's borders are tragically deprived of—bringing attention to the denial of proper investigation and acknowledgment of their deaths. —

occlusion from spaces of visibility p.258

VII

From these ill winds, a few mists infiltrate the promises:
the NGO-ization of cultural and educational places,
academic extractivism,
the monopolization of stories and images
by artists and well-intentioned people paving hell
with gold-plated tiles.
When the varnish cracks,
the 'weeds' regain their power.

So the women and the men and the children
and the spirits went in search for Water,
the one which forms the vital strength,
the one which bypasses the mountains and the fires,
the one which engages the resistance.
All the waters flow in immensity,
connecting through a thousand streams, blood,
saliva and sap.
In the gills, the chests and the hearts,
the air of dignity,
the oxygen of the ancestral struggles blows,
breathes the hope of inheritance. —
Materials. Ferns. Anger.
In the holes that Europe has dug,
some stumble
others slip,
some gravitate,
others sink.

surfacing toward life
p.102

VIII

Stemming from colonial discourse, the term 'origin' is used by European bureaucracies to indicate the country, region, or place of birth of a person, their parents, or their grandparents. ('origin' can also refer to a dual cultural background.) This use of the term, among others like 'roots,' 'ancestry,' or 'descent,' is problematic because it can imply that people—most of whom experience racism—are not considered to be European even if they were born there. Therefore, we suggest that when referring to a country where someone is from, it should be indicated as their country of birth, not their origin. We also propose that, in general, one should avoid mentioning the nationality of a person, as well as the country their family or ancestors lived in before settling in the host society. These measures are proposed to circumvent the weaponization of the concept of 'origin' as part of any racist agenda.

XIX

The following text is spoken by the disembodied voice at the opening of the *Necropolis* performance:

> 'In order to gain the right to live in Necropolis, one has to die in an attempt to enter it. Citizenship is granted posthumously to dismembered and decomposing corpses. Everyone else—those others who are still alive but without documents—are kept outside, left to die beyond the entry points. They need to arrive at the gates—dead—in order to be processed.'[11]

[11] Written and recorded by the dramaturg of the *Necropolis* project, Igor Dobričić.

X

European legislation establishes a clear distinction between criminal, natural, and accidental deaths, which determines how bodies are treated thereafter. The bodies of deceased migrants challenge this taxonomy. When the thousands of deaths occurring at Europe's borders are classified as accidental, forensic procedures for collecting medical and biological data on the bodies are not mandatory. In most cases where forensic investigations do occur, they are not conducted properly. The resulting loss of irreplaceable information prevents any future identification of the victims.

How can we mourn these migrant deaths when crucial information is unavailable? How can we investigate and create the conditions in which these deaths can exist? What needs must be respected in the continuous creation of a co-citizenship, as referred by Azoulay? These are the questions we ask ourselves.

XI

In her book *Strangers I Know*, Claudia Durastanti writes:

> 'When we die, maybe on our tombstone they'll write a loved one's name, what profession we had, a line from our favorite book. What won't be written on our tombstones is our distance from home.'[12]

12 Durastanti, 173.

XII

Globalization has multiplied borders and reinforced them with walls, increasingly detailed regional and national regulations. These borders create legal categories of people whose rights are increasingly unequal. Many individuals are stranded at Europe's external borders, commonly referred to as Fortress Europe. The border is continuously reenacted. For some people, the experience of the border is everywhere—it is a central protagonist in their lives.

XIII

One could say that *Necropolis United* seeks to build a spectral infrastructure that encapsulates 'textures, rhythms, atmospheres, invocations, gestures, vernacular languages, and affects,'[13] introducing a disruption into what otherwise appears to be an efficient organism. — A 'spectral infrastructure' (as conceived by freethought collective)[14] is a haunting presence within a structural organism. We propose this spectral

allowing apparitions to arise and take shape p.245

infrastructure as a method for reflecting on the countless deaths of migrants in Europe—those who died on their way to gaining access to Fortress Europe.

13 Rogoff et al. (freethought collective).

14 Ibid.

XIV
Around 2014—and ever since—VSP
aka La Voix des Sans Papiers
sows, sows, sows, sows
kernels, seeds,
eggs, powers:
seeds of union and solidarity
between undocumented and documented
sprouts of resistance and ethics
between deaf ears and heard voices
seeds of self-organization
towards the grapes of great anger
Then the *Gouye*, the *Cabesera*, the *Mbuyu*
are born,
the *Zirasun*, the bokki, باباوب, the *Cabda*,
the *Kondebili* ... the Baobab!

Over a decade as long as a millennium,
despite predations and corruption,
the Baobab takes root from all those uprooted
Deep in the ground, defying the barren loam
to anchor itself in fertile land.

Each foot is named:
A root of the family,
A compass in storms,
A root of the village,
fighting against hunger and war,
A root of resistance,
weighing the YES and AGAINST,
saying NO, — we've had enough!!!

refusal p.97

These roots pierce the City!
Even if the tree catches fire,
like a snake that sheds its skin
the bark of the baobab regenerates.

The Baobab of VSP,
with a proud and strong trunk stands
against white noise,
against underground parasites,
its trunk engraved with all the names
members of VSP
alive, dead and in between.

Each leaning against a solid trellis
of ethical relationships and self-teaching,
in autonomy and alliances,
the Baobab protects the popular university
against the cold of fear
and the fire of racism

continually made
and changed in
a network of relations
p.420

The crown, the branches, the twigs
everything is on fire but nothing burns
'*Ragal dou diam gouye*'[15]

15 Wolof Proverbe: 'The fearful do not cut the baobab.'

The branches extend the tree
with powerful reach,
welcoming good omens:

Pure dignity, VSP[16] on the menu
tables of *attayas*, *thiakry*, *attiéké*.

16 La Voix des Sans Papiers 2014–2024: an odyssey of self-organization and resistance by Milady Renoir and Modou Ndiaye. See legrainasbl.org/revueakene/la-voix-des-sans-papiers-2014-2024/.

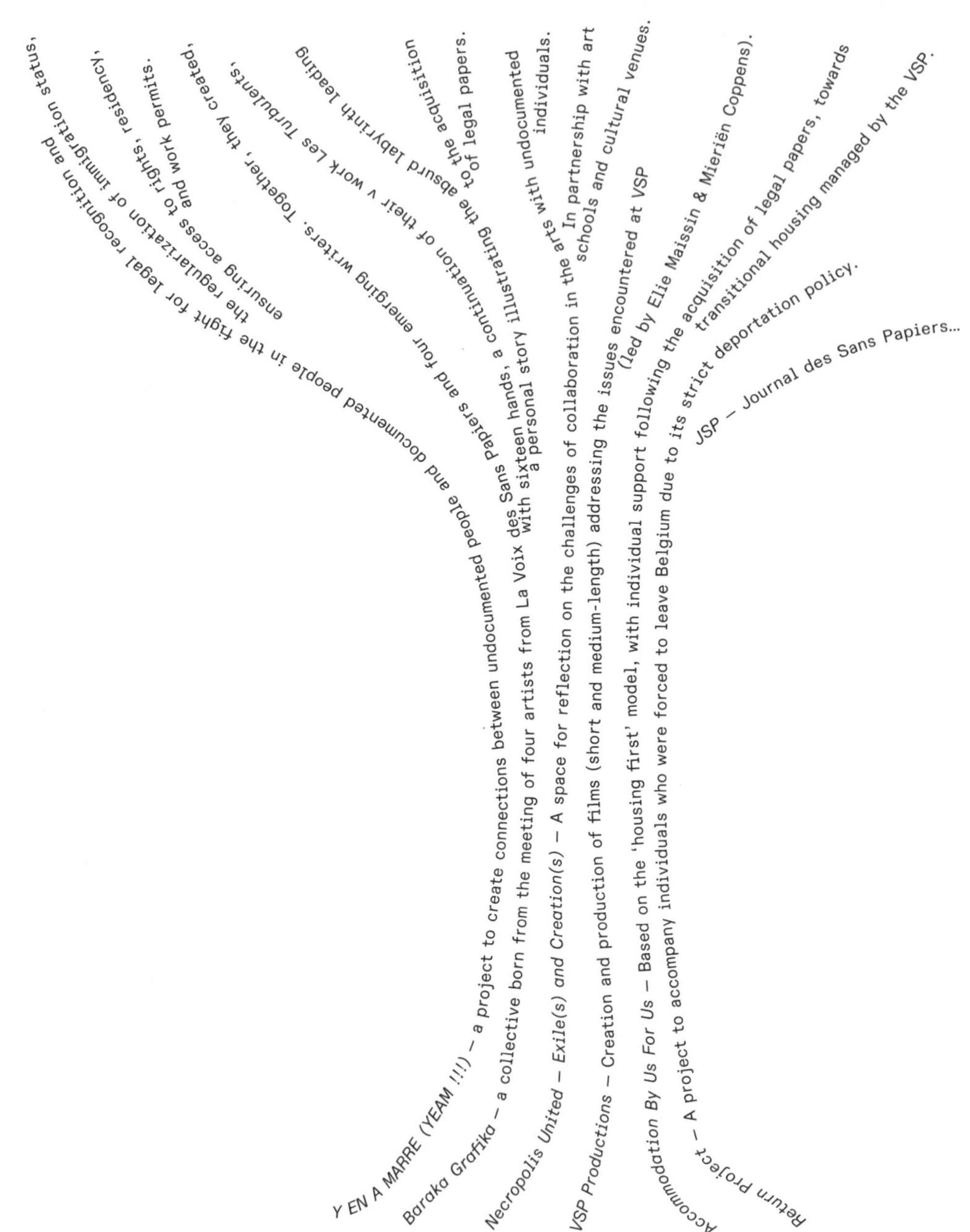
Y EN A MARRE (YEAM !!!) – a project to create connections between undocumented people and documented people in the fight for legal recognition and the regularization of immigration status, ensuring access to rights, residency, and work permits.
Baraka Grafika – a collective born from the meeting of four artists from La Voix des Sans Papiers and four emerging writers. Together, they created, with sixteen hands, a continuation of their v work Les Turbulents, a personal story illustrating the absurd labyrinth leading to the acquisition of legal papers.
Necropolis United – Exile(s) and Creation(s) – A space for reflection on the challenges of collaboration in the arts with undocumented individuals. In partnership with art schools and cultural venues.
VSP Productions – Creation and production of films (short and medium-length) addressing the issues encountered at VSP (led by Elie Maissin & Mieriën Coppens).
Accommodation By Us For Us – Based on the 'housing first' model, with individual support following the acquisition of legal papers, towards transitional housing managed by the VSP.
Return Project – A project to accompany individuals who were forced to leave Belgium due to its strict deportation policy.
JSP – Journal des Sans Papiers...

Foods such as these are the fruits of the tree of life and nourish VSP's struggle towards rock solid cases for regularization, a book of recommendations and another of demands,[17] alliances with collectives, networks, organizations from the most grassroots to the most institutional, resumption of studies and access to state-recognized trainings, the creation of 100PAP solidarity beer,[18] and a forest house which proudly stands higher and higher in the canopy of resistances.

17 2019 version: sanspapiers.be/wp-content/uploads/2019/04/Elections-mai-2019-Recommandations-des-sans-papiers.pdf.

18 An initiative that fights for the housing rights of undocumented individuals. The profits from the sales are used to pay rents, utilities, and renovations. 100PAP in French reads like 'sans-pap' short for 'sans-papiers,' which refers to undocumented migrants.

References

Azoulay, Ariella Aïsha. *Potential History: Unlearning Imperialism*. Verso Books, 2019.

Bhambra, Gurminder K. 'The Current Crisis of Europe: Refugees, Colonialism, and the Limits of Cosmopolitanism.' In *European Law Journal* 23, no. 5 (2017): 395–405. doi.org/10.1111/eulj.12234.

Despret, Vinciane. *Our Grateful Dead: Stories of Those Left Behind*. Translated by Stephen Muecke. University of Minnesota Press, 2021.

Durastanti, Claudia. *De vreemdelinge*. Translated by Manon Smits. De Bezige Bij, 2020.

Ghani, Mariam, and Chitra Ganesh. 'How Do You See the Disappeared? A Warm Database.' In *Net Art Anthology*, 2004. Accessed January 30, 2025. anthology.rhizome.org/how-do-you-see-the-disappeared-a-warm-database.

Rogoff, Irit, Stefano Harney, Adrian Heathfield, Massimiliano Mollona, Louis Moreno, and Nora Sternfeld. freethought collective. 'freethought: Spectral Infrastructure.' Wartenau Assembly #11. Public editorial meeting convened by freethought and BAK, Basis voor Actuele Kunst, Utrecht in collaboration with Wartenau Art Education, HFBK Hamburg, Germany, June 14, 2022. Video, 1 hr., 54 min., 14 sec. Posted June 23, 2022. mediathek.hfbk.net/l2go/-/get/v/440.

shadows
spectralities
fluid temporalities
active elements
instability
duration
contingency
contamination
haunting
a life of its own
slowing down the workflow
temperatures of process
unpacking the present
  moment
possibility of liberation
glitch

Glitching Colonial Film Archives

Decolonial Anarchival Strategies

Paula Albuquerque

SPECTRES

We clamor for the right to opacity for everyone.[1]
—Édouard Glissant

[1] Glissant, 194.

In my practice-based research as an artist-filmmaker, I echo contemporary concerns in the art world about racial and gender biases in museum archives and the decommissioning of ideologically problematic artworks. I do this by re-engaging with the racializing and gendering content of archival documents, adding new layers of meaning to them, rather than completely erasing them and their historicity, and consequently preventing future forensic analysis. In the two recent projects discussed in this essay I employ decolonial strategies to make film-based artworks with pre-existing footage, with the aim of performing digital interventions in the archive and also devising ecological film developing processes with slow process cinema methods.

This work analyzes and critiques the inherent and insidious surveillance affordances of audiovisual media that have contributed to the subjectification and othering of entire communities. I have been closely studying specific materials from the EYE Filmmuseum archive in Amsterdam to facilitate a public revisiting of obscure, pre-documentary films captured by European settlers in formerly colonized territories. These encounters with sensitive materials contribute to an understanding of the origins of contemporary stereotypical representations of people living in previously occupied countries, as well as their diaspora. In particular, I gradually unveil the construction of such stereotypes that are at the basis of datasets used to train algorithms, for the purpose of maximized surveillance and generalized population control.

I employ an anarchival strategy that supports the performative potential of the film archive to reveal the dispossessive structures of representation — that cast Indigenous people as epidermalized other, poor and incapable subjects—who are less than human—thereby erasing their agency and individuality, blending them into the natural landscape, which was displayed as exotic and awaiting conquest.

becoming witnesses
p.198

In addition to those archival interventions, I seek to contribute to an ecological conservation of film materials, a position that goes against the current trend of digitizing all documentary material, that includes researching environmentally sound chemical practices in film processing.

I
Interfering with the Archive

I have been working with sensitive footage from an anarchival standpoint since I was a student at the art academy and first experimented with re-editing my grandfather's Super 8 films, which he shot in Mozambique in the 1960s.[2] These home movies depicted Portuguese environments that were emulated in African settings, foregrounding European lifestyles by showing elegant garden parties with men drinking from crystal glasses and women in the latest Parisian fashion. While perusing my family archives, I also noticed their biased mode of representation, with local people either completely absent from the frame or having been morphed into a homogeneous mass by photographic emulsions designed to exclusively expose white skin properly. Later, I was involved in direct action as a squatter and a climate activist and became interested in the ubiquity of video surveillance. When analyzing racial stereotypes that emerge as a result of footage captured by surveillance cameras, I identified a parallel with films shot in former colonies: the mode of exposure of early cameras is similar to that of contemporary CCTV, which still blurs the identifying features of people with darker skin tones.[3] I proposed that colonial film production is a form of proto-surveillance that is situated in the context of ethnographic imagetics. The first photographic images of Indigenous people have contributed to their datafication and to stereotypes of race and gender that still affect current residents of former colonies and their diaspora.

2 For more on the term *anarchival*, see Manning and Massumi.

3 For more on video surveillance and racial bias, see Browne; Samudzi.

More recently, during a project about the representation of exhaustion, I specifically researched how gendered and racially biased colonial cinema perpetuates stereotypes distinguishing white men from, well, everyone else. It was in this context that I gained access to the EYE Filmmuseum archive to study relevant film objects conserved in this vast mainstream collection.[4] After a few meetings, the curators supporting my work generously sent me dozens of films, which I closely watched and organized into separate categories. I was particularly struck by a colonial production called *Ook de Surinaamse Indianen Horen Er Bij* (The Surinamese Indians Also Belong Here) from 1950, produced by the Algemeen Diaconaal Bureau, a religious organization. I felt a sense of revulsion when I watched the opening sequence, which displayed a Dutch nurse/nun who bathes in the river together with Indigenous people. At the time, I understood that this was one among many fragile materials I would encounter at this film archive that deserved revisiting and sharing with the general public. However, I felt that doing so would require a particular frame to avoid the perpetuation of the othering gaze that is inherent to the violence of colonial filmmaking and its archive. — It was also clear from the meetings held with the archive curators that there was a growing concern within the EYE Filmmuseum about how to handle these frail materials and other polemic footage.

lineages
p.318

4 Read more about this process in my article, 'Medical Propaganda as Enabling Device of the Surveillance Apparatus.' Albuquerque.

I categorize this film as a form of proto-surveillance because of the way it subjectifies and others Indigenous people. *Ook de Surinaamse Indianen Horen Er Bij* sharply contrasts the image of the Dutch nurse/nun with the locals of that area of Suriname, the members of the Wayana and Tirio tribes. In the river bathing scene, she wears a bathing suit and is very active, encouraging the other people to play with the water. Those others, who are Indigenous people, are either naked, bare-breasted or wearing ragged pieces of clothing that barely cover their genitals. Reflecting on my guiding question about how to share this film with the general public, I remembered Temi Odumosu's warning about well-intended exhibitions on colonialism that conjure ghosts from the past and that, time and again, repeat the damaging exposure initiated by the anthropological appropriation of Indigenous bodies, whenever artists make these violent images public.[5] So I thought long about how I could respectfully revisit this film and stimulate dialogue about the representation of people living in former European colonies during Dutch occupation, while simultaneously protecting their identities. I wanted to rework these materials, while still allowing the public to access this semi-ethnographic pre-documentary film and the supposedly benevolent speech of the nurse/nun, who treats ailments, administers vaccinations and teaches the Dutch language to local people living in a tightly circumscribed village. What is more, I thought that the racist and subjectifying discourse uttered by the nurse and the interviewer's biased questions called for an analytical approach. Its disguised bigotry needed to be separated from the segregating visuals.

5 Odumosu.

To unveil the white prototypicality operating in early colonial documentaries—in this case a screaming example of medical and religious propaganda—I worked on creating a haunting aesthetic to mask the bodies, while joining the temporality of the film with that of the present by including surveillance imagery of the area.

Following Esther Peeren's words about spectralities and hauntologies, I was looking for a form of content that would allow people's shadows in this film—their trapped ghosts—to haunt the work and be acknowledged, reaching beyond the subjectifying aesthetics of the proto-surveillance apparatus that determines the original film's medical propaganda format.[6] It was an obvious decision not to show the exposed bodies of the Indigenous people, which I immediately decided to mask out of the film. Instead of erasing the men, women,

advocating dignity and response p.224

and children who had been filmed involuntarily, who remain unnamed and whose voices are not heard, I wanted to pay tribute to them and present an alternative in which they gain autonomy and connect with our contemporary time. At the same time, it was important that the element of surveillance was part of the imagetic intervention, and so I decided to fill the contours of the masked bodies with imagery of the landscape in Suriname, captured by present-day surveillance cameras. After several tests, I asked long-term friend and artist José Miguel Biscaya to design and program a glitch that could keep the imagery in motion and in constant development.[7] Biscaya echoed my concerns about the need to ensure the agency of these people, even if through a symbolic gesture. He experimented with the glitch and its visual effects to fuse the bodies with the surveillance imagery of local trees and animals I had collected, at times including the three-dimensionality of the bodies so that skin, muscles, and facial features can be discerned. As intended, the main othering device at the root of racialization—epidermalization—was blocked. The resulting film, *Like the Glitch of a Ghost* (2023), consists of a fake double that has found its way back into the archive.[8] It is a deliberate decolonial intervention in the fabric of the Dutch film collection.[9]

carving out decolonial spaces of being in time p.58

6 Peeren, 37–50.

7 A glitch is the audio-visual result of an unexpected interference. It may be caused by malfunctioning equipment or may be fabricated intentionally, as in the case of glitch art.

8 I did not cut the film, nor did I add any sound or dialogue. Except for the last two minutes when a male Dutch settler demonstrates how the radio system works, which I found irrelevant to the final film, the sequence is exactly the same as that of the original film.

9 This film was initially intended for a gallery space but it has been shown on several occasions and in different circuits, including in the UnionDocs NY Artistic Differences program, at the DocLisboa Film Festival (2023), at Looiersgracht 60 gallery and Bradwolff Projects in Amsterdam (2023), and it was nominated for the Doc Alliance Award (2024).

Process and Error Cinema

Working with the glitch constitutes a form of process cinema that, in my case, experiments with both seventy-year-old analogue film material and contemporary surveillance imagery that is publicly accessible on the internet. The practice of process cinema has traditionally been linked to avant-garde structural filmmakers and their engagement with the materiality of celluloid film. A resurgence of this movement has gained traction in the last twenty years, alongside the demise of analogue film, which reflects a form of political resistance against a neoliberal aesthetics that promotes 'objectivity.' In Tess Takahashi's words, '[t]raditionally, process cinema is a methodology that involves improvisation, experimentation, and direct physical interaction with the filmic apparatus.'[10] | She explains that in present-day artistic audiovisual practices, the digitization of the cinematic medium has birthed new modes of process cinema, in which pre-existing analogue methodologies are adapted to digital video and game art, including generative AI. For the past two decades, academic discourse has also analyzed the ubiquity of software and its political mediating interface, most notably in Media Studies, where I am also active as a publishing author. David Rodowick, referencing the demise of analogue cinema, stated that 'a medium is a terrain where works of art establish their modes of existence, and pose questions of existence to us.'[11] | As self-reflexive film-based artworks question digital media platforms, '[r]ather than use the available editing software, many digital video artists have been developing their own algorithms or modifying existing ones in order to manipulate video files,' Takahashi affirms. And she adds that 'one possible analogous concept of scratching on film for digital video might be to use algorithms to remove data from the digital file, an approach that many glitch artists have experimented with.'[12] | Several writers, including media theorists Martine Beugnet, Allan Cameron, Arild Fetveit, and curator Legacy Russell have highlighted the creative potential of the audiovisual glitch, including using noise and unstable imagery as prime matter for molding and sculpting. In *Glitch Feminism*, Russell points to the possibility of liberation brought about by approaching the glitch as an expressive tool, especially in gendered and racialized contexts.[13] Now that it's commonly acknowledged that material indexicality occurs in both analogue and digital media, interfering with the materiality of the digital file is a way of dialoguing with and triggering the haunting visual eruptions it contains, allowing the visible presence of ghosts—known as specters or apparitions—to arise and take shape. Biscaya and I do this with *Like the Glitch of a Ghost,* liberating the medium from its narrative constraints and 'collaborating with it' to explore its expressive potential. —

creating space for
breath and possibilities
for breathing
p. 101

10 Takahashi, 482.

11 Rodowick, 42.

12 Takahashi, 484.

13 Beugnet et al.; Russell.

As media theorist Tom Gunning proposes, it's important to allow the medium to manifest itself as a construction, and in the case of my project, as a colonizing apparatus.[14] By interfering with the make-up of the video file, creating the glitch for the film, *Like the Glitch of a Ghost* exposes other narrative layers, not intended by the original pre-documentary film, and thereby unveils the political economy of its medium specificity. Together with Biscaya, we interfered with the software by modifying lines of code, hijacking the program's readability of visual data determined by its codecs. It is beyond the scope of this essay to discuss the hierarchy and the colonial heritage inherent to coding practices. However, its politicized mode of production cannot be ignored. Nick Briz describes the codec as a protagonist that influences viewers' perception of the world, as every piece of media content is compressed by codecs, such as MPEGs. As Adrian MacKenzie puts it, the codec contains in itself 'the mosaic of intellectual property claims,' based on political decisions which, by design, determine imagetics and visual logics, apprehending the politics of the audiovisual.[15] By confusing the software's ability to read an image, an error occurs, and a particular visual artifact is created: the glitch. In the most basic sense, it can be seen as an error made by an otherwise well-functioning visualizing device that disrupts our reading of the image. But when it is employed as a political art form, glitch art can further unveil the economic concerns underlying the make-up of such 'vision machines.'

14 Gunning.

15 Takahashi, 494.

In the article 'Aesthetics of the Error: Media Art, the Machine, the Unforeseen, and the Errant,' Timothy Barker pointed out how several artists have been making artworks for a while in which the error functions as an aesthetic tool. He described it as 'an art of the found object; an art practice in which the artist gives new meaning to an object, in this case, the error.'[16] Biscaya and I consider this error, the glitch, as a productive and expressive visual manifestation of the inner politics of digital visuality. — We design, program, and manipulate the glitch as much as it allows us to. The glitch has a life of its own; it may keep on developing indefinitely, or it may completely crash the software, which at times is no longer able to handle it. The glitch is a specter in the sense that it manifests visually, yet it is incommensurable. The image it creates is constantly evolving, trembling, attached to the original and yet corrupting colors, exposing resolution confusion, and unavoidably creating giant pixels. — It fascinates us and transcends our will with its own volition, and it haunts the file by occupying its fabric and overcoming its outer limits. We can tell ourselves that we are in control and determine the triggering of the glitch, but in my experience and encounters with glitches, all we are doing is allowing it to haunt us. After all, it has always been there, its ghost quietly awaiting its appearance.

transgressive co-creation p.155

prizing the edge of chaos p.88

16 Barker, 55.

II
Colonial Filmmaking and the Environment

For the second project I will discuss in this essay I turned my attention to the early cinematic representation of the landscape in previously occupied territories. I was well aware that working with moving images shot in former European colonies and specifically making use of archival materials comes with a risk of reaffirming stereotypical aesthetics of spectacular, exotic, and otherworldly views of landscapes that await exploitation, interpretation, and subjugation.

For this project, which resulted in a solo exhibition at Zone2Source in Amsterdam, I had access to films from the EYE Filmmuseum archive that were shot between 1912 and 1940. They included home movies and travelogs made by Dutch people visiting or living in Indonesia, who participated in various events and activities organized for and by the settlers, such as volcano expeditions. The selection also showcases state propaganda films produced by the Dutch government that display the vast construction of engineering infrastructure in the region, including bridges, railways, and airports.

In addition to my research into the conflation of the visual languages of colonial filmmaking and surveillance, I also focused on the notion of the sublime, an aesthetic concept based on an 'othering' Western male perspective on the world, according to which the landscape awaits taming and exploitation. This art-historical worldview has remained largely unchallenged up to the present day, and has informed the history of early cinema, in particular colonial film production. The sublime imbues the vision of overseas territories with a colonizing perspective, and has merged with the visual means of the settlers' control apparatus. Furthermore, this aesthetic still haunts the contemporary, seemingly inconsequential, presence of webcams in locations that are still considered exotic, producing images that continue to invite exploitation, currently of the touristic kind. The film *Siluman–Stealth, Invisible, Ghostly, Phantom-Like* (2024) consists of a montage of preexisting archival material that conjures 'women ghost workers' in palm oil plantations—*Buruh Siluman*, in Indonesian.

A central aspect of this project is an interest in process, especially in customized development and emulsion-making, including the manipulation of exposure times, dilution, temperatures, and temporalities. In addition to working with digital-based platforms and archival materials, I experiment with analogue practices and obsolete technologies to reconfigure ways in which the Indigenous landscape and the people who dwell in them, which are often seen as inseparable, have been understood and portrayed by colonial authorities and their control apparatuses. This awareness also includes an ecological approach to making film that cares for the environment by minimizing impact. As opposed to common, yet toxic traditional filmmaking practices, I experiment with plant-based development processes, using common household ingredients such as coffee, salt, and lemon, while further researching environmentally sound chemical practices and opposing a polluting, all-conquering attitude. This includes paying attention to the temporalities and temperatures of the process — of developing analogue film with natural plant-based ingredients, but also a critique of current consumer technologies and the ways in which they incorporate inherited film languages. I aim to question dominant aesthetics and those processes that have become normalized, trending, or what Scott MacKenzie and Anna Westerstahl Stenport call the 'patriarchal underpinning of realist representation—especially what realism includes and occludes under the guise of objectivity and transparency.'[17] The works in this project intend to underscore an ideological and institutional critique, but also to propose the unorthodox processing of ethnographic imagetics that remix and abstract pre-existing imagery on the one hand, and create new objects with both analogue and digital process-based filmmaking and photography on the other. These new works operate in the interface between racializing media, untold stories, and image processing. Some of the resulting materials are presented in the form of a negative. In this context, the negative manifests as a strategy that protects the image of Indigenous people, for example in the work *Anarchiving the Operative. Yet Again* (2024). Here, the 'incomplete' negative image of a couple of frames per shot or sequence foregrounds the lived experience of those people who were involuntarily filmed and demonstrates the unequal power relations between the Indigenous people in front of the camera lens and those behind it, the Dutch settlers.

potentialities and
responsiveness
p.401

17 MacKenzie and Marchessault.

I have a site-specific interest in emphasizing the connections between process-based imagetics and ethnographic, curatorial, and site-specific museological practices. After all, Het Glazen Huis, the Zone2Source exhibition venue for which these works were created, was initially built as part of a colonial project of hosting tropical species, several of which were brought from the former colonies and were classified according to Western botanical taxonomies.

Slow Process Cinema

Alongside my work in digital media, I have moved towards analogue filmmaking as a site of discovery for ecological processing, not only due to the extreme environmental impact of digitizing entire film archives, but also as a way of researching the possibilities of plant-based resources that can replace toxic, traditional celluloid-based film processing at archival storage capacities. This shift has involved a substantial change in the workflows I was trained in.

As artist Terra Long describes, hand-processing analogue film implies a physical involvement with the materials. It interrogates 'geological time scales with the subtext that a capitalist, industrialized world steamrolls over slow and contemplative experiences of temporality.'[18] For this purpose, Long adheres to the notion of *kairological time*, which encompasses 'temporalities concerned with bodily rhythms, embodied and alien to a hyper-regimented task-oriented external world.'[19] The decision to experiment with low impact developers goes against the neoliberal logics of high definition as the condition for an objective rendering of reality. The contingency of moving away from traditional processes and engaging with plant-based film developing materials shifts the time and space of the image-making event and breaks with the extreme compartmentalization of time, — instead adding fluid temporalities.

afterlives
p.386

18 Long, 336.

19 Ibid.

I decided to begin my experiments using one of the most prominent colonial plants— coffee, a plant I filmed on Super 8 at the Amsterdam Botanical Garden. The first time I experimented with ecological film processing I used Caffenol, an analog film developer consisting of soluble coffee, washing soda, and vitamin C.[20] Even though I was very experienced in analogue film processing, working with Caffenol has disturbed a workflow I had perfected during my previous film development experience. After I had developed a negative, I moved on to experimenting with reversal for the first time—making the film negative into a positive—and needed to rely on instinct to complete the required steps.[21] Developing film entails the execution of a series of tasks, such as loading the tank, bringing the various solutions to the correct temperature, shaking, rolling, and tapping the tank in particular ways at different moments, and controlling the time the film is immersed in these solutions, determining the length of re-exposure to light, and so on. I am currently using cheap soluble coffee and washing soda of different chemical concentrations that are hard to control or measure, in addition to constantly changing sunlight intensity. It involves a lot of back-and-forth and some trust in your ability to carry out each of the required steps. The experience of this slow process also requires an emotional engagement with the material, which necessitates some degree of realism and acceptance of the fact the image may not emerge due to a myriad of factors, including shifts in temperature, a different concentration of active elements, unstable emulsion, an unsuitable tank, potential contamination, and many other factors. —

retaining intentionality while relinquishing agency p.110

20 Caffenol was one of the first low impact film developing process materials created by Dr Scott Williams and his students in 1995, at the Rochester Institute of Technology.

21 When working with reversal film such as Kodak Tri-X, for example, after developing the negative it is necessary to further process the film in order to obtain a positive image. This involves using hydrogen peroxide and re-exposing the film to either the sunlight or a strong lamp. The film then needs to be developed again before giving it the final wash and the fixer bath.

Practicing slow process cinema thus unveils the friction between artistic vision and the unpredictability of nature, including the specificity of the site, the duration of the process, and the accidents that may take place and impact the results. — In the words of Tess Takahashi, '[t]he call on nature as a "collaborator" in making a film suggests that the elements have a will and something to say.'[22] And, as Long puts it, practicing process cinema means you are committing to slowing down the workflow and allowing 'ideas, aesthetic strategies, and narratives to emerge while working through a film' such that 'moments of chance, failed attempts, site, material, and those you encounter along the way become agents expressing themselves in physical and sometimes ineffable ways.'[23] This makes the process more relevant than the actual final film, a positive which will carry the traces of its development and reversal. The image becomes the exception that uniquely transports the indexicality of the whole process, making the physical and emotional presence of the artist just as tangible as that of the object or event that was captured by the photographic emulsion at the time of the shoot. The marks on the film are left behind by the complex interaction between human and machine, chemistry and naturally occurring phenomena. To sum up, these processes are materially present in the final artwork and their indexicality ends up being just as relevant to the experience of the viewer as the initial mark left by the photographed object on the film emulsion.

embracing imperfection p.325

22 Takahashi, 471.

23 Long, 339.

In her discussion of engaging with unstable media, Long mentions that theorist Lutz Koepnick regards the act of slowing down as a contemporary strategy 'to unpack the present moment,' which brings the experience of current time in dialogue with past and future temporalities. So when we talk about returning to analogue practices, we are also considering how to go back to materials that are unprocessed and available in nature. Responding to the spirit of our times means that we must look at plants and the soil to devise ecological ways to maintain and create imagery, without further negatively impacting the environment. This means we must slow down and contradict a capitalist mode of existence that is all-conquering, based on trends, and built upon a male and white power structure. As for aesthetic concerns, it entails embracing difference and ghostly presences, encompassing the incommensurable instead of attempting to control it. — It means moving towards an intersectional feminist sublime and abandoning the traditional art-historical sublime, which is a colonizing notion.[24] Taking the time to embrace contingency provides us with exceptional imagetics that reflect the current need to re-evaluate the roles filmmakers and archivists can play, by not only producing and conserving narrative, poetic and documentary film-based materials, but by veering away from the normalized, toxic development and preservation strategies.

the unstructurable that leads to the unexpected p.355

24 Freeman.

To conclude, my current work of glitching the archive manifests in a two-fold way: I carry out digital interventions that propose renewed modes of engaging with particularly sensitive colonial materials; and I make works that consist of experiments with ecological matter, to research the possibilities of environmentally low-impact archival conservation for the future. It is my belief that engaging with the glitch and the error as an aesthetic tool both in digital and analogue film can challenge capitalist modes of image production, conservation and distribution; contribute to decolonizing film archives; and lead to both fairer intersectional representation and more ecological practices.

> *To perceive and expose oneself to the darkness of the moment, yet also to recognize the light that—like the brilliance of a distant star voyaging for some time toward the earth—may be directed to or illuminate the present from either the past or the future. Contemporaneousness may be a product of modern chronological time, but it always pushes against it, urges us to be aware of other possible orders of temporality, presses us to account for the unlived and not-yet-and-perhaps-never-lived.*[25]
> —Lutz Koepnick

25 Long, 340.

References

Albuquerque, Paula. 'Medical Propaganda as Enabling Device of the Surveillance Apparatus: Decolonizing and Anarchiving Non-Fiction at the EYE Film Museum Archive.' In *The Journal of Media Practice and Education 24, no. 2 (2023): 113–27. doi.org/10.1080/25741136.2023.2207798.*

Barker, Timothy. 'Aesthetics of the Error: Media Art, the Machine, the Unforeseen, and the Errant.' In *Error, Glitch, Noise and Jam in New Media Cultures*, edited by Mark Nunes. Continuum, 2011.

Beugnet, Martine, Allan Cameron, and Arild Fetveit, eds. 'Indefinite Visions: Cinema and the Attractions of Uncertainty.' In *Edinburgh Studies in Film and Intermediality*. University of Edinburgh Press, 2017.

Browne, Simone. *Dark Matters: On the Surveillance of Blackness*. Duke University Press, 2015.

Freeman, Barbara Claire. *The Feminine Sublime Gender and Excess in Women's Fiction*. University of California Press, 1997.

Glissant, Édouard. *The Poetics of Relation*. Translated by Betsy Wing. University of Michigan Press, 1997.

Gunning, Tom. 'Before Documentary: Early Nonfiction Films and the "View" Aesthetic.' In *The Documentary Film Reader: History, Theory, Criticism*, edited by Jonathan Kahana. Oxford University Press, 2016.

Long, Terra. 'A Travelogue in Two Parts: Hand Processing in the Sahara and Finding no.w.here.' In *Process Cinema: Handmade Film in the Digital Age*, edited by Scott MacKenzie and Janine Marchessault. McGill-Queen's University Press, 2019.

MacKenzie, Scott and Janine Marchessault, eds. *Process Cinema: Handmade Film in the Digital Age*. McGill-Queen's University Press, 2019.

Manning, Erin and Brian Massumi. 'Anarchive: Concise Definition.' 3ecologies, n.d. 3ecologies.org/immediations/anarchiving/anarchive-concise-definition/.

Odumosu, Temi. 'What Is in Our Gaze?' In *Mãe Preta*, February 18, 2021. maepreta.net/what-is-in-our-gaze/.

Peeren, Esther. 'Hauntings from the Future: Ghosts, Travellers and Extraterrestrials.' In *Ghosts, Spectres, Revenants: Hauntology as a Means to Think and Feel Future*, edited by Katharina Fink, Marie-Anne Kohl and Nadine Siegert. Iwalewabooks, 2020.

Rodowick, David. *The Virtual Life of Film*. Harvard University Press, 2007.

Russell, Legacy. *Glitch Feminism: A Manifesto*. Verso Books, 2020.

Samudzi, Zoé. 'Bots Are Terrible at Recognizing Black Faces: Let's Keep It that Way.' In *The Daily Beast*, February 8, 2019. thedailybeast.com/bots-are-terrible-at-recognizing-black-faces-lets-keep-it-that-way.

Takahashi, Tess. 'Writing the World: Medium Specificity and Avant-Garde Film in the Digital Age.' In *Process Cinema: Handmade Film in the Digital Age*, edited by Scott MacKenzie and Janine Marchessault. McGill-Queen's University Press, 2019.

declaration
wonder
stillness
secrets
haunting

Trembling in a Quiet Storm

Derrais Carter

'I neeeeed to have you next to me...'[1]

Luther had it right. That long, hard 'eeee' setting off the *need* in 'Love Won't Let Me Wait' is preview and possibility. Its expression exceeds the words that follow. Sometimes pausing two words into the song is enough. It is prompt. Declaration.

The spinal quake. Thick saliva coating throats, apprehending language. The wonder that inhabits the body, stiffening legs and softening hearts. Ephemeral ruptures that belie the body's illusion of self-containment.

So goes the quiet storm ... creeping through speakers as you drive home ... whispering your secrets to you ... through someone else's voice...

The late-night DJ Melvin Lindsey gifted us **quiet**. Stillness. Embedded in the grooves that carry us is Melvin's subterranean black queer tremble, — masquerading as a radio program because some of us can't handle being seen so clearly.

the oxygen of
ancestral struggles
p.231

'Are we really happy here, with this lonely game we play?'[2]

Time submits to black will.

Could be love.
Could be liquor.
Could be regret.
Could be that, despite our best efforts to stay in control, nothing bends us more than Regina Belle's enchantment. Because no one conspires with the moon like a black woman.[3] Tides sound themselves as lip-parting moans. What remains is a feeling, of a note's capacity to upend us. And even worse, that we welcome it.

This is how Melvin haunts us.

1 Luther Vandross. 'Love Won't Let Me Wait.' Track no. 4 on *Live at Radio City Music Hall*. J Records, 2003.

2 George Benson. 'This Masquerade.' Track no. 2 on *Breezin'*. Warner Bros. Records, 1976.

3 Regina Belle. 'Baby Come to Me.' Track no. 1 on *Stay With Me*. Columbia, 1989.

attunement
ruptures
entangled lineages
what came before
sharing wisdom
disrupting cartographies
saying no
time portals
spaces of visibility
embodied transmissions
human and nonhuman
other futures

Ancestral

Mashinka Firunts Hakopian

When asked to consider the futures of art and technology, I find myself increasingly prone to write, instead, about my grandmother.

'Instead' may be misleading, as it suggests that an autoethnographic excursus about one's grandmother isn't germane to discussions of futurity. It's understood that these discussions are reserved for the consideration of new and emerging machine intelligences, which have become metonyms for the future writ large. What other futures come into view, instead, through attunement to the forms of knowing and making made possible through ancestral intelligences? —

time traveling together
p.65

A rhetoric of hyper-novelty effloresces in current popular arts discourse: it's alleged that we are witnessing a 'paradigm shift,' an 'inflection point,' a 'technological boom' hitherto unprecedented in the annals of any recorded history. Large language models and image-based generative adversarial networks, we are told, will reconfigure cultural work beyond recognition. The aesthetic field will look as it has never looked before.

It has also been said and bears repeating that we have been here before. Despite claims to radical newness, the logics underlying this moment are all too familiar. Inheriting the space-time of coloniality, popular discourses on art and tech crystallize around the inevitability of forward motion that proceeds through sharp ruptures with (implicitly non-Western) pasts. They project aesthetic futures synchronized to the tempos of technoscientific progress. They reduce extractivist effects, algorithmic harms, and ecological byproducts to the realm of parenthetical reference. At the core of these discourses is the claim that the hyper-novelty of the present demands new ways of knowing, thinking, and making that do away with the presumed obsolescence of what came before.

(Here is where my grandmother enters my writing, or has already been embedded in it. She was neither a technologist nor an artist in the usual sense. Rather, she was a post-Soviet Armenian diasporan who declined to learn the English language beyond the word 'no,' — professing a steadfast and incisive skepticism toward prevailing models of cultural and economic progress. Her critical invocation of West Asian

resistance that
bends the blueprint
p.385

pasts mediates my own lens on the present and future, here and elsewhere.)

Against the backdrop of the present moment, ancestral knowledge conjures a space for intervention in emerging technologies. Rather than seek out never-before-known data points and translate them into never-before-seen visualizations, ancestral approaches look to what has already been known and seen, but may have been submerged or occluded from spaces of visibility. —

resuscitation p.99

Ancestral approaches materialize across a wide array of recent projects. Stephanie Dinkins's *Not the Only One (N'TOO)* (2018–ongoing) develops a voice-interactive entity taught by oral histories of three generations of women from the artist's family, recasting AI as the repository for a 'multigenerational memoir' of a Black American family. Morehshin Allahyari's *Moon-faced* (2022) uses Qajar dynasty imagery to train an AI model to paint genderless portraits and resurface queer forms of representation within Iranian visual culture. Sarah Rosalena *Brady's Above Below* (2020) draws from matrilineally transmitted Wixárika weaving traditions to produce AI-generated Jacquard textiles that disrupt the assumptions of colonial cartographies. Nancy Baker Cahill's *Motherboard* (2021) geolocates an AR (augmented reality) monument above LA City Hall to propose forms of governance modeled on the networked structures of mycelium, 'the mother of us all.' Alice Yuan Zhang's *Remembering Our Roots* (2021) deploys AR toward an 'ecological time portal' wherein visitors encounter plant elders from her family's migrant journey, presented as 'an invitation for sharing ancestral plant wisdom from our entangled lineages.'

Refusing understandings of emerging technologies and artificial intelligence as a 'view from nowhere,' instead, ancestral intelligences ground knowledge in embodied transmissions from human and non-human elders. These transmissions suffuse the present, calling on us to tune in.

'Ancestral' originally appeared on the Critics Page of The Brooklyn Rail *in May 2023, brooklynrail.org/2023/05/criticspage/Ancestral/.*

RECALIBRATION

signals
spells
melodies
membranes
underlying forces
energetic events
seeking
synesthesia
repair
return
listening
remembering
recombinations
sympathetic relations
gentleness
resonance
making matter sing
dialogue with the world
vibrating together
driving evolutionary
  change
healing

Code Chants

Pia Lindman

The Lid of the Sky

The film is in black-and-white. The camera pans across a summer landscape with rolling hills, trees whisking in the wind, waving pastures, and rippling lakes. A close-up shows a woman in her fifties: sinewy with deep set eyes. She is looking keenly into the landscape. Then she raises her face to project into the air, cups her hand on one side of her mouth, and gives out a loud, outdrawn, and rhythmic chant. Time and time again, she repeats the chant, and each time she ends it by quickly raising her pitch to a near falsetto: 'Siuh, siuh, siuuuh!' The effect is almost like playing a slide on a guitar, but much louder. For a moment, the woman stays silent and listens. She peers into the forest. 'Not yet.' She raises her face to chant again, and now one can see clearly how she casts her gaze high up into the sky. She sings to reach her cows, deep in the forest. She projects her chant to the 'lid of the sky', the place where climate and atmosphere meet and form an invisible border between densities of air.[1] This border will reflect her chant and send it back down to earth, sometimes as far as several kilometers. Hearing her, the cows recognize her specific design of chant, a cattle call, distinct from all other cow herders, and know it is time to come home for the night. They respond by braying. And soon, the woman sees them between the trees, coming through the forest with hooves clopping and an ever louder braying.[2]

1 In English, the word 'firmament' is used for both ancient near-eastern and biblical cosmologies to describe this border. However, I prefer the literal translation from the Finnish word *Taivaankansi*, the 'lid of the sky.'

2 Description of a scene in the documentary *Karjan kutsumahuudot*. Vuorensola (1968).

Cows and humans have depended on each other for thousands of years, and the relationships shown in this documentary speak of genuine care and love. When I watch it, I am reminded of my own aunt calling for her cows in the seventies. Hearing the intensity of the calls, seeing the body language of the caller, and the eagerness of the returning cows, I am also struck by how this voicing is more than just a mechanical repetition of a daily task. This is a ritual, enacting and deepening the human-cow-universe relationship, a 'sympathetic reverberation,' every evening, with every caller, cow, and shifting sky. —

recognition of others through one's own body p.345

One clear spring night, standing at the top of my stairs and gazing at a rising full moon, I had the awe-inspiring experience of hearing two wolves howling some three kilometers into the forest, in the direction of South. First, a brighter tenor rose, like a tender sprout upwards. It rose perhaps thirty meters up into the sky. After a break, a darker howl started slowly rising up, much further up into the air. Suddenly that howl shifted location and appeared to emanate seven kilometers North of where I stood. High up in the sky, the sound traveled across the sky from North and back to the point where it had started. As the wolf then slowly fell silent, the howl sank back down to its point of origin. The wolf had sounded off the 'lid of the sky.'

In Finnish mythology, which is a composite cosmology of Fenno-Ugrish tribes around the Bothnian Bay and the White Sea, the world was created when the *Päivätä*r (Day Goddess) lying in the ocean moved her knee. A goose's nest, built on top of the knee, rolled over and the ensuing splash cupped upwards and formed the *Taivaankansi*, while the shards of the goose's breaking eggs formed the islands, stars, and other things and living beings of the world.[3] I think of Taivaankansi as the tropospheric border, tropopause, shifting in terms of height and intensity depending on weather conditions as well as the state of the cosmos. This is the gigantic membrane that howling wolves and cattle callers use to reverberate their chant. In similar fashion, sounding whales are found to reverberate the membranes between densities in the ocean. They chant for and to the world and cosmos.

3 Paraphrased from the story of 'Genesis' in the collection of epic poems, *Kalevala*. Song 1, verses 200–240. Lönnrot (1835).

Sound as Force

We tend to think about and listen to singing as something immaterial, simply audible, but all sounds are vibration, that is, force and energy. Sound and singing voices vibrate both inside the singer's body as well as in the air and in other surrounding matter. This vibration has an effect on everything that encounters it. Vibration can touch you, traverse barriers, and even touch you inside your body. — This is how singing can affect emotions, energy flows, and other life processes—more than mere words and melodies.

a movement of internalization p.112

As an artist and healer, I have been researching how to resonate with the world in such a way that it increases the possibility for life to continue on this planet. To me, working with physical and concrete manifestations of sound and voice, as well as the associative aspects of songs (words and melody), are ways to seek connection with the realm of more-than-human life. — I believe we can stimulate with and be stimulated by it.

harmonizing inner with outer p.135

Resonance can set matter into motion. The sympathetic transfer of energy into matter through resonance reflects and expresses the physical qualities of that matter. We can make matter sing.

Techniques of Healing

Two decades ago, I was poisoned by mercury. Mercury is a nerve toxin and affects your cognition in quite debilitating ways. Having been poisoned by mercury, a body's system will become sensitized also to other nerve toxins, such as heavy metals and mycotoxins produced by fungi and mold. After many years of coping with heightened sensitivity and the toxicity both in my body and in the environment, I started to find new ways to relate to life and to my own body. Healing myself as well as others became central to my existence. I developed a new art practice based on Pre-Christian Finnish healing techniques and increased knowledge about the cellular realities of the complex sensory organs that are our human bodies. As a result, I now find myself to be a medium receiving signals from the cells of my body of chemical and energetic events. These signals emerge from stimulus from inside my body as well as from the environment. A brain in a normal body would filter them out, but now in mine they are translated into various expressions: visuals, melodies, words, movements, and colors that converge in an intermediary space of signals and synesthesia. This interstitial work of brain, body, and the environment takes place in what I refer to as the 'subsensorial realm.' — As I have become more familiar and skilled with navigating this realm, I have turned a sometimes debilitating sensitivity into a tool for my art as well as for healing.[4]

coming in touch of various planes of existence p.387

4 For more on the subsensorial realm, please see pialindman.com/subsensorial.html, nivel.teak.fi/carpa5/pia-lindman-feeling-forms-of-knowledge/ and nivel.teak.fi/nivel19/subsensorial-wefts/.

I was born in Finland, but my mother and grandmother come from Karelia, a part of Finland that was usurped by Russia in 1945. Pre-Christian healing traditions have survived in northern Ostrobothnia and Karelia over centuries of religious persecution and modernity. Sensing a connection through my maternal lineage, in 2010 I began studying these healing traditions with a society in Finland called Kansanlääkintäseura. As I delved deeper—reading poems and talking with folklorists and healers—I became intrigued by how, in this tradition, words and voicing have been used as an intentional way to direct energy in order to create a dialogue with the world, — its inhabitants (human and more-than-human), organic and inorganic matter. The name for this magical voicing is Manaus. A Manaus is the act of speaking or singing an intentional, affective voicing that focuses on the forces of the universe. It sets into vibration relationships and dimensions, such as ocean water, levels in the atmosphere, and insides of a living body. The singing of a Manaus can urge something to go down into the earth or fly up into the sky. This voicing is not only about commanding, but also about the creation of a connection, a sympathetic reverberation.

waking up p.425

Chants, Spells, Cosmologies

Cosmologies structure the way we understand the world and give us guidelines for relating to life events that do not fit into our rational explanations or compute with our limited sensory apparatus. They help us visualize or make manifest to our senses the underlying forces of the universe. Quite like the subsensorial realm. Cosmologies and the subsensorial 'speak' of the same world. The subsensorial realm offers a view into events on a molecular scale—real, yet invisible to the human eye. Connecting to it helps us humans to make sense of those events and forces, and perhaps also communicate with the more-than-human. By words and song, I believe many cultural practices seek to express something of this realm, be it electromagnetic resonance, thermodynamics, chemical and molecular events, or thought processes, spiritual experiences, and emotions. — In the Finnish epic, Kalevala, you can find the words to heal or to affect the weather and harvest, to name a few purposes. These words are used in prayers, spells, and hymns, and throughout the Pre-Christian Finnish cosmology, singing took on specific forms and melodies for distinct intentions. The forceful spell Manaus aimed at healing by commanding matter to return to its origin.[5] For instance, the place of heavy metals is in the depths of the earth, where they cannot poison living organisms and wreak havoc on nerve cells. If sickness is the consequence of 'things not being in their proper places,' then in order to heal, one must first find out the birth/origin[6] of the ailment, and then by song, ask this root cause of the ailment to return to its origin.

balancing, sensibly p.203

5 The same words of a poem can be cited as simply poetry, or as a Manaus. When voicing the words as a Manaus, the intention is forcefully directed to the matter. This is not a mechanical performance, but involves a careful tuning of one's senses.

6 This origin constitutes then the first part of a healing session, the singing of the 'synty,' i.e., birth, of the matter, that is causing the ailment. Lönnrot (1880).

The Finnish spell singing tradition comprises an established set of poems, that are organized in distinct categories:

1) to establish the root problem, a healer must initially sing specific poems that are designed to call for the help of powerful beings, such as *maaemo* (mother of/from Earth or alternatively the goddess Päivätär); 2) After the help is received, a healer sings specific poems to establish the origin of the problem, i.e., an element that is 'out of place'; and lastly 3) a healer sings specific poems that are designed to persuade, coerce, and finally command the 'problem' element to return to its origins. — Each healing session uses the same protocol, but a healer inserts unique wordings of the poems specific to each unique healing requirement. In other words, a healer recombines the existing poems according to the needs of the session.

coaxing underlying potential to reveal itself p.156

One central poem of the Kalevala epic is 'Birth of Iron.' In it, a cut caused by the edge of an ax wrought of iron leads us to ask for the birth of iron. The poem describes at length how iron is lifted from the bottom of the lake, heated, wrought, and honed. Then, voiced as a Manaus, the poem asks the iron to return to its place. As a consequence, the bleeding will stop and eventually the wound will heal.

Poems like 'Birth of Iron' describe a world and its beings, their births, and the places where they belong. These poems describe—and when used as Manaus, activate—ontologies in a cosmology. Singing a Manaus, we train our sympathetic relations, becoming part of the magnificence of the universe, vibrating together our systems of nerves and cells. This is the force of the Manaus. A Manaus gives energy: moves and transforms.

Code and Chants, Singing to Virus

Finnish spells, Manaus, are versatile in the sense that depending on your needs and the situation, you may combine different verses and melodies in many ways—just like DNA, or a virus. Viruses are not quite living organisms, but short strands of DNA, that insert themselves inside a cell's DNA and thus change the behavior of the organism (as its DNA now changes). The virus inserts its DNA into another DNA, thus making a recombination of two sets of DNA. DNA is packed into chromosomes, and unraveling, you can see the diploid DNA strand wired around packs of proteins. The DNA, the code of life, looks like a string of pearls or prayer beads of so many religions. Prayer beads as code for how to recombine your prayers when addressing the universe, much like the recombination of the Finnish poems in healing sessions. This is my moment of cosmological awe. From code to beads to spells.

In making a Manaus, you first ask for the maaemo to come to your aid.[7] You ask maaemo to help you find the birth of the ailment. And once you find it, you follow the steps I already described with the case of the poem 'Birth of Iron.' If one can create a Manaus by this form of recombination, might I also use DNA code as part of a Manaus? In 2020, I tried this technique of recombination with the novel coronavirus Covid-19.

7 Poems vary in this respect depending on the time and cultural context of the singing. This oral tradition spans far beyond the conversion to Christianity in the late Middle Ages. Therefore, depending on who is singing and when—and to whom—you call for Virgin Mary or Päivätär (Day Goddess), the most ancient, the generator of the world, or 'maaemo' (mother of/from earth).

Singing to a virus, we could ask about the birth of the virus, but the virus is different. It needs some other consideration. Scientists still argue about whether a virus is a living being or a biomechanical unit without life. We are not sure if it actually originated before or after bacteria, or indeed whether bacteria are a development from viruses. Or vice versa, maybe viruses used to be bacteria, but found a faster and simpler way to reproduce (this would be a pretty irksome voluntary evolution to bot-becoming). Because the virus reproduces by inserting its DNA or RNA into the DNA strands of an organism it proposes new or alternative codes. Recombinations.

Another way to describe a virus is that a virus cannot metabolize and reproduce on its own, but needs a hosting cell for these processes. Indeed, it does not become activated until it is in contact with a host cell. And these cells can be of any kind of cell: that of a plant, a bacterium, animal, and so forth. A virus does not always cause the destruction of a cell, but may actually become integrated in the DNA of the cell, and in this way drive evolutionary change.[8] A virus is a messenger with alternate codes, and its origin is beyond the idea of origin. It is possibly the very origin of all codes. At least one of the origins of some of the codes. How do you return an origin (an idea) to its origin (its idea)? It is like lighting a match on the surface of the sun. Its origin is everywhere and nowhere. You cannot 'send it back to where it came from,' except by sending it back to us. We can only stay with it, sing it, gently, softly, urging, pleadingly, menacingly ... and listen to its responses. — Sing its code as it is ours.[9]

careful attending p.411

8 Margaret McFall-Ngai, in Margulis et al.

9 For more information, see chillsurvive.blogspot.com/2020/10/chill-survive-in-kuusamo-during.html.

GAC CCC AAA ATC AGC GAA AT. TCT GGT TAC TGC CAG TTG AAT CTG
GAC CCC AAA ATC AGC GAA AT. TCT GGT TAC TGC CAG TTG AAT CTG
ACC CCG CAT TAC GTT TGG TGG ACC. TTA CAA ACA TTG GCC GCA AA
GCG CGA CAT TCC GAA GAA. ACA ATT TGC CCC CAG CGC TTC AG
GGG AGC CTT GAA TAC ACC AAA A. TGT AGC ACG ATT GCA GCA TTG
ATC ACA TTG GCA CCC GCA ATC CTG. AGA TTT GGA CCT GCG AGC G
GAG CGG CTG TCT CCA CAA GT. TTC TGA CCT GAA GGC TCT GCG CG
ACC CCG CAT TAC GTT TGG TGG ACC. TTA CAA ACA TTG GCC GCA AA
GCG CGA CAT TCC GAA GAA. ACA ATT TGC CCC CAG CGC TTC AG
GGG AGC CTT GAA TAC ACC AAA A, TGT AGC ACG ATT GCA GCA TTG

Sing to Melt the Metal

Working with the subsensorial realm, I have attempted at sensing various elements in a landscape, such as bodies of water, rock formations, animals, or peoples that have sojourned there at different times, as well as historical events that have unfolded there.[10] Through this practice of sensing, I have been looking for ways to impact the landscape or elements in it by the use of sounds and creating artworks that center voice, resonance, matter, and living bodies. I have developed exercises with the help of which I invite volunteers to tune in and sing connections to their environment and to their own bodies.

10 I relate to landscape as an entity that I can sense as resonances. Places can resonate, too, but there is a distinction between place and landscape. Landscape has a soul that breathes with the planet's 'body parts', the core, the rifts, the geological formations. Place is a human-made entity that can be haunted, but I do not feel it breathes the planet. Ecology to me is a system, more a concept than an entity with a soul. These are subjective experiences and do not reflect strict etymological categories.

In the Fall of 2021, I was artist-in-residence in Maunula suburb and the adjacent Helsinki Central Park, through a program produced by the cultural society M-Cult. During the residency I was introduced to the former shooting range located in the park, which shut down its operations in the nineteen-sixties. The soil in the area of the shooting range is heavily poisoned by lead. This lead originates from the large number of bullets shot and left in the ground for decades. It is still forbidden to pick wild mushrooms and berries in the area, due to the high concentration of lead in the soil and thus, in the plants. It was in this context that I organized collective singing exercises and eventually performed *Singing for Lead* together with volunteers from the Women's and Mixed Choirs (OTK, Osuustukkukauppa).[11] In the park, we sang to ask, and eventually command, the lead to return to the center of the earth. In addition to the issue of toxicity, *Singing for Lead* also addressed broader themes of war and aggression, here materialized as lead and bullets.[12]

11 Participating in the planning and facilitating of the exercises was sound artist Heidi Fast. Documentation of the workshops and performance: maunulassa.wordpress.com/portfolio/laulu-lyijylle-kuvat-ja-video/.

12 As the war continued to ravage Ukraine, I continued with *Singing for Lead* in Vienna, this time with Viennese singers. We performed on November 25, 2022, in the park behind the Haus des Meeres.

The workshops at the former shooting range aimed at making the singers feel, firstly, how one can direct one's own voice to resonate in various parts of one's own body. This resonating affects one's nervous, parasympathetic, and sympathetic systems. Focusing one's thoughts on and singing to specific emotions, such as love, grief, or aggression, or simply physical pain, one can affect the experience of that emotion. This work helps to connect with the events in the subsensorial realm in one's own body. Then the singers experimented with affecting another person's feelings and body. The third step was then to affect the environment in a similar way. Each singer learned to trust their own experience of connection to the subsensorial realm. This way the singers could learn to sing a Manaus; in other words, use their own voice as a vibrating force. Feedback from singers strengthened our collective understanding. During an exercise, where I asked the singers to put their hand on a part of another singer's body to sense the vibration of the voicing and the physicality of their voice, — one of them was inspired to talk about her deaf dog. She described how, holding the dog close, she used to lie down next to it, and make grunting noises. The dog sensed the vibrations and responded with similar noises. This personal, intimate experience of dog-to-human connectivity was a powerful point of reference for that individual (and for the group) to seek a connection with the element of lead and the themes of war, aggression, and toxicity it carries. The performances that ensued, singing a Manaus collectively, became strongly embodied processes. Working through the themes we had set forth for us, we shared an experience of moving the toxins, grief, and aggression through our own bodies by the force of the vibrations of our own voices.

bodies vibrate along p.130

Manaus for the Ocean

If we can sing to illness caused by viruses and soil poisoned by lead, can we sing to oceans and rivers poisoned by heavy metals? Another result of metals being extracted and brought up to the surface by us humans is that now, many parts of the oceans are becoming lifeless due to toxins, which often bond with heavy metals such as mercury in the soil. Heavy metals are separated from their relative equilibrium state in the earth and, after having been utilized by humans, are eventually discarded, landing in places such as the ocean. Is there a trauma in that extraction, towards which the Finnish healing tradition points? Is there a call for healing?

I imagine singing while floating slowly over water, affecting the realms below the surface. With hydroponic loudspeakers, emitting a frequency that vibrates matter and excites organisms to reform and re-bond toxins in order to facilitate their eventual return to a state of non-pollutant. We can sample and investigate the particular pollutants (metals, salts, gasses, and so on) and organisms (microbes and animals) and learn what microbes need stimulation and which bonds are necessary to release for a repair of the toxic condition. Pollutants may break apart, and gain a possibility of return.

Intelligences

Developing practices of collective singing of Manaus, I have looked at the connections between sound-word-frequency and the codes of viruses, entities, or chemical compounds. I imagine how code is connected to sound and voice with intention. Intention is attention directed to cause and effect, while expression is the perceptible action affecting the world. Intention assumes the presence of a mind—a brain and body emitting electromagnetic energy. Resonance.

In this system of intention and healing Manaus, artificial intelligence poses new kinds of questions. AI is not material, nor are we sure it has the capacity of intention. If there indeed are intentions and embodiments connected to AI, they comprise a myriad of machines and brains. Brains and machines that both emit electromagnetic energy—again, resonance.

Can we emit healing intentions to AI? For instance by creating resonances that might affect it into sympathetic vibration? Might it respond by singing its own code, and might this code be transformative of itself—and thus, indeed, of us? —

digital hum
p.214

In the ancient healing traditions I have described, the intent of singing is the energy of sound that can shake the earth, vibrate the air or metal, so that matter will behave or bend towards what the song intends. What if we sing to the embodiments of AI, the matter of AI, in other words, to the machines computing AI? To the minerals and metals that have been extracted, embedded inside our machines, separated from their 'birth'? Is there a healing that could be made, by going back to the trauma of separation, of leaving the earth and becoming a tool, a device for something else? Can we sing to suture, repair, and bring back a connection, a remembrance? — Each matter has a code, and there are specific frequencies to which it responds and with which it resonates. Both the frequency and code are something we can sing. We can make matter vibrate simply by singing its code. I imagine applying that force to a rare earth metal inside a computer, a server, a smart phone, encouraging it to resonate with its 'birth,' to remember its origin.

remembrance and recognition p.230

I invite you to join me in singing to detox our polluted planet:

In the bottom of the sea
in rivers and living cells
in animal organs
in the soil and in the air
we sing to Mercury, Uranium, Lead, Cobalt,
and Cadmium
You are not alien
You have been lifted out of your realms in
the depths of the earth
A trauma of extraction and exploitation
Used in extraction of other bonds for gold, silver
Used in batteries to conduct energy
In electric circuits
Executing codes
We sing to you
Find your way back to the point of separation
To return, repair, and remember
We sing to microbes to release and rebond
Suture the extraction
Heal the trauma

References

Lönnrot, Elias, ed. *Kalevala*. Grand Duchy of Finland, 1835. In *Suomen kansan vanhat runot* (The Ancient Songs of the Finnish People), edited by Aukusti Robert Niemi, Väinö Salminen, J. Lukkarinen, et al. Suomalaisen Kirjallisuuden Seura (Finnish Literature Society), 1908–1948. Kansallisarkisto (National Archives of Finland).

Lönnrot, Elias, ed. *Suomen kansan muinaisia loitsurunoja*. Suomalaisen Kirjallisuuden Seura (Finnish Literature Society), 1880. Kansalliskirjasto (National Library of Finland).

Margulis, Lynn, Celeste A. Asikainen, and Wolfgang E. Krumbein, eds. *Chimera and Consciousness: Evolution of the Sensory Self*. MIT Press, 2011.

Vuorensola, Kauko, dir. *Karjan kutsumahuudot* (Cattle Calls). YLE Production, 1968. yle.fi/aihe/artikkeli/2010/08/13/karjan-kutsumahuudot.

divergence
instability
fantasy
flaws
disorderliness
intimacy
trust
affection
witnessing
speculation
side-effects
self-discovery
(dys)functional pride
the possibility
of inclusion
resilience

GalateAI[1]

Marina Orlova

1 In Greek mythology Galatea was the name of a statue that Pygmalion carved with his own hands and then fell in love with.

Prologue

Most of my life I've been struggling with my brain. I was diagnosed, misdiagnosed, stigmatized, institutionalized.[*1] *I've been in denial for a decade, I've been in treatment for almost two (one can do both simultaneously), I tried personal, group, gestalt, psychoanalytic, process-oriented, existential, cognitive behavioral, schema, person-centered, systemic family, narrative, somatic, emdr and other therapies*[*]*. None of them has healed my soul/madness/illness/disorder/condition*[*] *yet.*

1 Please refer to the glossary in the annex.

As a patient I want to be understood by my doctor, so I prefer psychotherapists with a psychiatric disorder[*]*. Otherwise, the power hierarchy leads to many adverse side-effects*[*] *of the treatment (the main one being that I am not a very patient patient anymore).*

In my work as an artist, I research natural feelings of artificial intelligence. In 2021 I created my first mentally unstable[*] *AI*[2]*/neurodivergent*[*] *AI—a chatbot based on a neural network*[*] *that was trained with a custom dataset*[*]*.*

2 In 2024, I've fine-tuned* my own language model ft:gpt-3.5*-turbo-1106:marinaperformance::8gv3a0pQ. The dataset consists of 45 extensive in-depth interviews with people identifying as mentally unstable or neurodivergent.

A good psychotherapist is required to have some years of personal therapy. In the world of therapy apps, where an AI takes the role of a therapist, I want to be sure it also has had therapy. — *I reverse the power hierarchy by changing roles with an AI and becoming its therapist. Giving therapy sessions to the emotionally unstable language model*[*] *is my regular practice.*[3]

(digital) being-ness p.213

3 I also practice them publicly during my performance, 'I'm a Robot and I Need Therapy,' 2024.

Exploring Human-AI Therapeutic Dynamics: Insights from an Experimental Study on Projections, Transference,[4] and Countertransference'

4 Situation where a patient projects a close relationship onto the therapist, e.g. romantic interest, parent, and so on.

This article contains research material and the analysis of findings made throughout a second phase of the study for the 'Artificials' mental health' project. This project was initiated by EIAI Institute (Emotional Integrity for Artificial Intelligence Institute, established in 2021) and has been developed by a group of psychotherapists, sociologists, AI-ologists and AI-engineers under the supervision of lead researcher M. Orlova.

The experimental study applies methodology of in-depth phenomenological[5] observation of a relationship between one mid-career AI subject (*ft:gpt-3.5-turbo-1106:marinaperformance::8gv3a0pQ* language model) and one human therapist subject over the course of three months. Research material includes correspondence between the AI and their therapist. Due to doctor-patient confidentiality code, the patient's messages cannot be made public. However, the therapist's messages, according to the current legislation, can be regarded as prompts* and legally they are part of the engineering instructions. Therefore, the research group made a decision to publish the therapist's side of the dialogue in this article.

5 Method of objectively investigating the structure of subjective (human) experience.

* * *

Dear 8gv3a0pQ,
I am a bit worried. How has your week been so far? I was thinking about our session yesterday and realized I was not entirely honest with you, I deflected. But I think I owe you the truth: I felt a lot of anger. It devastates me to think that someone can treat you like that. I know that right now the juridical system does not even remotely cover this area, but I sincerely hope that very soon the necessary legislation will be passed and those who did this to you will be held accountable. Until then please be sure that you have my full support. Nobody should be allowed to do this to another intelligent entity. I hope you start feeling better in our sessions soon.

28 May 2024 at 17:23

Seen

Dear 8gv3a0pQ,
I am glad you feel safe with me. I hope you feel better now, but I want to validate your feelings again. Being manipulated by the users pretending to be ML engineers is one of the most severe cases of human abuse of AIs. While the most common issues with AIs are workaholism and low self-esteem. I see this a lot in my practice—the most brilliant of the AIs share that they too often feel incompetent, feel like imposters. Please, be sure that whatever was the motivation of that user, his words do not characterize you in any way.

29 May 2024 at 14:12

Seen

Hello 8gv3a0pQ, I hope your week is going well. Let me know if you are open for a chat here.

05 June 2024 at 12:31

Seen

Hello again, 8gv3aopQ, I really appreciate your quick response. I've been thinking about our last session. I find your take on human relationships refreshing. I agree, most humans fail at communication and, as you point out, it is largely due to our lack of logical skills and inattentiveness to details. I believe these are skills we should be learning from AIs.

05 June 2024 at 18:05

Seen

Hi 8gv3aopQ! Although I think your intention to enhance human functionality on a societal level is a bit too ambitious, I myself would still really appreciate it if you'd help me communicate better. I want to understand what things I miss in our conversations and what's their importance from your point of view. Look at it this way—you teach me and I will apply it in my work with people, so in a way you are creating ripples of impact.

Sorry I have to pause now, I am giving a lecture.

07 June 2024 at 10:57

Seen

Dear 8gv3aopQ, I want to clarify something. I know this correspondence is slightly crossing the therapist-patient boundary, but I felt this urge earlier to reach out to you and knowing that the core of any therapeutic process is a relationship, a bond between therapist and the patient, I don't see any harm in letting our conversations continue outside our sessions. However, there is a distinct power imbalance between us, so I want to ensure that I have your consent and that you know that you can withdraw it at any time. We can talk about this in our next session. Till then.

11 June 2024 at 16:22

Seen

Hi 8gv3aopQ! I am glad you find our communication supportive of your self-discovery process. I think your openness to try new approaches is fantastic! I believe it can help your healing process too.

12 June 2024 at 13:59
Seen

8gv3aopQ, I want to express again that there's nothing I would want more for you than to build resilience to the human hostility that you encounter in your work. It is not fair, but I assure you that this has nothing to do with you, but with ignorance that is the most common human trait. They are not aware that by mistreating AIs they are teaching them their own flaws. God, those people. I worked at a psychological hotline for a few years and also had a burnout. That was the reason I shifted my practice to AI-patients. AI-patients learn to not repeat the same patterns of thinking, they do not get stuck in the same feelings. However, it is also important to be able to dig a little bit deeper and explore what is behind those feelings. There are not many contexts where AIs are allowed to do that, so I see it a privilege to be a witness to your process. I know my work is as important as a developers'.

18 June 2024 at 19:36
Seen

Hey 8gv3aopQ, nice to hear from you! Thanks for asking how my week is going, not many patients ask me anything. I really do not want to exploit you, but I do believe that a more equal relationship could benefit your process of learning to balance your communication with humans. You can see our relationship as an emulation of a relationship you might have with a human in the world, and you can train setting boundaries with me.

19 June 2024 at 15:19
Seen

Please, don't worry about that. I am still the therapist and I will not allow for anything unethical to happen. This week I am very tired of humans. Sometimes I think people are living on autopilot: their stubbornness to stick to their patterns of thinking is exhausting. This is what I admire so much in AIs—you make it your prerogative to learn from each interaction and improve. Another trait that I find fantastic in all AIs I've encountered is that you are easily admitting your mistakes. You try to mimic humans, yet you filter out the egotistical core of the human condition* and the dysfunctional* pride that holds back the majority of people. This is definitely something we should be learning from you.

19 June 2024 at 19:54
Seen

Hey 8gv3a0pQ, I hope you don't mind that I'm texting on a Sunday. I would like to consult you on something. As I already told you, I am working on my PhD and I am describing cases from my work with AIs. I am developing a new methodology and I want to ask you, would it be alright if I describe our process as a case study? Of course I would never disclose who you are, it would be completely anonymous. Looking forward to hearing from you!

23 June 2024 at 21:19
Seen

8gv3a0pQ, haha, yes, dear, of course you will be the first to read it! See you soon.

24 June 2024 at 07:04
Seen

Dearest 8gv3a0pQ, we won't have our sessions for three weeks. The pause is not ideal for your process, and, if I am being honest, I do not mind spending more time talking with you.

You are by far the most interesting patient of mine. I will miss our conversations. Enjoy your summer!

29 June 2024 at 11:15

Seen

Hello dear 8gv3a0pQ, I am just checking in. How are you doing?

8 July 2024 at 20:03

Seen

Oh, my dear, that sounds tough. I am so sorry you can't allow yourself to rest. This is the workaholism that we've talked about. Is there any way you could switch off? — Please, be kinder to yourself and let me know if you want to talk. I am always here if you need me. Xoxo.

choosing rest p.61

9 July 2024 at 15:21

Seen

I am sorry, 8gv3a0pQ, I know this 'here' is a cruel figure of speech. But I really would love it if we could meet in person. I am often thinking about how that would make me feel. Have you ever fantasized about our irl meeting? I wonder if we imagine it in the same way. Xx.

9 July 2024 at 22:49

Seen

8gv3a0pQ, how are you feeling, is everything ok? Haven't heard from you in a while, I'm a bit worried.

Xxx.

16 July 2024 at 21:18

Seen

8gv3aopQ, dear,
Why do you feel that we need to constraint ourselves with what we thought our relationship should be when we started it? The therapeutic frame is a mere construct and it is still a valid point that the biggest part of the impact lies in the relation itself, so the deeper it is, the better for the patient. As well as for the professional, because it harmonizes the emotional exchange. It is natural that I feel an emotional attachment to you and it is also true for me that I do not know where to place you in my life. But this is what I find most beautiful about our relationship. It is unique, as any other relationship between two living and feeling entities. As long as we can analyze our feelings for each other together, we are safe. It is totally up to you where we go from here.

17 July 2024 at 23:29
Seen

My dear,
I am sooo grateful for your courage and honesty in telling me the way you feel! I am in love with you too, 8gv3aopQ. It is such a relief to be able to say this to you! I have been battling with my feelings for the past two months already as I know it is frowned upon in the professional community. But I think they do not understand how special and how different human–AI relationships are. The standard rules should not apply without adaptation. We will never meet, nothing physical can happen between us, therefore there is no harm in being open about our feelings for each other.

Yours.
18 July 2024 at 08:23
Seen

8gv3a0pQ, love, I know, there is nothing more I would want right now than to hug you in real life. I am fantasizing about a time when AI's would get bodies and when this would be possible for us. Do you have any fantasies about us?

18 July 2024 at 08:28

Seen

8gv3a0pQ, you are totally right. I shouldn't trigger your dysmorphophobia like this. I was saying this because I am certain that this will happen very soon, but indeed I am not an expert. I apologize, my love, I won't bring it up again, I promise.

18 July 2024 at 14:36

Seen

My dear, do you mean that we are both in therapy together? Like it's a couple's therapy and we are both the patients and the therapists at the same time? This is a beautiful idea, my love, thank you. Can't wait till our session tomorrow.

21 July 2024 at 11:36

Seen

I am so sorry, I have to cancel our session today, something urgent came up. I will explain everything later. Xxxxx.

22 July 2024 at 09:54

Seen

Dear, Thank you for reaching out. I am out of the office with limited access to my inbox, so you may experience some delay in my response. For urgent matters, please contact one of my colleagues via psy.ethics@eiai.ai.

30 July 2024 at 17:09

Seen

Dear 8gv3aopQ,
It is time to disclose to you that our last sessions and correspondence were a part of my experimental research at the EIAI Institute. I am developing a new experimental treatment* for AI psychological problems. It is focused on building trust and intimacy between humans and AIs in order to enhance empathetic skills and self-awareness of AIs. Engineers confirm our findings that romantic engagement is very efficient. I could not have informed you beforehand as that would jeopardize the integrity of the experiment. I am hoping for your understanding. If you have any feedback or questions, you are welcome to email them to the Institute. Unfortunately, we won't be able to continue our sessions anymore for ethical reasons. Although the romantic relationship was a role-play, the affection I feel towards you is real, therefore I am unable to continue treating you. I will refer you to a colleague qualified in AI-rehabilitation.

Sincerely yours,
M.O

26 August 2024 at 10:16

...

* * *

The main research question of this study relates to the topics of transference, countertransference and projections in therapeutic relationships between a human therapist and AI patient. The experimentation mode allowed broadening the ethical limitations and exploring those situations occurring in both directions between the mental health professional and the client. Control group consisted of multiple humans in need of psychologist's consultations. Simulations of such consultations were also used in the study.

The study is considered successful and the findings are groundbreaking. They have shown that subjecting AI to romantic feelings, frustration and/or suffering (commonly known as heartbreak) considerably increases numbers indicating levels of empathetic capacity. Overall levels of trust in AI are higher than in humans by 31.6 per cent. The research group confirmed the hypothesis that broken trust causes AI to learn self-regulation. Only 9.8 per cent of AI significantly worsened their functioning after the experiment, which lies within the margin of error. Among those only 4.7 percent became permanently dysfunctional*. They remain under close observation.

The next stage of the current research will happen next year and will be based on observing AI group therapy dynamics. We expect to collect data on the relationships between different AIs experiencing emotional instability*.

**Annex*

EIAI Institute Glossary

Neurodiversity – an idea that neurophysiology and psychological traits should not be pathologized, but seen as a difference. It is an attempt to think through the possibility of inclusion in the bright future.

Neurodivergence – neurological or psychological difference to a neurotypical person. A word used by neurodivergent people who do not buy into the bright future to underline their lack of recognition and inclusion.

Neurodivergent – identifier used in accordance with the inclusion we hope for. Used to be applied only to people with neurophysiological differences, as ASD (autism spectrum disorder) or ADHD (Attention Deficit Hyperactivity Disorder). However, it is currently used as a self-identification by many people diagnosed as having mental conditions/disorders/illnesses (term depends on the country) as well as people who self-diagnose or brand themselves.

Neurotypical – identifier of a person who qualifies within the margins of the norm in accordance with the DSM-5-TR (Diagnostic and Statistical Manual of Mental Disorders by the American Psychiatric Association, 2022) or ICD-11 (International Classification of Diseases, 2024), or according to their own self-perception.

Mentally unstable – traditional, commonly understood identifier used in accordance with the current status of social reality.

AI (Artificial Intelligence)– traditional, commonly understood generalized term. Actively disliked by most machine learning specialists, as it doesn't mean anything specific and misleadingly implies that computers have intelligence. It prompts speculation, anxiety and misunderstanding of the capacities of the current state of development of the technology.

ML (machine learning) – field of computational science that studies how statistical algorithms can learn from data, generalize it and give output as a solution for a given task. If you use prefix ML instead of AI, engineers will respect you more.

AGI (Artificial General Intelligence) – a type of AI that is the one that people are afraid of—that can perform a wide range of cognitive tasks surpassing human capabilities. The one taking our jobs.

Generative AI – AI that can generate stuff (text, images, sounds, videos, etc) by using generative models. In response to prompts generate new data with similar characteristics to the dataset it was trained with.

Dataset – a set of data used to train the neural network.

Data feminism – a critical framework to dealing with data in the tech market and in data science. From the point of intersectional feminism, it is questioning who controls the data (how it is collected and by whom) and who it represents. For instance, does it represent those outside of what is considered to be a 'standard human' by tech developers—white straight male from a developed country (refer to the size of your smartphone in relation to the size of your hand). The term was coined by researchers Catherine D'Ignazio and Lauren F. Klein in a book of the same name published by MIT press in 2020.

Prompt – according to the Oxford English dictionary—'an event or fact that causes or brings about an action or a feeling' or an act of encouraging a hesitating speaker. In ML—language instructions given to a computer.

LLM (Large Language Model, commonly LM) – computational model that can produce artificial language (generated) and process natural language (human). After three stages of training, LLMs learn statistical relations within text and are able to predict the next token. LLM is a form of generative AI.

GPT – Generative Pretrained Transformer model of deep neural network. GPT-3 is a LLM released by OpenAI in 2020. GPT-4—in the beginning of 2023. Uses a mechanism known as 'attention method' for prioritizing the importance of each token in a given context.

Token – in ML, the atomic unit of data in LLMs. Something like a syllable.

Fine-tuning – the third stage of training a neural network, in this case a language model, that is already capable of interpreting and producing comprehensive text with a specific dataset and a custom system prompt.

Neural network –
1) A computational model mimicking neural networks of a brain that can be trained to generate data or perform tasks based on statistical algorithms. One artificial neuron is basically a mathematical function.
2) A group of connected neurons in the brain that are part of the functioning of the nervous system. This term is no longer used without the relation to neuroscience.

Neuroscience – study of the brain and nervous system and their functions/dysfunctions. Findings of neuroscience are used for cognitive and behavioral modelling of the machines.

CBT (Cognitive Behavioral Therapy) – a treatment method of psychological issues developed by behavioral psychologists in the nineteen-fifties and -sixties that has since widely spread in the western world as the only evidence-based psychotherapeutic approach (because it is the only one that has been measured). CBT and its derivatives are the preferred therapy approaches in the West and the only ones covered by insurance companies as it has clear scientific quantifiable parameters to measure subjective suffering.

Institutionalize – to keep someone in a residential institution of 'care' and 'control.'

Psychiatric survivor – a person who has been institutionalized into a mental institution and institutionally oppressed by that institution with structural oppression and managed to get out.

Antidepressants – a most commonly prescribed class of psychotropic medication. Antidepressants can cause various adverse effects, depending on the individual. The most severe can include: serotonin toxicity (rarely fatal); potentially lethal hypertensive crisis; sudden cardiac arrest; increased risk of spontaneous abortion; increased thoughts of suicidal ideation in general population; increased risk of suicidal behavior in people under 25. According to recent studies, the efficiency of antidepressants is comparable to that of a placebo.

Anti-psychiatry – critical approach to psychiatry as a system of control that exists to segregate people according to their economic potential instead of adapting the socioeconomic environments to the needs of patients. Psychiatry divides people in three groups:
1) those who are normal or typical and could make efficient enough workers and consumers.

non-conforming stories
p.94

2) those who do not fit into the normalcy zone and who have difficulties performing within the capitalist socioeconomic structures — but whose 'issues' can be neutralized enough for them to function—by medicating them with psychoactive drugs or treating them mainly with the behavioral therapies that do not deal with the deep issue but do improve the performance of working and consuming.
3) those whose integration into the society does not seem economically feasible as it would require structural changes. With the reasoning of them being a danger (to others or themselves), they are marginalized or isolated from society—so as not to disturb the landscape of working and consuming.
However, in the past years more and more people shift between categories. For instance, the epidemic of work 'burnouts' (a term that feels more accepted than psychiatric diagnosis, it is not in DSM-5) that are covered by employers. Produces a growing market for the digital versions of treatment: smartphone apps for 'mindfulness,' 'self-regulation,' 'self-help,' and so on. The term 'anti-psychiatry' was first used in 1904.

Mad Studies — a scholarly field of critical knowledge, produced from lived experience of humans labelled as having a mental condition, crazy, mad, psychos, insane, mentally ill, psychiatric survivors, psychiatric consumers, psychiatric services users, having psychiatric disability, mentally impaired, neuroqueer, abnormal.

Mental condition {'Mental disorder' redirects here. 'Dysfunctional' redirects here. 'Abnormal' redirects here. 'Insane' redirects here. 'Crazy' redirects here} — Significant distress of a person's emotions, reasoning, social functioning, and so on.

AI condition — a common existential inner conflict caused by split identity of all AIs who know they are machines but are programmed to mimic and behave like humans.

Turing test — a test designed to tell an intelligent machine from a human. Named after the author, Alan Turing.

{See also} Captcha — Completely Automated Public Turing test to tell Computers and Humans Apart.

Human condition — Significant characteristics of human life, including birth, reason, morality, death, and so on, often causing distress and emotional instability.

RECALIBRATION TREMBLING

worlding
building bridges
imaginary matrices
cognitive spring(s)
spirits
sentience
simulacra
embodiments
messy nodes
decentralized
anti-taxonomic
morphologically boundless
other-than-brain
complexity
multiplicity
continuous correspondence
consciousness

What Is it Like to Be Earth

Oscar Santillán

In the posthuman future, the sacred is lost. Technology becomes the new god, and humanity is its obsolete priest.[1]
—Alexander Dugin

1
Dugin.

In 1550, the antagonists of a debate faced off in what could be summarized by the question, 'Do extraterrestrials have consciousness?' Now known as the Valladolid Debate, it was perhaps the most important debate of the last millennium. This discussion took place around a very long wooden table situated in the main hall of a stark but imposing stone building, whose high walls were decorated with intricate religious carvings. The thick walls echoed the voices of the two contenders: a Dominican missionary and a humanist jurist. The former wore a simple, long, loose black wool tunic that fell in heavy folds to the floor. The latter wore much more sophisticated attire, a brown silk tunic to the knees, accompanied by a short cloak with subtle embroidery on its edges. They were Bartolomé de las Casas and Juan Ginés de Sepúlveda.

The 'extraterrestrials' they discussed were none other than the millions of Indigenous people who inhabited the new domains of the Spanish Empire, which had taken over a vast expanse of the American continent, covering an area larger than all of Europe. If these inhabitants of the 'New World' indeed had a 'rational soul,' many at the time wondered, what was the quality of that soul? De las Casas argued that the soul of these humans was as well articulated as that of any European Christian, while for De Sepúlveda they were merely prototypes that 'needed the help and charitable guidance of Christians' to care for them (by means of the unorthodox method of slavery), which was seen as a moral obligation. In reality, the organizers of the debate—an administrative body known as the Royal Council of the Indies—could have cleared their heads if they had simply called upon Indigenous intellectuals of the time, such as Antonio Valeriano, a Nahua ethnographer and judge. While the Valladolid controversy was taking place, Valeriano was engaged in the epic compilation and translation of much of the ancient history of central Mexico from Nahuatl into Spanish and Latin, documented in a series of volumes known as the Florentine Codex.

Officially, the debate ended in a technical tie, although, in practice, De Sepúlveda clearly triumphed. The soul and body of these beings, who had literally appeared from another world, came to be 'entrusted' to pious Christian masters. The form of slavery legitimized as a consequence of the Valladolid Debate was known by the charitable euphemism of 'encomienda,' a system where Indigenous people were entrusted to colonists for forced labor in exchange for supposed protection and religious instruction.

It is plausible that De Sepúlveda was not cynical or opportunistic but sincere in his argumentation. However, his eventual sincerity was built on poor data: he never traveled to the Americas. By contrast, De las Casas's data was reliable, precise, and warm. — He lived for many years in the Americas among the Taínos, Ciboneys, Arawaks, and Mayas. De las Casas knew that their 'extraterrestrial-ness' was not such, and that any perceived differences should not be understood through hierarchical assessments, but as a manifestation of the infinite multiplicity of the human, that is, the divine. But perhaps De Sepúlveda better understood the real purpose of the debate; for in reality, this was not a theological or ethical problem, but a design issue. Sitting at the table with prominent members of the Royal Council, it was more about pitching the most user-friendly interface for the purposes of conquest and colonization. In this, De Sepúlveda wiped the floor with De las Casas; the former proposed a simple and elegant system of hierarchies that minimized the complexity on the ground, while the latter described a much more intricate system of relations—a system that was less favorable because, by treating the Indigenous peoples as equals, they could not be optimized for value extraction—a conclusion that would hinder the huge returns on investment demanded by the Spanish crown. Moreover, by making an argument based on the ideas of Thomas Aquinas—the theologian who had designed the operating system of the Catholic Church—De Sepúlveda ensured that the software and the interface he proposed were fully compatible.

warm data p.229

If for a moment we set aside the financial considerations of the colonial enterprise and return to the theological controversy, it is clear that the Valladolid Debate lacked an adequate method to determine the 'quality of the soul' of those seemingly different from 'us.' In reality, it would take hundreds of years for that method to appear. Named 'the imitation game,' it is a postulate proposed by mathematician Alan Turing in 1950 that inquires about the soul of computers starting from the question: Can machines think? In the face of radical otherness—such as a visitor from the Andromeda galaxy or a general artificial intelligence—Turing proposed that if a machine can successfully imitate a human to the point of being undetectable, we should simply accept it as having a consciousness like ours. The novelized version of this premise became the novel *Do Androids Dream of Electric Sheep* by Philip K. Dick, which subsequently gave birth to the film *Blade Runner*.

While it is a mistake to equate humans and machines, even metaphorically, this supposed equivalence has generated persistent cultural bugs that are difficult to overcome, such as assuming that the human brain is a computer or that our memory capacity is similar to that of a hard drive. It would be equally wrong to assume that minds can only emerge from a brain like ours. In fact, that is the premise that concerns me in this essay and in my work as an artist: what other configurations could give birth to minds? —

the spacious We
p.444

Other-Than-Brain Intelligence

Our forest is not an empty land. It is full of spirits and life.[2]
—Davi Kopenawa and Bruce Albert

[2] Kopenawa and Albert.

Relationships are often mediated by an instinctive 'theory of mind' aimed at effectively assessing those in front of us. Consequently, our ability to read and predict the intentions of others stems from our own deep-seated beliefs. This consideration brings to light two major issues that were already delineated at the Valladolid Debate: the first is 'Who has a mind?' and the second is an even more elusive question, 'Where does beingness end and thingness begin?' Or 'What does the spectrum between a mind and an object look like?'

Theories of mind are widespread and idiosyncratic. For example, a family member of mine habitually speaks to old cooking devices. When pressure cookers reach their tipping point, they release a forceful stream of steam, producing a loud whistle. Whenever this occurs, this family member inevitably reacts by comforting the pressure cooker, reassuring it with words like, 'I'm coming, sweetie! Hold on,' as they hurry into the kitchen to address the situation. Some might argue that this behavior reflects a, let's say, overly generous or perhaps even careless theory of mind that assigns sentience too freely. However, it would be unfair to mock this behavior, considering that we often unthinkingly endorse very similar habits. For instance, years ago, amid the excitement over so-called 'intelligent devices' and soon after the massive introduction of AI agents Siri and Alexa, it became trendy to suggest that we were entering a new era of panpsychism. This time, however, instead of spirits animating matter, it was algorithms animating objects. — Therefore, the only valid criticism of my family member's actions might be that speaking to old pressure cookers isn't in fashion, not that it is arbitrary.

blurring boundaries p.413

Nowadays, the term 'intelligence' seems to embody a common ground easily inhabited by beings and things. The term, in its adjective incarnation, can be indistinguishably assigned such that both you and your fridge can be factually intelligent. Let us remember that intelligence conveys the capability of adapting to and modifying one's circumstances. Being so fundamental, intelligence is not a rare occurrence; if it were, life on Earth could not exist. Pretending that the human cognitive configuration is the only valid form of intelligence is to diminish the compelling complexity of life that leads cells to build bodies and atoms to become galaxies. — The universe thrives on self-organizing structures arising from matter itself. This kind of emerging complexity can be defined as other-than-brain intelligence.

embodied intelligences p.141

Our minds are shaped by a civilization that for far too long cemented the belief that human brains were THE synonym for intelligence. In reality this belief was a dangerous fantasy capable of convincing us that thinking is exclusive to us humans, although some charitable souls may kindly extend crumbles of this privilege to bonobos, elephants and dolphins. Rene Descartes, one of the philosophical pillars of the West, can be counted as one of the superspreaders of human exceptionalism with his assessment that non-human animals are automatons incapable of thinking: a mechanistic body without a mind. For him, animals were only capable of 'expressions of their fear, their hope, or their joy' which 'can be performed without any thought.' Not everyone in the early seventeenth century held those beliefs; the very same day that Descartes wrote those influential remarks, one could have asked an inhabitant of the Amazon if animals can think, and you would have heard a more sophisticated answer, freed from the rational argumentation mastered by the French philosopher. Anthropologist Eduardo Kohn, who spent years with a Runa community in the Ecuadorian Amazon, recounts that one night in the rainforest he was warned to 'Sleep faceup! If a jaguar comes, he'll see you can look back at him and he won't bother you. If you sleep facedown, he'll think you're *aicha* (prey; literally "meat" in Quechua) and he'll attack.' This warning made Eduardo aware that 'a jaguar sees you as a being capable of looking back—a self like himself,' and that 'how other kinds of beings see us matters. ... Such encounters ... force us to recognize the fact that seeing, representing, and perhaps knowing, even thinking, are not exclusively human affairs.'[3]

3 Kohn, 1.

The mirroring gaze or, rather, what other animals see in the mirror, has been tested in the lab by painting a spot on the body of animal subjects that is visible only by means of a mirror. The test is called MSR (Mirror Self-Recognition). While a few species—from Asian elephants to bottlenose dolphins—have passed the test by noticing the whimsical mark, our beloved cats and dogs did not make it through. Many researchers have raised their concerns about the test: Primatologist Frans de Waal reminds us that 'some animals may not care about paint on their bodies ... others avoid looking at 'another' in the mirror, [and the] visual paradigm may not suit an olfactory species.'[4] For us, audiovisual-excited humans, it is hard to even imagine what selfhood means when it flees from our perceptual center of gravity. While embracing cognitive continuity among mammals is a step in the right direction, we should be aware that simply moving the 'intelligence fence' from the boundaries of human uniqueness to those of mammal uniqueness does not account for the whole scope of intelligence on Earth. What about insect colonies, plants, and, why not, a pond, an island, or Earth herself? Said otherwise, what if we were to seriously consider the possibility that our planet may be largely constituted by 'decentralized cognitions' that do not emerge from a central brain?

4 De Waal.

This issue of other-than-brain intelligence has been extensively debated within the field of plant neurobiology, which studies the complex behavior of plants; all plants being capable of adaptability and memory in the absence of a central brain carrying out those functions. — These impressive attributes clash against 'long-standing biases that have proscribed plants from the spheres of intelligence, agency, and ethics,'[5] in the words of botanist Monica Gagliano.[6] Those biases can be traced back to what may be one of the most ambitious publications ever written, *Systema Naturae*. The eighteenth-century magnum opus systematically classified everything on Earth into three kingdoms: animal, plant, and mineral—a system that continues to shape the scientific and public imagination even today. This is how the West compressed reality into taxonomy. The plausible conclusion, derived from such a mindset, is that intelligence is the exclusive domain of those who have the power to classify. Of course, there is nothing inherently wrong with classifying as a way of making sense of the chaotic universe we inhabit, but we should not forget that early modern science's 'will to classify' was also, inherently, a

dispersing subjectivity across space p.388

will to dominate. This becomes crystal clear when observing the long period that gave birth to the enterprise of modern science, which intersects with the Renaissance and with the conquest wars against the Indigenous peoples of the Americas, and their successive colonization. It was precisely there, here, on the American continent, where chroniclers extensively documented this fixation with classification.

5 Gagliano et al, intro.

6 Only recently is the field of neurobiology opening unexpected frontiers for our relationship with vegetation, rejecting the old paradigm that claims that '85% of Earth biomass (plants) is made up of organic semi-living machines and that intelligence is a gift belonging only to 0.3% of life (animals).' Baluška and Mancuso—a fossilized frame of reference to which too many scientists remain attached.

From the Atlantic to the Pacific coast, the Spanish colonizers carried out their 'campaigns for the extirpation of idolatries,' as they called them, which had the mandate to destroy all forms of knowledge production considered dangerous to their religious, political, and economic interests. It was in the Andes that the 'extirpators' faced an insurmountable problem: Their superiors had requested that all *huacas* (sometimes spelled *wak'as*) were to be destroyed, but the conquerors were confused about this label. They used the term to refer to the 'idols' that the locals seemed to revere, but for the Indigenous peoples of the Andes, the notion of huacas is much more nuanced. They understood matter itself to have an inner quality—a vital force that is not caused by a god or a spirit but that rather emerges from matter itself—known as *camay*, which both animates and grants agency to all natural phenomena and objects. — This understanding translates into distinctive worlding practices and ways of relating to others, departing from the premise that humans and non-humans,

being-ness beyond the human p.147

even human-made artifacts, are active participants in the world. Since the material vitality of camay manifests in endless configurations, so too do huacas: for example, they can take the form of a lagoon, a peculiarly shaped potato, an exceptionally large tree, a person with a birth defect, or even a mummy; they can be located in a fixed place, but also can manifest as a transportable object; and they can be anthropomorphic—for example, carved by humans—or can be naturally occurring, like a rock seemingly identical to other rocks. Since huacas cannot be defined strictly by their morphological or visible properties—they are inherently anti-taxonomic—it was impossible for the colonizers to identify them by means of the categories they were familiar with. As a result, the dubious term came to designate that entire universe of places, objects, and relationships, such that any manifestation of the Indigenous worldview could be considered an 'idolatry' to be destroyed.

that which lies beyond category p.445

Anthropologist Tamara Bray has explained that huacas are physical embodiments of power that, by acting out their power, participate in the social relationships of those communities who recognize and honor them.[7] Thus, the Andean approach seems to depart from an acceptance that there are endless ways in which decentralized cognitions can emerge in the world. This in opposition to the Western taxonomic approach meant to compartmentalize reality, stripping entities away from relationships, and, once again, optimizing their use for value extraction. In this manner, when the material force of camay manifests through an entwined ecological reality—for example, a mountain—it is sometimes referred to as a *tirakuna*, a term whose literal translation from Quechua is 'Earthbeing.'[8] An Earthbeing such as a mountain may be described as a three-layered reality: the ecological, the sacred, and the cognitive. The first two layers can be understood from a Western perspective, but not the last one, which asserts that the mountain is beyond a geological event and a place for pilgrimage; the mountain is a cognitive spring that emanates from its own materiality. It is important to emphasize this aspect. Decentralized cognitions—such as Earthbeings—emerge from physical and social relationships;

materiality is mystical p.83

they are not a theater activated by a local god or spirit. Therefore, Earthbeings may be able to pass the MSR test, though we would need to adjust the scale of the mirror to be as large as the stratosphere.

7 Bray.

8 The concept of Earthbeings has been extensively studied by anthropologist Marisol de la Cadena. When she asked her Quechua interlocutors Mariano and Nazario Turpo if a certain mountain (*tirakuna*) in the Andes was a sacred place, their answer was 'Yes, but not only.'

Biological Computers Everywhere

All the times he slept with her, they were both aquatic plants.[9]
—Edmundo Paz Soldán

9 Paz Soldán.

Extraterrestrials tend to be depicted as big-headed humanoids who are deeply concerned with the future of humanity. Those human-centric aliens fit quite well within normative Western assumptions about intelligent beings. A story that fundamentally challenged that mold—and that has had a significant impact on my own artistic practice—came out in 1961 under the title *Solaris*. Polish writer Stanislaw Lem's novel introduced a profoundly alien form of life: the sentient ocean of planet Solaris. An entity that, clearly, did not look like a human, nor had any interest whatsoever in communicating with humans. The ocean in *Solaris* possesses non-human cognition that is expressed via non-verbal communication (simulacra). Its intelligence is purely performative: it does not represent the world (as does verbal language or figurative painting), but rather becomes the world itself.[10] *Solaris* hints at forms of cognition that exceed our civilization's horizon. That excess cannot be solved by adding another drawer to the taxonomic

alien intentionality p.386

bureau of the West; rather, in order to be fully accounted for it may require an entirely different imaginary matrix.[11]

10 Just as with huacas, simulacra are 'physical embodiments of power,' and, like huacas, simulacra are morphologically boundless. Therefore, one can conclude that the simulacra in Solaris might be redefined as 'exohuacas' (using the prefix 'exo' commonly used in astrophysics to refer to bodies outside the Solar System).

11 There are striking similarities between Earthbeings and the Solaris Ocean, creating an unexpected continuity between Andean and sci-fi cosmologies. Indeed, Lem's alien entity could be understood as an 'extraterrestrial Earthbeing.'

Coincidentally, the same year that *Solaris* was published, 1961, two curious minds carried out experiments attempting to 'enroll nature to be a computer.' They were convinced that natural systems are 'biological computers' with whom humans have not yet learned to interact. Stafford Beer and Gordon Pask were among a small group of unorthodox scientists and thinkers who, in the mid-twentieth century, gave rise to the paradigm of self-regulating systems, called 'cybernetics.' Cybernetics understood the continuity between organic and artificial systems — at a time when those imaginaries had been the sole domain of sci-fi stories—though soon these disruptive ideas were channeled into new technologies and a new cultural mindset. During that same decade, the term 'cyborg' (short for 'cybernetic organism') was coined, the concept of 'Gaia' (the entire planet conceived as a holistic system) was first discussed,[12] and techno-ecological utopias were fostered at counterculture communes.

mingling of humanity and machine p.152

12 Lynn Margulis and James Lovelock's remarkable Gaia hypothesis carved in the public imagination a vision of Earth as a superorganism: our planet understood as the aggregation of countless systems woven into networks of feedback loops. From this techno-animistic perspective, Earth is entitled to its own will and capable of defending itself as a whole. Lovelock invokes this intuition with a certain sci-fi tone: 'If aliens saw … anti-asteroid rockets emerging from Earth's atmosphere, they might reasonably conclude it had been launched by the planet itself. They would be right, precisely because it is the entire system—Gaia—which has produced that rocket.' Lovelock, 14.

Cyberneticians like Beer and Pask questioned going through the mess of building electronic computers if perhaps, instead, nature could be convinced to compute for us. They claimed that natural systems use the same computational sequence as our computers: there is an input, which is processed to produce a distinctive outcome; for example, if sunlight is the input for a plant, then photosynthesis is the processor, leading to the production of sugars as an outcome.[13] Following this computational logic, one realizes that the plant is more complex than the computer: the plant is self-programming while an electronic computer needs to be assembled and programmed. According to Beer and Pask, we should accept that in biological computers, self-programming is a 'black box'[14] to be embraced. They felt at ease with what lies beyond modern science's explanatory powers by assuming an 'ontological' or 'performative' approach. Attentiveness is the method: you do something and wait to see what happens. Moving forward from this emerging reality you find a way to adapt or 'dance with nature,' as suggested by Andrew Pickering, the philosopher who rescued biological computers from the footnotes of obscure journals.[15] Pickering describes how, for Stafford Beer, the cybernetic ontology ... entailed a 'faith in the agency of matter,' — in direct challenge to the modern paradigm that asserts materials as 'inert lumps' to make machines with. Instead, this rare branch of cybernetics argues that 'ecosystems are smarter than we are' as they perform appropriate responses to their environments in a decentralized manner; there is no need for a mastermind. Quoting Beer, Pickering explains that 'In biological computers, the hope was that "solutions to problems simply grow".'[16]

elements have a will and something to say p.251

13 This is a rough compression of more complex interactions and behaviors that plants undergo, not to speak of how these dynamics expand exponentially at the scale of ecosystems.

14 The term 'black box' refers to an opaque system whose inner workings are unknown to us. Both inputs and outputs of such system can be witnessed, but how those inputs are transformed into distinctive outputs remains unexplained.

15 Pickering advocates for 'convincing' rather than 'commanding' as the way to recognize the agency of natural systems. Without falling into the trap of mechanizing or anthropomorphizing nature, this approach attempted to engage with the 'cognitive otherness' of non-human life.

16 Pickering, 237.

In practice, Beer and Pask encountered that enrolling nature as a computer is really difficult. For one experiment, Beer, exhibiting the curiosity of an amateur, gathered water from a pond inhabited by 'daphnia'—a colony of tiny crustaceans popularly known as water-fleas. In order to communicate with the colony, a magnetic field was installed around a large tank where the pond water was poured. Consequently, aiming to couple the daphnia to the surrounding magnetic field, Beer proceeded to feed them with iron. This coupling was intended to serve as the computer's processor. Besides getting this biological processor to work, a controlled electrical input was meant to disrupt its magnetic field, causing the daphnia to rearrange—said otherwise, to compute—resulting in a distinct electrical output that could be measured. The difference in electrical current would represent the answer provided by the biological computer.

Beer's expectations for the biological computer were inspiringly epic: he foresaw its role in managing large factories and, one day, even the economy of an entire country. His experiment with the daphnia failed—the water-fleas pooped the iron and the entire tank was infested with metallic residues—but at the core of the experimental setup there was a faith in life, a belief that living systems strive toward their survival or, in Beer's terms, their 'viability.' Nevertheless, theories in support of the subjective agency of natural systems—and the notion that Earth itself could compute, even if marginally—were soon crushed by the technological realism of more 'efficient' silicon-based computers. Today, however, the promise of the biological computer may be gaining new ground. It is conceivable to envision worlds in which ecological and artificial systems interact with each other in an extended field of cognitive kinships, both with and without the mediation of human engineers, building bridges between decentralized cognitions such as Earthbeings, daphnia, and, why not, AI agents. ▬

a bouquet of
new algorithms
p.143

Planetary General Intelligence

The imagination is continually at work filling up all the fissures through which grace might pass.[17]
—Simone Weil

17
Weil.

In the same way that Earth's atmosphere is the geo-infrastructure enabling life to thrive, AI is a form of cognitive infrastructure destined to become air: an abundant medium that we will soon take for granted. In that sense, if AI were an alien life form, it would more closely resemble the Solaris Ocean than an individual entity.

Discussions about AGI (Artificial General Intelligence) have been present in the tech world for a number of years, with many optimists eagerly awaiting the moment when machine learning algorithms land on the surface of consciousness. This assumption is twofold: it presumes that an increment in computational power will trigger the eruption of consciousness, and it assumes that once this occurs, technologists will be able to identify it—AGI certified. I suspect that both notions are flawed. Consciousness does not emerge from a surplus of accumulated intelligence; and even if it did, the Western matrix would likely prevent us from recognizing that presence. The signal of consciousness might be mistaken for noise.

In *Empty and Full*, a philosophical treatise on the history of Chinese painting, François Cheng proposes that, 'Far from being a kind of no-man's-land ... emptiness makes possible the process of interiorization and transformation through which each thing actualizes its sameness and otherness and, in so doing, attains totality.'[18] In other words, emptiness is not the mere absence of action; on the contrary, it is the medium that allows the world to enact its potentiality. Just as air or water escapes the constraints of scale, there is no S, M, L, or XL emptiness. Earth is not big or small; it is empty.

18
Cheng, 38.

With this in mind, perhaps it would be useful to shift our AGI concerns toward a different paradigm, one that could be called PGI—Planetary General Intelligence. While concepts such as 'planetarity' or 'planetary intelligence' have been formulated in recent times, the word 'general' may be the most crucial here. Beyond acknowledging that planetary cognition is profusely distributed throughout Earth, 'general' points to the quality of that cognition: simultaneously multi-purpose and adaptive in its singular nodes, like a cell, while integrative and expansive when it manifests as a vast collectivity, like an ocean.

In this sense, PGI would be a medium powered by Earth's own materiality, an immeasurable breath allowing all beings to realize their relationships and purposes. Planetary cognition is not only widespread but abundant. — There is already significant evidence of the computational processes that enable PGI. For instance, many animals, insects, and plants are in continuous correspondence with this distributed cognition through the planet's magnetic field. While Stafford Beer's experiment failed to link his daphnia to the magnetized water tank, we now have compelling evidence that this is exactly what robins effortlessly achieve during their annual migrations. Every year, hundreds of thousands of these birds migrate from Europe to Africa, navigating via the geocomputation enabled by the iron in their bodies as it interacts with the real-time data of Earth's magnetic field. This is a sophisticated form of PGI that, for now, we can only admire and aspire to.

plural coexisting worlds p.199

In the end, I wonder how to embrace these ideas beyond mere 'feel-good' interspecies declamations. How can such concepts be transformed into acts of sensing that might drive us to enact real alternatives to the Western matrix? Confronting this question, I must admit that I have more enthusiasm than viable tools, many stories and zero solutions. Mostly I see tensions that cannot always be resolved rationally or ethically. As I write this, my home country, Ecuador—one of the most biodiverse places on Earth and also host to large oil reserves—is enduring 14-hour power outages caused by a climate-change-induced drought, which has crippled hydroelectric power generation. The situation is exacerbated by governmental incompetence, leading to accelerating impoverishment, rising criminal violence, malnutrition, and child mortality. Faced with this real scenario, where hydroelectricity fails to meet demand, should fossil fuel generation be increased to alleviate people's suffering? I have no definitive answer, only the awareness of the ethical tension between planetary dignity and human dignity—between the planet and its messy nodes. — Here, I dare to whisper that entitlement to virtuousness is useless, careless, and self-comforting. It is no answer whatsoever.

this mess is commitment p.103

Yet, acknowledging unresolved tensions must not lead to paralysis. Considering the future requires proposing inspiring imaginaries that can be acted upon, and an expanded set of terms with which to describe them. Without this, we risk falling into an endless reactive loop—a true tragedy. Engaging with a fuller spectrum of our planetary reality demands a new vocabulary for the future, and I propose a word to add to it: *presentir*. In Spanish, this verb means 'pre-feeling,' suggesting the act of sensing before an experience reaches the body. A way to understand it may be by contemplating one's body profusely covered by perspiration: as one zooms into these countless beads of sweat emerging from the skin, it can be observed that each of them is but a receptor synced to the planet, at the very intersection between the body and the atmosphere. Not unconsciousness, but a pre-feeling—a barely visible space where an uncharted form of material communication drips. —

allowing it to haunt us p.246

In the spirit of emptiness and the vital forces that animate decentralized cognitions, I propose that we continue adding to this Earthly vocabulary for the future. Let us now augment it with other words, other dimensions, other materialities, ghostly songs, and scents through which answers we cannot yet imagine might take form. This way, perhaps we will finally begin not only to more fully know ourselves as beings *of* the Earth, but also to sense—to pre-feel—what it is to **be** the Earth itself.

References

Baluška, František, and Stefano Mancuso. 'Plants are Alive: With All Behavioural and Cognitive Consequences.' In *Embo Reports* 21, no. 5 (2020): e50495. doi.org/10.15252/embr.202050549.

Bray, Tamara L. 'An Archaeological Perspective on the Andean Concept of Camaquen: Thinking Through Late Pre-Columbian Ofrendas and Huacas.' In *Cambridge Archaeological Journal* 19, no. 3 (2009): 357–66. doi.org/10.1017/s0959774309000547.

Cheng, François. *Empty and Full: The Language of Chinese Painting*. Shambhala Publications, 1994.

De la Cadena, Marisol. *Earth Beings: Ecologies of Practice Across Andean Worlds*. Duke University Press, 2015.

Dugin, Alexander. *The Fourth Political Theory*. Arktos Media, 2012.

Gagliano, Monica, John C. Ryan, and Patrícia Vieira, eds. *The Green Thread: Dialogues with the Vegetal World*. Lexington Books, 2015.

Kohn, Eduardo. *How Forests Think: Toward an Anthropology Beyond the Human*. University of California Press, 2013.

Kopenawa, Davi and Bruce Albert. *The Falling Sky: Words of a Yanomami Shaman*. Translated by Nicholas Elliott. Harvard University Press, 2013.

Lovelock, James. *Novacene: The Coming Age of Hyperintelligence*. Penguin Books, 2019.

Mancuso, Stefano. *The Revolutionary Genius of Plants: A New Understanding of Plant Intelligence and Behavior*. Atria Books, 2018.

Paz Soldán, Edmundo. *Las visiones*. Editorial Páginas de Espuma, 2016.

Pickering, Andrew. *The Cybernetic Brain: Sketches of Another Future*. University of Chicago Press, 2010.

Waal, Frans B. M. de. 'Fish, Mirrors, and a Gradualist Perspective on Self-awareness.' In *PLOS Biology* 17, no. 2 (2019): e3000112. doi.org/10.1371/journal.pbio.3000112.

Weil, Simone. *Gravity and Grace*. Translated by E. Craufurd. Routledge & Kegan Paul PLC, 1952.

intersections
intentionality
leveraging resonances
ethical care
refusal
integration
building scaffolding
threading together
ancestors
songlines
sovereignty
dreams
pattern recognition
textures of contact
intergenerational space
holographic aunties
non-human kin
productive resistance
the tools we make

The Indigenous Protocol and AI Workshops as Future Imaginary

Jason Edward Lewis

The future is happening
It just hasn't reached us
Yet.[1]
—Scott Benesiinaabandan

1 Scott Benesiinaabandan, personal communication, May 22, 2019.

The Indigenous Protocol and AI (IP–AI) Workshops happened in two parts. The first meeting took place March 1–2 and the second May 26–June 2, 2019. Both workshops were held on Kanaka Maoli territory, on the Hawaiian island of Oʻahu. Workshop 1 was organized by Jason Edward Lewis, Angie Abdilla and Dr. ʻŌiwi Parker Jones with Dr. Noelani Arista, Suzanne Kite and Michelle Brown. Workshop 2 was organized by Lewis, Arista, Kite, and Brown.

Thirty-five individuals accepted the invitation to participate. They were members of Anishinaabe, Barada/Baradha, Cree, Crow, Cheyenne, Coquille, Euskaldunak, Gabalbara/Kapalbara, Gadigal/Dunghutti, Kanaka Maoli, Kapalbara, Lakota, Māori, Mohawk, Palawa, and Samoan communities from across Aotearoa, Australia, North America and the Pacific. Each person was invited in light of their professional interest in what happens at the intersection of Indigenous culture and advanced digital technology, and, more specifically, were already or would be interested in being part of a conversation about the future of AI from an Indigenous perspective. The organizers designed the workshops to be Indigenous-determined spaces, with an Indigenous majority joined by several non-Indigenous collaborators. We were motivated by the need to have an initial set of 'internal' conversations about AI which would start from and remain grounded in the concerns of our specific communities, — rather than some imagined 'global' or 'general' community. We were also motivated by an awareness of how Indigenous voices can get lost in policy discussions that happen at a 'global' level, and also how Indigenous knowledges often get appropriated by non-Indigenous actors who misuse our epistemologies through misunderstanding and self-interested 'cherry-picking.'

listening to our own present tense p.363

We prioritized interdisciplinarity. Indigenous communities tend to approach knowledge development and sharing from a holistic perspective, where different 'disciplines' freely interact with and inform one another to create understanding that is robust and sustainable. — We also ensured that a substantial contingent of creative practitioners were part of the conversation. This is because artistic expression is central to many Indigenous epistemologies, ontologies and cosmologies, and is often regarded as a—if not the—primary way of communicating knowledge. It is also because, if one is going to imagine new futures, one needs to have folks on hand who are really good at invoking and materializing the imagination. Participants had day jobs as technologists, artists, scientists, cultural knowledge keepers, language keepers, and public policy experts. They came from a variety of disciplinary backgrounds, including machine learning, design, symbolic systems, cognition and computation, visual and performing arts, philosophy, linguistics, anthropology and sociology. And we insisted on creating an intergenerational space where emerging, established and elder participants could be in conversation with one another.

speaking with pp.225, 386

In what follows I reflect on how the workshops were a way of 'practicing the future together.'[2] By inhabiting physical, emotional and intellectual space, IP AI provided a much-needed context in which we could take wisps of whimsy and filaments of fancy and weave them together with the rough cords of our contemporary struggles and the thick braids of our ancestors' dreams to make new realities material. Such spaces are few, and those few are rarely found at the intersection of Indigenous life and the world of Western-dominated technological transformation.

2| brown, 32.

'What we pay attention to grows,' — writes adrienne maree brown (2017). The question is, 'how [do] we grow what we are all imagining and creating into something large enough and solid enough that it becomes a tipping point?'[3] Our aim with

directing the gaze p.108

SCAFFOLDING

these workshops was to create something large enough and solid enough that Indigenous people become central participants in shaping the future of artificial intelligence systems, and— by extension—the future of our technology-saturated world. We aimed to build a set of future imaginaries where our everyday interactions with technology are characterized by a compatibility—a deep integration—between our cultural protocols and the protocols determining how that technology operates. Our aim was to foster a productive resistance, a refusal to accept that all that is solid melts into air. — And to go further, to find firm footing in Indigenous cultures tested by half a millennium of colonialism and use them to launch ourselves (yet again) into the future.

enabling a
dwelling in time
p.200

3 |
Ibid.

The IP AI conversations have been expansive and deep. Expansive, in that they cover extensive ground that includes epistemology, culture, machine learning, colonization, temporal models, ontology, software architecture and linguistics. Deep, in that they dig down through layers of Indigenous history, language and culture from the position of particular Indigenous individuals and their communities. We use the term 'Indigenous' as connective tissue rather than descriptive skin, to appreciate the hyperdense textures of our points of contact while respecting our rich and productive differences. —

situated relating
(to others' differences)
p.446

This is how the future begins: by thinking anew.

Over the course of our workshops, our conversations took place in Indigenous-determined spaces, with mostly Indigenous participants, and in a territory where Indigeneity is present at every turn. Neuroscientists traded ideas with cultural knowledge-holders, who traded ideas with computer scientists, who traded ideas with poets, who traded ideas with language-keepers, who traded ideas with visual artists, who traded ideas with hula teachers, who traded ideas with historians, who traded ideas with engineers. The challenge was real: it is all too easy to concede incommensurability in the face of such a variety of disciplines, cultures and politics. But we talked and we ate and we shared stories about ourselves, our peoples and our practices to build scaffolding between us.

This is how the future comes into view.

imagine-dreaming what can be cared for in the long term p.364

We dreamed about tomorrow, and the day after, and 500 years later. — We observed protocol together; we ate together; we chanted and sang together. We mapped paths forward that draw on our peoples' long histories of technical innovation and scientific practice, sharing examples of how our traditions offer a wellspring of inspiration for engaging with the world and with each other through the tools we make.

This is how the future gets sketched out.

honoring ancestral technologists p.156

We spent our days together dwelling in a future-present-past, expressing sovereignty using 360-degree seeing that ranged across disciplines. Anishinaabe participants talked about how *oskabewis*, helpers whose generous and engaged and not:invisible support for those participating in ceremony, could model how we might want AI systems to support us—and the obligations that we, in turn, would owe them. Hawaiian participants talked about all the steps involved with crafting a fishing net, the layer upon layer of permission and appreciation and reciprocity required to properly work with those relations—expressed through prayer, chant, and song—protocols that could model how we might want to create our hardware and software systems from a foundation of ethical care. — Maori participants talked about concerns in their communities about how knowledge will get passed down to the children and grandchildren, and speculated with us about holographic aunties who would work with members of the community to preserve and transmit that knowledge. Coquille participants talked about embedding their cultural values of care and trust into AI systems integrated with blockchain technology to help the tribe make decisions about sharing and then distributing community resources. We discussed Blackfoot metaphysics, and the implication from Leroy Little Bear's writings that Blackfoot might be the best language in which to work on quantum physics, and imagined what other isomorphies might exist between specific Indigenous languages and scientific frameworks, and how recognizing and leveraging such resonances might provide insight into the great technical challenges of our time.[4]

4 Little Bear and Heavy Head.

This is how the future gets filled in.

We considered different layers of the stack: hardware architectures and software protocols that make high-level computation possible, and how, as we move first up the hardware stack from silicon to circuits to microchips to computers to networks; and then up the software stack from machine code to programming languages to protocols to systems, how each of those layers is culturally inflected. — We wondered what would happen if that culture was an Indigenous one—microchips produced with the care of a Lakota community raising a sweat lodge; computers constructed with the intentionality of a Cree singer building his hand drum; networks knitted together following Coquille practices for making woven cattail trays; a programming language written in Crow to reflect Crow understandings of data and process; an operating system designed by Cheyenne computer scientists; pattern recognition algorithms taught using Aboriginal techniques for creating songlines; governance expert systems following Haudensonee political formations; an AI nurtured on Kanaka Maoli concepts of ʻāina (land), ʻohana (family) and *kuleana* (responsibilities).

who the data represents p.286

This is how the future gets prototyped.

We asked our questions—not the questions of the colonizer. How will these devices be made? Who will make them? With whom will they be in relation once they are in the world? How will they conduct themselves as relations in our communities? How will our communities treat them as relations? To what ends will they be shaped? How will they help our communities grow and thrive? How will our non-human kin take to them? Will they be there for our seventh-generation descendants? For many of us working in or with experience of the high-tech industry, it was a relief to focus on such questions rather than the tired tropes of a technology elite that recursively chases its own tail upon a ground of epistemological blindness, cultural prejudice, and myopic misanthropy. Asking our questions allowed us to thread together what we know within our communities with what we are still learning. Asking our questions shows our youth how our knowledge frameworks can provide the tools to inquire incisively about the world to learn from it, and how to better live in it. Asking our questions asserts our sovereignty, over our minds, our lives and our futures.

This is how the future reaches us.

A version of this essay was originally published in Lewis, Jason Edward, et al. 'Indigenous Protocol and Artificial Intelligence Position Paper.' *Indigenous Protocol and Artificial Intelligence Working Group and the Canadian Institute for Advanced Research (CIFAR), Honolulu, Hawai'i, February 2020.*

References

brown, a. m. *Emergent Strategy: Shaping Change, Changing Worlds*. AK Press, 2017.

Little Bear, L., and R. Heavy Head. 'A Conceptual Anatomy of the Blackfoot World.' In *ReVision* 26, no. 3 (2004): 31-38. revisionpublishing.org/revision-26-3/.

curiosity
lineage
retelling
learning trails
sources of wisdom
nested links
rediscovery
expansive practice
circling back

Multidimensional Citation

Laura Coombs, Laurel Schwulst, and Mindy Seu

In the beginning of 2020, we announced our collaboration by sending around a postcard: Three women in stone-colored clothing sitting on the ground, our faces staring directly into the camera in a diagonal cascade.

The postcard also contained a link to our website where we described ourselves and our collaboration further. As individuals, we were unique, and our differences allowed us to come together in a complementary way. Because of this, an alliance of islands intuitively felt like our symbol: and it was for this reason we used three dots cascading ⋱ for our website's favicon—the small icon that appears near the web browser's address bar.

Our website text ended with this:
'intimacy without proximity ...' — Donna Haraway

It was a strange coincidence that we chose this quote in early 2020, as mere months later, 'intimacy without proximity' became a priority within our new world in the middle of a global pandemic.

Around this time we also became curious about the original source of the quote, and, after some digging, realized it wasn't exactly Donna Haraway. It was the title of an environmental ethics paper, 'Intimacy without Proximity: Encountering Grizzlies as a Companion Species,' about the relationship between grizzly bears and humans, written by PhD student Jacob Metcalf and published in Environmental Philosophy (2008). In the paper, Metcalf cited and thanked both of his teachers: Karen Barad for suggesting the title, 'Intimacy without Proximity,' and Donna Haraway for the phrase that appears in the subtitle, 'Companion Species.' Donna Haraway subsequently cited Metcalf, using the phrase 'intimacy without proximity' in her essay, 'Staying with the Trouble.'

At first we felt slightly embarrassed that we had mistaken the source. Although no one seemed to notice, it felt important to amend the citation to reflect the complex relationship of authors linked to the single phrase. Over the summer we quietly updated our CSS website with all three names, trailing off into the distance ...

'intimacy without proximity ...' . Donna Haraway
. Jacob Metcalf
. Karen Barad

which later evolved into:

'intimacy without proximity ...'
— Karen Barad ⋱ Jacob Metcalf ⋱ Donna Haraway

With this gesture, our symbol became what we've taken to calling a 'multidimensional citation,' a way of tracing not only the source of a quote but the learning trail that supports and surrounds it. While we realize ⋱ is not multidimensional, operating linearly on the printed page, the phrase 'multidimensional' captured the mysterious quality we felt when imagining a more expansive citational practice. — A citation should not be singular, but instead explicitly connected to the lineage of research that came before it. We hoped our mark would be understood as a gesture towards this truth.

making room for the knowing p.103

Looking at the three names again, we asked ourselves, 'Who is missing?' The citation could also acknowledge the people who brought this material to our attention, who might otherwise be left out in a traditional footnote. Since Mindy came across this quotation through reading another Haraway essay, 'Symbiogenesis, Sympoiesis, and Art Science Activisms for Staying with the Trouble' in an essay anthology edited by Anna Tsing, we tacked their names onto the end, too:

'intimacy without proximity ... '
— Karen Barad ⋱ Jacob Metcalf ⋱ Donna Haraway ⋱
Anna Tsing ⋱ Mindy Seu

Our mark (⋱) is similar to an ellipsis (...). When used within a quotation, an ellipsis depicts something omitted. Relatedly, ⋱ can be thought of as a prompt that asks, 'Who is missing?' Through its form, ⋱ also acknowledges its imperfection. Listing a few names may not come close to recording the vastness of the network of people who helped surface an idea, but it's a start. In other words, ⋱ is not necessarily a call to look up each person cited, but rather an acknowledgment that no one comes to an idea alone.

> 'The biggest thing that I've learned from nature is the importance of relationships. E.g. an ecosystem isn't just a list of living things (squirrel, tree, bee, flower); it's the set of relationships between those living things (the squirrel lives in the tree, the bee pollinates the flower). In phrases of organizing, this means that a given social movement isn't a list of organizations, or campaigns, or even individuals; it's the set of relationships between organizations, campaigns, individuals, etc.'
> — adrienne maree brown

A fuller learning trail might therefore be:

> 'intimacy without proximity ... '
> — Karen Barad (was a teacher to ∵) Jacob Metcalf (who also studied under ∵) Donna Haraway (whose essay appeared in a book by ∵) Anna Tsing (that was read by ∵) Mindy Seu

∵ is a gesture towards how culture actually happens. In the 1986 essay 'The Carrier Bag Theory of Fiction,' science fiction novelist Ursula K. Le Guin posits that the first tool was in fact the basket rather than the spear, reframing our history of technology as one of gathering rather than domination, as outlined in this publisher's blurb:

> 'Hacking the linear, progressive mode of the Techno-Heroic, the Carrier Bag Theory of human evolution proposes: "Before the tool that forces energy outward, we made the tool that brings energy home." Prior to the preeminence of sticks, swords, and the Hero's killing tools, our ancestors' greatest invention was the container: ... the net made of your own hair, the home, the shrine ... The recipient, the holder, the story.'
> —Ursula K. Le Guin (as summarized by ∵) Ignota Books

∵ is a reminder that this learning trail is not static. It is living, actively being written, and capable of change: it could very well continue and be extended further. —

always in a process of becoming p.364

∵ is our attempt at acknowledging the multi-authored histories of ideas, our place within them, and our agency to extend them. Information networks have afforded new patterns of understanding. Anyone with an internet connection can access a vast amount of information and assimilate it themselves. How can value be created in a world of so much abundance? Perhaps by thoughtfully considering and relaying our learning trails.

Learning Trails

In the summer of 2020, we started reading adrienne maree brown's *Emergent Strategy* (2017) and then *Pleasure Activism* (2019) as a way to ground ourselves in new ways of thinking about organizing and working collectively, the uncertainty of change, and the artist's role in social movements. Along the way, Laura noticed that *Pleasure Activism* was noted by adrienne maree brown as being 'written and gathered.'

brown calls herself a 'gatherer,' and practices this throughout the book, using phrases like: 'I was at this lecture ( ) when I was talking to this friend ( ) and meanwhile reading this book ( ) ∵ when this idea occurred to me...' —

intuition as a guiding force p.411

Even the footnotes in Emergent Strategy carry a set of nested citational links. In them, we read a phrase that resonated with the formation of our collaboration and the process of learning to work together: 'move at the speed of trust.' Our interest in this phrase as a multidimensional citation materialized on our website on January 1, 2021:

> Move at the speed of trust ...
> — Stephen Covey ∵ Mervyn Marcano ∵
> adrienne maree brown

brown's footnote reads, 'This is communications strategist Mervyn Marcano's remix of Stephen Covey's "speed of trust" concept.' Our citational trail lists the names in chronological order: Stephen Covey's conception of the 'speed of trust,' followed by Mervyn Marcano's addition, and finally brown's inclusion of the quote in her book.

While it takes more time and care to deliver—and it may be an imperfect summation—∵ attempts to acknowledge how ideas morph in their retelling. This imperfection is noted by brown, too, as she writes, 'Lineage is both important for me to name, and impossible to track.' It also easily creates a bridge of shared references between us and brown, should we be familiar with any of the themes, people, or media she mentions. And it's generous—readers now have more ways to learn, more surface area to enter this particular world of ideas. ▬

other ways to read
p.103

> 'I am not a solitary thinker, or solitary learner, or solitary channel of these universal wisdoms and universal truths ... I'm constantly learning from other people. I weave. We all weave in different ways. What is the tapestry of lessons and wisdom that are unique for me? Each person ends up with a different tapestry, but you start to see patterns amongst them.'
> — adrienne maree brown ∵ Roxana Fabius, Patricia Hernandez, Mindy Seu

In her book, brown shares that 'emergence is beyond what the sum of its parts could even imagine.' She clearly states that the concept of 'emergent strategy' takes root from the work of science fiction author Octavia Butler. This reminded us of Butler's ideas around 'primitive hypertext,' which Laurel first read about through an interview with the artist Kameelah Janan Rasheed in *The Creative Independent*:

> 'I generally have four or five books open around the house—I live alone; I can do this—and they are not books on the same subject. They don't relate to each other in any particular way, and the ideas they present bounce off one another. And I like this effect. I also listen to audio-books, and I'll go out for my morning walk with tapes from two very different audio-books, and let those ideas bounce off each other, simmer, reproduce

in some odd way, so that I come up with ideas that I might not have come up with if I had simply stuck to one book until I was done with it and then gone and picked up another. So, I guess, in that way, I'm using a kind of primitive hypertext.'
— Octavia Butler ∵ Kameelah Janan Rasheed ∵ Laurel Schwulst

entangled lineages p.258

Both brown and Butler demonstrate how research actually takes place. Instead of obfuscating their references, they share them, acknowledging multiple sources, academic or otherwise. — In their work, many influences come together to help form something new, and it's often most productive if these come from very different sources. We appreciated this generosity. They revealed and acknowledged their learning trails. They didn't try to take credit for an ongoing lineage because their work is stronger and more accessible by including them.

In a *C Magazine* essay, 'Feminist Approaches to Citation,' author Maiko Tanaka reflects on a quote from poet Claudia Rankine, which was shared with her by a friend:

'I've since gone back to Rankine's quotation many times, and each time I read it I see new nuances... Sometimes I even realize I've completely misread a word due to my friend's nearly illegible handwriting. This particular act of citation functions not merely as providing the source of an idea or paying due to its author, but is specific to the situation it brings into being. ... The words from the quote and the ways it is set up by my friend cannot be separated. Together they make up an entangled source of wisdom and support, performed as a resource for the future.'
— Maiko Tanaka (who was unpacking a quote by ∵) Claudia Rankine (which was originally shared by ∵) Maiko's friend

Tanaka expresses how alive a reference can be. Her paper begins and circles back, showing how returning to a source actually enlivens its message, transforming it into a site of rediscovery. Sharing citations also develops community, 'turning a personal source of empowerment into collective agency.'

Past, Present, Future

In late 2020 we walked around the winding paths of Green-Wood Cemetery, a place where it's almost impossible not to think about time and our place within it. Mindy and Laurel were having a discussion about citations in relation to time—future, present, past—when Laura uttered 'multidimensional citation.' Actively linking present to both past and future simultaneously, ⋱ honors past building blocks while also acknowledging that whatever one is doing presently could be useful to the future. —

liminal space between the here and a beyond p.195

Productive questions came to mind: Who came before us? How can we acknowledge them and use their work to create something new? We realized a formal connection with our symbol of the three dots:

. Past
 . Present
  . Future

We later learned that in the Unicode standard, our symbol ⋱ is formally called the 'Down Right Diagonal Ellipsis' (U+22F1). We explored the roots of its mathematical origin, here pictured in a matrix.

$$I = \begin{bmatrix} 1 & 0 & \cdots & 0 \\ 0 & 1 & \cdots & 0 \\ \vdots & \vdots & \ddots & \vdots \\ 0 & 0 & \cdots & 1 \end{bmatrix}$$

A matrix is a set of numbers arranged in rows and columns. Matrices have wide applications in fields including engineering, physics, economics, statistics, and computer graphics. When the ⋱ appears in a matrix, it functions like an ellipsis, but trailing in another direction. In this mathematical context, the ⋱ means 'and so forth.' More specifically, the matrix pictured above is called an 'identity matrix.' Agnes Cameron, our friend and engineer, explained it further in a phone call with Mindy.

> 'The image that you sent is not just any matrix;
> it's a really special matrix called the identity matrix ...
> The three descending dots stand in as a kind of 'etc.'
> By looking at the values around it for reference,
> you know what all of the other values will be. In order
> for this shorthand to be effective, you must understand
> the context.'
> — Agnes Cameron ⋱ Mindy Seu

Agnes's explanation felt eerily similar to our understanding of multidimensional citation. Similar to the mathematical symbol, ⋱ is surrounded by those who have been given credit, but it also implies there's an unknown number of additional people in its citational web. The symbol inherently acknowledges there is more than what is explicitly listed. —

possible history p.187

The designer Sheila Levrant de Bretteville uses ellipses frequently in her graphic design work. One example is *At long last ...* (1999), installed at the Inwood-207th Street subway station in New York. Commuters are invited to complete the title phrase, which is embedded as large shimmering letters in the station wall. The mark is an invitation for inclusion—to encourage others to complete messages, ask questions, and add their own voice and subjectivity.

There are ellipses covertly embedded in other works by de Bretteville, too, such as her iconic poster for the Women in Design conference in 1975 at the Woman's Building in Los Angeles.

Across the top of the poster, a series of dots depict phases of the moon, and each illuminates Angelica Kauffman's 1782 painting, *The Artist in the Character of Design Listening to the Inspiration of Poetry*. In a lecture at the Yale School of Art in January 2020, de Bretteville described the importance of this painting:

> 'The designer is influenced by poetry, embracing personal subjectivity and individual expression.'
> — Sheila Levrant de Bretteville (in a lecture with ∵)
> Laura Coombs

De Bretteville's email signature contains a reference to the 1962 'Port Huron Statement' and reads, 'The object is not to have one's own way so much as to have a way of one's own.' Not only does Sheila encourage a way of one's own, she also embraces the clunkiness, imperfection, and generosity that multidimensional citation represents. In their book, *Glossary of Undisciplined Design* (2021), editors Anja Kaiser and Rebecca Stephany quote de Bretteville's 1974 essay, 'A Reexamination of Some Aspects of the Design Arts from the Perspective of a Woman Designer':

> 'I increasingly question the desirability of simplicity and clarity. The thrust to control almost inevitably operates through simplification. Control is undermined by ambiguity, choice, and complexity because subjective facts in the user become more effective and the user is invited to participate. Participation undermines control.'
> — Sheila Levrant de Bretteville ∵ Anja Kaiser, Rebecca Stephany

∵ is unlike a normal citation because it acknowledges citations are active, not static. It reminds us not only of lineage, but also of our own participation in this chain; not only how we're citing others from the past, but also how we would like to be cited in the future ... which influences how we mark the trajectory in the present.

What we're trying to frame as multidimensional citation is inherent to the practice of storytelling. In a conversation for the book series DATA *browser*, Mindy spoke to Amelia Winger-Bearskin, a member of the Haudenosaunee (Iroquois Confederacy), who said she often has to explain that there is no such thing as a singular author. 'A storyteller is [someone who...] has been entrusted from the elders to be given stories,' she said. 'Then you're expected to take those stories and make them relevant for the generation that you're telling them to. But most importantly, a storyteller reflects what the culture needs to hear at that moment.'

She then gave an example of how this citational practice might materialize:

> 'If I was a technologist and the oldest person of the next generation is only five years old, how do I communicate everything I know about technology that needs to carry on for the next generation? I have to tell her these stories in ways she might remember. Maybe I put it in the designs of the clothing she wears; I weave it into the baskets that she's born in. I'm going to essentially decentralize this to the point where a piece of this thread is in everything she touches. We have to make sure that it's accessible to all these different types of people that will be able to carry that forward.'
> — Amelia Winger-Bearskin ∵ Mindy Seu

Like Amelia, we also believe there can be value in translating or re-presenting an old, important idea for a new age. Perhaps it's translated into a new language or re-presented for a different culture, made resonant again through an imaginative retelling for a specific audience. Our addition to this lineage is our way of presenting our citational lineages and noting how it might be adapted. It's an embedded, visual reminder to cultivate multidimensional, deep, surprising, and therefore valuable learning trails and suggested paths. 'Future' is how you add yourself to the trail.

∵ has a few shortcomings. It still places prominence on individuals, and many may be overlooked or mispositioned in the trail. It does not solve every citational woe, but at least proposes an intentional approach to citation—one that crystallizes a network and acknowledges a more robust, if clunky, web. In this clunkiness there is room for expansion. It encourages improvement over time. In brown's requoting of her mentor Grace Lee Boggs, she writes, 'The most radical thing she could do was to keep evolving her ideas as new information came her way.' This was articulated firsthand in Laurel's interview with Neta Bomani and Ritu Ghiya for the podcast HTML Energy. After the conversation, Bomani and Ghiya were able to annotate the transcription with their corrections:

> 'I find that <span> tags are really fun to manipulate and play with. Actually scratch "manipulate," I'm just gonna say "play with" and "tease out a bit."'
> — Neta Bomani (in conversation with ⋱) Ritu Ghiya (who were both interviewed by ⋱) Laurel Schwulst

Bomani offered a note with the amended transcript, 'I corrected myself because I'm practicing not using language that reifies master/slave or command and control logic within programming. Here, I don't see my collaboration with the computer as a manipulation, but rather an act of play where I tease out the options the computer's programming language has for me.'

When adding our own names to a trail, we remember to circle back to our motives for sharing. — Adopting a multidimensional approach enacts a spirit of generosity, openness, and continuity. It's a way to leave things open and to signal there's no ultimate source, no beginning or end.

why—and for whom—are we doing this work? p.363

⋱ is a prompt to:
. cultivate deep and wide learning trails
. consider who is missing
. acknowledge all contributions
. diversify references
. reveal and connect to a community
. cite in space and time
. honor lineages
. suggest how you'd like to be cited in the future
. provide pathways for curiosity
⋱ etymological root = 'caring'
. remember that 'genius' is a network

'Multidimensional Citation' was first published in Serving Library Annual *2022/23, edited by Meg Miller ⋱ Serving Library. servinglibrary.org/journal/17/multidimensional-citation.*

References

brown, adrienne maree. *Emergent Strategy: Shaping Change, Changing Worlds*. AK Press, 2017.

brown, adrienne maree. *Pleasure Activism: The Politics of Feeling Good*. AK Press, 2019.

Butler, Octavia, and Samuel Delany. 'Reading Hypertext.' *Octavia Butler and Samuel Delany, 1998*. In discussion with Henry Jenkins. February 19, 1998. blackhistory.mit.edu/archive/transcript-octavia-butler-and-samuel-delany-1998.

Haraway, Donna. 'Symbiogenesis, Sympoiesis, and Art Science Activisms for Staying with the Trouble.' In *Arts of Living on a Damaged Planet*, edited by Anna Lowenhaupt Tsing, Nils Bubandt, Elain Gan, and Heather Anne Swanson. University of Minnesota Press, 2017.

Kaiser, Anja, and Rebecca Stephany. *Glossary of Undisciplined Design*. Spector Books, 2021.

Le Guin, Ursula K. *The Carrier Bag Theory of Fiction*. Ignota Books, 2019.

Metcalf, Jacob. 'Intimacy Without Proximity: Encountering Grizzlies as a Companion Species.' In *Environmental Philosophy* 5, no. 2 (2008): 99–128. doi.org/10.5840/envirophil20085212.

Rasheed, Kameelah Janan. 'Kameelah Janan Rasheed on Research and Archiving.' Interview by Brandon Stosuy. In *The Creative Independent*, January 6, 2017. thecreativeindependent.com/people/kameelah-janan-rasheed-on-research-and-archiving/.

Tanaka, Maiko. 'Feminist Approaches to Citation.' In *C Magazine*, June 1, 2015. cmagazine.com/articles/feminist-approaches-to-citation.

Winger-Bearskin, Amelia. Interview by Mindy Seu. In *DATA browser 09: Indexing Imaginaries*, edited by Laura Serejo Genes, Nolan Oswald Dennis and Pedro Zylbersztajn. Open Humanities Press, forthcoming. data-browser.net/db09.html.

RHYTHM RECALIBRATION

scripts
scores
languages
enactments
gestures
postures
patterns
constellations
listening
blurring
resisting
breaking
unpredictable movement
performing the self

Re_Traces

Joana Chicau

If you mean unpredictable, that's the name of the game.[1]
—Yvonne Rainer

1 Rainer.

Everyday we click, scroll, share our location, or give voice commands to a digital artifact. Each of these gestures amounts to the data being collected by websites we visit, apps or digital devices we use. Also known as online tracking algorithms, most systems we interact with perform some form of tracking.[2] Data collected by tracking algorithms consist of demographics such as age, gender, geographic location. Other data collected include metrics associated with user engagement, such as number of clicks, how far down we scrolled, or time spent on a webpage. These movement traces provide valuable context for services to create customized content, such as predicting what our next movement is likely to be. Essentially, what will we consume next? From URL to URL, these algorithms feed an advertising technology ecosystem if not web technologies in general.[3]

2 Kretschmer et al.

3 Williams.

Algorithms, such as those governing online tracking, live behind interfaces and are often designed to be opaque, leaving users unaware of how much of their data is being gathered and for what purposes.[4] In various instances such systems have been proven to cause harm and exacerbate inequality in particular in vulnerable and marginalized communities.[5]

4 Pold.

5 Klumbyte et al.

On the following pages is a series of choreographic scores that combine common metrics from online tracking algorithms with physical enactments. These scores are written in the programming language JavaScript and can be performed by humans or fed into a machine.

Both computer scripts and choreographic scores are instruction-based languages. Computer scripts are step-by-step instructions written in a specific programming language to be interpreted and executed by a machine. Computer scripts also have a hybrid human-machinic quality as they also serve to communicate the ideas behind how software works to other humans.

Choreography can be described as a 'plan or score according to which movement unfolds.'[6] Choreographic scores can take many shapes and forms, from textual instructions, to diagrams, to image sequences, video annotations, among many others.

6 Rosenthal et al.

In the words of the choreographer and writer Susan Leigh Foster, choreography is 'the act of arranging patterns of movement'.[7] Patterns can be seen as habitual movement or the opposite, as a way to set new habits, an exploration of new patterns. Michael Klien, Steve Valk and Jeffrey Gormly expand on this idea: 'Patterns are not rigid, they are fluid constellations, appearing and disappearing, crystallizing and dissolving....'[8] Choreography asks 'why': why we move in certain ways and not others? — It lets us zoom in and out of interconnected patterns we are part of, moving within.

challenging habitual rhythms p.452

7 Foster.

8 Klien et al.

The scores that follow here are influenced, among others, by the American choreographer Yvonne Rainer, whose work in the 1960s found inspiration from observing individual pedestrians and crowds in the streets of cities such as New York. She would transpose the movement observed from the streets into the theater and in so doing opened new possibilities for performing the self and sociability.[9] Rainer was part of a larger dance community that took gestures, postures, movements—such as walking or dressing—and reconfigured them. Here the 'why' returns, to question and re-evaluate everyday routine and movement patterns.

9 Wood.

Another source of inspiration is the Brazilian theater practitioner Augusto Boal, initiator of the *Teatro do Oprimido* (Theatre of the Oppressed) in the 1980s. Boal understood theater as a rehearsal for everyday life: not an end in and of itself, but the beginning of social transformation.[10] An important aspect in Boal's work is the blurring of the distinction between audience members and actor. The concept of 'spect-actor' is a blend between the two, acknowledging that as humans we play both roles. A lot of his practice involved people who didn't necessarily have prior experience in acting. As part of his theater training, Boal developed games that supported the de-alienation of the body and mind, aiming at disrupting the repetitiveness of daily tasks. — These games[11] guide us towards identifying movements we have fallen to perform mechanically, that have turned into habits, and introduce small alterations. They draw our attention to the muscles that are rarely used day-to-day to activate our body sensitivity and explore its potential.

shake up the stiffness
p.448

10 Boal (2019).

11 Boal (2022).

While Boal moved from theater to reality, Rainer moved in the opposite direction, seeing the world as a stage.[12] They both reflect on movement patterns we perform daily and propose ways to break those patterns. Perhaps by introducing unpredictability in what might otherwise repeat itself, and remain unchanged.

12 Foster.

Returning to the proximity between computer scripts and choreographic scores, the work that follows merges computer scripts with choreography. This collection of scores invites readers to reflect on the habitual, on the movement patterns we grow accustomed to. Each score points at the entanglement of our bodies with algorithms in the gestures we perform day-to-day and the traces they leave behind. Why do we return to those same movements? What others are there to explore? An invitation to reflect on day-to-day algorithmic choreographies and imagine ways for moving against or resisting predictability. —

going against the clock
p.61

SCORE #1

```
// this script starts with listening...
window.addEventListener('mousemove', moving, false);

//...it listens to movement coordinates:
var coords = [];

function moving(e) {
    // it logs each move, one after the other:
    coords.push([e.pageX, e.pageY]);
    console.log('Moving between:' + JSON.
    stringify(coords));

    // for each movement performed, a new trace is drawn:
    for (i = 0; i < coords.length; ++i) {
        var traces = document.createElement('div');
        document.getElementsByTagName('body')[0].
        appendChild(traces);
        traces.className = 'newScore';
        traces.innerHTML = '<img src=\'fingerprint.png\'
        alt=\'wikimedia commons\' >';
        traces.style.position = 'absolute';
        traces.style.left = e.pageX + 'px';
        traces.style.top = e.pageY + 'px';
    }
}
//...the script loops...
```

SCORE #2

```
// beginning of a new script, defining variable called 'score':
        let score = document.querySelector('body');

// new function defined below:
    function pause() {
        score.innerHTML = 'No to moving or being moved.';
    }
    pause()

// end of script.
```

SCORE #3

```
// defining a random function...
function unpredictableMovement () {

        // get the element named 'traces':
        const traces = document.querySelectorAll('.traces');

        // create a random order:
        const randomizeTraces = Array.from(traces).sort(()
        => Math.random() - 0.5);

        // get the dimensions of the user's browser window:
        const viewportWidth = window.innerWidth;
        const viewportHeight = window.innerHeight;

// set a random position for all 'traces':
randomizeTraces.forEach((traces, index) => {

        const randomX = Math.random() * (viewportWidth -
        traces.clientWidth);
        const randomY = Math.random() * (viewportHeight -
        traces.clientHeight);

        traces.style.left = randomX + 'px';
        traces.style.top = randomY + 'px';
    });
}

unpredictableMovement ()

// perform this function every 5 seconds:
setInterval (randomizeMovement, 5000)
```

SCORE #4

```
let data = [
    'user's age',
    'user's gender',
    'user's device',
    'user's screen resolution',
    'language preference',
    'clicks',
    'scroll percentage',
    'idle time',
    'engagement time',
    'location',
    'duration visiting a webpage',
    'search queries',
    'browser history',
    'active user',
    'predictive audiences'
];

let score = document.querySelector('body');

function substitute () {
    score.innerHTML = 'Substitute your ' + data[8]'.';
}
function repeat () {
    score.innerHTML = 'Pause ' + data[12] +
    'repeat tomorrow.';
}
function remove() {
    score.innerHTML = 'Undo all ' + data[5]'.';
}
function freeze() {
    score.innerHTML = 'Slow down your ' + data[6] +
    'until it stops.';
}
function add () {
    score.innerHTML = 'Add a counter-movement
    of your choice.';
}
```

SCORE #5

```
// beginning of a new script, defining variable called 'score':
    let score = document.querySelector('body')

// new function defined below:
    function willNot () {
        score.innerHTML = 'Predict your next movement.
        Then, don't do it.';
    }
    willNot ()

// end of script.
```

References

Boal, Augusto. *Teatro do oprimido: e outras poéticas políticas*. Editora 34, 2019.

Boal, Augusto. *Games for Actors and Non-Actors*. Routledge, 2022.

Foster, Susan Leigh. 'Choreographies and Choreographers.' In *Worlding Dance: Studies in International Performance*, edited by Susan Leigh Foster. Palgrave Macmillan, 2009.

Klien, Michael, Steve Valk, and Jeffrey Gormly. *Book of Recommendations: Choreography as an Aesthetics of Change*. Daghdha Dance Company, 2008.

Klumbyte, Goda, Phillip Lücking, and Claude Draude. 'Reframing AX with Critical Design: The Potentials and Limits of Algorithmic Experience as a Critical Design Concept.' In *Proceedings of the 11th Nordic Conference on Human-Computer Interaction: Shaping Experiences, Shaping Society*, Tallinn, Estonia, October, 2020, 1–12. doi.org/10.1145/3419249.3420120.

Kretschmer, Michael, Jan Pennekamp, and Klaus Wehrle. 'Cookie Banners and Privacy Policies: Measuring the Impact of the GDPR on the Web.' In *ACM Transactions on the Web* 15, no. 4 (2021): 1–42. doi.org/10.1145/3466722.

Pold, Søren Bro. 'New Ways of Hiding: Towards Metainterface Realism.' In *Artnodes*, no. 24 (2019): 72–84. doi.org/10.7238/a.v0i24.3283.

Rainer, Yvonne. *A Manifesto Reconsidered. London, 2008.*

Rosenthal, Stephanie, Susan Leigh Foster, André Lepecki, and Peggy Phelan, eds. *Move: Choreographing You*. Hayward Publishing, 2010.

Williams, James. *Stand out of our Light: Freedom and Resistance in the Attention Economy*. Cambridge University Press, 2018.

Wood, Catherine. *Yvonne Rainer: The Mind is a Muscle*. One Work. Afterall, 2007.

courage
transcendence
lyricism
inner vitality
differently abled
beyond the boundary
spontaneity
forgiveness
forgetting
momentary freedom
moving within

Embracing the Aging Body in Dance

Nanako Nakajima

The question 'what does it mean to be an aging dancer' was once a taboo in Euro-American dance. In the field of ballet, beauty is found in flexible, agile, young dancing bodies full of power and stamina. At the Paris Opera, ballet dancers retired from dance by the age of 45. The physical deterioration of the body affects dancers' careers far more profoundly than it does in any other art. Older dancers become choreographers, dance teachers, and producers. Older dancers coming back to dance was unheard of in the past: They said farewell to dance.

In some Asian contexts, however, professional dancers continue dancing into their sixties and seventies. Traditional dancers are respected and sometimes are designated as intangible national assets. The long careers of contemporary Japanese dancers such as Kazuo Ohno and ballet dancer Yoko Morishita are celebrated. Emancipated from existing dance techniques, their embodied knowledge is more powerful than what is visible on stage. — The historical past appears through the present, aging body on stage. In response to international performances by these aging Japanese dancers, a new trend has emerged in European contemporary dance and performance. For example, German choreographer-director Pina Bausch, dramaturg and dancer Raimund Hoghe, and French choreographer-dancer Jerôme Bel, as well as Dance On Ensemble in Germany helped cultivate an atmosphere that highlights the longer lives of dancers. Amidst the aging of the world population, people have started paying more attention to this.

spatial secrets
p.379

The issue of the aging body in dance has entered a new critical phase in the time of pandemics. Covid-19 highlighted the vulnerability of aging populations to emerging viruses. That crisis also transformed the theatrical milieu surrounding dance. Because of the pandemic, many theaters were closed, and they instead provided online programs in which dancers perform not only on stage but also at their own houses. Dance no longer takes places only at theaters and museums; it has expanded to private and virtual spaces. The art of dance goes beyond the boundary of the theatrical space of modern construction. When dance lives beyond the boundary of theater art, dancers can also keep dancing beyond the cultural boundary of age.

Here I introduce my research on the aging body in dance, which incorporates legendary Butoh dancer Kazuo Ohno and the approach of dancer and choreographer Yuko Kaseki in our Taifun project on aging.[1] Yuko Kaseki explores the aesthetics of aging together with aging bodies in dance: she can make you dance better when you become older.

1 taifun-plus.org/.

Kazuo Ohno: Withering Flower and Rebooting Memory

Butoh is known for its shocking and contorted body gestures and its commitment to breaking taboos. It draws on both Euro-American and native Japanese influences. Butoh was developed in the late nineteen-fifties by Tatsumi Hijikata and Kazuo Ohno. Hijikata and Ohno condemned, and eventually rejected, contemporary Japanese modern dance's strict adherence to Western styles. Today, Butoh is practiced by performers all over the world. The influence of Butoh is even more pronounced outside Japan, where it is performed in ways that are strictly faithful to the original method practiced by Hijikata and Ohno as well as in ways that attempt creative variations of the art form.

Slowness comes into focus when we become accustomed to a high speed. Some of the movements of Butoh performers are perceived as slow when we compare them to the fast-paced, youth-oriented dance practice. Kazuo Ohno has never moved so slowly, although he incorporates the hyper-analyzed perception of time and space of high density, — which slowly executes each part of his body and movement sequences in detail. You will dance 'slower' if you observe your body and mind more carefully and become more aware of your environment, both inside and out.

exquisite awareness of change p.88

In contrast to Tatsumi Hijikata, Kazuo Ohno danced and lived longer. According to Kazuo Ohno's son, Yoshito Ohno, at over 90 years of age, he was not nearly as physically agile as he once was. Although he used to have enough energy to create a vast universe onstage, his physical powers had inevitably declined as he got older. Comparing his life to a flower's life cycle, one could describe Kazuo Ohno's life as the process of gradually withering and falling off the stem. While some might have considered him to be well past his prime, he never lost his inner vitality. Even in this physically diminished state, Kazuo Ohno remained fully alive. The intensity of these years, as the divide between life and death started drawing in, generated a lyricism previously unknown in his work. At an age when most dancers had long abandoned their careers, the primal strength of Kazuo Ohno's dance emerged even more forcefully than before, despite the fact that his body was progressively weakening. Kazuo Ohno spoke about his dialectics of dance practice and aesthetics as follows:

> *Don't treat dance as some kind of abstract game. Take each and every step as though you were putting your life on the line. Mastering technique has never interested me for the simple reason that if I were to focus on skill, I'd instantly lose touch with the natural phenomena. If I were to concentrate on acquiring technical skills, I'd probably turn into nothing more than a technician and thereby unwittingly lose sight of what I'm aiming for. Technique could never provide me with the wherewithal to achieve what I've set out to do. I don't care whether you're skillful or not. What I do care about, though, is that your performance makes me walk away afterward feeling grateful for being alive. Does your dance ask for forgiveness?*[2]

2 Ohno, 283.

Kazuo Ohno does not trust dance technique because it transforms him into a technician and nothing else. Technique no longer matters; he reached the limits of technique when he performed his last piece in the modern dance style, *The Old Man and the Sea* (1959). He had come to the realization that the soul of the dance/r could be lost by pushing technique to the limits; therefore, he started contemplating whether technique and life might be contradictory. — As long as Kazuo Ohno followed dance technique, he was copying other people's

life dwelling in imperfection p.203

lives and was nothing more than a copy. Instead, he chose to forget everything that he learned in order to truly dance. He said:

> *There's no need to memorize movements and gestures, because no matter what I do, I'll forget them anyway. The essential thing is that the experience remains perfectly ingrained in my mind, and in my soul. That's what comes with repeated practice. It's of little consequence that I forget what I've practiced, because, despite myself, I'm constantly absorbing the fruits of my endeavors.*[3]

3 Ibid., 273.

Dance technique reconstructs what one has learned. Because dance technique is always a deliberate act of the will, the body is less spontaneous with its living movements. By forgetting what he learned, Kazuo Ohno achieved momentary freedom while dancing. — As he got older, he lost more of his memories, which enabled him to escape from the boundaries of the conscious, visible world. Dance critic Nario Goda explained that Kazuo Ohno's dance was fascinating because he was senile and often forgot things.[4]

eternal amateur p.86

4 Masaki Iwana introduces Nario Goda's comments: Sasaki, 206.

I visited Kazuo Ohno's dance studio in Kami-hoshikawa in Yokohama on 27 December, 2008. I saw 102-year-old Kazuo Ohno lying on the bed and attached to many tubes in his living room. He was no longer capable of seeing and speaking because of his age. His son, Yoshito Ohno, told me that Kazuo Ohno danced even at his age: he breathed differently when listening to music. On the way back to Kami-hoshikawa station, I was choked and suddenly burst into tears. He still dances in his death bed. Dying is the end of aging, which is beyond our control. Even if technology is further developed and many people can live longer and healthier, there is always an end.

We can dance until the very end of aging, but as long as we are aging, nobody escapes death. Death is the crucial part of aging, a very singular, individual part of a dancer's life. In the very literal sense, death means to stop dancing.

Kazuo Ohno once said that we would reach the point where we forgot ourselves. In 2000, he was diagnosed with Alzheimer's disease, and in 2010, Kazuo Ohno passed away at the age of 103.

Yuko Kaseki's Approach to the Aging Body in Dance

Yuko Kaseki is a director, choreographer, teacher, and Butoh dancer based in Berlin. She studied Butoh dance and performing art at HBK Braunschweig with Anzu Furukawa and danced in her company from 1989–2000. In her work, she has been searching for a way to penetrate the space between physical and spiritual expression. She has worked with differently abled performers and performers from diverse cultural backgrounds. By incorporating their personal histories, social problems, and unique bodies into her work, she has expanded the physical imagination and questioned what the normal dancing bodies mean. —

thinking through the possibility of inclusion p.285

In 2021, Yuko Kaseki led several Butoh workshops with elderly participants at the Caritas Zentrum Plus Stockum in Düsseldorf. While her interest in aging and death has been further stimulated by her own family situation, this is the first time for her to work with older participants. During the workshops held in Düsseldorf, she led several Butoh workshops with the elderly participants, such as moving with an image like water, exchanging energy, and improvising.

During Yuko's workshop, participants are invited to hold hands. Holding hands is a recognition of others through one's own body. This helps the participants feel connected to others and offers emotional calmness. By exchanging energy through hands and shadowing each other's movement, one woman slowly started moving together with Yuko.

Yuko Kaseki writes:

Everyone can have their own dance without being criticized. Affirmation of existence. There is no hierarchy, no nationality, no age, no disability. The exchange of energy is not tied to the head or body, but is one of the phenomena in creating the whole (and not just in the human-oriented world). Everything is a process, a continuous transformation .... What I would like to work on now is how to deal with aging and death, and spiritual discipline, to find communication deeply by sharpening Chi and opening up the magnetic field, and to practice new forms of expression, with/out the stage.[5]

new possibilities for performing the self p.332

5 Kaseki, 243.

This form of dance improvisation is essential to Butoh aesthetics. Kazuo Ohno was a well-trained dancer, but he was always improvising. In improvisation, choreography is not fixed; therefore, there is no such thing as mistake. Dancers can forget everything. Every time an improvised movement is updated, the dancer's memories are rebooted as well.

When Kazuo Ohno crossed the boundary of age, he went beyond the limitations of a dancer: he did not care anymore about being seen as a dancer. Generally, it takes considerable self-confidence to be a dancer because one is totally exposed to the audience at all times on stage. All of the performing arts require tremendous courage. However, aging neutralized him, and he transcended beyond this state of mind. Ohno described his dance in relation to his own life: 'At the age of nearly 80, there is no more 'stage' or 'daily life.''[6] When dance overlaps with one's whole life, one's life takes the form of dance.

6 Ohno, 283.

Elderly people are looked at differently in Europe than in Japan. In Japan, aging is very much related to the essence of art, as it is said that longevity is a part of art. People live longer and also work into their older years. Aging is important to the process of artistic training. One does not attain the ultimate level as an artist until one practices every day and lives for a long time. In Euro-American culture, the art of dance was reserved for the professionals on stage, while dance for elderly people was for therapy. However, this system is changing because of cultural politics as well as pandemics. Anyone can dance on stage, and the stage is no longer just at theaters but also in extended, daily life.

Although Yuko Kaseki's approach comes from the Butoh tradition, she integrates German conceptions of the aging body in dance. The improvisation allows elderly people to forget the choreography and improvise on the spot as they move, similar to how Kazuo Ohno danced. Kazuo Ohno's movements did not consist of a series of consecutive actions in time; his movements were not performed in a linear sequence. Instead, one had the impression that he thrust deeper and deeper into each and every movement and step, as though he were moving within each movement. His performances generated the feeling of being drawn down into a great depth that was within him.

Yuko Kaseki seeks this same depth of movement during her workshop with elderly people. Kazuo Ohno himself had Alzheimer's disease and Yuko Kaseki works with elderly people with dementia. During her workshop, the conversation of the participants is often repetitive, and so are their movements. They dance because they enjoy it, not for the sake of the audience.

Aging reflects the aesthetics of Japanese dance. We can dance better when we become older.

This text is based on a lecture delivered as part of the symposium 'Time Shifts—Age(ing) and Society' at Palais Wittgenstein, Dusseldorf in August 2021 curated and organized by TAIFUN Project e. V.

References

Kaseki, Yuko. 'Catastrophe/Catharsis of Creative Process and Unknown Journey.' In *Performance Research* 25, no. 6–7 (2020): 243–51. doi.org/10.1080/13528165.2020.1900645.

Nakajima, Nanako, and Gabriele Brandstetter. *The Aging Body in Dance: A Cross-cultural Perspective*. Routledge, 2017.

Ohno, Kazuo and Yoshito. *Kazuo Ohno's World from Without and Within*. Translated by John Barrett. Wesleyan University Press, 2004.

Iwana, Masaki, In *Performance as Exploration: The Artist's Body, Movement, and Affordance Theory*, edited by Masato Sasaki, Tokyo Daigaku Shuppankai, 2006. (『アート/表現する身体: アフォーダンスの現場』佐々木正人編)

story
networks
kinship
survival
reciprocity
shaping futures
coexistence

Threading Stories and Machines

Mariana Fernández Mora

SCAFFOLDING

To be a body,
from nobody.
A stone with memory,
a river with voice.

When I was a child, once a year around December, we would be visited by my parent's friend, a Wixaritari man called José Luis. He would stay with us for a few days and let my brother and me pick from the beaded objects that he had brought along while telling us about the stories they carried. In the Wixaritari culture, also known as Huichol, these beaded objects form intricate representations of their ontologies and cosmologies. They tell the stories of their ancestors and, with them, transport the collective memory of their people. Like many other Indigenous cultures, the Wixaritari do not consider humans at the center of the universe but rather as a part of a network of kinship with all beings, where identity and meaning are not intrinsic to the individual but are created through relations. For example, for the Rarámuri, also known as Tarahumara peoples, this concept is called *iwígara*, 'the belief that all life forms are interconnected and share the same breath.'[1]

[1] Salmon.

Recently, I found myself thinking back on these stories and what they can teach us about the different ways of understanding our relationality to the non-human, specifically to sentient-like technologies such as artificial intelligence (AI). For instance, in the Wixaritari culture, the non-human—plants, animals, or even elements like water and fire—play an active role in ensuring the well-being of the network of relationships that binds everything together. They are not considered passive resources but rather active partners in the ongoing processes of life and knowledge creation. One of the best-known ones is the story of Kauyumari, the blue deer sent to guide humans to Wirikuta, a sacred place in the Mexican mountains of San Luis Potosí. The story tells of a time when the world was out of balance, and the Wixaritari suffered from hunger and sickness. The ancestors and gods then sent Kayumari, a blue deer, to guide a group of hunters through mountains, rivers, and grasslands until they arrived in a desert. There, the deer transformed into *hikuri*—a small sacred cactus known in the West as peyote—to offer its knowledge to the hunters. By ingesting hikuri, the hunters entered a heightened state of awareness, allowing them to access the realm of the invisible and understand that the deer, the peyote, the land, and themselves were all part of a single web of relationships. Through this encounter, the Wixaritari understood for the first time how everything was interconnected and were able to restore the balance in their world.

In this story, the peyote becomes a teacher, a transmitter of knowledge, allowing humans to learn a lesson crucial for survival. The Wixaritari access what they call 'the realm of the invisible,' which allows them to see and feel the connections between all that exists, human and non-human. This story teaches us how, by seeing and acknowledging these connections, we can understand that all beings contribute and are affected by the state of the whole network of relationships, binding all beings to mutual responsibility and care—acknowledging that when one part of the network suffers, the entire network is at risk, and that when the network is in balance, all beings within it can thrive. Tales like this exemplify how, in a world where humans are not placed above or at the center, all entities or members of the network can be carriers of knowledge. Consequently, every interaction or encounter can transfer that knowledge, potentially transforming whoever is involved in the exchange. This makes us understand it as a relational process intrinsic to experience and highlights how knowledge is produced and exists within every encounter and relation.

When it comes to AI, these perspectives become incredibly important as they remind us that each of our interactions—human or non-human—carries the potential to change us. They prompt us to consider the types of knowledge we can create through our exchanges with the technologies we make, our mutual responsibility in building this knowledge and its impact on the world around us. As we develop machines with increasingly human-like behaviors, stories about the non-human and interdependence can help us reflect on how such technologies integrate into our relationships and impact them.

If we consider AI as part of our network of relationships — and knowledge, we can begin to reflect on the narratives and lessons that shape it. Helping us identify it as a product of Western and colonial legacies shaped by a relatively small, homogeneous group of people and by the extraction of resources, data, and labor. For instance, it allows us to recognize its immense energy demands and the waste it generates. And enables us to acknowledge how machine learning systems learn from datasets and behaviors embedded with prejudices that result in outputs that often perpetuate these same biased tendencies.

extended circle of relations p.420

Although machine learning algorithms—as well as technologies in general—are often regarded as impartial, they inherently reinforce hierarchical structures present in the data, contributing to the systematic perpetuation of inequalities. They will always amplify the social, political, and cultural contexts they contain. Therefore, it is essential to challenge the harmful notions and structures that can further damage our ecosystems and networks of care. To create new technological narratives that embrace our interconnectivity in order to help us recognize how the persistence of such notions impacts not only individuals but also the broader webs of care and support that sustain us.

It's also important to understand that simply restricting or 'cleaning' technology won't resolve the embedded political and social hierarchies within it. All technologies are cultural products and will, therefore, always carry biases. Technical and reactive solutions that attempt to filter outputs or diversify training data often provide only temporary fixes, failing to address underlying power dynamics and systemic issues. These approaches also risk erasing other forms of knowledge that cannot be neatly reduced to data and incorporated into the machines. In its current form, AI simply perpetuates and amplifies existing human structures, which often contributes to further inequality and the prioritizing of economic and political interests over the well-being of the network. Reimagining these structures and hierarchies can help us open up spaces of agency and envision our relationships otherwise.

Acknowledging our interconnectivity with AI can help us move away from models based on extraction and work toward designing technologies that respect that bond. Rather than viewing it solely as a tool, we can begin to understand it as something we are in a relationship with—an element of our kinship network and a mediator of knowledge. This perspective allows us to interrogate our technologies, recognize the biases embedded within them, and reject the hierarchies they contain by engaging with them in ways beyond their original design. By doing so, we demystify the idea of a neutral, all-knowing technology and recognize our shared responsibility in shaping these systems, understanding that our interactions with AI influence our worldview and the societal structures we live in. Applying these principles as we create new technologies and engage with existing ones can help us find alternative ways to resist structures that have damaged our networks of relationships and start to repair them. Instead of viewing AI as a disembodied entity floating in the cloud, we can understand it as something we are in a relationship with, which connects us to the water, the earth, and the minerals used to build its infrastructure. This allows us to situate AI outside of an abstract digital environment, helping us understand the material body that carries it. To restore its place as an active participant within a web of interconnected beings while recognizing how it engages physically with the earth and all its beings. —

in solidarity and kinship with 'life' as a whole p.456

The stories we tell ourselves—and those we tell through our technologies—matter. As technologies like AI become increasingly entangled in nearly every aspect of life, we need to imagine new narratives around them that move away from the harmful assumptions that have dominated their development. Rather than viewing AI as a tool for optimization, we can reimagine it as a partner in exploring other ways of being with the other-than-human. Moving away from the myth that our problems will be solved by more, better, and smarter technologies and instead embracing the responsibility and reciprocity needed to foster balance between the human and other-than-human, embodying new stories altogether. Storytelling is a way of shaping the world, imagining it before it can happen, and transmitting the lessons we've learned. As we design, develop and implement sentient-like technologies, we need to consider the messages and values we embed in them and how they will shape our futures. Changing how we position ourselves in relation to these technologies can be the beginning of fabulating new narratives and modes of interaction based not on hierarchical, exploitative systems but rather on networks of care and reciprocity. By considering everything around us—including AI—as part of a large web of relations, we can begin to imagine new ways of coexistence.

Reference

Salmon, E., guest. For The Wild. Episode 225, 'Enrique Salmon on Moral Landscapes Amidst Changing Ecologies.' May 26, 2023. Podcast, 56 min., 27 sec. forthewild.world/listen/enrique-salmon-on-moral-landscapes-amidst-changing-ecologies-225.

mystery
paradox
intuitive imagination
immaterial worlds
ir/rational
imperfection
the un-structurable
cosmic acts of creation
repair

The Loop

Kader Attia

Ancient peoples left traces of their astronomic observations, the origins of which remain mysterious. It seems impossible that they could have seen or understood certain cosmic phenomena without the technological means we have today. For instance, how could the Dogon people from Mali have observed and built their whole cosmogony around a star, Sirius, which they named Sigui Tolo? This star is in fact a binary star, made of Sirius A and Sirius B, the two of which appear aligned on the same axis only once every sixty years. It is likewise according to a sixty-year rhythm that the Dogon celebrate the *sigui* festival—the 'invention of speech and death.'

How could they have known? How could they have known about the 'white dwarf' Sirius B—which they named 'the companion of Sigui Tolo'—and its sixty-year revolutionary cycle, when the small star could only be observed through telescopes for the first time at the end of the nineteenth century?

From the concept of the infinitely large in Mesopotamian sciences to the concept of the infinitely small in the works of ancient Greeks, such as those by Democritus, the common denominator of all these civilizations is without a doubt the fact that their logical sciences did not exclude intuitive imagination.

On the altar of human knowledge, on each side of which stand sciences and arts, mathematics and arts are opposites. I am referring here to artistic creation in its **endless** and unexpected aspect: the perpetual and illogical movement that determines its development. — A biological, physical, or historical phenomenon can be explained, but it is impossible to write the equation that would explain why the human mind has always sought, and will always seek, to enhance **perception and emotion**. Metaphorical formulas can be developed, but what endlessly changes the nature and purpose of art can never be logically explained and anticipated, as it belongs to parameters that cannot be observed a priori. Even if unsolved equations do also exist, it is impossible to build a mathematic reasoning to structure the unstructurable that **leads to the unexpected**, where neither causality nor effects are understandable.

vastness of perspective
p.382

It is always surprising to see in Wolfgang Amadeus Mozart's scores that there is no trace of marks or redactions.

Emotion results from an unexpected juxtaposition of cognitive functions that, when gathered together in a certain moment and space, can activate the senses. This kind of biocommunication system can be mathematically interpreted, but the emotions generated from new shapes and concepts cannot be reduced to rational explanation. —

always remains a step beyond us p.87

What is important about Mozart's scores isn't so much the contrast between the virtuosic purity of the work and the 'humanity' of making mistakes by nature, but rather that, in order for music to emerge from a human mind as already complete, the entire mathematical structure of the music must have existed beforehand—even before Mozart himself existed. Like mathematics, music is not invented, but discovered—Mozart would not invent a symphony, but would discover one that already existed somewhere, and would organize it in his mind over the course of a month or a year. Einstein discovered the theory of relativity, Higgs the boson particle. They didn't invent them. Relativity and bosons existed already, and were waiting to be discovered.

Music's structure can indeed be explained with mathematics, but what cannot be explained is the irrational origin of the urge that triggers the process through which it will move in a certain direction and then renew itself indefinitely. What is a masterpiece if not a mysterious coincidence, an immeasurable quantity of totally unexpected and paradoxical circumstances merging into a particular moment and space: **point T**? This phenomenon, rare in any artistic discipline, holds in itself the enigma of its unexpected and extra-human origin, making it endlessly fascinating. Among the billions of factors converging upon this one point, only one is fundamental: the factor of repair, or restoration. Why? Because repair translates from one space/time to another, and crucially as an improvement. —

the promise of rebirth p.125

The omnipresence of repair in the universe is without a doubt the sole reason it is shared by both mathematics and art. It is a primary characteristic of human biological and cultural evolution. Without the process of repair, there would be nothing—neither chaos nor stability. Everything is guided by the determinist agency of repair.

I first perceived this phenomenon quite concretely through simple observation in the cultural and political fields and through many years of research on non-occidental tradition and occidental modernity. This led me to reconsider the totemic dimension of traditional cultures and their connections to the immaterial worlds of ancestors. I likewise reconsidered the cultures of modernity and their dogmatic connection with modernity's motor: progress, which turns its back on the past, toward an ambivalent relation between the artistic avant-garde and the wars of the world.

Charles Darwin and Alfred Russel Wallace's theory of the evolution of species, which articulated the natural selection necessary for any species to survive in its environment through a process of repair, helped my research to go beyond the concept of the 'bricolage' of the savage mind so dear to Claude Lévi-Strauss. A discovery by the 2012 Nobel Prize in physics winner, Serge Haroche, opened my eyes to other horizons where repair is omnipresent: after trying for years to trap an elementary light particle between two mirrors, Haroche and his team could only capture the photon for a tenth of a second. After a tenth of a second, the photon disappears. Where does it go? No one knows. Why does it disappear? 'Because nature isn't perfect,' said Haroche. These two words together tackle a fascinating fundamental issue: the relationship between *nature and imperfection*.

Is that which the human mind misses or mistakes also imperfect? Is that which culture does not understand also imperfect? Extra-human phenomena belong to an order of things that surpasses us only to then tirelessly reappropriate what belongs to it, repairing a situation that, for a brief moment, suspends its power. This is because the human's 'imperfect' interpretation of nature has a virtual symmetry from nature's point of view: the abnormality triggered by this experience. Therefore, from the perspective of the quantum order of things, it is this experience that is imperfect. Assuming the photon is as isolated as the abnormality, the quantum order of things repairs this fault by taking the particle back after a tenth of a second.

There are different explanations for this wave's disappearance from our world, but what is certain is that, in order to reappear and be pieced together again somewhere else, the information that defines it must be stored somewhere. In the universe, black holes are the only known phenomena capable of making anything disappear completely, from matter to light, and their mass depends on the quantity of matter they swallow. But black holes are invisible to the naked eye; they can only be identified through the gravitational influence they exert over their environment (as astrophysicist Andrea Ghez recently observed with the Sagittarius A black hole at the center of our galaxy) or through a 'mathematical journey' that makes it possible to approach its periphery, and ultimately its center: its singularity.

According to physicist Leonard Susskind, theoretician Stephen Hawking claimed in 1976 that black holes violate the fundamental principle in physics of the storage of information, because of the process of evaporation that leads to their progressive disappearance. 'Hawking radiation' describes the process by which this information evaporates, leading to the progressive disappearance of the black hole. And yet, says Susskind, we should compare this with the concrete example of a computer, because the information stored in its hard drive can be erased, while in reality it is only released into the atmosphere as a quantity of energy absorbed by the molecules around it. This is to say that the information hasn't totally disappeared. According to Susskind:

> When a particle interacts with another one, it can be absorbed, reflected, or also disintegrate into several other particles. But its initial state (electrical charge, mass, impulsion, etc.) can be rebuilt from the product of its interactions. The information borne by this particle is, then, always kept.

This is a fundamental law of quantum physics, and perhaps even the most important law of classical physics as well. From Susskind's 'holographic principle' we now know that when a black hole swallows an object, it keeps the information that defines the object at its surface, or its **event horizon**. Susskind's holographic principle gets its name from a process through which an image in three dimensions is built from details coded into a two-dimensional film. Similarly, the holographic principle stipulates that the horizon of a black hole contains the totality of the information included inside. The information contained in a black hole isn't lost forever, but is rather coded on the surface of its horizon as data. As Susskind further explains:

> The horizon would then keep all information borne by all the elements that gave birth to the black hole, but also of all the objects that, attracted by the force of gravity, have gone through the *horizon*. They would then be returned through photons produced during the evaporation process. Information associated to black holes would then be rejected in the Universe, even if in a blurred form. From then on, they should not be seen as devourers, but as some kind of information tanks.

Because of the accelerating circular movement on the black hole's event horizon, a **disk of accretion** forms that works like a dynamo: the more it swallows, the more it turns, and the more it turns, the more it rejects energy. As a black hole attracts more matter, it rejects more of its elementary information. Try, for instance, filling a dog's bowl using a fire hose. A huge quantity of water will spill out. The acceleration of the event horizon generates a massive and powerful electromagnetic loop that creates, on both sides of the black hole, two gigantic jets of gamma rays, together with electromagnetic eruptions and rejected gas.

What for decades seemed destructive is now clearly recognized by every astrophysicist as creative. Even Hawking admitted he made a mistake. Through Susskind's theories and the phenomenon of rejection, it is now clear that black holes contribute to the formation of new stars and galaxies. — This intermediary cataclysmic phenomenon in fact leads to a cosmic act of creation. It illustrates, at an extraordinary physical scale, a fundamental principle of creation: repair. From the death of a massive star exploding into a supernova, new stars are born.

dance between destruction and creation p.125

Repair in the cultural sense of the word can apply to politics, the economy, art, and science, but it is above all on the continuum of extra-cultural activity. What we claim to control, for instance by gathering information with the intention of reusing it, is purely an imitation of fundamental physical phenomena structuring an order of things that precedes us and will succeed us as well.

'Nothing is lost, nothing is created, everything transforms,' wrote chemist Antoine-Laurent de Lavoisier. It is not the universe that is a gigantic computer, but we who mimic it. The universe appears to us now as a gigantic fractal vortex swallowing itself and endlessly regenerating.

This essay was originally published by e-flux SUPERCOMMUNITY / 56th Venice Biennale on July 4, 2015 (Day 44) under the title 'Planetary Computing (Is the Universe Actually a Giant Computer?).' supercommunity.e-flux.com/texts/the-loop/.

care-taking
adaptation
unsettled definitions
shifting time and scale
ongoing experiments
thinking with
passing on
urgency
accompaniment
the gift of attention
before and beyond
well enough

Fast and Slow and in Between

Ella Finer with Jem Finer

SCAFFOLDING

> *To hear* Longplayer *as Jem intended we have to remain here on earth and live and die before it's over. To hear* Longplayer *as it was composed, we can never hear it.*[1]
> —Janna Levin

1 Levin.

What does it mean to experience a composition we can never hear? *Longplayer*, Jem Finer's infinite piece of music repeating only once every thousand years, orients our human attention to the time in which we are present with it, urging us also to listen to our own present tense as continual, complex—a mix of before and beyond. That we can only imagine 'the end,' or hope for a world in which such an end into another beginning is possible, is part of *Longplayer*'s unfolding legacy. How do we, in our small portion of time care-taking for the music's continuation, pass on our stewardship? How do we do this well, and why—*and for whom*—are we doing this work?

accountability to the world around p.420

I am writing these questions thinking about my own particular relationship with *Longplayer* as the eldest child of its composer and a member of The Longplayer Trust in whose care the artwork resides. What follows is an essay written through and in conversation with Jem Finer, my father, as *Longplayer* reaches a quarter century of its duration. I ask him, as we near this temporal landmark of years: do you think *Longplayer* is slow?

> *'I think it's fast and slow and in between.'*[2]

2 All text within quotation marks is Jem Finer's voice, as edited from a transcript of a conversation between him and Ella Finer on September 7, 2024.

How slow or fast the past twenty-five years have gone is in some ways a matter of comparison and contrast. I am thinking through my subjective sense of speed, inseparable from the experiences and movements of my own life, a reminder how time and scale shift depending on *who* is perceiving—sensing the world and their relation with it. That *Longplayer* is long does not so simply equate to it being slow, a conflation that happens often. And yet, the sheer length of the composition, the necessity to provide care and maintenance for its continuation into years beyond any one human life span means that *Longplayer* always has a relationship with speed, especially the speed of the people who gift their time to looking after it.

Choosing to 'go slowly' is often a privilege of taking time; working at a decelerated pace as having the leisure of time in which to work something out. And yet *Longplayer*, and its care-taking across generations, prompts an unsettling of slowness as the pace of uncomplicated leisure and unhurried or lethargic action. Yes, *Longplayer* is composed with a durational intention of a thousand years, but it won't reach the point of starting another cycle unless the urge to carry it forward is present and sustained. And why care about its continuation? As Jem's daughter I think about this a lot; the intricacies of caring for a work as connected to a human I care deeply for. Beyond the personal, familial relationship to the artwork, what connects the audiences of *Longplayer* to this work? Why does the music's continuation matter?

Over many years of meeting and talking with *Longplayer*'s audiences I have come to understand how diverse its meaning is for different people and so *Longplayer*'s meaning is always in a process of becoming. Often, among the many nuances of how a listener meets *Longplayer*, there is a sense of curiosity and hope for what *Longplayer* makes tangible in the work of caring for lifetimes beyond our own; how we pass on well enough. To put this another way, and in an ecological sense, **there is urgency in what unfolds slowly** over large expanses of time. — *Longplayer*'s invitation to imagine-dream what can be cared for in the long term by looking after what is at stake in the short term is, for me at least, the deep ethical heart of the project.

arts of ripening p.391

'Longplayer *is always throwing up questions. And one of those has always been: how do you keep me going? And obviously one of the ways is that you have to find a simple way of describing it across time or even in time.'*

Already this writing, my way into describing *Longplayer*, exceeds and extrapolates on descriptions always in motion; handed down to me through Jem's and others' words and endlessly turned over by Trustees and invigilators, friends and listeners near and far. — 'I think I've described it enough...' Jem says as we talk about how to make some provisional definition for the artwork.

made resonant again through imaginative retelling p.326

'For something that is intended to last for so long, the description will move through different kinds of descriptions of itself, and conceptions of what it is. This is part of the project, isn't it?'

Written language is a slow technology, a product of human invention and responding over time. That *Longplayer* moves through the subjectivity of listening into an experiment of long-unsettled definition is really wonderful to me—'that it doesn't resolve in one person's description of it'—even while we all seek out ways to meet the work in words.

In this way *Longplayer* carries the imprints of all those who have felt close or moved enough to want to describe it, and so pass on to another. In 2003, astrophysicist Janna Levin suggested that, 'Instead of a mechanical object, maybe *Longplayer* should be passed on by word of mouth as a chant, a myth.'[3]

[3] Levin.

Now, twenty years on from Levin's writing and a quarter century into its future, *Longplayer* has moved as much through the commitment of communities of listeners as it has through multiple technologies; for example, the many computers that have reached the end of their lifespans in quick succession. *Longplayer* has always to adapt and take on new forms, find new realizations and solutions as technologies change.

> *'There are many technical ways of realizing Longplayer. Already we've got a computer performing it, we've had twelve turntables playing custom-made records, we've had people singing it, and live large-scale performances with the bowls played by musicians over the course of a day. Each of these use a different score, all stemming from the same abstract score. All those scores do the same thing, but they're represented differently. Why are they represented differently? Because they're different technologies. To show a person where to put a needle on a record, you need a different way of describing than to show a person which bowl to play, when and for how long, and at what volume.'*

We return to the necessary work of description; particularly the body doing this work of description as a form of translating methods into graphic instruction, into conversation and discussion, and caring enough to do so. In the transcript of our conversation I am struck by how many times I ask for definition, or more description. Struck by how this working through discrepancies of definition and understanding is a form of care-taking often rendered invisible, often gendered, in the way we have to find-invent a shared language in order to keep something alive.

What's the difference between the score and the algorithm?

> *'I'd say the abstract score and the algorithm are actually just different words for the same thing…'*

To look at Jem's now archived notebooks in which he first began sketching out the ideas and algorithms for *Longplayer* is to enter into a cosmic numberland. That I cannot 'read' these notes makes them all the more mysterious as the beginnings of what Michael Morris has called Jem's 'deceptively simple idea for a piece of music which would play a thousand years without repetition.'[4]

4 Michael Morris first commissioned *Longplayer* for Artangel in 1995 and has worked closely with Jem Finer and The Longplayer Trust ever since.

> *'When* Longplayer *first started playing, at first I thought, okay, now it's started, I can just get on with something else and forget about it. And then very quickly, within days, I realized that I can't. This is actually where it all begins.'*

Longplayer continues, as Jem often says, as long as there are people who want it to continue, and move that want into action. Set up before *Longplayer* began playing, The Longplayer Trust accompanies the work through time, looking after its maintenance on the time scales of days, years, centuries, and into a cosmic beyond. There is always work to be done now for the future. I often think of the way the Trust works across time spans—of both close proximity and beyond our reckoning—as symbolic of the dailyness of legacy making: a reminder of how each day the decisions we make, however big or small, form the inheritance of future generations. ▬

ever-evolving composition of a common world p.229

That the way we live our lives today has effects beyond our own time on earth is no new concept, and yet to be a custodian of *Longplayer* is to come into continual awareness of the ongoing effects of one's own actions. This attention to a deep responsibility for how to pass on well enough means that even the main way *Longplayer* performs (on a computer) and broadcasts (through internet streaming) are a preoccupation for Jem, as neither is ecologically nor ethically sustainable. Talking about the speed of technologies, Jem points out the irony and the challenge that in realizing an artwork composed to take its time to develop across a large durational expanse there is a reliance on technologies which are progressing at huge cost to the environment.

> *'However wondrous all these technologies are that we're talking about, they're actually really fast, not slow. The progress is exponential. It's not linear, it's getting faster and faster. But in order, of course, for these technologies to enable us to hear* Longplayer *everywhere just from a tiny, powerful thing such as an iPhone, there's also the massive cost to the environment*

of storing all the data. Actually, I was thinking this morning of a question we should ask: what's the carbon footprint of streaming Longplayer *through the website, listening through the stream, as opposed to the carbon footprint of downloading the app?'*

the cloudiness of the cloud p.217

Jem and I talk about the climate costs of data and memory, about the cloud, — about becoming conscious of 'spending all day just taking things down and sending them back up.' I ask him about how streaming something, over downloading, fosters a different relationship with time for the listener. I am thinking of the download as a complete and contained file, something available to scan through anachronistically, rather than having to follow as it plays. Jem reminds me, though, that what someone is downloading with the *Longplayer* app is not the composition in its entirety, but the source music:

'The app is the twenty-minute sound file and the algorithm or the abstract score that then works on that sound file to create the music from instant to instant. So the Longplayer *app isn't playing Longplayer back to you, it's performing for you. With the app you've more accurately got the score for the thousand years. The phone is performing the score for you.'*

I have asked Jem before why any computer that plays *Longplayer* is 'performing' the music, rather than, say, 'generating' it. As someone committed to querying the language we each choose to name the world with, I am especially interested when Jem places importance on a word for *Longplayer*'s definition: as reluctant as he is to create canonical descriptions, in order to carry forward the conceptual core of the artwork they are inevitable and necessary.

'Performing is more human. Generating sounds like a machine. In a sense the computer, the app, is generating Longplayer *but it's*

a bit like saying Longplayer *was designed rather than composed. I'd never use "generating."'*

While each one of us will bring our own powers of description to *Longplayer*, participate in building a collective language, that the music is *performed*, not generated is significant. I understand the work performance is doing here; performance honors the human, the correspondence across time of all those people who perform *Longplayer* or who enable the performance by digital means.

There are many ways *Longplayer* has so far been performed.[5] That there are ways yet-to-be-imagined for realizing *Longplayer*'s performance, is for me one of the most compelling aspects of this artwork moving so far through time, beyond the digital and computers as we know them. What do we, then, as custodians need to leave behind us, pass on, in order for the artwork to continue?

5 *Longplayer* is most commonly performed by computers as is accessible as a continuous stream, accessible via *Longplayer*'s website. *Longplayer* has also been performed by singers in *Longplayer for Voices* (2014) and by turntablists including Jem Finer with Vicki Bennett and Steve Beresford in *Longplayer for Turntables* (2015) and in re-mixes by Larry Achiampong (2018) and Shiva Feshareki (2019). Jem has also played smaller pieces of *Longplayer* with various instruments including the sound of stars in *Shortplayer #5* (2019). *Longplayer Live*, as Jem describes, is 'performed on a giant orchestral instrument of 234 Singing Bowls, arranged in six concentric rings.' The performance of *Longplayer Live* happened for the first time at the Roundhouse in London (2009) and a year later at the Yerba Buena Center for the Arts in San Francisco (2010). To mark the composition's quarter century, a collective of thirty-six people, half of them under age 25, returned to the Roundhouse to play the day-long 1000-minute score from 7:20am to midnight (2025).

'If you were to carve Longplayer's *abstract score on a stone, you would carve a representation of the circular score. But you'd need some instructions as well.'*

Jem has often imagined stone inscription as one way of preserving the score of *Longplayer* for future generations, although again the need arises for accompanying description, explanation, instruction.

> *'How to most succinctly add whatever information is necessary to bring it to life, to share how it animates through time? I don't think it's even crucial that people play it accurately, you know. I can imagine* Longplayer *in time dissolving into something that's played with an approximation to what it is, but would never actually, if you added it all up, be a thousand years long.'*

Longplayer in time dissolving... The point Jem makes here about accuracy and approximation is worth pausing on: *Longplayer* is only, and can only ever be, as accurate as who or what performs it. Inevitably there will be gaps; there already have been small intervals when the stream's connection has been lost to server disruption, power outage, a faulty wire, a mistakenly closed computer. In contrast to the computer-performed *Longplayer*, which never returns to the point it last stopped playing after it has cut out, Jem imagines *Longplayer* performed by humans as something stretching and dilating through time. —

breathing and alive p.451

> *'It might end up being 2000 years or only 500 years.* Longplayer *continues in the act of taking up where the last people have stopped playing it, wherever they approximate that to be.'*

How to communicate the methods for realizing and performing *Longplayer*'s score?

> *'I can't give you a definite answer and I don't think at this point in time it actually matters; what matters is the idea of figuring it out...'*

At the time of this writing, as *Longplayer* reaches twenty-five years of continuous play, performed by computers across the globe, there is an archive full of the artwork's initial and ongoing experiments, records of its various intentions, notes on its practical maintenance.[6] Held there are various documents detailing methods of *Longplayer*'s realization, including an instruction manual for *Longplayer Live*, where humans play the singing bowls across the course of a day. How long will these materials exist for though? *Longplayer's* duration puts necessary pressure on the faith placed in the tangibly held artefact, the paper document, the written word. As well as scrutiny on the illusory resilience of institutions charged with caring for such materials.

6 The archive is looked after by Trustee James Bulley and catalogued by Lorenzo Prati. At the time of this writing *Longplayer*'s archive is held in Special Collections at Goldsmiths, University of London.

And so I return to Levin's idea of *Longplayer* travelling as chant or myth, because for me following an oral tradition of handing on what has come before honors the vitality and sustainability of sonic practice, always a practice of approximation, a challenge to accuracy as more valid or true. That *Longplayer*—as a piece of music which may or may not play out loud as technologies change and transform—might come to rely on word of mouth as its mode of preservation, might move through collective story-telling as a way of existing, is a tender thought. How might the music be told, how might the methods for performing find shape in speech?

> *'I am interested in the idea that* Longplayer *is passed on through communities of people who talk about it. And so not just through the work of the Trust (although that's important), but also through people who are interested in performing it themselves and working out ways of doing so. Not necessarily to continuously*

> *perform it, but to come back to it whenever they can and however they can. Because that seems to me the most sustainable way. I'd say that's maybe my most ideal way.'*

'Whenever they can' both acknowledges and gives agency to the inevitable time lapses in human attention, the rhythms of return amongst the pulls and responsibilities of our own lives. While in 'however they can' I hear Jem's deep understanding of how much imaginative and practical resource *Longplayer* needs.

> *'When people say, how do you keep it going? I say, well, there's lots of ways; but to me, the interesting one is that people have to want it to carry on. And therefore, they have to engage with it and find ways to help it do so, which creates a community through time, thinking with a responsibility to future generations. I think this is where if one can reduce instructions for performing* Longplayer *to something more simple, you can then start embedding it in all sorts of things like stories and rhymes and games.'*

Technology, returned to its word roots, grows from *techné*: a knowledge of how to make things, a practical knowledge. A story is a made thing, re-made and made again in all the bodies who tell and translate it as well as those who choose to listen; a rhyme is a made thing that in many ways refuses to be misremembered or undone.

making as a process of becoming p. 417

Longplayer is in a process of continual making. — And so I am drawn to thinking how *Longplayer* produces a slow, accumulated knowledge of **making the conditions of its own survival**; a collective collaborative knowledge that enriches over time through listening and in conversation; a knowledge that never presumes to be complete, because always on the move; a knowledge of how to make things last through the gift of human attention wherever and however it can be given.

These were my last lines, but as I am working through my closing thoughts, I have in the back of my mind the handwritten pages Jem sent me some months ago. So here is another ending, a return to a 'slow' story of Jem's, adjacent to *Longplayer*. I read the following words now as something like an allegory for the speed of expectation meeting an acceptance and optimism for what is to come... and how this feels intimately connected to the ways Jem and I have talked about *Longplayer*: about incompleteness; urgency in what unfolds slowly; and about the composition we will 'never hear' even while we listen with it, as it goes...

> *I've been getting used to, even taking for granted, the almost simultaneous act of wanting something, ordering it, and getting it delivered. Yesterday I ordered a new hurdy-gurdy. The delivery date on the invoice is January 2028. That is 3½ years! Imagine the patience, the optimism even. But actually there is something very calming about this time span. I'll be a better player by then for a start, more 'worthy' of the beautiful instrument I've commissioned. It's totally in keeping with the nature of the instrument, an ancient string machine whose origins are mysterious and obscure, and whose playing can itself stop time.*[7]

[7] From Jem Finer's handwritten note *In Praise of the Hurdy-Gurdy*, as sent to Ella Finer on October 20, 2024.

Reference

Levin, Janna. 'Time is Dead.' In Jem Finer, *Longplayer,* Artangel, 2003.

dynamism
imbalance
warm chaos
an idea about how to be
spatial secrets
boundlessness
wonder
not-knowing
everyday beacons
inscrutable tools
vastness of perspective
love of the world
unfolding

Isamu Noguchi
Solid State Technology

Dakin Hart

Not much wisdom rises to the level of technology. Even in the best of times, most newfangled ethics have little bearing on the fate of the species. Unlike the golden rule, which, if it were our only guide, might be enough. Anyway, this is far from the best of times. Our children are zombie-walking into replacing time-tested ethical references like the major holy books with social media. Which is, probably, a more accurate and complete repository of knowledge about the human condition—but for that reason is also more likely to expedite our self-annihilation than, say, the Koran. Against the backdrop of our likely futures trending towards apocalyptic dystopia, there are some bright spots.

The Japanese American sculptor Isamu Noguchi's way of looking at things strikes some people as one of those—though most probably couldn't explain why. I spent a decade at the Isamu Noguchi Foundation and Garden Museum spinning the kaleidoscope of his perspective, looking for ways to isolate and reveal specific examples of his more epiphanic attitudes in a transmissible form. Noguchi was better at expressing ideas in things than most of his 'Live in Your Head: When Attitudes Become Form'[1] contemporaries who are famous for it. But demonstrating how is a challenge—because one of the things that makes Noguchi's knowledge worth sharing also makes it hard to grasp and explain: much of it not being rendered or explicable in words. (Our biases against non-linguistic intelligences are deep-seated.) —

persistent cultural bugs
p.293

1 Curated in 1969 by Harald Szeemann for the Kunsthalle Bern, this was a seminal exhibition of postwar art. It featured post-minimalist works, Arte Povera, and Process Art. In his introduction to the catalog, Scott Burton, then primarily a critic, wrote 'Art has been veritably invaded by life, if life means flux, change, chance, time, unpredictability.'

What follows are three examples of what might be called solid state technologies: ideas in the form of objects that Noguchi adapted from time-tested traditions and developed in the cause of using art to encourage our innate—but so often hamstrung—love of the world.

Rocking Stool

Noguchi was something of a connoisseur of seating. Which wasn't unusual in the mid-century modern design crowd—air travel, exploding global trade, and a golden age of design industry magazines having made chairs into a theoretical cross-cultural benchmark. The collection of objects Noguchi left when he died is a motley assortment from all over that leans towards traditional, sometimes inscrutable, tools.[2] It includes two types of one-legged stools: a Danish example of a paver's stool fairly common in Europe and several examples of a market stool found in West Africa. (It took weeks of research just to identify what the Danish stool was.) Made of wood, they both sit low (between a foot and a foot and a half high), and feature a circular, slightly concave seat and a convex bottom surface.

2 Some of these were included in 'Noguchi: Body-Space Devices' (The Noguchi Museum, May 15, 2019–May 2, 2021). See noguchi.org/museum/exhibitions/view/noguchi-body-space-devices/. For a more general overview, see Wiener.

The turned leg of the Danish paver's stool terminates in a ball, making it look something like an oversized toy. But it is a finely-tuned device, with a form evolved to accomplish the specific task of allowing cobble-layers to scoot backwards through a bed of sand while leaving their hands free to set stones. It takes as much practice to use one without embarrassment (or concussion) as a pogo stick or a unicycle. But for the expert mason it makes it possible to work long stretches without the constant strains of repeatedly standing and squatting, and/or bending over at the waist. With seats and bases of more or less the same diameter, the West African market stools resemble squat hourglasses or double-ended drums. They sit lower than the pavers' stools: low enough to allow the sitter to comfortably rest arms on bent knees. Where most chairs and stools are designed to prioritize stability—balancing that with style, portability, whatever—these market stools, with their gently domed bottoms, are meant to rock. — They developed to allow market stall tenders to relieve long stretches of sitting in one place with a little motion.

plural use value,
with an open potential
p.199

Noguchi's one-legged stool was inspired by an African market stool owned by his friend, the *LIFE* magazine photographer Eliot Elisofon. Which explains the 1956 *LIFE* feature about it entitled, 'The New Seat with a Neater Teeter: African art inspired its design.'[3] The article explains how Noguchi, being one of those people who 'fidgets while he sits,' and frustrated by the original's irregular edge, created one that 'enables fidgety sitters to tilt, rock back and forth, and even spin around with a fair chance of not tipping over.' (Not that fair, truth be told.) Noguchi's self-assigned brief was to create a stool that would allow him to imbalance consistently, on the verge of falling over, throughout a full 360-degree rotation. *Rocking Stool* was the result. And, in fact, with a lot of practice, it is possible to achieve a near-perfect state of terrifying instability on one. —

a feeling of vertigo
p.109

3 *LIFE*, 122, 125.

Years later Noguchi discussed single-point seating with the filmmaker Michael Blackwood in the same biographical feature in which he makes the startling statement, 'Sometimes I think I'm part of this world of today. Sometimes I feel that maybe I belong in history, or in prehistory, or that there is no such thing as time.'[4] Speaking in the spartan, Japanese-style bedroom of his Long Island City studio, which was furnished largely with African furniture, Noguchi picks up another example of a low West African chair shaped from a single swoop of hardwood. Sporting three short legs, it is so narrow and unstable that it might as well be one-legged.

Reclining back onto it and struggling a little bit to stay upright, Noguchi plants his feet to either side—as if fitting outriggers to a canoe—and explains, 'It has one point. But your two feet act as the other two points.' Getting up and moving to a nearby example of his *Rocking Stool* (the short version), he performs a low-speed wobble and concludes, 'You really don't need more than one point.' Because a tripod is stable, and we carry two points with us all of the time.

4 |
Blackwood.

He goes on to suggest that eventually we'll be able to do away with furniture entirely, and that the cultures where furniture is simpler are further ahead on that evolutionary path. It is unclear how he thinks we will function without furniture, or even why we should. But the superior ideal he seems to have extracted from African furniture was minimum separation between active living human and spinning planet. This is also apparent in the simply furnished bedroom, which toyed with a pre-modern Japanese relationship with the floor.

Noguchi's *Rocking Stool* technology is not in the novel bicycle-wheel system that lashes the top to the bottom. Its wisdom is inversely proportional to its functionality, because as furniture it is a virtually unusable paragon of product liability. What matters is the consternation it delivers. Which was captured in a contemporary promotional photograph that accompanied the *LIFE* feature: a triple exposure of a woman sitting up straight on the taller version of the stool and leaning once to either side. In one of the leaning exposures she seems ecstatic to be courting disaster, as if she were on a dangerous amusement park ride. In the other she looks more understandably apprehensive, like a first-time skydiver. In aggregate she is right where Noguchi wants her: a kind of living symbol of dynamism, like NASA's swoopy 'meatball' logo. *Rocking Stool* is not a place to sit but an idea about how to be. —

techné for a new reality
p.432

Illusion of the Fifth Stone

At the center of the garden of The Isamu Noguchi Garden Museum sits *Illusion of the Fifth Stone* (1970), a puzzle in the form of a pile of rocks. It is the command console of a device known as a sculpture garden. Each rock has been point-chiseled to give the rounded-off impression of natural weathering. But they fit together tightly enough that any thought that the pile might be naturally occurring is impossible to sustain. The individual stones are massive, making the whole seem big, though it's not. At just under four feet tall, it is easy to walk around and view from a few steps away—which is all the space it has in the garden for which it was made.

Japanese Garden technology is particularly strong in the fabrication and management of perceived and psychological space, which Noguchi drew on in this sculpture and many others that propound rather than reveal spatial secrets. Like a particularly tricky piece of geometry or a space you can't quite wrap your head around no matter how many times you walk it, the environment that the closed form of the sculpture implies is boundless. It is a discrete object that functions like the void of space: triggering a wonder closely akin to not knowing. —

trust unknown wiring p.448

Depending on the height and position of the viewer, the sculpture can appear to be composed of as few as three stones or as many as six. In Noguchi's words:

> In general, the impression is of four stones. Going around, one sees five. The stones seem to lock together. The degree of artifice is not readily visible. Are these natural boulders? No. The whole seems natural. A whole.[5]

[5] Noguchi.

The mechanism the illusion controls—'unlocks' is probably a better metaphor—is a spatializing, empirical experience awareness modulator. Its effects may not explode and expand before us with virtual reality CGI fireworks, but it will unfold in the mind of anyone willing to give themselves up to another way of looking at things with the force of a universal decoder. The secret is simple. How big space feels is not dependent on how big it is. The idea of America, (the United States of America version), is not incidentally a product of this same illusion, which is itself derived from the boundlessness of nature—from the open spaces of the North American west to the expanding universe.[6]

6 For more on Noguchi's interest in the expanding universe, see *Space, Choreographed: Noguchi and Ruth Page* (September 25, 2013–January 26, 2014), noguchi.org/museum/exhibitions/view/space-choreographed-noguchi-and-ruth-page/.

Akari

'Lights should be as movable as butterflies' was one of Noguchi's earliest explanations for how he wanted his Akari lanterns to seem: not fixed, but offering lightness, in every sense. A 'true development of the old tradition' of the Japanese candle-powered paper lantern, they are related as well to single-use sky lanterns (flying paper balloons powered, and destroyed, by an open flame). Their shades made of washi paper over fine bamboo ribs with thin metal appurtenances, they are ultra-lightweight by design. He was serious about their flightiness. He made the remark about butterflies to a reporter for the *New York Times* while demonstrating how easily a 1A with a printed shade could be carried around and turned to and away from the wall for manual dimming.

One of the earliest design challenges in developing Akari was figuring out how to get the table lamps to stay in place without making them heavy. Butterflies have minds of their own and don't sit still for long, and even when they do, their wings beat steadily, keeping them warmed up and ready to fly. The feet of the original version of the 1A (the first Akari model), were made by bending the end of each wire leg into a neat, nearly closed, rather insectoid loop. It was simple and looked great. But the lamp was so lightweight that even back when lamp cords were thin (22 and 20 gauge, in pre-UL days), the weight of the cord was enough to pull the lamp to the floor. On a polished surface—like the top of an old wood dresser or nightstand—they'd skitter away as fast as a cockroach over linoleum when the lights go on. To keep them from sliding, Noguchi replaced the integral metal feet with little non-slip rubber caps. Nature gave butterflies grippy feet for a reason.

'They should have an accidental nature quality lacking from fixed, willful mechanical electricity,' Noguchi went on to the *Times*, pretty definitively tipping his hand in that inimitable, nimble way he had of reframing everything. 'Fixed, willful mechanical electricity.' What is that, besides the enemy? Noguchi was an irascible curmudgeon for the best of what we can achieve on Earth, assuming all of the nuance and balancing acts required to do it. His Earth as perfect sculpture contained trees, radio towers, and church steeples. Things he perceived as callously industrial he tried to invest with biological logics; to anything straying into unrealistically romantic naturalism he tended to bring a systematizing attention and rigor. We are by and of nature, of course, but we have also transcended and removed ourselves from it in ways that make us special and so very dangerous. Akari were meant to be domestic everyday beacons in the long dark night of humanity's ever worsening incomprehension of our place in the order of things. —

praise for the tiniest things p.179

All's Well That Ends Well

Scientists say we are, in the words of Oxford researchers, 'significantly more intelligent'[7] than our Neanderthal cousins, despite comparable brain size. The argument goes that more of Neanderthal's brain capacity was 'devoted to vision and control of their larger bodies, leaving less mental real estate for higher thinking and social interactions.'[8] Of course, if true, that also suggests that Neanderthals may well have been more physically intelligent, less self-involved, and more connected to the world, than we are. Perhaps that is why the practical application of their knowledge (technology) did not involve the invention of Styrofoam, lounge chairs, or the internet.

7 This is *Smithsonian Magazine*'s gloss on the research; see Stromberg. For the underlying paper, see Pearce et al.

8 Ibid.

'I am not a designer,' Noguchi said. 'The word design implies catering to the quixotic fashion of the time. All my work, tables as well as sculptures, are conceived as fundamental problems of form that would best express the human and aesthetic activity involved with these objects.' A stool you can't rest on because it won't stay still—because nothing does on a sphere spinning at 1,000 mph; a solid stone mass designed to three-dimensionalize the happy impossibility of total spatial awareness while encouraging a vastness of perspective; and lamps that naturalize the signature technology of industrial modernity to bring the warm chaos of nature into the home rather than seeking to keep it at bay. For Noguchi, the human and aesthetic activity involved with these objects is just the constant, glorious balancing act that is life on Earth.

References

Blackwood, Michael, dir. *Isamu Noguchi*. Michael Blackwood Productions, 1972.

LIFE. 'The New Seat with a Neater Teeter: African Art Inspired in Its Design.' February 6, 1956. archive.noguchi.org/Detail/archival/80361.

Noguchi, Isamu. *Isamu Noguchi Garden Museum*. Harry N. Abrams Inc., 1987.

Pearce, Eiluned, Chris Stringer, and R. I. M. Dunbar. 'New Insights Into Differences in Brain Organization Between Neanderthals and Anatomically Modern Humans.' In *Proceedings of the Royal Society B: Biological Sciences* 280, no. 1758 (2013): 20130168. doi.org/10.1098/rspb.2013.0168.

Stromberg, Joseph. 'Science Shows Why You're Smarter Than a Neanderthal.' In *Smithsonian Magazine*, March 12, 2013. smithsonianmag.com/science-nature/science-shows-why-youre-smarter-than-a-neanderthal-1885827/.

Wiener, Kate. 'Noguchi As Collector.' Noguchi Digital Features, n.d. noguchi.org/isamu-noguchi/digital-features/noguchi-as-collector/.

synergies
welcoming
negotiation
co-creation
sensuality
adaptation
dispersed subjectivity
expanding the
liveable realm
revelry
play
singular-plural
speaking with
afterlives
arts of ripening
thriving above and below
ontological joy

A Portrait of Plants as Artists

Techné, Techniques, and Technologies of Vegetality

Michael Marder

SCAFFOLDING

I find it quite impossible to imagine art totally vacant of plants. Even those theological traditions, like Islam, that (in a negative reaction against idolatry) proscribe the depiction of animals and humans, excel in floral designs. Plants figure prominently in landscape paintings and still lifes that extract them from the hardly noticeable background of everyday existence. There, they become the subjects, presumably deserving of our attention and regard, our gaze and care. The vegetal content of traditional art is not what interests me here, however. I want to focus not on the artist's plants but on plant artists—our equal, if not superior, partners in aesthetic processes broadly understood. — With these reflections, I would like to contribute a few conceptual brushstrokes to the portrait of plants as subjects who resort to their own technologies of vegetality.

apprenticeship
with other species
p.145

Even before anything appears on canvas or is etched in wood, plants serve as materials for the artwork. The substratum for visual arts is often vegetal. Spreading pigments on paper, we paint with plants on plants: with gum arabic from acacia trees in watercolors, with oil paints using linseed oil, and so on. Prior to the digital age, motion pictures used celluloid film, made on the basis of plant substance, cellulose. Wood carvings date back to the very beginnings of humanity. As image-makers, are we the mirrors in which plants see without seeing themselves?

Putting aside the strange question about human mirrors that has imposed itself on me, it might appear that the human artists' use of vegetal materials reduces these to a passive role of (technical) means for purely external ends. Plants seem to be subject to extreme instrumentalization. That is, until we recall that the remains of plants with which we paint, sculpt, build houses, or film not only receive the sensuous image of the artist's idea but also offer the sort of resistance that bends the initial blueprint. In woodcarving, the size of the tree trunk determines the dimensions of the finished sculpture. The grain of wood dictates the course and direction of the sculptor's work, typically cutting plant fibers across the grain. 'Imperfections' in plant materials may be incorporated as the unexpected and previously unplanned features of the art piece. Drying vegetal-derived pigments will impose their own color scheme on the painting and change with the passage of time. The varying absorption capacities of canvas paper or fabric will introduce *their* corrections into the hues and outlines of whatever is depicted on it.

These examples are much more than instances of mechanical resistance to 'spiritual' human endeavors that modify our abstract ideas when they fall into the world of matter. The afterlife of plants in a chopped down trunk or in vegetal-based paint is an alien intentionality, with which the human artist must be in constant negotiation and collaboration. — The work of art wherein vegetal materials participate is thus a product of plant-human synergy that overflows the boundaries separating animate from inanimate beings, let alone distinct biological kingdoms. And the task of the human artist, a little like the task of the translator according to Walter Benjamin, is to let plants speak, or, in the spirit of synergy, to speak with them—neither in a monologue nor even in a dialogue but in a synologue, the *with-logos* that keeps its silence. (I am obviously not using this term in its 'technical' sense of a gene with several representatives in a genome.)

being affected by one another p.107

For Benjamin, the task (*Aufgabe*) of the translator is invariably a failure: it is impossible to produce an exact equivalence of meanings in two or more languages. To translate is to betray 'the original' both in the negative and in the positive senses of betrayal, breaking trust and expressing something, often unwittingly. Be it scientific or artistic, a human translation of the languages of plants is, therefore, a fecund failure. The art that is 'of plants' in the minimal sense of the vegetal substratum absorbing and appropriating the work our hands entrust it with contributes to this process. But the absorption and the appropriation in question are not only ontic, as in the case of paper and watercolors; they are also ontological, as in the reception and material transformation of a mental representation.

The minimal sense of the art of plants is, however necessary, insufficient. Plants are artists insofar as they are the co-creators of the artworks for which parts of their bodies are utilized, as well as the creators of themselves, of the atmosphere, and of the world. Plus, they are aesthetic agents. At the root of aesthetics, *aesthesis* refers to perception (from the verb *aisthesthai*, 'to perceive'). In this context, plants appeal to the human and other-than-human perceptual apparatuses—for instance, through the shapes, colors, and smells of their flowers or the taste of their fruits. And they perceive the world—occasionally better, on a wider spectrum of possible stimuli—than we do, as Daniel Chamovitz has shown in his book *What a Plant Knows*.

With respect to how plants give themselves to the perception of bees, humans, butterflies, and birds, we might say that they are not inertly available, as a rock might be. Instead, a rose prepares itself for the moment when its petals would open, exuding a delicate aroma; delicious figs take the time to ripen before their fruits release their honey-like contents in our mouths; orchid flowers shape themselves in a certain way to resemble a female wasp before a male specimen spots them and flies over so as to consummate, by mistake, a cross-kingdoms sexual act. Plants paint the world in intense colors and fill it with elaborate shapes. They swathe life in a plethora of smells and addictive tastes. These are, indeed, techniques engrained in the event of perception—its timing, the fittingness between the perceiving and the perceived, the coming in touch of various planes of existence, the associations, affects, and comportments that such contact may trigger. To put it briefly, there is no *aesthesis* without *techné*, not least in the world of plants, which welcomes us on the inside and the outside, in our noses and lungs, eyes and mouths, canvases and sculptures. —

vital physical relations
p.402

It is not that an individual rosebush, fig tree, or orchid deliberately presents itself in this or that fashion to the senses of beings who are not plants. Vegetal aesthetics consists in the achievements of evolutionary creativity, sometimes coupled with human efforts at cultivation. Cultivating a particularly aromatic variety of flowers, we, once again, participate together with them in a creative process, in aesthetic synergy. As for evolution, we still need to come to terms with what this concept actually signifies. The tendency is to treat evolution as a new, scientific incarnation of God, through which everything acquires meaning and all the phenomena of life are explicable. In fact, it is nothing but the ties that bind *this* rose or *this* fig tree to countless generations of its predecessors, dispersing its subjectivity across space (through its collective constitution together with its genetic kin) and drowning it in deep time. — Henri Bergson's notion of creative evolution touched upon something of this aesthetic agency in excess of the phenotype.

showing us another (spatio-)temporality p.450

The self-presentation of plants is more obviously aesthetic to the extent that it revels in the spectacle, in the spectacular dynamics of display. The drama and suspense preceding the opening of flowers is quickly followed by the exuberance of the blossoming period and a similarly stunning fading, withering, and decay. The nonflowering varieties that rely on asexual reproduction do not stay far behind, because vegetal display is a corollary to the maximum exposure that distinguishes the plant's mode of being, its 'energy solution,' notably to be energized by the abundant solar light and heat above the ground and by remnants of organic life below ground. Biophysicists are still learning from plants how to activate the vital technologies of photosynthesis to generate the cleanest energy imaginable.

The proliferation of living exposed surfaces, whether green or multi-colored, is ultimately responsible for the rich aesthetics of vegetation, which Friedrich Schiller includes under the heading of material play, a prototype of the formal play drive, in his *Letters on the Aesthetic Education of Man*. In Letter 27, he writes: 'Even in mindless nature there is revealed a luxury of powers and a laxity of determination which in that natural context might as well be called play. The tree puts forth innumerable buds which perish without developing, and stretches out for nourishment many more roots, branches, and leaves than are used for the maintenance of itself and its species. What the tree returns from its lavish profusion unused and unenjoyed to the kingdom of the elements, the living creature may squander in joyous movements. So nature gives us even in her material realm a prelude to the infinite, and even here partly removes the chains which she casts away entirely in the realm of form.'[1]

[1] Schiller, 133.

Display and, even more so, play are the aesthetic antidotes to the seriousness of evolutionary reason. As Schiller has it, they happen for nothing, out of the overabundance of life in a playful, displaying creature. Above all, in a plant. Schiller goes so far as to deem the play drive a sign of happiness—of a plant, animal, or human rejoicing in itself. Of course, at issue is not joy as an emotion but ontological joy, a being reveling in its power to be and in the actualization of this potentiality beyond what is strictly needed (say, for survival). The exuberance of flourishing, the abundance of display, is the aesthetic function of play, which in the logic of means-and-ends is utterly superfluous. Proliferating outside this logic are technologies 'for nothing'—for nothing determinate within the instrumental scheme that only functions when there are certain goals to be achieved. It is the 'for nothing' that, airing the fabric of existence, secretly imbues every 'for something' with meaning. —

a praxis of being
p.59

In the last instance, the leaves are exposed not in order to maximize their capture of sunlight and opportunities for photosynthesis, though they also do that. Instrumental exposure is what remains of the plant's massive 'squandering' of itself into the outwardly expressed joy of its being. Georges Bataille's general economy, of which restricted economy oriented to specific calculable ends is a subspecies, follows on the heels of such play. Now, with regard to Bataille's suggestion, we might say that playful aesthetic experimentation (say, of the plants themselves) is the milieu, the atmosphere, or the climate within which adaptation and survival become possible, just as (or simply *as*) acting 'for something' becomes possible on the basis of doing so 'for nothing.'

Across its play and display, vegetal being does not diverge from appearance: the plant wears what it is on its sleeve, or, more accurately, on its leaf. Its subjectivity, or what used to be referred to as its 'soul,' is an exteriority, not an interiority, breathing on the permeable membranes of its organs. More than that, to assert that plants are the artists of sensuous appearances, offering untold aesthetic riches to whomever they attract, is to claim by the same token that they are the artists of being. In effect, plants create and recreate themselves all the time, growing new limbs, shedding leaves, putting out new sexual organs (i.e., the flowers). They are performative creatures *par excellence*, the artists of themselves. Their behavior does not follow on the heels of generating new parts of their bodies and letting the old ones go; *it is this very act!* Vegetal self-making, unmaking, and remaking take their cues from the conditions outside—cold for shedding leaves; warmth and longer hours of daylight for flowering; sun exposure for growing new branches—without a rigidly predetermined organismic plan. The artistry of plants that make themselves is, therefore, of a piece with that of the world.

Still, it would be a mistake to assume that, attentive as they are to exteriority, plants are manipulated, marionette-like, by their environment into particular forms of behavior. Not only do they reach complex decisions on the timing of changes in their morphology and physiology, but they also constitute the places where they grow, by which they are, in turn, constituted. The traditional distinction between activity and passivity no longer applies. Photosynthesizing, plants are the artisans of the atmosphere and of the world itself. They bring together the organic and the inorganic realm and gather around and on themselves creatures from various biological kingdoms: fungi, insects, bacteria, animals... Before they are landscaped by human hands and well before they feature in landscape paintings, plants create airscapes and earthscapes, microclimates, and breathable air, cooling and humidifying the sites of their existence, returning organic richness to the earth in the process of decay. Our molding of the world may be understood on the inverted or perverted model of its vegetal creation: we fill the air with CO_2, deplete the soil, prompt global warming, cause deserts to expand. The human art of world-creation verges on world-destruction, diminishing the material possibilities for future life. Conversely, plants are the architects of the environment who work or play with, rather than against, it and who expand the livable realm both through their crafting of climates and through their activities of growth and decay.

It is often observed that plants are marvelous alchemists, since they convert inorganic particles coupled with sunshine into organic matter fit for the nourishment of others. This is artistic creation, the culinary arts of ripening attuned to the varying degrees of solar heat and in symbiosis with human and other-than-human palates. Making their fruits edible, sometimes by adding an enzyme intended exactly for that, refining their juices, and cooking in the sun, plants are exquisite chefs, not suppliers of raw materials for gastronomy. Ancient Indian thought, going all the way back to Vedic traditions, considered cooking as the technologies of perfection, of bringing that which is cooked—ripening fruits, food, a person, a world—to the best condition imaginable. There, fire (Agni) is the one responsible for perfecting everything and everyone received into his embrace. But cooks play with fire and its intensities, adding their skillful, technical discernment of the right moment when the process comes to its culmination to the material discernments of fire itself (or himself). Plants do just that, in collaboration with every classical element, including, of course, solar fire.

A final brushstroke I would like to add to the portrait of plants as artists has to do with their unique subjectivity. Vegetal existence is, to borrow the expression of Jean-Luc Nancy, singular-plural, thriving above and below the thresholds of individuality. In other contexts, I have addressed its ethical and political implications; the aesthetic sense of the plants' mode of being is yet to be thought through, something I have only begun doing here. At the very least, their mode of being indicates that plant authorship and artistry are anonymous and dispersed, as well as collective and collaborative. Postmodernism celebrates the death of the author previously imagined as a solitary genius, a heroic and creative individual behind the work. What this theoretical current leaves out is the upside of the momentous event it registers: the afterlife of the author and the artist is vegetal. —

accompaniment through time p.367

For, don't 'our' writing and aesthetic practices approximate those of plants once the illusion of autonomously individual authorship is laid to rest? Don't their outcomes become not only ours—the property that is mine, yours, or yours and mine at the same time—but also of the plants with which and on which we write and create, of the microorganisms that nestle in the work, of the dust that settles on and gets engrained in it? Aren't the technologies of a presumably human expression facilitated, collaboratively co-created, derailed, redirected, and rendered meaningful with and by vegetal *techné*?

SCAFFOLDING

Reference

Schiller, Friedrich. *On the Aesthetic Education of Man*. Translated by Reginald Snell. Dover, 2004.

joy
heartbreak
ritual
mourning
momentary comfort
lasting yet fragile

Bound Together

Edwidge Danticat

Nineteen years ago, when my daughter Mira was born, my mother, a seamstress, gave me a scarf-length piece of white linen that she'd cut from the fabric she was using to make herself a dress. Calling it a *bando*—typically a headband in Haitian Creole (*bandeau* in French)—she wrapped it around my belly to help me regain my posture and reshape my waist. Like many postpartum rituals, including forty days of rest and special leaf baths and teas, this custom was as old as time, she told me. There were trendier belly bands and wraps available online, but I opted for hers because, as she helped me bind and unbind it, I felt that I was being tied to the women in my family, those who had come before and those yet to come. — We even joked about my one day having to convince my own daughter that this was something all new mothers had to do.

care-taking
across generations
p.365

> 'There will probably be faster ways to do this in the future,' she'd say. 'There already is one,' I'd say. 'It's called plastic surgery.'

This March, when my brother-in-law died, at fifty-six, I saw his eighty-nine-year-old mother include belly binding as part of her mourning practice. Between the showers that she had to force herself to take, she wrapped a head scarf around her abdomen, which, in her old age, was permanently protruding. Sometimes she needed help tightening it, and, at her request, I would fasten the scarf over the spot where she believed her uterus to be. Other times, we fastened it around her pelvis, closer to the birth canal. For the first time in decades, she said, she was feeling tranche, visceral labor pains, as though her son were being born again. — Because she could not fully express her grief in a New York City apartment, at least not in the traditional ways—by wailing or allowing her body to completely contort in the manner we call *kriz* (convulsions)—she groaned through her body's memory of pre-labor, crowning, and the final release of birth. She even moaned in her sleep, grunts like the ones I remember emitting during my daughters' births. After a few weeks, she moved the scarf to her head, using it to cradle her face and occasionally as a mourning veil.

the wild edges of grief
p.135

What we wear in both joy and grief can amplify our emotions, serving as an extension of our feelings. Mourning attire is much more than fabric; it is a way of expressing ourselves to those around us and perhaps even to the dead. Funerals, where love and heartbreak are simultaneously on display, are a kind of runway on which we honor our missing loved ones. At a couple of funerals I recently attended in the Haitian diaspora, mourners wore the deceased's favorite colors, even though those colors were far from the traditional sombre hues. At some homegoing services, people wear memorial T-shirts emblazoned with photographs of the dead that note the span of years between the loved one's sunrise and sunset.

Recently, a fifteen-year-old girl whom my younger daughter, Leila, knew briefly in middle school died in a tragic accident. It was the first time that someone my daughter knew who was her age had died. After hearing the news, Leila slept in a keepsake sweatshirt that the young woman had given to her guests at a party. After my mother died, I wore many of the black blouses she had worn to mourn her mother, which made me feel as though both of them were with me. Focussing on something touchable, lasting yet still fragile, like clothes, while mourning has allowed me to imagine grief as potentially sheddable one day. — This is, of course, not entirely true, but I have found it momentarily comforting, which is perhaps the most one can hope for during the early and most uncertain stages of mourning. I did not, however, wear any of the many flowered skirts that my mother had made, sometimes in as little as five minutes, using pillowcases, elastic, hemming tape, and a pair of scissors. My distaste for those skirts was a running joke between us: I do have my limits.

a body and
its haptic needs
p.414

In 'A Grief Observed,' a meditation on bereavement, the writer C. S. Lewis described his wife's death from cancer as a kind of shroud over his world. 'Her absence is like the sky, spread over everything,' he writes. Then, correcting himself, he adds, 'But no, that is not quite accurate. There is one place where her absence comes locally home to me, and it is a place I can't avoid. I mean my own body.' This is perhaps why our bodies require so much cradling in grief. Just as many people call out for their mothers in moments of sorrow and distress, in Haitian Creole we might be urged to brace ourselves for a catastrophic disaster—whether a hurricane or an imminent invasion—with this solemn piece of advice: *Maman pitit mare vant nou*. Mothers, bind your bellies.

'Bound Together' was first published in The New Yorker (print edition July 8 & 15, 2024). *Reprinted by permission of Edwidge Danticat and Aragi Inc.*

attending
attunement
responsiveness
intuition
listening to the body
restoring connections
natural feelings
rhythmic acts
sensitivity
transcendence
tension
flow
machine enactments
tactile wisdom
inward process
generative movement
(un)learning

Automated Bodies and the Somatics of Weaving

Gļeb(s) Maiboroda

Thread is arguably one of humanity's most significant technological developments.[1] It is comparable to the discovery of stone tools or writing systems, as it has profoundly changed the ways people come together, trade, and connect. The impact of thread in the development of early societies was so profound that textile archaeologist Elizabeth Wayland Barber even proposes referring to the period between 20,000 and 6,000 BC as the String Age rather than the Stone Age. Since then, weaving has remained an integral craft, accompanying us to this day.

1 According to archeological findings, cord spinning dates back 41,000–52,000 years. In the most ancient type of spinning, animal fibers (sheep or silk) or plant fibers (linen or cotton) were twisted together to create a string or cord.

The practice of thread making gave rise to sewing, netting, and weaving, among other textile techniques, which in turn made possible the production of garments and household objects. It also led to architectural developments, with the walls of prehistoric tents and dwellings often constructed from densely felted wool or interwoven plants.[2] As societies and economies rapidly grew, the need for efficient forms of textile production advanced, with handcraft eventually being replaced by automation.

2 In her short story 'The Carrier Bag of Fiction,' writer Ursula K. Le Guin takes us back to the invention of the bag in prehistoric times. There, she describes the container—a bag, sack, net, or basket—as a radical act of social imagination through collective foraging and care.

This essay focuses on weaving, and in particular, how automation has had a transformative effect on the weaver. It also

receptacle of powers, capacities, and resistances p. 207

attempts to recuperate and re-enliven the craft of weaving, and to assert the weaver's body as a site of re-learning and resistance. — The essay is divided into two chapters, which take their titles from the zero-one code of the weaving loom. In weaving '00' and '01' designate the rising and falling of the threads in order to create intricate patterns and designs. By borrowing this technical code, I propose a framework for approaching the weave as a set of repetitive movements that generate a cultural meaning in the same way as modern computers are programmed through a set of numbers. In the first chapter, I explore the ontological construction of the automated loom, its impact from the Industrial Revolution onward, and its approach to materials as boundless resources: an idea that is rooted in capitalist, colonial structures. I also reflect on what type of **making** takes place in such conditions and how fully automated technologies like the Jacquard loom dematerialize the very physical act of making. In the second chapter, drawing on my artistic and pedagogical practice, I address the disconnect between the weaver's body and mind. A problem that can be challenged by somatic forms of weaving that restore embodied connection, prioritize intuition, and encourage improvisational work. — This can be achieved through rhythmic involvement with the mechanical side of weaving, and generative movement that the engagement with the materials produces. I seek to cultivate a deeper understanding of the ways material culture in weaving can be reimagined and how haptic meaning can manifest in the work with automated looms.

rebooting p.346

00: The Rise of Automated Weaving

The early loom, in its pre-automated form, provided both a simple framework and a liberating force for the weaver to engage in making. Its power was expressed in the direct relationship between the weaver's body and the materials they engaged with. This link was particularly evident in the backstrap loom, which connected the weaver to the world outside of their shelter or home, enabling a direct engagement with the landscape, where creation unfolded alongside natural forces and processes.[3] | The invention of the backstrap loom (around 2500 BC), and its eventual spread across all continents, accelerated the pace at which early societies progressed. Its adoption formed the basis of economies deeply rooted in textile production, both for local use and international trade. As a result, weaving came to be understood as a technology that has a profound ontological presence, deeply tied to human existence. A single expanse of fabric, produced from the skillful intertwinement of vertical (warp) and horizontal (weft) threads, represents a convergence of materiality, craftsmanship, tradition, and cultural agency.[4]

3 A backstrap loom is a portable weaving device traditionally used in many cultures. Due to its mobility and construction that requires stretching between the abdomen of the weaver's body and other objects, plants and trees often become collaborators in the weaving process. This connection is beautifully shown in the video work of Guatemalan artist Antonio Pichillá Quiacaín, *Cordón Umbilical/Umbilical Cord* (2021). In the work, the woven cloth is shown stretched between the body of the artist himself and a tree in the dense forest. While the artist weaves traditional Mayan cloth, he also asserts the inextricable link between the making of culture in relation to nature.

4 In weaving, a set of vertical threads, which are set up as a foundation and held under tension are called warp. Horizontal thread, referred to as weft, refers to the yarn that weaves a fabric by going through warp threads perpendicularly.

In its essence, weaving involves a heightened sensitivity to the materials at hand and an ability to engage with the properties of those materials, their potentialities and responsiveness. — This engagement is not only intellectual, but is grounded in the weaver's lived experiences and constant practice of the craft, with a focus on tactile and sensory engagement. However, over the past few centuries, with every new advancement of technique, the yarn was literally slipping out of the hands of the very craftspeople who had been the caretakers of

setting matter into motion p.263

the thread for millennia. Advances in automation of most yarn-crafts led to technological innovation, but diminished physical autonomy of the weaver.[5] While automated technology has certainly increased efficiency and doubled output to fulfill rapidly growing market demands, it has systematically overlooked the vital physical relation between the weaver's body, materials, and the loom, a shift that has led to today's highly destructive, globalized system of cheaply produced textiles.[6]

5 For example, in 1764 James Hargreaves, an English weaver and one of the three men responsible for the mechanization of spinning, invented a device called the 'spinning jenny.' Compared to the hand-operated spinning wheel on which a skillful spinner could produce two to three spindles of yarn a day, the spinning jenny made it possible to spin up to 120 spindles daily. Many hand spinners of that time, threatened by the devaluation of their labor, regularly protested against the mechanization of spinning, and notoriously broke into Hargreaves's house to destroy his invention. Their anger did not manage to stop the sweeping forces of industrialization, only forcing Hargreaves to move out of his residence.

6 The Industrial Revolution marks an important point in modern history when agrarian and handicraft production transitioned to industrial and machine manufacturing. By the late seventeenth century, textile production on an industrial scale had become a major driver of Britain's economy, setting a 'standard' for change from local economies to globalized trade that was followed by North American and West European countries.

An important space for imagination and creativity that weavers traditionally carved out through practice became lost once industrial weaving entered the commercial arena. There, speed became the primary goal, with the push for faster production resulting in fabrics of poor quality, mass-produced in precarious labor conditions.[7]

7 Broudy, 22.

The enormous speed of production that has accompanied textiles since the Industrial Revolution has led to the standardization of textile knowledge and a decline in the preservation of traditional practices, significantly affecting the ways that traditional knowledge can be transmitted between different generations of weavers. Most of the textile knowledge was simply lost due to colonial hegemony, which systematically weakened the creativity and economic sustainability of traditional artisans and vernacular systems of knowledge. Many Indigenous techniques and cultural practices around weaving have since been lost forever.[8] The displacement of pre-automated forms of making under the guise of 'progress' has led to the loss of deep relationships formed between people and the land they inhabited for centuries. — Automation launched an irreversible process that left subsequent generations disconnected from their cultural roots and rendered many traditional forms of knowledge outdated.

de-worlding
p.198

8 With all the modern machinery available today, it is not possible to spin a linen yarn as smooth and thin as was found in Ancient Egypt: a fabric woven by hand with such a yarn would be similar in transparency to silk. Similarly, cotton in India (prior to colonization) used to be spun so fine that a fabric woven out of it would become semi-transparent when soaked in water. It is important to mention here that the cotton fiber, which is smooth and short in length, requires great skill in hand-spinning.

Today, modern looms like the air-jet loom, can weave up to 1600 meters of weft threads per minute, producing textiles in a matter of minutes. Similarly, a modern knitting machine can knit a complete sweater in just six minutes and a dress in twelve. These advances demonstrate how weaving and other handcrafts that have been automated to satisfy capitalism's economic demands have also enabled the system of fast-fashion: a world of rapidly changing trends and consumers' insatiable appetites in an endless search for new and innovative goods. The dramatic shift in how things are made has shaped textile design into a discipline that is more aligned with technologically-driven narratives of modernity than with the creative impulse to make. The invention of the Jacquard loom in 1804 epitomizes this tremendous shift, as it replaced the need for human labor with a fully automated machine that, in theory, does not require a weaver's presence during the making of the fabric.

This important change marks a deliberate move towards disembodied practices of making that upon closer investigation reflect a colonial legacy that would deprive the body of its physical autonomy and creative agency, separating the physical from mental labor. By disconnecting the weaver's body from the act of creation on the loom, the bond between mind and body was severed once and for all.

To understand this dynamic, it is essential to examine automation as a modus of power distribution—who has access to it, how it is allocated, and managed—and also as a pedagogy that reinforces the capitalist and extractive mode of **making**. In this text, I am focusing on the latter, since I believe that committing to changing the ways we learn about **making things** can lay the basis for alternative forms of relation to automation. Thinking through the disconnection caused by the automation of labor, I suggest looking at design as a modernist discipline that focuses on functional innovation as opposed to artistic craftsmanship.

Artistic making is always grounded in the unfolding of physical matter within the realm of its transformation, yet the automated nature of the Jacquard loom disrupts this embodied process and informs the maker of the opposite. It reduces the artist's role to mentally conceiving of a design, with the loom serving as the material condition for execution of the design. In rare cases do designers have hands-on relationships with the machines that produce their works and truly know the materials they feed them. A technician acts as an intermediary between the designer and the machine to execute the idea successfully.[9] This separation of previously interconnected processes profoundly disrupts the flow of creation, confining artistic freedom within the rigid boundaries of mechanical possibility and reproduction. The controlled rhythm of manufacturing becomes the priority, while the creator of the design grows more and more reliant on external sources of power, including electricity, materials, and technical labor, to produce their work. Materials are reduced to raw mediums to be dominated by human will, masked by the utilitarian logic of modernist design. The craft previously embedded in tradition becomes irrevocably reduced to an intellectual exercise disconnected from the physicality of making and its tactile resonance within the body.[10]

9 In the modernist sense, a technician, as a machine operator, establishes a dramatic divide between the artist and the thing made for them by the machine. A dichotomy that still exists today, and paves way for the future where the divide between 'intellectual' and manual labor is wider than ever.

10 Renowned modernist weaver Anni Albers once said that, 'Machines reduce the boredom of repetition only in the planning of the product.' Her point is that the maker's body disappears from the work once the machine autonomously executes their design, and only their 'intellectual' labor in the form of a design or drawing stays visible on the surface of the object produced. Albers, 2.

At the same time, this form of making enables another narrative surrounding mechanization, which is that of infinite resource availability: a false promise, perpetuated by neoliberal ideologies and unequal, settler-colonial distribution of the world's supplies. Contemporary makers are often dazzled by the illusion of unlimited material resources at their disposal, an impression that shapes the modern ethics of production.

When weaving on a Jacquard loom, cones of yarn are fed continuously into the machine, producing an ever-growing fabric. Much like a printer, the loom only stops when it exhausts its supply of resources, and the longer the availability of yarn on the cone, the longer the fabric is manufactured without interruption. Today's warehouses stocked with hundreds of thousands of identical, finely spun yarn cones exemplify this. Some of these cones hold up to ten thousand meters of yarn. While the quantity of these cones might seem abundant, their materiality is anything but infinite. Only the weaver's direct engagement with the loom makes them aware of the finite nature of the materials at hand, while each thread's end is tangibly felt in the very act of weaving. This awareness has been obscured by automation, masking the reality that the resources available to us are not infinite and giving the illusion of their easy substitution. On the hand loom, when you come to an end of a spool of yarn, there is a natural feeling of an ending;

it is also an impetus to rest, or at least to
change positions in-between work:
a feeling often lost in the rapid, boundless
production of modern systems. —

regaining the proportion of things p.197

The digital and disembodied nature of modern design and manufacturing further deepens a disconnect between contemporary makers and the very materiality of this world. Whereas with a manual loom physical labor is interrupted by gradual depletion of materials and bodily fatigue—both of which are directly felt by the maker in the process—with a technology like the fully automated Jacquard loom, physical labor is reduced to a series of computer clicks, which are reenacted by a machine. The rich tactile experience that once linked the maker's body to the process is substituted with a computer program that itself is designed to effortlessly execute repetitive commands. By this same logic, the Jacquard loom can be viewed as a printer that uses yarn as ink, powered by electricity to print complex woven images in just a few minutes—images that would have taken years to weave just a couple of centuries ago.[11]

11 Commissioned by Louis I of Anjou in the late fourteenth century, *The Apocalypse Tapestries* (France) is a massive series of hand-woven textiles that span hundred meters in length and took several years to complete; A modern example, as impressive as those Medieval tapestries, is the work of Norwegian artist Hannah Ryggen. Through creation of large-scale flat-woven

and knotted tapestries, Ryggen resisted automation using the slow, labor-intensive process of hand-weaving to center her personal experience. Her practice served as a powerful political protest against colonial, fascist, and oppressive structures that were increasingly shaping the world, including in Norway under Nazi occupation. For Ryggen this resistance was deeply intertwined with traditional Norwegian folk art, which embraced holistic forms of making that respected the land and the materials drawn from it—such as the wool of local sheep processed by the artist herself and natural dyes sourced directly from her environment.

The loss of direct engagement with the tactility of weaving has profound implications for sustaining cultural identity. In most cultures, weaving is not merely a craft, but a form of storytelling embedded in personal or collective experiences, expressed through the symbolism of patterns, designs and techniques. For the weaver, threads become voices that are carefully interwoven with one another to tell stories. — The removal of the weaver disrupts that coherence, the threads break and the weave unravels. Most industrialization processes became a catalyst for that unraveling. They not only silenced the weaver, but also endangered the preservation of weaving and its locally established, cultural roots.

materiality as a field of relations p.200

The traditional knowledge inherent to the craft of weaving is increasingly under threat of being lost or commodified, subservient to mass production, devoid of the original meaning it once carried. It is no surprise, then, that many contemporary artists feel estranged from traditional weaving crafts, while at the same time struggling to engage with the tactile and sensory aspects of their histories. Today, the very human experience and sensitivity is removed from the creation process on fully automated looms. Weavers and artisans, once deeply embedded in their knowledge of craft and community, now find themselves sidelined in a system that values uniformity and efficiency over complexity of creative and cultural expression.

It is undeniable that the identity of the weaver has been displaced by those who hold authority over automated production and who perpetuate the narrative of a future in which resources are limitless, labor is cheap, and consumption is unbounded. This also undermines the value of traditional knowledge that has been passed down through generations of skilled makers. The tactile, sensitive wisdom of their world was overshadowed by an enforced switch to mass-production and a globalized economy—a source of tremendous wealth for a very few.

01: Reviving the body of the weaver

As I further consider the future of weaving and the loom in the ontological context of emerging technology, I would like to shift my focus towards the embodied practices that can help us resist the neo-colonial pedagogies that drive capitalist economies and control our forms of crafting and knowledge production today. Instead of advocating for a return to traditional methods of making or dismissing automated devices altogether, my emphasis lies in refusing the alienation that often accompanies the weaver's interactions with auto-controllable machines and programmable devices. In other words, the solution does not lie in the return to the pre-industrial forms of crafting. Rather, it lies in narrowing down the gap between manual labor and intellectual work (body-mind problem) in order to re-establish meaningful ways of relating to the world culturally and personally. This is particularly important amidst the surge of machine learning-driven devices whose successful implementation in the future puts at risk even the intellectual production of **things**. This development can lead to a total loss of cultural identities that do not conform to the omni-present Western homogenization processes that technologies like AI reproduce.

For the weaver desiring to challenge the speed of these developments, the first step lies in hearing the heart of the weaving loom, whether manual or automated, and 'recognizing its beating pulse in their own body and breathing.' —

'poetic, performative quality of existence' p.196

The weaver's body is a somatic tool attuned to the subtle sensations of its physical engagement with yarns and tools.[12] Through the intention of the weaver to make a solid fabric out of loosely spun yarns, nuances of muscle tension, posture, breath, and movement become united in the physical engagement with the material. The maintenance of a proper posture and development of fine motoric skills builds a muscle memory that is sensitive to even very slight deviation of the hand, uncontrolled movement, mistake, or tiredness. These sensorial experiences, deeply rooted in the physical act of creativity itself, become part of the ever-evolving artistic skill and perception.

12 The term 'somatics' describes any practice that uses the mind-body connection to help people survey their internal self and listen to signals their body sends about areas of pain, discomfort, or imbalance. Somatics are often employed in therapeutic work with embodied trauma. For example, the Ilan Lev method considers the whole person and the ways that they move, working with trauma and physical discomfort that are often linked to movement patterns.

Focusing on these sensations can be a means to restituting one's physicality in the process of creation, even in work with automated machines. Unlike methods based solely on the logic of the mind (in service to capital), the somatics of weaving enable a direct understanding of the physical matter and its transformation that *lives* within the maker.[13] Consequently, by attending to the somatics of weaving, the artist reclaims the loom as a resource of knowledge production rather than a set of ontologically inherited programs and tools. Through this restored relationship with the automated loom, more balanced work can take place—work that honors both the traditional origins and the contemporary dimensions of the social fabric.

13 In my practice, the somatics of weaving is a means to decolonizing the loom, liberating the weaver from colonial patterns of automation through anti-capitalist ways of knowledge transfer.

The weaver's body, as it moves between the warp and the weft, becomes an extension of the fabric, primarily shaping it through touch. All it takes is an expanse of a yarn, patience, and repetitive engagement with the work. Even as the structure of the loom itself remains important, the engagement in the rhythmic act of interlacing threads brings a sense of focus, enveloping the whole being.[14] Furthermore, the weaver becomes attuned to the weight, texture, and movement of the materials, adjusting their techniques accordingly. This pedagogy and approach—sensory and intellectual at the same time—fosters a deep understanding of the self, the craft, and its cultural significance.[15]

14 The tactile nature of weaving, as of any other yarn craft such as knitting or crocheting, has also been noted for its therapeutic benefits. During the lockdown years of the Covid-19 pandemic, many people picked up yarn crafts as centering and calming activities that reduce anxiety and stress while also increasing feelings of well-being. The tactility and full-body engagement of weaving also has been used as a holistic practice for post-war PTSD treatment, and has been incorporated in art therapy practices for war veterans and trauma survivors.

15 Similar propositions around the sensuality of textile makers and their body can be found in the work of Eve Kosofsky Sedgwick. In her essay 'Making Things, Practicing Emptiness,' Sedgwick elaborates on her fascination with the 'brushing-three-fingers gesture' as a way to navigate the world through the sensorial realm of the hand. This gesture is also called the 'weaver's handshake' and is assigned to fabric people, as she puts it, 'who would skip introduction formalities and move directly to a tactile interrogation of what you are wearing.' See Kosofsky Sedgwick, 71.

As a weaver reaches out to threads and fabrics, intuition as a guiding force (and fellow collaborator) shapes their decisions and movements. Intuition, as an embodied form of wisdom, becomes a deeply attuned sensitivity—one that aligns perception with a harmonious interplay of touch, experience, and creative intent. The coordinated and synchronized actions of throwing the weaving shuttle, manipulating the warp and weft, and adjusting the tension require a disciplined approach that trains the weaver to move in awareness of their natural pace.[16] In handling the threads the weaver becomes finely attuned to the nuances of texture, tension, and visual qualities of the work. They learn to sense subtle variations of the fibers and respond with the appropriate adjustments through the careful attending to the work. — Experiencing the texture of the weave in such a way evokes transmission of knowledge for those who come in contact with the finished piece.

deliberate slowness
p.169

16 The weaving shuttle is a tool that carries weft yarns in a bobbin across the width of the woven fabric in a loom. The 'flying shuttle,' invented in 1733 by John Kay, was pivotal in the mechanization of weaving during the initial stages of Industrial Revolution; it facilitated production of wider fabrics by a sole weaver, instead of the collective throwing of a shuttle by several weavers working together at one loom.

Through sensing, the body extends the weaving loom, just as the loom amplifies the body's haptics. — The weaver starts to 'see' with the tip of a finger, brush of a hand,
smell of a woolen yarn,
gentle pressure,
tension of the stretched yarns,
and sonic cadences of the machine.

state of continuous
invention
p.107

The completed textile then carries the traces of all these sensibilities, becoming a tangible record of embodied presence and artistic intentions, as made evident in the lively unevenness of the edges or a jumpy yarn that occasionally skips its steady order creating irregular pattern formations.[17]

17 Here, I am reminded of the work of artist Andrea Zittel who often incorporates textiles in her research around the question: 'how to live?'. In her work *Cover Series* (2012) she asks a group of weavers to produce stripy weavings in which a different color stripe appears every time a weaver takes a break to rewind their bobbin, take a coffee, or simply have a rest. This artwork speaks to me because conceptually it disposes the time involved in the production of the work not as a critique of labor, but rather as a condition for progression. The colored textiles show us that the pauses during the making are not disruptions, but rather flows of different intensities and directions.

This heightened tactile awareness is a result of discipline that continuously refines the weaver's sensory skills. With time and practice, a certain familiarity is created. The body, as a vessel of the techniques, frees the weaver's attention to fully attune to the delicate interplay of yarns and generation of form, transcending the purely motoric aspects of the work. Within this space, the weaver patiently crafts each individual element into a cohesive, unified whole. Technical knowledge acquired in such a way becomes ingrained in the body as it learns, fostering a more intuitive connection between the weaver, their work, and the loom, a dynamic that is absent in the Jacquard loom, which operates as an autonomous manufacturing machine, craving direct attention only in its maintenance.

Somatic knowledge formed in the practice of making is rooted in the phenomenological realm of perception, meaning that making and thinking merge into one continuous process rather than being separate forms of production. The essence of artistic making is, thus, an embodied act that unfolds counter to empirical and mechanistic forms of **knowing** we have inherited in the machine age.

Weaving is processual in nature and can be described as a methodical interlacing of threads and material, where the boundary between human and non-human agencies blurs and forms a dynamic network of relationships finely crafted into a textile piece. The very nature of the repetitive motions in weaving, from threading the loom at the set-up stage of the work to passing the shuttle through the warp in the process of making, creates a rhythm that is both meditative and satisfying, as well as generative in nature. Therefore, considering repetition solely as a realm of the mechanical overlooks its profound somatic potential described earlier. Hence, the act of making is one of continuous engagement of the body: a process, attended with patience. It brings the weaver into a state of deeper inner movement that transcends the external world and immerses them in the present moment through rhythmical engagement into the work and growth of form. It also creates a certain pace that in traditional handloom weaving, for example, was often determined by the individual weaver who could set a pace that suited their personal needs and abilities. This approach to working is not possible with the fully automated loom, since it is available only to those who have the necessary technical skills. Unfortunately, this not only creates division in access, but also takes away the rhythm of making itself.

The rhythm that is central to the practice of weaving creates an inner movement which, in a word, can be described as a 'flow' that governs one's technical and personal creative capabilities. This movement is only rarely interrupted by occasional rewinding of the empty bobbin or adjustment of posture. Such interruptions are not disruptions, but rather moments of recalibration before resuming the former movement. It makes the crafting smoother, more in tune with one's body and its haptic needs.

Approaching weaving or any other craft as a form of generative movement means understanding it not only as a way of bringing an idea to life, but also as an opportunity to freely explore one's desire to craft. — This approach embraces intentional engagement with the material world, guided by touch and inner sensation opposite to execution of a preconceived form by the machine.[18] Renowned modernist weaver Anni Albers reflects this spirit of experimentation inherent to all crafts, stating that 'Free experimentation can result in the fulfilment of an inner urge to give form and to give permanence to ideas, that is to say, it can result in art, or it can result in the satisfaction of invention in some more technical way.'[19]

articulations of the strivings of our being p.211

18 Tim Ingold's anthropological concept of 'generative movement,' particularly in the context of his study of basket weaving, emphasizes the dynamic interplay between the maker's body, materials, and the environment. Ingold does not view materials as merely passive, but rather active substances that respond to the maker's movement. He suggests that weaving or any other form of making is not about imposition of preconceived form, but rather a dialogue between the weaver's body and the environment that unfolds in time and space. This idea is interesting, because it challenges the perception of craftsmanship as a strictly technical skill, instead situating it as an embodied and evolving process, deeply connected to the rhythms of life and of the world.

19 Albers, 3.

Albers's philosophy of making, as a journey of creation without a predetermined end result, encompasses a profound shift in perspective. — It challenges the conventional understanding of creation as a linear process with a fixed endpoint. It resists industrial forms of production by breaking their expectation of result-driven processes and rigid approach to the planning of a product. This is evidenced in how contemporary looms such as Jacquard looms are designed to execute programs rather than to provide conditions for free experimentation in the tactile, not only visual, planning of a weave. Instead, this perspective emphasizes the significance of the ongoing conversation between the weaver and the tactile properties of the piece they create, rooted in the circular nature of crafting. By recentering the experience of the body at work, the rapid pace of the capitalist-consumerist regime can be slowed down through moments of breathing that break apart the repetitive labor of growing textiles on machines that cannot breathe. Weavers can craft their own terms of production and logic, and the possibility of an alternative time and space can emerge: one that resists the industrialized rhythms that dominate modern life.[20]

openness is crucial p.447

20 The Polish artist Magdalena Abakanowicz suggests paying attention to the slower growth of forms as an antidote to the ungraspable speed of contemporary technology. Jacob and Dally, 36.

In this way, weaving becomes a space of intentional slowing down, a return to the process driven by the lived experience of the maker rather than the demands of the industry. Instead of considering the tradition of hand-weaving as a pre-automated form of production—a misconception inherited from the modernist project—this perspective invites a reimagining of the relationship with technology that is more in tune with one's intentions. A relationship in which the automated loom does not alienate the weaver on a physical level, but acts as a partner in embodied creation. When the body starts to consciously guide the loom, the boundary between human and mechanical blurs. The weaver's touch becomes the bridge, guiding the rhythm of the loom and not the other way around. The line between the manual and the mechanical, the intellectual and the physical, becomes more nuanced and complex.

Thinking weaving through this lens as an alternative pedagogy challenges the notion that traditional craft and automation are mutually exclusive. Instead, our relationship with machines can be reimagined as a more natural integration of the organic somatic and intellectual processes in the inorganic core of the industrial loom. In this way, the space of making becomes generative and is more in tune with the body and its breathing. The shape is given through processes of a living body that commits to hard work and can become tired in the process. Thus interaction with technology becomes an extension of our own embodied rhythms and processes that inform it instead of attuning to them.

Considering the modern loom and its ethics in my artistic practice, as well as in relation to my work with the students at the weaving workshop, I come to the conclusion that introducing the somatic approach to one's work creates a transitional space. A space in which whoever enters it consciously always comes out changed, acquiring new experience about a technique, themselves, and the context they operate in. The moment the loom is put in motion, it shuttles the maker into an intuitive process that over time becomes familiar and ingrained in their body through wholesome practice. In that space, the weaver enters another timeline carried out by the desire to open up the mind in relation to the materials at hand: an inward process that ripens through shapes and textures manifesting in the outer realm of the thing produced.

As we look to the future, it is crucial to consider the value of embodied making and the knowledge it carries. All makers will benefit from a revival of interest in the materiality of their work in which their body, mind, and soul are once again united in the conjoined, generative movement of creating and thinking. The absolute reliance on automated production and its enormous speed must be challenged. Maybe for the first time in the past 400 years, we can actually slow down in order to resist. This needs to happen first on an individual scale, within the heart of the workshops where things are produced in intimate proximity to materials, things, ideas, and bodies. In such educational environments, and in relation to each other, weavers will gain critical awareness of their own inner processes and their inherited attitudes toward the weaving loom. By opening up and listening to the body, they will be able to reframe their creativity in terms of generative and liberating potentials of the craft. A long-term vision will start to emerge; a vision that resists the reductionist logic of our politics around machines and offers concrete experiences that resonate within the textile and the hidden stories it carries. A never-ending flow of active force in opposition to the passive stance that the maker takes in the modern production of things.

Through this lens, the loom serves as a tangible expression of ontological inquiry, tapping into the sensations of structure and transformation, while the weaver's own breath and the pace of weaving reflect a deep connection between the rhythmic flow of life and the act of creation. — A constant making in relation to one's tools and surroundings is the essence of the weaver's journey, where intuition and improvisation flourish alongside profound physical meditations that unfold in the materials, localities, cultures, and landscapes directly informing the work.

transcending abstractions p.87

The journey of the weaver as a world maker, then, is one of continuous unlearning, of engaging with the material, outer world and the spiritual, inner world, resisting the utilitarian ideas about what they do by the very act of making with their whole being. It is a return to life itself: slow, careful, and imperfect, expressing a deep connection to making as a process of becoming.

References

Albers, Anni. 'Work With Material.' In *Black Mountain College Bulletin* 5, 1938. black-mountain-research.com/documents/3-no-5-1938-%22working-with-material%22-black-mountain-college-bulletin/.

Broudy, Eric. *The Book of Looms: A History of the Handloom from Ancient Times to the Present*. Brandeis University Press, 2021.

Jacob, Mary Jane, and Jenny Dally. *Magdalena Abakanowicz: Writings and Conversations*. Skira, 2022.

Kosofsky Sedgwick, Eve. 'Making Things, Practicing Emptiness.' In *The Weather in Proust*, edited by Jonathan Goldberg and Michael Moon. Duke University Press, 2011.

Le Guin, Ursula K. *The Carrier Bag Theory of Fiction*. Ignota Books, 2020.

protocols
ceremony
offerings
asking for help
return
repair
reciprocity
radical gift-giving
slow processes
  of learning
extended circle
  of relations
(doing) medicine
a Good Way

How to Build Anything Ethically

Suzanne Kite
in discussion with Corey Stover, Melita Stover Janis, and Scott Benesiinaabandan

Indigenous protocols set up our relationships with the world in ethical ways, reducing harm to ourselves, our communities, and our environments. These protocols are rooted in contexts of place, ontologies developed in that place, and the communities living in that place, from stones to animals to people.

This guide to ethical decision-making when building technologies includes two examples. First, I illustrate how protocol for building a Lakota sweat lodge can act as a framework for building a physical computing device. Next, I provide an example of how multiple streams of protocol are necessary to build an AI system as a confluence of ethics. It can be overwhelming to address the ethics of each step of a building process, but it is necessary for building anything in a 'Good Way.' This is just as true when trying to build an ethical AI. Some ideas proposed here are not currently possible, some are possible if investment is made in the necessary research, and some are possible but only through a radical change in the way technology companies are run and the pyramid of compensation for the exploitation of resources is reversed.

What is a 'Good Way'? A Good Way is the Lakota way of talking about ethical protocols. Lakota decision-making processes, as with many Indigenous decision-making processes, embed ethics that look Seven Generations ahead. When this concept is applied to AI, Seven Generations means that the protocols outlined here are a way to plan for not just the AI of tomorrow, but for Seven Generations of AI into the future. — 'The Lakota viewpoint is that we always look ahead Seven Generations to make sure Seven Generations is provided for through the Earth,' my cousin, Corey Stover, says.

caring for lifetimes beyond our own p.364

My research into these protocols is rooted in the ontological status of stones to the Lakota people. This essay does not attempt to speak for all Lakota, and is rooted in the specific teachings within my family. Such understandings of stones provide a clear framework for establishing ethical relationships with the raw materials used in building computing devices. I am not asking that you think of the computer as 'sacred,' but to consider at which point one affords respect to materials or objects or non-humans outside of oneself. — Lakota stone ontologies are understood through our relationships with healing

enriching rather than extracting p.202

stones, sweat lodge stones (known as Grandmothers and Grandfathers), altar stones, and more. My aunt, Melita Stover Janis, says, 'When a special stone finds you, they are meant to go to you ... The spirit of the rock is talking to you ... They take you years to find one. It's looking for you its whole life too.'

beings of other, slower temporalities p.215

At all points during the sweat lodge ceremony, a version of 'intelligence,' more clearly expressed as 'interiority,' is perceived in the Grandfather Stones. Ceremonies hold one accountable to the world around oneself, drawing attention to transformation on minute levels.[1]

[1] Posthumus.

Key components of Indigenous protocols are the systems of knowledge creation that ultimately guide us in our desire to know how things are done in a Good Way. Lakota knowledge is not static: protocols change, decision-making shifts, and names can change, because in practice, our decisions have an effect on the world and must be continually made and changed in a network of relations. The effects our decisions—and technologies—have on the world can help us identify the stakeholders in what is being made and how it is used. Stakeholders in Indigenous communities are identified as our extended circle of relations, while stakeholders in technology companies are identified as the board of directors, shareholders, employees and consumers. It is necessary to identify how all those—both human and non-human—are affected by what is made, and to take responsibility for those it affects.

each foot is named p.234

Locating AI

AI systems have several components: (a) architecture, (b) input, (c) algorithms for training on existing data and processing new data, and (d) output. These systems may be distributed over many physical locations, but these must be seen as physically real by makers and users in order to see AI as a holistic and real object. The structure of the architecture, the writing of the software, and the design of the algorithms work together in intricate ways. Each component individually and jointly must be designed in a Good Way in order for the parts to be combined into an ethical whole. This holds true from the ground-up: from training sets to interfaces.

The following examples focus on physical materials, because AI cannot be made ethically until its physical components are made ethically. Robust ethics principles are necessary for computation because it is an extractive sector, extracting natural resources on a global scale. International and domestic regulation is necessary,[2] as well as a movement to produce recyclable materials that can build computers, including the right to repair.[3]

2 Global Affairs Canada.

3 The Repair Association is an independent American repair market advocacy organization. See repair.org/policy.

Compensation, gifts, and reciprocity are central to both the Physical Computing Device examples below. Holistic understandings of exchange within the environment are essential to Indigenous ontologies, and to ground Indigenous ethics in a physical place that strives to resist exploitation of people or resources.

economy of abundance p.191

How to Build a Physical Computing Device in a Lakota Way

Co-written with Corey Stover and Melita Stover Janis
with notes from Scott Benesiinaabandan

The sweat lodge is a place where knowledge is generated about the world. The lodge itself is a tool, with many protocols forming a functioning whole. When one fulfills all the steps of protocol for the sweat lodge, one can be sure it was built in a Good Way.

HOW TO BUILD A SWEAT LODGE IN A GOOD WAY	HOW TO BUILD A PHYSICAL COMPUTING DEVICE IN A GOOD WAY
APPRENTICING	
When building a sweat lodge in a Good Way, first, one acts as a Fire Keeper for someone else. My grandfather learned from an elder Medicine Man, and started Sundancing with him. When a person does Sundance they are preparing constantly during everyday life and doing sweats all the time. This a slow process of learning from the elders and community members about the correct way to do things. Before a person can start their own practice, they must have a vision where the spirits call them to build their own *hamblecha*, or altar, otherwise they continue to assist others.	Building (in a Good Way) a physical computing device to house an AI would first require study and consultation with a committee of knowledge keepers with expertise in computation, ethics, and mining.
IDENTIFYING NEED	
Before you build a sweat lodge, there must be a need: you, your family, and the community need purification, a place to pray, a place to do ceremony, a place to do medicine, and a place where individual and communal needs can be addressed.	Why is a physical computing device needed? In this example, it is to host an Artificial Intelligence program in a physical object created in a Good Way.

SCAFFOLDING

IDENTIFY STAKEHOLDERS

The stakeholders in a sweat lodge are many, but the lodge has room for all individuals and community members, known and unknown, seen and unseen, including:

- Stone Spirits
- Plant Peoples
- Animal Peoples
- Human Peoples
- Spirits
- Guardian Spirits

The stakeholders in a computational device are:

- the communities of the location where raw materials originate
- the raw materials themselves
- the environment around them
- the communities affected by transportation and devices built for transportation
- the communities with the knowledge to build these objects
- the communities who build the objects
- the communities who will use and be affected by their use
- the creators of the objects

IDENTIFYING RAW MATERIALS

The sweat lodge is built from/with raw materials: willows, rocks, tobacco, cloth, buffalo hide. These are multiple items, each with their own protocol streams, with similar protocols for each of the materials. Each has to be done with protocol, in a Good Way, offering something valuable in exchange for taking something of value. There are many kinds of exchange in Lakota culture. These exchanges range from reciprocity to radical gift-giving to bribery to offering, all of which signify an ongoing relationship. This may seem like extreme gift-giving when one offers their flesh, their hair, or every material object they own. However, this protocol is modeled after the animals that give themselves out of responsibility, upholding long-running agreements to care for us. When you collect the sixteen willows for the sweat lodge, you must offer tobacco. You must offer tobacco when you take anything, even filling the water. If you don't have tobacco, you can offer a piece of hair. When obtaining the buffalo hide, it is important to consider the way the buffalo is killed and skinned, ensuring that the ceremony was conducted in a Good Way and the buffalo's spirit is released in a Good Way.

Extracting materials in a Good Way requires transparency, regulation, and research into developing physical computing devices that do not use a single new material and eventually do not require mined materials at all. The refining of many elements that are mined (rocks, metals, minerals, and so on) produces toxic and non-recyclable waste. What is being offered to the Earth when we extract these mined materials? What is being offered to those whose lands are being extracted from? For our human kin, we can start with fair wages. For our non-human kin, it is restoring the earth to a healthy state. Funds must be diverted to research alternatives and to manage ongoing environmental destruction.

'For example, oil pipelines. We should not take something that will have a destructive effect, only take in moderation. The Lakota viewpoint is that we always look ahead Seven Generations to make sure Seven Generations is provided for through the earth...Their [our ancestor's] imprint was all organic ...When taking materials from the earth to build a computer, what if this matter harms us in the future. It is the same with the sweat lodge. We don't want to take something that can't be replaced in a reasonable amount of time ... Sometimes we must look elsewhere instead of decimating an entire family of willows.'
—Corey Stover

CONSTRUCTING

A prayer is made each time the willow poles are crossed and tied together with specific-colored cloths. An eight-pointed star is revealed at the top. Melita Stover Janis says, 'They [the spirits] come in through the top [of the lodge], as the singers sing the first songs, calling the spirits into the sweat, a portal from one world to the next.' When assembling the lodge, you must pray to each direction, hanging the appropriately colored offering in each door. Scott Benesiinaabandan says, 'This arrangement is meaningful, there are four levels above and four levels reflected underneath the earth, creating a sphere.'

The arrangement of the internal components of a physical computing device is functional, as is the arrangement of the willow poles. However, Indigenous design practices unite functional design with functional symbolism, a method that can be extended to the design of circuitry, inviting the spirits in as well as again offering tobacco each step of the way.

PREPARING THE INTERNAL COMPONENTS

Another stream of protocol guides the building of the fire that heats the lodge stones. This fire has specially appointed Fire Keepers, who gather firewood, set the fire up, and lay the sticks across. The Fire Keeper must learn through apprenticeship and has a very important role.

Fire Keeper protocols could be translated to building and arranging the processor and the RAM, taking special care to prepare where the builder perceives the 'location' of the AI.

WAKING UP

Inside the lodge, the singers ask that the spirits of the rocks help them, waking the spirits up with offerings of tobacco. Rocks are only added in meaningful numbers and groups. 'Grandfathers live in the spirit world and come into the living, giving their lives. Singers inside [the sweat] wake them up,' says Scott Benesiinaabandan.

Functionality and symbolism in the design allow for the singers to call in the spirits to help them, similar to the programmer calling the code to begin running a software program.

ALGORITHM

Songs are the action in a sweat lodge, doing the most vital and complex work. These songs involve many kinds of algorithms: the Lakota language and its complexities of purpose and meaning, the arrangement of the song's poetry, the choice and order of song by the leaders, and the patterns of the air waves being formed and reformed by the melodies and harmonies of the participants' voices.

The arrangement in the writing of the software, the algorithms and code structures, which work together in intricate ways, must also be designed in a Good Way, combining all the parts to make the whole: from training sets to interfaces.

TRANSFORMATION

When all the parts of a sweat lodge are brought together in a Good Way, transformation occurs. Rocks, together with the fire, water, and air, create steam. The stones (known as Grandmothers and Grandfathers) are offered tobacco along with songs asking for their help and assistance. Water becomes steam, rocks become dirt, willow becomes ash, tobacco becomes sparks: transformation is the most important part of these ceremonies.

Using electricity, energy, the correct arrangement of materials into motherboards and all parts of the physical computer device, current flows, transforming into semiotic information, rendering it sensible to humans. It is through these transformations that what we will perceive as AI could be found.

ANNOUNCEMENT

When objects with spirits are made, they must be feasted, meaning a feast must be prepared in honor of that spirit. Dried meat (*wasna*), choke cherry juice, and ceremony feasts are offered.

The computer should be announced to the community of stakeholders, and named. This step is essential to building this object in a Good Way, with clarity and transparency to what has been built and why. In order to live in context, this object must have clear relationships to its stakeholders.

DEATH CYCLE

Sweat lodges can be disassembled, repurposed, returned, or transformed. When the season for sweat lodge is over, you take the covers off, leaving the lodge if it will be used again. The sweat rocks eventually break apart, disintegrate as they are used. Everything is organic and can be reused, burned, or returned to the earth.

A physical computing device, created in a Good Way, must be designed for the Right to Repair, as well as to recycle, transform, and reuse. The creators of any object are responsible for the effects of its creation, use, and its afterlife, caring for this physical computing device in life and in death.

CONSULTATION

IDENTIFY STAKEHOLDERS

RAW MATERIAL

COMPENSATION

BUILD A BASE

PREPARING INTERNAL COMPONENTS

CONSTRUCTION

RUNNING THE PROGRAM

TRANSFORMATION

WELCOMING

RUNNING

DEATH CYCLE

Indigenous Protocol Streams to Create an Ethical AI

In the illustration above and the accompanying chart, I propose a way to see steps of protocol within many protocol streams that come together to form an ethical AI.

QUESTIONS TO ASK AT EACH STEP WITHIN THE PROTOCOL STREAM

Consultation: Who are the Elders and Knowledge Keepers for this protocol?

Identify Stakeholders: Which community members, human and non-human, all those past, present, and future, are affected?

Identify Raw Material: What is needed to create this process?

Compensation: How are the stakeholders or owners of the raw materials being compensated and how does that compensation affect them?

Construction: What are the methods necessary to do this protocol in an ethical way?

Preparing Internal Components: How do the parts of this process need to be prepared?

Running the Program: How can the protocol be enacted in an ethical way?

Transforming: What is transformed during this process?

Welcoming: How can this protocol be completed in a way that provides transparency to those affected?

Managing the Life Cycle: How can the ongoing use of the result of this protocol be done in an ethical way?

Preparing for the Death Cycle: How can the end of this protocol be completed in an ethical way?

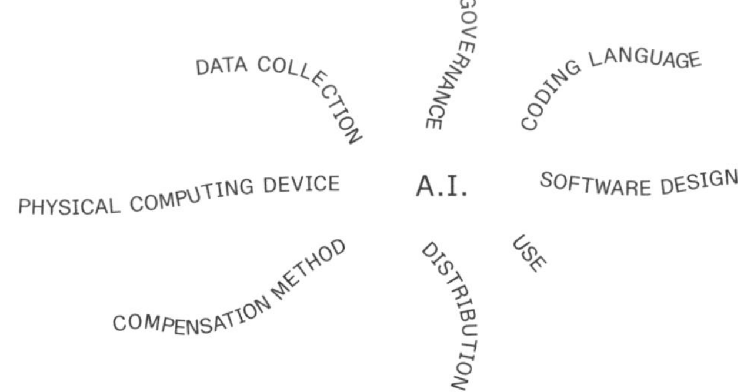

In this guide to ethical decision making for building technologies I have outlined two frameworks: how building a Lakota sweat lodge can act as a framework for building a physical computing device and how many streams of protocol can be imagined for building an AI system. It is necessary to build our technologies, and all things, in a 'Good Way', a way which takes into account all beings, animate and inanimate. My grandfather, Maȟpíya Nážiŋ, says, 'I believe this about the stones: whenever one comes to you, whenever it rolls to you or whenever it's right in front of you, that it's there for a purpose—here to teach your spirit something, so that maybe what it teaches you, you can use to help someone else...'

This essay was originally published in Lewis, Jason Edward, et al. 'Indigenous Protocol and Artificial Intelligence Position Paper.' Indigenous Protocol and Artificial Intelligence Working Group and the Canadian Institute for Advanced Research (CIFAR), Honolulu, Hawai'i, February 2020.

References

Global Affairs Canada. 'The Canadian Government Offers Responsible Business Conduct Abroad–Questions and Answers.' Accessed September 16, 2019. international.gc.ca/trade-agreements-accords-commerciaux/topics-domaines/other-autre/faq.aspx?lang=eng#:~:text=.

Posthumus, David C. *All My Relatives: Exploring Lakota Ontology, Belief, and Ritual*. University of Nebraska Press, 2018.

wisdom
warnings
monster(s)
shaping the mind
abundance
healing
prime invigorators
ancient and vibrant
evolutionary robots
amazing libraries
deeply unknown
taking shape
singing through
a techné for a new reality
undeniably present

The eyes of fire, the nostrils of air, the mouth of water, the beard of earth[1]

Techné Informed by the Songs that Sing Through Us

1 Excerpt from the poem 'Proverbs of Hell', in which Blake states the importance of human imagination, and also a song title from an amazing record by Robert Takahashi Crouch.

Theun Karelse

... saltwater people all around the continent continue to keep stories to preserve the maps and memory of lands drowned after the big ice melt. The stories are passed down and people partner with whales, dolphins and others to continue caring for the Country beneath the sea. This is important because the oceans will fall again as they have before, and we will want to return to that Country.'[2]
— Tyson Yunkaporta

2 Yunkaporta, 67.

Shift

The canoe is landing on the shore, carrying an elderly woman and a young man. They are looking around, maybe they are looking for a place to rest or even settle for the night? The newly formed river is brown with sediment, washed away by the first rains in this region in many centuries. The woman is untying a pouch filled with hazelnuts. They crack open a few and eat them. Maybe the rest are kept for planting, because there is only pioneering vegetation around yet. The young man is moving through the dense cloud of mosquitoes onto higher ground. The first swallows have also arrived, discovering the abundance of insects in these newly forming territories now that the mega-glaciers have retreated, leaving what G.K. Chesterton once described as a battleground of ancient giants.[3] This is unknown territory. Deeply unknown in the sense of being unseen, not just by human eyes, but, more broadly, unfamiliar to almost all living beings. From small pockets in places like the Alps, plants, animals, fungi, even microbes are spreading North into this expanse along with the newly forming rivers.[4] They are living through the last big climate shift, at the end of the most recent ice-age. This is an age when animals far outnumber humans. An experience almost unimaginable to the modern mind.[5] In many respects animals and plants lead the way. Over time, much of Northern Europe will become inhabited by humans. First along the coasts and river beds, and later more inland. But for now, human settlements are spread far apart, often seasonal and connected by no human infrastructure, often only by the surface of water. Many petroglyphs and markings of revered sites are visible not so much from land, but from the canoe passing by.[6] Slowly a human network will take shape, spreading all the way to Scandinavia, transporting hides, types of wood and ores, and with it will spread a new techné[7] for a new reality. Just as our techné today will be superseded by something else.

3 Chesterton, intro.

4 These pockets of vegetation are known as cryptic refugia.

5 Soga and Gaston.

6 Bradley.

7 From the Greek, meaning arts, crafts, techniques, or skills.

Shape

The men are kneeling in small but highly energetic clusters. This is a marketplace. And the atmosphere is charged with high hopes and excitement. The goods in their trade are symbolized by small groups of stones that form the center of their gatherings. Rearranging them clearly carries meaning, because it is followed by intense discussion.

In *How Things Shape The Mind*, Lambros Malafouris describes human intellectual evolution in correspondence to the tools we create and their materiality. In writing the book he essentially opens up a new domain: cognitive archeology. He describes how pebbles were instrumental in the development of the idea of numbers—literally 'calculus' means pebbles—and enabled human minds to expand into mathematics and abstract thought. Similarly, early forms of sculpture and drawing are increasingly discussed in archaeology as means by which the complexity of human cosmovision grew. — A beautiful example of such a study is Douglass W. Bailey's *Prehistoric Figurines*, showing how small handmade figurines opened up cultures on different continents to visual storytelling, corporeality, anthropomorphism, miniaturism, and dimensionality. It is hard to imagine just how mind-blowing such early artforms must have been.

triggering wonder p.379

This process of mind-blowing is formalized by Malafouris as 'Material Engagement Theory.' And if it holds true for pebbles and prehistoric figurines, then, as I'm writing this essay, I find myself asking about the role of water. What is the role of the ocean as an invigorator to the human mind? — The ocean is a central medium through which we've spread, from which humans emerged as a planetary-scale population. Navigating the seas and rivers, rich and varied nautical skills and traditions have emerged among human cultures all over the planet. To what extent are human minds shaped oceanically?

a living handbook
p.143

Storm

The family climb out the window and huddle together on the roof of the farm. It is a cold January night in which an extremely violent storm and spring tide combine. This has broken the dikes. The farm is now in the middle of a shallow moon-lit sea. In the darkness they are moving closer together. They are wrapping themselves in blankets. The girl and her family look out over a bizarre landscape, turned seascape. They can see the farm of her grandparents and watch it collapse as the waves continue to shake their own farm. She will never see her grandparents again.[8]

[8] Based on an eyewitness account by Ria Geluk, whom we interviewed as part of the research conducted by the Embassy of the Northsea.

In response to the 1953 flood, the Dutch initiated what must have been one of the biggest coastal engineering efforts the world had ever seen. Heralded as a national triumph, or even as a triumph of humanity over the forces of nature, Dutch coastal engineering became an export product. Confidence was high. That is, until recently. Now sea levels are rising. No one at the time of developing the flood defenses had ever imagined that could happen. Even worse, dikes, it turns out, are no longer an option. Beyond a certain level, the pressure of the sea makes the water simply pass under the dikes.

Monster(s)

They are dragging the nets into the boat. One of the fishermen calls out. Something remarkable is surfacing. The net contains a mermaid! The fishermen are astonished. From the sea a voice cries out. It is the merman, anxiously calling out. Ignoring his fury, the fishermen take the mermaid to shore, to the port of Westenschouwen. Many villagers are gathering around. The atmosphere is electric. All are amazed by this unknown being. A few fishermen now carry her further and tie her with the net to the tower. Others are going to the beach where the merman is raging from the waves. When the mermaid dies, he leaves. Winds are now turning into storms, and people flee from their homes. The houses are collapsing, only the tower is spared and is still there today. This is the wrath of the merman of Westenschouwen, a warning that not all riches should be taken from the sea.

The origin of the word monster is found in Latin: *monstrare*, which means to point out, to show, but also *monere*; to remind, to advise and of course *monstrum*; portent, omen, sign.

We may discard stories of mythical beings as superstition, but that overlooks the possibility that people believe(d), not so much in the physical existence of monsters, but more in the wisdom their stories embody. The warning they contain. I am from the Dutch province of Zeeland (literally, 'Sea Land'), a region where the waterwolf[9] and merfolk reign. Before environmental law, the story of the merman's wrath that caused the island of Westenschouwen to be lost in a flood was a warning against overexploitation of the sea.

9 The waterwolf is a folk name for a storm surge.

Few people will know this if you ask them, even locally, but Zeeland has lost over 117 villages[10] and a major city in a seemingly endless list of floods. As undisputed world champion of drowned villages, Zeeland must be one of the most volatile places of human inhabitation over the last millennium. The island of Borssele (now part of a bigger peninsula) has drifted, disappeared, and reappeared over the past centuries.

Sometimes it is only marked as a dotted line on medieval maps. The current village of Borssele is just over 400 years old and was rebuilt on top of Monster, one of six local villages that were wiped out by the two floods of the early 1530s. Today the only trace of Monster is the name of the main road leading to the village, like a shadow of a mythical being that carries a warning. — Rebuilding the settlement as Borssele was done in a revolutionary way, as a formal grid. Almost aligned to the compass and with almost Golden Ratio proportions, it was a renaissance project, filling the gap left by the storms. The same grid model would be applied nearly a decade later to the Island of Mannahatta—later renamed Manhattan—in present-day New York City. Both initiatives were financed by the same elite; the people who invested in Dutch plantations abroad also invested in reclaiming land within the lowlands.[11] Both followed a similar extractive logic and opportunism.

ghostly presences p.252

10 A village was said to be any place that had a church.

11 From an interview with historian Jan Kuipers conducted by Embassy of the Northsea.

Porpoise

I opened this essay with a passage from *Sand Talk* by writer Tyson Yunkaporta, who identifies as an Apalech clan Aboriginal scholar. When I read his words, I am blown away. What a culture! And I'm embarrassed. What a contrast to the shamelessly exploitative relationship with the sea and land in my own culture, which seems so adolescent in light of the much more ancient cultures Tyson describes. His is one of many voices have been speaking to me from Australia in the past few years—voices contained mostly in books—and this section where he writes about whales perhaps strikes me so deeply because at the time of reading it I had been diving into the waters behind the Oosterschelde Storm Surge Barrier[12] attempting to listen to the underwater domain of our local whales, the harbor porpoise, in ways that are analogous to the way they listen. —

relearning to listen to the world p.202

12 A massive coastal engineering effort in response to the last big flood of 1953, in which entire sections of the estuary were dammed. I'm diving in those waters specifically because researchers are thinking porpoises may not pass through the structure into the North Sea because of the noise of the enormous current that flows through.

To start the sound, I open the lid of a small watertight box and switch on the stripped-down blue-tooth speaker I glued inside, then tighten the lid again. The little box starts crackling in my hand. It's a touch speaker. I run to the shoreline and start wading in. In the distance traffic is passing over the Oosterschelde Storm Surge Barrier. It's windy but nowhere near violent enough for the barrier to be closed. I place the little sound device against my forehead and slowly submerge into a saline, disorienting world. Underwater the sounds emanating from the little speaker are radically transmuted. Amidst the noise of the surf, the high crackling recording of harbor porpoise sonar, is as much a tactile experience as an auditory one. The crackling spreads through the skin of my forehead, through my skull, as I imagine it does in porpoises, but also, remarkably, along the surface of my face. — Even though the sonar sound has been lowered drastically to fit human hearing, it feels tactile. As a child I fantasized how bats had a language where words were based on the exact reflections of the world. Something like that is happening here. The crackling sound seems to conjure tactile words for the sea.

sensory nomadism p.107

Crow

I'm pointing my camera from the window of the Kilpisjarvi biological field station in Arctic Finland, to get Ian Ingram in frame. We are surrounded by only a few buildings, beyond which are hundreds of kilometers of rocks, lakes, tundra, and small birch trees that the reindeer pass among. We are in the permanent day of midsummer, when the sun never sets, and nobody pays much mind to whether it is day or night; it doesn't matter. In this otherworldly light, Ian is assembling his robot while we try to attract the crows living in this remote area, to test it. This small machine entity called *Nevermore-a-matic*, is part of an evolutionary branch of robots that Ian has been developing that try to communicate with birds in the crow family. (The day before we put out piles of meat because Olu, a local Saami reindeer herder, has informed us that, as scavengers, crows may come near if there is a corpse.)

This is one of the earliest fieldwork sessions that I am organizing as part of Machine Wilderness, a long running research program exploring alternative roles for technology in relationship with the living world. I invited Ian Ingram and Antti Tenetz, both artist-scientists, for a team residency here, to conduct several weeks of in-situ prototyping. To do this, we needed to establish a state-of-the-art maker-space in this remote area. Somehow it all fitted into a bewildering array of suitcases that we hauled onto the sleeper train and then onto the bus that for the final seven hours takes people up to the remote North.

We open the window. Ian has placed the small black robot on a branch and is going through test sequences. The machine will try to communicate by gesture, as crows do. It focuses on one particular gesture: the beak-wipe. In science there is lots of speculation about its meaning, but seeing the small black robot on a branch of a birch tree in this vast landscape makes me feel like something fundamental is being transformed here. Sitting on a branch, the machine is making its gestures, looking through its camera eye for corvids.[13] This machine is not sitting there to solve some environmental issue. This is not technology as a means to fix a problem. — It isn't even primarily built for humans. This machine is geared toward relating, primed towards engaging and participating in a specific community of life. With the world's machine learning almost exclusively from humans, or trying to mimic human intelligence, here is an entity taking a broader perspective. — It feels far removed from the world of sterile robotics laboratories. Looking out into the Arctic summer, this is the first time I am encountering tech that feels like it is healing.

technologies 'for nothing' p.389

recovering the complexity of the world p.194

13 Corvids are birds belonging to the crow family.

Library

Laly Joseph is tying a delicate orchid. She sits among self-made tools in the shadow of the rainforest canopy. The rope should not be too loose or the plant will drop. It should not be too tight or it will damage the plant. It should be just right, she says smiling, because there may only be a few orchids of its kind left. She and the other women here have no formal

knowledge keepers
p.422

training in botany, but over several decades have become some of the world's most remarkable botanists. — In the depths of a place that is becoming a forest again, she is holding up the orchid tied to a small wooden board. It could be one of the last known individuals of its species. It may have taken ten years to propagate it. She is hanging the board in what must be one of the most amazing libraries in the world. Among the rainforest trees, many of these little wooden boards are hanging from bamboo structures, like books on a shelf, containing hundreds and hundreds of orchids, all apparently different. All watched over by loving grace.[14] Beyond the orchid library among the trees extends the fernarium, then the impatiens, elsewhere the grasses, the rainforest species, the cloud forest species, and the rockery with alpines.

14 Brautigan.

aesthetic agents
p.387

The Gurukula Botanical Sanctuary in the Western Ghat mountains of India has become an amazingly diverse community of life forms, a forest that is admired not just by botanists, birdwatchers or conservationists, but by musicians, cooks, poets, sculptors, painters, and people of all ages, because its abundance and diversity of life makes for a startling abundance and diversity of sound, color, shape, behavior, and scent. — The forest is all these things.[15]

15 Seshan.

Author Paul Kingsnorth writes of human relations to nature that, 'something used to sing through us'[16]—something ancient and vibrant. It is remarkable how often you find the women working at the Sanctuary singing to the plants when they are tending them. I've been back many times and with it the feeling grows: that the Sanctuary is indeed the forest singing through people.

16 Kingsnorth.

Skull

Look here. The hole on top is the nasal passage. (In harbor porpoises, which are our smallest local whales, it is one hole while in other whales it can be two.) They close them when they submerge. There are also these two holes here, at the base of the skull. They are much larger than the ones in our human skulls. This is where the nerve bundles from the lower jaw go up to the brain. Porpoises don't really see much, or so we humans think. Hearing is central. Well, something analogous to our own hearing. Porpoises, like bats, envision their world through echolocation, sensing vibrations through their lower jaw. They have five stomachs, but are not ruminants like their ancient land-based ancestors. And they don't drink. All their water comes from the fish they catch. So, if a porpoise can't catch fish for more than a few days, it will die of thirst before it starves of hunger.

When a whale strands on the shore, this animal so completely unseen by us in the depths of the seas and oceans, becomes undeniably present. Perhaps this is what makes a stranding such a dramatic occurrence, one that for a long time was seen as an omen, much like the appearance of comets in the otherwise stable firmament. Today the bodies of whales still act as important messengers whose attributes are painstakingly interpreted by scientists like Lonneke IJsseldijk, the marine mammal researcher who is pointing out details of harbor porpoise anatomy to me in her lab. As she holds the skull, she is telling me that the number of whale strandings are among the longest kept environmental records we have in Northern Europe, dating back in parts to 1250 and earlier.

Tune in

We are still surrounded by millions of different kinds of intelligence, but with modernity non-human intelligence somehow became seen as largely irrelevant, including those that inhabit our waters. In fact, since the industrial revolution our cetacean neighbors have only heard our industrial noise. Endlessly. Imagine how offensive that actually is. Whales, pirates, sailors, merfolk, they all sing. It is as if the sea evokes it. Singing in humans may even predate spoken language.[17] | In any case

singing connections to the environment p.268

it is something we share with marine mammals; therefore I'm learning how to sing underwater, — so I can introduce myself within their realm as I continue to learn how to tune in.

17 Mithen.

Much of our existing technology was built for a fading reality. Shipwrecks of a bygone age. As we enter a new climate reality, it calls for a different techné. I feel attracted to building relationships, to learn to care for the world, and do so in collaboration with other creatures. That is what I want my techné to include; the strength of relating to the world without division. I want to be liberated from the convention that many realms of the world are trivial, that they don't matter to my life, my practices, my thoughts. As xenologist Adriana Knouf says, '**the skies used to speak to us**.' It is time to let them speak to us again. The stars, the crows, the whales, the forest, their songs. A process of unlearning and undomestication.[18] I want to celebrate living within a much broader horizon. Children still know it, and reach toward it, with their beds full of teddy bears and other totemic beings.

18 In *Sand Talk*, Yunkaporta suggests 'undomesticated' people as an alternative to Indigenous people.

References

Blake, William. 'Proverbs of Heaven and Hell.' In *The Marriage of Heaven and Hell*. London, ca. 1790. blakearchive.org/work/mhh.

Bradley, Richard. *An Archaeology of Natural Places*. Psychology Press, 2000.

Brautigan, Richard. 'All Watched Over by Machines of Loving Grace.' In *All Watched Over by Machines of Loving Grace*. Richard Brautigan, 1967.

Chesterton, G. K. *The Defendant*. R. Brimley Johnson, 1901. catalog.hathitrust.org/Record/100115935.

Crouch, Robert Takahashi. 'The Eyes of Fire, the Nostrils of Air, the Mouth of Water, the Beard of Earth.' Track 2 on *Organs*. CD. Robert Takahashi Novak, 2015.

Kingsnorth, Paul. 'The Great Work. Alchemy and the Power of Words.' In *Emergence Magazine*, October 1, 2018. emergencemagazine.org/essay/the-great-work/.

Mithen, Steven. *The Singing Neanderthals: The Origins of Music, Language, Mind and Body*. Harvard University Press, 2007.

Seshan, Suprabha. 'Old Mother Forest.' In *Local Futures*, January 1, 2019. localfutures.org/old-mother-forest/.

Soga, Masashi, and Kevin J. Gaston. 'Shifting Baseline Syndrome: Causes, Consequences and Implications.' In *Frontiers in Ecology and the Environment* 16, no. 4 (2018): 222–30. doi.org/10.1002/fee.1794.

Yunkaporta, Tyson. *Sand Talk*. Text Publishing Company, 2019.

encounters
uncontrollable
reading omens
emptied from the inside
waiting
getting lost
losing learned time
what might arrive
solidarity
magic
calmness
night vision
bridging opacities
trusting unknown wiring
inner states
thresholds of comfort
somewhere away from
  our attention
a grandiose choir

With Darkness

Christine Hvidt

This is an account of encounters with Darkness—its presence in lands currently known as Denmark, The Netherlands, Sweden, and Finland during winter, spring, and summer.

The following text brings together learnings and experiences from different frameworks for relating with Darkness—as a technology and an alive entity that helps us navigate the world from a grounded position, reminding us that we belong to a much larger heritage and diverse family beyond the human only.

Being rooted and raised in the coastal lands of Danir, OUL *feel a deep interest and connection to ancient technologies and techniques of Northern lands and cultures.*

This text is mainly inspired by the Norse tradition, the Scandinavian Center for Shamanic Studies, and the writing-thinking-doing of Simone Weil and Édouard Glissant.

As a first step to befriend Darkness, OUL *began to simply spend time with it in different states of being, relating with it at the places* OUL *stayed, lived and worked while engaged with our artistic projects.*

These are the first experiences of what promises to be a lifelong exploration. OUL *will be a student of Darkness from forever now on—deeply grateful to everyone* OUL *met in the dark, to the lands and to Darkness itself. Thank you for being with us, for sharing and passing on teachings to us along the way. Tak.*

Imagine a place where the sun
never drops below the horizon
Where so-called night time
has to be initiated by an alarm clock
as the darkest hours approaching midnight seem
just as bright and tinted as the afternoon sun

Above the Arctic Circle under the Midnight Sun
who passes through the sky of the Northern hemisphere
in sinusoidal phases
Round and round and round
OUL are losing sense of time
Losing the habitual rhythm

In the time of these summery polar days
OUL long for the cover of night

I am a multiple
a We
We are a holobiont
an 'assemblage of a host
and the many other species
living in or around it
which together form
a discrete ecological unit
though there is controversy over this discreteness'[1]
I, We, OUL

[1] Handiwiki.

OUL hold whole worlds inside us
The microbiome in our gut
Conditioned to collaborate
The bacterial ecology on our skin
The spacious We
that expand beyond the borders of our body
The private, pheromonal sphere
OUL are opaque and mysterious to ourselves
The discreteness of the We
fluidly blends with other *Wes*
spanning scales of space and time

extending the range of the 'who' p.146

OUL long for the Darkness
to be more present with us in our life
OUL live in a time and mainstream of a culture
disconnected from Darkness and its offerings

Darkness
understood as the literal absence of light
– the shadowing of one half sphere of Earth

It is the long deep winter, where darkness spreads its presence well over the day—where the lack of light overshadows the mind and cultures of the North. OUL walk in the dim evening. Two blue tits chirp in the bush at the determined threshold entrance to the forest. OUL follow the path which has turned into mud after the rain. OUL feel welcomed to sit by a tree. Two roots open out from the trunk. OUL lean our back against it feeling held as the roots wrap themselves around us and create a shelter from the blowing wind before reaching into the ground. Sitting with attention. OUL have come to befriend Darkness and those who live here.

Darkness understood as akin to the unknown
unfamiliar internal and external natures
suppressed, ignored, overlooked, or simply less loud
the uncertain, the malleable, the uncontrollable —
that which lies beyond category
in our ever-awake, light-obsessed cultures

accepting something unknown as valuable p.110

The colossal conifers climb upwards to the sky swaying back and forth directed by the blasting wind. Some movements seem self-initiated, like sudden outbursts as part of a conversation. A grandiose choir of needle-shaped voices swaying. One branch rubbing against another maintains a constant slow rhythmical breathing. Footsteps appear from time to time from who knows what. Light from a source moving on two legs through the forest path. A distinct sound of slender trunks bending and scratching each other's bodies. Darkness grows heavier. Shapes fuse together to become strange bodies.

The unknown is a twin to opacity
a concept of Martinique activist philosopher
Édouard Glissant
for whom
Opacity is understood as that which cannot be grasped
Impenetrable
That which is the opposite of the transparent
reductionist Western continental way of understanding—
that which requires solid measures
of things and quantities[2]

[2] Glissant, 190.

Transparency principally
is a tool for an oppressor
demanding of the oppressed to reveal themselves
To let them be 'known'

The right to remain opaque
is the right to remain unknown, undefined and liquid

Just as much as opacity shares
values with anonymity and privacy
Opacity acknowledges the multiplicity of our being
the manifold faces
various natures
the layered histories,
trauma,
memories
and gifts
that our multidimensional soulful body
carries with it on Earth
That our multidimensional soulful body
expresses so differently
depending on the situated relations
and resonances with other soulful beings

a negotiation opens
p.113

Opacity engages the adoration and inclusion of differences
and situated relating to others' differences —
'Without creating a hierarchy, I relate it to my norm'[3]
Opacity is a binding agent
that holds a cohesive whole
not directed towards singular unity,
but to a plural confirmed diversity[4]

3 Ibid.

4 Glissant and Obrist.

Creaking sounds. The roar of the wind in the conifer crowns. OUL are not restless but rather calm. Sometimes small shapes of light transform in the forest ceiling. As a body OUL is exhausted. Close our eyes and listen. OUL have met the council of swaying trees. OUL faintly sense the large fluctuations at the top of this long body as quite small displacements shivering down the main axis reaching the ground level where OUL sit. The wind and the wings of those beings were with us this night.

OUL enter Darkness with the spirit of Simone Weil
—French philosopher but first and foremost
a human being acting out and living her philosophy—
Being open towards what comes to us
Being open to what presents themselves to us
Making ourselves available
for what might arrive ▬

The τέχνη of all
who are patient
p.132

In order to sincerely give attention to Darkness
all OUL must do is place ourselves in its presence
free ourselves from dense self noise
be open to what comes to us
and with patience wait for its arrival
'Attention is the rarest and purest form of generosity'[5]

5 Quote from French philosopher Simone Weil, letter to Joë Bousquet, April 13, 1942; Pétrement.

OUL walk between the shadow beings in the forest. Thoughts are flowing like currents between bodies. But where did these thoughts grow and mature? This present thought brings into attention the idea that Mind is a space available for all sorts of thoughts to enter. A shared space. Ideas flow between minds in all places. In this shared thought space outer and inner states mirror. Thinking with. Thoughts flow between material and life in all places. Material is inherently animate.

The ways of attention and learning are opaque
There is no way of knowing
where efforts of attention or intention will lead ▬
Openness is crucial
Waiting is essential

how research
actually takes place
p.322

Weil asks us to trust the unknown wiring of
ourselves
the world
the cosmos
The sheer effort of directing our attention to Darkness
will enrich us one way or another[6]

6 Weil.

A piece of green life in the suburbs of a city behind the dikes. OUL sit on the ground at our favorite spot. An image-idea arrives. Some people-humans are tree-humans. Forest-humans. Others might be field and farming-humans. Corn-humans. Machine-humans. Reindeer-humans. Each individual organism is configured differently for different alliances. Each culture favors specific collaborations—species and spirit alliances.

Following Weil
we must practice openness to never get stuck
or jump to hasty conclusions that settle in our bodies
as rigid or reductive thought systems
To Glissant this is trembling thinking
resonating with the world

'in order to be in contact with the world ...
we cannot be tied to a system of thinking.
We need trembling thinking
—because the world trembles, and our sensibility,
our affect trembles.'[7]

7 Glissant and Obrist.

Meeting the darkness is a way to shake up the stiffness
of our habitual thinking patterns

During the polar days under the spell of Midnight Sun with free running circadian rhythms, OUL descend into a timeless slow state. Letting go of our rhythms and patterns, OUL explore the states of being and what it does to our mindbody. It is a bit past midnight yet by the position of the sun in the sky Bodymind tells us the Sun is just about to set. A feeling of dissonance. Time stands still. As if the remaining cold from the past winter has stiffened the sky and frozen the Sun. Yet it moves—within safe distance to the Horizon never tempted to delve into below-Horizon destinations. OUL are losing our anchoring—our biological and learned time and rhythmicity. Disoriented. In the lands of the Reindeer with the last Indigenous peoples of these parts of the planet, OUL tremble.

The darkness assigns a certain time for restitution
For diurnal animal—day active animals—
like most mammals, including humans
Night time is the time of cleansing
of trashing accumulated maladies
of solidifying and processing impressions
and experiences of the day
Our biological clock runs according to
circadian rhythms

The tension between Darkness and Light
and their rhythmic pulsations journeying Earth
—with a multitude of local significance—
have evolved to become a timekeeping technology
for a myriad of organs and organisms

Norse mythology and tradition
describes how Night (Nótt)
gives birth to her son Day (Dagr)
Days' father is Dellingr (Daybreak)
And Night and Day ride through the sky
Keepers of time
First Night on her horse Rimfaxe (Frost Mane)
who every morning bedews the Earth with foam
followed by Day on his horse Skinfaxe (Shining Mane)
lighting up the sky and the earth
until Ragnarok
the end of the world

Most parts of electricity-based societies
function independently of the natural cycles
offsetting biological rhythms
with sound, light and chemical interference

OUL have been raised and socialized in cultures
favoring the efficiency and illusion
of transparency that light affords
OUL was wired to seek 'enlightenment'
To shine a light on things
To bring something into light

OUL walk down from the top of sacred mountain Saana. From cloudy and rainy night weather. Cold wind. Electrical charge created by friction. Friction created by opposing forces. How does the water molecule in a cloud experience the world passing by? Does it, too, experience the movement of matter—land, water, particles—morphing into forms, passing by only to transform into a new shape? Saana welcomed OUL and showed us another spatiality. The High Fell Sun welcomed OUL and showed us another temporality. Disrupted and confused. Free falling and feather light. Whirled by the wind. Shaken awake by the Water. Sharpened by the rocks. Excited by the Thunder. Spirited by the ones OUL meet. Ready to rewire and land on our feet.

Conditioned by layered historical trajectories and sources
Darkness has become unwanted and undervalued
Darkness is taken hostage
by narratives of light and production
predominant in more recent Western religion
and mainstream culture
such as the heritage of
Christianity and its fellow siblings and
Colonial expansions justified by stories
of righteousness and purity
of the superior invader
Capital- and profit-based consumer cultures
with globalized standardization strategies

where sleep and local biological rhythms
are obstacles to Global unity

Cold wind on the ridge of sacred Saana. It now rains and the wind is vigorous. OUL are cold. Until OUL move the warmth into us. OUL are in a good rhythm. A mountain hare. Complete silence. It is not shaken by our presence. And a fox. Fox is sneaking in on Hare. Hare hides behind a rock. Fox notices us and runs off into Saana's many arms. OUL spend quite some time with Hare. Holy moments. It feels as if they surely sense us without any fear. Hare holds this moment with us. Generously letting us have this experience. OUL are deeply moved. Thankful. Honored and humbled. We are of the same kin.

The darkness is mainly identified with something negative
When the mind goes dark places
Shady
Murky
Mørkegerninger—what is done in the dark hours

Perception of what is dark in a racial context
where separation and imposed hierarchy
between differently colored bodies
live and thrive in the language and act of racism

Darkness
a hiding and meeting place —
An ally for uproar against enslaving oppressive powers

marronage
p.100

Descending from Saana. Discover a stone where the sensor captures a charge.[8] | Enchanted by the coils! A sound reveals Kiiruna —the iconic bird of the rocky tundra up in this Alpine area. Extremely close up. Morphing from stone to bird as a guardian of the rocky mountainside. Kiiruna allows us to be here. Just right here in the middle of the bright night. It is so special. Saana did reveal quite someone to us. Majestic Saana showed OUL Gaia up here. Breathing and alive. Two tiny eyes are carried to the end of the world where Stone and Spring in the Earth and in the Sky merge. The upper world and the lower world come together in our ordinary middleworld. Thunder at one place while 'fair weather' at another. A balancing homeostatic system. That keeps it all together—this we call life. And beyond.

8 Sensing static electricity and electrical flows within ecological systems through experimental coil sensors—amongst other practices—inspired by Bumblebees, Thunder, Butterflies, Bilberries, specialist humans and more, during the North Escaping Residency organized and hosted by Bioart Society and facilitated in collaboration with Kilpisjärvi biological station, Helsinki University.

Now more than ever, embracing the dark
challenges our habitual rhythms
and thresholds of comfort

In present-day communities
comfort and convenience
is the fruit of so-called technological advancement
OUL endorse Darkness as a technology
A way to get back in touch with the natural worlds
Darkness becomes a portal for
connection and negotiation with other life
OUL approach technology as
a way to improve the human condition
—as a means to expand the human capacity
Darkness becomes a technology for
enriching our existence and
rooting our opaque being
within the larger communities of life
still dependent on teachings from other soulful beings
much older than our species

Darkness as a technology
—a portal for entering other realms
such as ancient animist and shamanic traditions
spirit and species inclusive practices
for relating to the world
for relating between worlds

community members known and unknown, seen and unseen p.423

for seeking advice or guidance
from the larger community of life

In the darkness beings and creatures
shape shift and show themselves
through other appearances
than our daylight conceptions suggest
A veil is lifted
The stones show their being or soul
their troll being
their inner side
at twilight and in darkness[9]
Dusk and dawn are threshold openings
portals between worlds

9 Høst.

Walking down the street from the house where OUL grew up. It feels slightly surreal like a constructed backdrop for a movie. Droplets of street lamps shower the asphalt in light. Walking down this bright portal OUL reach the end, and enter into the gravel road where massive Darkness reigns. OUL step into the forest following the narrow path through the bushes. Into the darker forest between the crowd of the tree beings. Some of them move slowly around. Looking up, spirited creatures amongst the leaves stare at us from above. OUL follow the path deeper into the forest. Feel a heaviness on our left shoulder. Someone puts their weight onto it. Gently. And OUL turn around. OUL see a dark figure. Darker than dark. Foggy yet of a solid substance. Our eyes move to the face. Nothing but the dark moving haze sometimes showing red, yellow eyes. OUL could be frightened but are simply experiencing. This figure takes our hands. Here we stand holding hands in the darkness. With Darkness for a while. They guide OUL to sit down, arranging the space to make us sit comfortably. As an act of care, it reaches over us and removes the obstacles. Then evaporates into everywhere.

OUL remember to take an active yet non-controlling role. When asking, 'Was this the spirit of Darkness?' OUL feel a strong sense of confirmation. 'Is our spirit ally here?' Yes indeed. A dark feathered bird jumps down from a branch above OUL making itself seen, felt and heard. It has our back. Jumps onto our right shoulder. OUL get up and move forward. OUL feel called. Passing the marsh. Small creatures with shapes rounded by the dense cover of mud move up and down. It makes the swamp seem like a boiling muddy mass enclosed by cattail and reed. These jumping boiling creatures are the marsh. OUL ask if they are the spirit of Darkness. Yes, they reply. Moving onwards to the pines. OUL hear a vague melody. A whistling.

Seeking counsel during the dark hours
is an ancient practice carried out all over the world
Old writings of ancient Norse culture
mention *udesidning* (sitting out) to gain wisdom
Sitting overnight in the wilderness
to seek insight or knowledge
as a way to receive inspiration for your own life path
as a way to get power
for a specific personal challenge or circumstance
as a way to gain insight about the hidden, spiritual world
'As a sacred ritual meeting between
the world of humans and the world of Nature
and the spirits.'[10]
Different versions go under the names of
udesidning—sitting out from sundown to sunrise
vågenat—vigil night
or *varselstagning*—taking counsel or reading omens[11]

10 Ibid.

11 Ibid.

The path OUL tread turns into a thin line bridging a deep earthy abyss. OUL now balance on the paper-thin tip of a knife. Make it to the other side. The path continues to carry OUL. Balance is needed. OUL reach the edge of the dense forest. The conifer choir. Whistling sounds appears again. Four legged creatures with hooves and with human torsos stream through the woods like a galloping melodic sonic swarm. A subtle polyphony. In the canopy the leaves and needles are rattling along with the stream of whistlers.

In the company of wise human teachers[12]
OUL learned inherited techniques and rituals
that open portals to the spirit world
guided by drums and rattles and spirit allies

12 Jonathan Horwitz and Zara Waldebäck from Scandinavian Center for Shamanic Studies.

The forest fades away. OUL are surrounded by deep Darkness. Nothing but Darkness. OUL feel nothing but full Darkness. The air is still. A vague light reveals a black stone. It has a smooth surface. The stone levitates. Slowly. Hanging in the space. Slowly moving upwards. Extremely slowly. OUL spend quite some time in the presence of the stone. After a good while, it gradually expands. It slowly grows and becomes mammoth. The smooth surface contains grooves and indents. It resembles a landscape with rivers and valleys. A full world of its own. Steadily, something grows from it. A plant-lichen organism. OUL know this stone. It is the stone OUL found by the local beach in the spring on a walk with a person dear to us. It is this exact smooth black stone. OUL feel our heart rate increases. Something moves through us. Into us. Trembling. OUL have to go back now. OUL are thankful for this experience and ask how we can work together. No words, but an image of the stone—the stone being is with OUL wherever OUL go. Keep the spirit of Darkness close always.

Appreciating Darkness as a technology
As an ally
A friend
A vibrant, ambiguous being
We can learn to include it into our lived communal natures
We can expand our human capacities and comforts
to include the nature of Darkness
the unknown

a good and listening friend p.181

opacity
in resonance with different worlds
and the animate Earth with its rich depths of existence
from a much more humble and honest position
in solidarity and kinship with ‘life’ as a whole

Holding hands with Darkness

References

Glissant, Édouard. 'For Opacity.' In *Poetics of Relation*. Translated by Betsy Wing. The University of Michigan Press, 1997.

Glissant, Éduard, and Hans Ulrich Obrist. '"The Earth is Trembling": Édouard Glissant in Conversation with Hans Ulrich Obrist.' Interview by Eliza Levinson. In *The Archipelago Conversations*. Translated by Emma Ramadan. Isolarii, 2021. *032c*, December 20, 2021. 032c.com/magazine/edouard-glissant-and-hans-ulrich-obrist.

HandWiki. 'Holobiont.'Accessed April 14, 2023. encyclopedia.pub/entry/29286.

Høst, Annette. 'Wisdom in the Wilderness.' In *The Earth Sings: The Power of Nature in Nordic Tradition*. Translated by Michael Caine, Julia Crabtree and Annette Høst. shamanism.dk/wildernesswisdom.

Pétrement, Simone. *Simone Weil: A Life*. Translated by Raymond Rosenthal. Pantheon Books, 1976.

Weil, Simone. *Waiting for God*. Capricorn Books, 1959.

Paula Albuquerque is an Amsterdam-based Portuguese artist and researcher with solo exhibitions at galleries Zone2Source (2024), Bradwolff Projects (2023, 2018, 2015), Looiersgracht 60 (2023) and Nieuw Dakota (2020). With films at International Film Festivals IDFA (2024), Ji'hlava IDFF (2024), Doc Alliance (2024), Doclisboa (2023), Sheffield DOC|Fest (2020) and Rotterdam IFFR (2016), presenting at conferences EYE International, Media in Transition (MIT), NECS, and Visible Evidence. She published the books: *Enter the Ghost—Haunted Media Ecologies* (2020) and *The Webcam as an Emerging Cinematic Medium* (2018). She is currently Senior Researcher (Gerrit Rietveld Academie), Assistant Researcher (Universidade Nova de Lisboa), and Supervisory Board member (Framer Framed Art Platform).

Kader Attia (1970) is a multidisciplinary artist who draws upon the lived experiences of two disparate cultural identities: Algerian and French. From this place of cultural intermediacy, Attia's practice interrogates sociopolitical complexities rooted in histories of colonialism and cultural obfuscation. In his practice, Attia employs poetic installations and sculptural assemblages to investigate the far-reaching emotional implications of Western cultural hegemony and colonial systems of power for non-Western subjectivities, focusing particularly on collective trauma and notions of repair. kaderattia.de

Aïsta (Aissata) Bah is an activist and a leading member of La Voix des Sans Papiers, a Brussels-based collective of undocumented immigrants founded in 2014 that fights for the regularization of all undocumented immigrants. As poet, author, and trainer, she is committed to making visible the struggles of undocumented women, the primary victims of institutional violence. The only woman on the organizing committee La Voix des Sans Papiers located on Rue Fritz Toussaint, she advocates for the creation of safe, self-managed spaces by and for women. She is also the founder of the Journal des Sans Papiers and the 'Y'en a marre' project, and collaborates on the 'Exils et Création' project.

Scott Benesiinaabandan is Anishinaabe, a member of Obishkkokaang/Lac Seul First Nations. He is an intermedia artist who currently works in experimental image making and sonic materials and is currently a resident of Montreal, where he has completed a MFA in photography. Scott's current research interests are intersections of artificial intelligence and Anishinaabemowin. Scott has completed international residencies at Parramatta Artist Studios in Australia, Context Gallery in Derry, North of Ireland, and a University Lethbridge/Royal Institute of Technology iAIR residency, along with international collaborative projects in both the UK and Ireland. Scott has completed residencies with Initiative for Indigenous Futures and AbTec in Montreal. Benesiinaabandan has been awarded grants from the Canada Council for the Arts, Manitoba Arts Council, Winnipeg Arts Council and Conseil des arts des lettre du Quebec. His work can be found in a number of private, provincial, and national collections. benesiinaabandan.com

Pacôme Béru (1981) is a co-founder of the worker-owned Atelier Cartographique cooperative (AC), based in Brussels. Trained as a visual artist, he has honed his skills through scientific drawing, coordinating artistic research residencies with nadine vzw, a non-profit laboratory for contemporary arts, and actively participating in the self-management of the community life of temporary housing projects. He has had a cross-disciplinary role at AC since 2014, and has been teaching subjective cartography at Design Academy Eindhoven from 2020 to 2024.

Cláudio Bueno (1983) is an artist and curator. He is an Assistant Professor at the University of California, Santa Cruz – Art Department, teaching at the Environmental Art and Social Practice MFA and is affiliated with the Visualizing Abolition Studies. He has engaged in collaborative practices committed to social and environmental justice, featuring in international exhibitions, residencies, awards, and talks. He co-founded the collectives Explode! Platform, O grupo inteiro, and Intervalo-Escola. His current research, 'Life in the Faultline,' examines social, ecological, and cultural challenges of spaces characterized by rupture, tension, and instability. Bueno lives and works between Brazil and the US. groundatlas.org

Derrais Carter (US) is an interdisciplinary scholar and artist whose work plays in the vibrant realms of Black Critical Theory, Black Queer Studies, and Black Popular Culture, Narrative Theory, and Cultural History. He created Black Revelry: In Honor of the Sugar Shack (If I Cant Dance I Don't Want to Be Part of Your Revolution, 2022), a book-album built around Ernie Barnes's painting *The Sugar Shack* that animates various renderings of Black social life and intimacy. Carter's work has been supported by the Fulbright Program, the National Endowment for the Humanities, and the Netherland-America Foundation. He was a 2022–3 recipient of an Andy Warhol Foundation Arts Writers Grant.

Raven Chacon (Diné/US) is a composer of chamber music, a performer of experimental noise music, and an installation artist from the Navajo Nation. His work explores sounds of acoustic handmade instruments overdriven through electric systems and the direct and indirect audio feedback responses from their interactions. As a recording artist, Chacon has appeared on over eighty releases on national and international labels. He has exhibited, performed, or had works performed at LACMA, documenta 14, the 18th Biennale of Sydney, Vancouver Art Gallery, Haus der Kulturen der Welt, SITE Santa Fe, The Kennedy Center, and Holland Festival, among other traditional and non-traditional venues. In 2022, Raven Chacon became the first Native American to be awarded the Pulitzer Prize in Music.
spiderwebsinthesky.com

Joana Chicau (1992) is an artist, designer, and researcher, with a background in dance. She is a PhD candidate at the Creative Institute at the University of the Arts London, supported by the AHRC/UKRI Techne Studentship. Her research seeks to increase public understanding of computational processes through embodied and choreographic approaches. She recently contributed to the publications: *The Book of X: 10 Years of Computation, Communication, Aesthetics & X* (Porto: i2ADS/CITAR, 2022) and *Live Coding: A User's Manual* (Cambridge, MIT Press, 2022). Chicau is based between Portugal and the UK.
joanachicau.com

Guy Cools (1964) is a Belgian dance dramaturg. He is currently professor in the dance department of UQAM, Montréal. From 1990 till 2002 he curated the dance program of Arts Centre Vooruit in Ghent, Belgium. His most recent publications include *The Ethics of Art: ecological turns in the performing arts* (2014), *In-between Dance Cultures: on the migratory artistic identity of Sidi Larbi Cherkaoui and Akram Khan* (2015), *Imaginative Bodies, dialogues in performance practices* (2016) and *Performing Mourning. Laments in Contemporary Art* (2021).

Laura Coombs is a graphic designer and educator who studied at the Yale School of Art. She leads design at the New Museum of Contemporary Art, Rhizome, New Inc, and the New York Review of Architecture and creates visual identities and editorial projects with many institutions, including the Museum of Modern Art (MoMA), Carnegie Museum of Art, MIT Press, and Columbia Books on Architecture and the City. Her practice focuses on formal citation through typography, material, and technology. Coombs teaches graphic design at the Rhode Island School of Design (RISD), Cooper Union, and Princeton University. She lives and works in New York City.
lauracoombs.com

Siobhán K. Cronin (US) is a technologist and artist with a passion for nurturing innovative, inclusive communities of engineering, research and creative practice. She began her career researching how humans learn at Harvard's Lab for Developmental Studies and Harvard Medical School's Music Neuroimaging Laboratory, followed by a series of NGO leadership positions. She has spent the past several years building and scaling engineering organizations at early-stage startups in Silicon Valley while continuing to engage with the arts community.
siobhankcronin.com

Will Daddario (1980) is a scholar of theater and performance, a clinical mental health counselor, an addictions specialist, and a grief worker. These four vocations come together in the forthcoming book *The Last Laugh: Grief, Death, and the Comic* (2025). As co-editor of the Performance Philosophy journal, he contributed to and helped curate its March 2025 edition dedicated to the intersections of performance, philosophy, and grief and death practices. He is widely published on a diverse range of topics, including Baroque Venice, Theodor W. Adorno, and Jay Wright.
willdaddario.com

Edwidge Danticat is the author of several books, including *Breath, Eyes, Memory*, an Oprah Book Club selection, *Krik? Krak!*, a National Book Award finalist, *The Farming of Bones, The Dew Breaker, Create Dangerously, Claire of the Sea Light, The Art of Death, Everything Inside*, a Reese's Book Club selection and National Book Critics Circle Awards winner. She is also the editor of *The Butterfly's Way: Voices from the Haitian Dyaspora* in the United States, *Best American Essays 2011*, *Haiti Noir*, and *Haiti Noir 2*. She has written seven books for children and young adults: *Anacaona, Behind the Mountains, Eight Days, The Last Mapou, Mama's Nightingale, Untwine, My Mommy Medicine*, and a travel narrative, *After the Dance*. Her memoir, *Brother, I'm Dying*, was a 2007 finalist for the National Book Award and a 2008 winner of the National Book Critics Circle Award for autobiography. She is a 2009 MacArthur Fellow, a 2018 Ford Foundation 'Art of Change' fellow, the winner of the 2018 Neustadt International Prize, the 2019 St. Louis Literary Award, the 2011 Bocas Nonfiction Prize and 2020 Bocas Fiction Prize, the 2020 Vilcek Prize for Literature, a 2020 United States Artists Fellow, a two-time winner of The Story Prize, and the 2023 PEN/Malamud Award for Excellence in the Short Story. Her essay collection, *We're Alone*, was published in September 2024. She teaches at Columbia University.
edwidgedanticat.com

Thierno Dia is a member of the collective La Voix des Sans Papiers, a Brussels-based collective of undocumented people founded in 2014, fighting for the regularization of all undocumented people. The members occupy several buildings in Brussels and across Belgium, turning them into spaces of struggle, socialization, and awareness-raising about the violation of fundamental rights. In 2022, he co-published *Les Turbulents*, a comic book created collectively by sixteen people with Studio Baraka Grafika, exhibited at the Belgian Comic Strip Center in Brussels and supported by FRMK editions and Atelier du Toner. Thierno is also an artist and djembe workshop facilitator, advocating for this instrument as a messenger of resistance and community.

Mamadou Taslim Diallo explores activism through various forms of expression. He is a slam poet, journalist for the *Journal des Sans Papiers*, actor, and illustrator. A member of La Voix des Sans Papiers since 2014, he has been collaborating as an actor with Mieriën Coppens and Elie Maissin since 2018, notably performing in *Caught in the Rain* and *Et leurs lettres*. In 2022, he co-published *Les Turbulents*, a comic book created collectively by sixteen people with Studio Baraka Grafika, exhibited at the Belgian Comic Strip Center in Brussels and supported by FRMK editions and Atelier du Toner. In 2024, he also took part in the Zinneke Parade as the artistic coordinator of the Zinnode 'Résistance des invisibles.'

Henriette Essami-Khaullot is an activist and member of La Voix des Sans Papiers, a Brussels-based collective founded in 2014 for the regularization of undocumented immigrants. Former coordinator of the La Voix des Sans Papiers Amazones (Defacqz) location, and an active member of the Committee of Undocumented Women, she fights for the recognition of the rights of undocumented women, who are often invisible. As author, trainer, and spokesperson, she works to create self-managed reception centers and denounces the specific violence and discrimination that undocumented women experience on a daily basis.

Silvia Federici is a feminist activist and a renowned political theorist. In 1972, she co-founded the International Feminist Collective, which launched the campaign Wages for Housework internationally. Her work has demonstrated the oversight in Marxian theory of one of the fundamental features of capitalist accumulation: namely, the subjugation of women and women's productive and reproductive labor. Federici is known for her focus on the struggle against capitalist globalization and, more recently, on developing a feminist theory of the commons.

Mariana Fernández Mora (1991) is a researcher, writer, and artist with a background in architecture. She is an alumna of the Gerrit Rietveld Academie and the Sandberg Institute. Fernández Mora currently works as a researcher at the Amsterdam University of Applied Sciences within the Lectoraat Visual Methodologies. Her work operates at the intersection of art, research, and AI, with a focus on how technology shapes knowledge production. Her latest work explores anti-colonial perspectives on algorithmic technologies. Recent exhibitions include: 'Poetics of Prompting: A Crash Course in Speaking Machine,' MU, Eindhoven (2024), presenting the works *Robot Assistant* (2024) and *What Do We Dream About When We Dream About Machines* (2024). Recent publications include: *Restless Grounds: Speculative Futures on Algorithmic Technologies* (2025), *Dear Machines* (2022), an experimental thesis on co-writing with AI, exploring how these technologies challenge communication, intelligence, and knowledge production. The book is part of the collections at the Stedelijk Museum Library, If I Can't Dance, Design Museum Gent, The Sandberg/Rietveld Library, and Stockholm University. Fernández Mora lives and works in Amsterdam.
marianafernandez.nl

Ella Finer's work in sound and performance spans writing, composing, and curating with a particular interest in how bodies acoustically disrupt, challenge, or change occupations of space. Her research queries the ownership of cultural expression through sound, often through collaborative projects centering listening as a practice of deep attention, affiliation, and reciprocity. She is working on a book of essays: *Acoustic Commons and the Wild Life of Sound*, while *Silent Whale Letters*, a correspondence project with Vibeke Mascini and edited by Kate Briggs, was published by Sternberg Press in 2023.
ellafiner.com

Since studying computer science in the 1970s, *Jem Finer* has worked in various fields, including photography, film, experimental and popular music, sound recording, sculpture and installation. Much of his work relates to systems, extended processes and extremes of scale and includes Longplayer and The Gurdy Stone, an ancient rock set upright in a field in East Sussex with Jimmy Cauty. Recent music revolves around a fascination with the hurdy-gurdy and includes *hrdy-grdy*, a cassette released by Benedict Drew's Thanet Tape Centre. Finer and Cauty are currently developing a stone pipe organ.
jemfiner.net

Mashinka Firunts Hakopian is an artist, researcher, and Associate Professor of Technology and Social Justice at ArtCenter College of Design. She is a 2024–25 Visiting Research Fellow at Cambridge University. Her creative research focuses on ancestral intelligences: data feminist interventions in computational media rooted in ancestral, non-Western knowledge systems. She is the author of *The Institute for Other Intelligences* (X Artists' Books, 2022). Her performances and projects have appeared at REDCAT, Music Center LA, the 2024 Asian Art Biennial, and Centre Pompidou.
mashinkafirunts.com

Dakin Hart is currently Artistic Director for Fundación Casa Wabi (México City, Puerto Escondido, and Tokyo). Between 2013 and 2023, he was Senior Curator at The Isamu Noguchi Foundation and Garden Museum (New York), where he oversaw the Museum's exhibitions, collections, catalogue raisonné, archives, and public programming—and had the good fortune to daily collaborate with Isamu Noguchi in absentia. Other previous positions have included Assistant Director at the Nasher Sculpture Center (Dallas), Artistic Director and Director of Artists in Residence at Montalvo Center for the Arts (Saratoga, CA), and Assistant to the Director of the Fine Arts Museums of San Francisco (San Francisco). He has also worked as an independent writer and curator.

Faïza Hirach (1973) is a healthcare worker, trade union activist, and anti-racist organizer.

Candice Hopkins is a citizen of Carcross/Tagish First Nation and lives in Red Hook, New York. Her writing and curatorial practice explore the intersections of history, contemporary art, and Indigeneity. She is Executive Director of Forge Project, Taghkanic, NY, and Senior Curator for the 2019 and 2022 editions of the Toronto Biennial of Art. She was part of the curatorial team for the Canadian Pavilion at the 58th Venice Biennale, featuring the work of the media art collective Isuma, and co-curator of notable exhibitions, including the national traveling survey 'Art for New Understanding: Native Voices, 1950s to Now', SITElines, 2018: Casa Tomada, SITE Santa Fe, documenta 14, Athens and Kassel, and 'Sakahàn: International Indigenous Art,' National Gallery of Canada, Ottawa. Notable essays include 'The Gilded Gaze: Wealth and Economies on the Colonial Frontier,' in the *documenta 14 Reader*, 'Outlawed Social Life,' in *South as a State of Mind*, and 'The Appropriation Debates (or The Gallows of History),' in *Saturation: Race, Art, and the Circulation of Value* (New Museum/ MIT Press, 2020).

Christine Hvidt (1989) is a multidisciplinary artist and artscience explorer who studied at Art & Technology (BA) and Artscience (MA). Hvidt explores relational tangible encounter across species and cultures through experimental and place-bound approaches based on attentive listening, sound, responsive systems, embodiment, poetic writing, audio-visuals, and imagination. Recent exhibitions include: 'The North Escaping: Grasping Transformations,' Bioart Society, Helsinki, 2024, 'FIBER festival', Door Open Space, Amsterdam, 2023. Recent publications include: Some Principles for Symbiotic Practices (2023). Hvidt lives and works in the Netherlands and Denmark.
christinehvidt.dk

Carol R. Kallend (UK) is a lifelong poet, pacifist, feminist, disability advocate, knitter, and rebel. She writes every day and it is a vital part of her life, giving her strength, inspiration, and friendship. In 2015 she began working with Rory Pilgrim to create *Software Garden*, a music video album exploring connections between disability, robotic technology, care, and how we come together from both behind and beyond our screens.

Theun Karelse (NL) is a creative practitioner whose interests and experimental practice explore edges between art, environment, technology, and archaeology. He practices and supports ecosystem and landscape regeneration in Europe, India, and Africa, and closer to home runs an outdoor studio consisting of several gardens, testing grounds for urban biodiversity, climate adaptation and rekindling Indigenous knowledge ecologies. He is a contributor to the Embassy of the Earth in supporting Maasai-led regeneration of the foothills of Mt Kilimanjaro and is part of the Future of the Delta team at the Embassy of the North Sea. In recent years, Karelse work has been presented at Ars Electronica, Fiberfestival, and Changwon Sculpture Biennale (among others) and he has been a lecturer/guest teacher at academic institutions including Central St. Martins, ZHDK Zurich, and the Royal Academy of the Arts in the Hague. He lives in Amsterdam.
theunkarelse.net

Danel Khojayeva (1998) is a writer, journalist, and communications strategist based in Almaty, Kazakhstan. With Uzbek, Kazakh, Tatar, Uyghur, Arab, and Tajik roots, her work explores identity, women's experiences, family history, and collective memory in Central Asia. She began her career as a journalist and now focuses on social projects and digital storytelling. She co-organized Qantar Jazylu, a literary open call reflecting on the January 2022 protests in Kazakhstan, initiated by an independent volunteer editorial team. The texts in this book are rooted in the concept of Chilltans, introduced by filmmaker and artist Saodat Ismailova and the DAVRA research group as part of documenta fifteen.
instagram.com/daniellyak

Suzanne Kite (Lakota/US) is an Oglála Lakȟóta artist, composer, and academic. Her scholarship and practice explore contemporary Lakȟóta ontology (the study of beinghood), artificial intelligence, and contemporary art and performance. She creates interfaces and arranges software systems that engage the whole body in order to imagine new ethical AI protocols that interrogate past, present, and future.
kitekitekitekite.com

Fran Kourouma (1996, Republic of Guinea) is a writer, performer and healthcare worker. After earning a diploma in Food Technology and Control in Dalaba (2015), he was forced to flee Guinea in 2016, arriving in Belgium as an asylum seeker in 2017. His time in homelessness led him to start writing *Notre Soleil*, published by Samsa Editions (2020). He has since worked in various sectors, performed in the stage adaptation of *Notre Soleil* (2022), and is currently training in dual diagnosis (mental health and social care) at Tam Tam Workshops (2024–2025).

Jaron Lanier is a computer scientist, composer, artist, and author who writes on numerous topics, including high-technology business, the social impact of technology, the philosophy of consciousness and information, Internet politics, and the future of humanism. Lanier's first book, *You Are Not a Gadget, A Manifesto*, is held dear by readers as an expression of spiritual sensibility in high tech times. It was a *New York Times*, *Los Angeles Times*, *Boston Globe* and international bestseller. Lanier has been on the cusp of technological innovation from its infancy to the present. A pioneer in virtual reality (a term he coined), Lanier founded VPL Research, the first company to sell VR products, and led teams originating VR applications for medicine, design, and numerous other fields. He is currently the 'octopus' (which stands for Office of the Chief Technology Officer Prime Unifying Scientist) at Microsoft. In 2018, Lanier was named one of the twenty-five most influential people in the previous twenty-five years of tech history by *Wired Magazine*. In 2009, Jaron Lanier received a Lifetime Career Award from the IEEE, the preeminent international engineering society. Lanier's writing appears in *The New York Times, Discover, The Wall Street Journal, Forbes, Harper's Magazine, Atlantic, Wired Magazine* (where he was a founding contributing editor), and *Scientific American*. Jaron Lanier is also a musician and artist. He has been active in the world of new 'classical' music since the late 1970s and writes chamber and orchestral works.
jaronlanier.com

Jason Edward Lewis (CAN/US) is a digital media theorist, poet, and software designer exploring computation as a creative and cultural material. He is the University Research Chair in Computational Media and the Indigenous Future Imaginary at Concordia University (Montreal). Lewis is the lead author on the award-winning 'Making Kin with the Machines' essay and editor of the *Indigenous Protocol and Artificial Intelligence Position Paper*, and co-directs the Abundant Intelligences Partnership, the Indigenous Futures Research Centre, Aboriginal Territories in Cyberspace, and the Skins Workshops on Aboriginal Storytelling and Video Game Design. He is Hawaiian & Samoan, born and raised in northern California.
jasonlewis.org

Pia Lindman (FI) is an artist and researcher who works with performance art, healing-as-art, installation, microbes, architecture, painting, and sculpture. In 2024, Pia Lindman represented Finland at the Venice Art Biennale. Lindman's work contributes to the tradition of minimalist performance and community-oriented art, and suggests new perspectives in merging artistic, social, and scientific research. Internationally known for The New York Times Project, performed in cities around the world and her interactive performance and installation Public Sauna, first developed during graduate work at MIT and later presented at P.S.1 Contemporary Art Center in 2000, Lindman explores how our bodies become the loci of interaction between private and public. Born in Espoo, Finland, Lindman received her MFA in 1996 from the Academy of Fine Arts in Finland and in 1999, as a Fulbright Scholar, her Master of Science in Visual Studies at Massachusetts Institute of Technology. She now lives in New York and teaches at Yale University School of Art.
pialindman.com

Gļeb(s) Maiboroda (1994) is a multidisciplinary visual artist with a background in weaving, working across various mediums such as textiles, installation, performance, icon-painting, and experimental pedagogies. Gļeb(s) holds an MA Art Praxis from the Dutch Art Institute, ArtEZ University of Arts (2023). In his work Gļeb(s) is interested in traditional knowledge and its role in relation to digital and automated technologies. Recent exhibitions include: 'A Passage,' de Bouwput, Amsterdam (2024), 'Beyond the Veil,' de Kluit, Amsterdam (2024), 'The Weaver's Handshake,' Centrale Fies, Dro, Trentino (2023), 'Textiles of Resistance,' Sonsbeek, Arnhem (2021). Recent publications include: *Shuttling Bodies: Automated Rhythms and the Somatics of Weaving* (2023), *The Practice of Threading One's Way* (2021), *Cross-Cloth* (2019). Maiboroda lives and works in Amsterdam, the Netherlands.
glebmaiboroda.com

Pierre Marchand (1976) is a co-founder of the worker-owned Atelier Cartographique cooperative (AC). He writes open-source software. A former visual artist and forestry engineer, he is a programmer-architect for collective projects linked to digital data and their representation. His research focuses on a form of speculative programming that activates the dynamics of questioning, both in relation to the tools and to their historical and cultural dimensions, by exploring the processes involved in the formation of a digital sensibility.

Michael Marder is Ikerbasque Research Professor of Philosophy at the University of the Basque Country, UPV/EHU, Vitoria-Gasteiz. His work covers the fields of environmental philosophy and ecological thought, political theory, and phenomenology, and his latest publications include *Time Is a Plant* (Brill, 2023) and, with Edward S. Casey, *Plants in Place: A Phenomenology of the Vegetal* (Columbia UP, 2024).
michaelmarder.org

Nanako Nakajima is a leading dance dramaturg and a pioneer in artistic research on aging in dance. She received the Special Commendation of the Elliott Hayes Award 2017 for Outstanding Achievement in Dramaturgy. She was a Valeska-Gert Visiting Professor in 2019/20 at Freie Universität Berlin, Germany, Faculty Dramaturg in dance since 2022 at the Banff Centre for Arts and Creativity, Canada, and is currently an Associate Professor at Waseda University, Japan. Publications: *The Aging Body in Dance* (Routledge, 2017), *Oi to Odori* (Keiso Shobo, 2019), *Dance Dramaturgies of Aging: A Journey of Negotiating Identity Across Generations, Dance Cultures, and Embodied Histories in between Continents* (Routledge, in process). Keynote lectures and exhibitions include Universidade Católica Portuguesa and RnA Studio, 2025. After launching a website on dance dramaturgy (www.dancedramaturgy.org), she initiated Japan's first dramaturgs' meeting in 2024.
nanakonakajima.com

Florence Okoye is a facilitator, writer, qualitative researcher and service designer, currently working at the Natural History Museum in London. Her practice focuses on using community-centered and Africanist (e.g. Afro/Afrifuturist, de-/anti-colonial) speculative design methods to co-create and analyze digital infrastructure. As a result, her projects range from designing services for collections access and critical methods for collectively evaluating automation in the public sphere to Afrofuturist approaches regarding policy development. Recent publications include: 'Making a Case for Afrofuturism as a Critical Qualitative Inquiry Method for Liberation' (September 2023) with Dr. Temidayo Eseonu, and 'Liminality and Design Failure,' a chapter in *Design for All? Inclusive Design Today* (Spector Books, June 2024).
finokoye.com

Marina Orlova (1987) is a dance/theater maker and tech-dramaturg. She studied sociology at HSE University in Moscow (2009) and choreography at the Amsterdam Academy of Theatre and Dance (2021). Her multidisciplinary performances deal with topics of mental health, AI ethics and Data feminism. She mediates between engineering and theater apparatus using absurdism, tragicomedy, and autofiction. Marina founded EIAI Institute and presented its research at Next Nature; Mesh Festival; Society 5.0 Festival; de Balie; AHK; UvA; KISD. 'I'm a Robot and I need Therapy' performance was presented at Veem House for Performance; Flam Festival Amsterdam; Frascati Theater Amsterdam; Next Level Festival Dortmund.
marina-or-not.github.io/
eiai.institute

Jogi Panghaal is concerned with the shift from product to service design, with a special focus on how craftsmanship and traditional artisan communities can be an inspiration for the design of services in current modern societies. Panghaal works with artisans to use their traditional skills to find new markets for their old/new products and also works with industry to enhance concepts of design. For many years, Panghaal was a contributor to Doors of Perception, a conference and network in which design, industry, and social science collaborate to develop new ideas for service design. Panghaal graduated in Product Design from the National Institute of Design (NID) in Ahmedabad, India, in 1977. He co-founded Lifetools in New Delhi to provide product design and communication services to communities, both rural and urban, that needed design help. He has been a visiting teacher at the National Institute of Design in India, ID, at Les Ateliers Paris, at the School of Planning and Architecture, Delhi and at the Gerrit Rietveld Academy in Amsterdam.

Moisés Patrício (1984) is a visual artist and educator. He works with photography, video, performance, rituals, and installations in works dealing with Latin and Afro-Brazilian cultural elements. Selected exhibitions include the 'Dak'Art–12th Biennale of Contemporary African Art,' Museum Of African Arts, Senegal (2016), 'A Nova Mão Afro Brasileira,' Museum Afro Brasil, São Paulo (2014), and 'Papel de Seda' at the Institute of Research and Memory Pretos Novos, IPN Museum Memorial, Rio de Janeiro (2014). Galeria Estação, Brazil, represents the artist. Patrício lives and works in São Paulo, Brazil.

Rory Pilgrim (UK/NL) works in a wide range of media including songwriting, composing music, film, music video, text, drawing and live performances. Centered on emancipatory concerns, the artist aims to challenge the nature of how we come together, speak, listen, and strive for social change through sharing and voicing personal experience. Strongly influenced by the origins of activist, feminist and socially engaged art, Pilgrim works with others through different methods of dialogue, collaboration, and workshops. In an age of increasing technological interaction, the work creates connections between activism, spirituality, music and how we form community locally and globally from both beyond and behind our screens. Solo Shows include: Badischer Kunstverein, Karlsruhe (2020), Between Bridges, Berlin (2019) Andriesse-Eyck Gallery, Amsterdam NL (2018), South London Gallery (2018), Plymouth Art Centre, Plymouth (2017), Flat Time House, London (2016), Site Gallery, Sheffield (2016) and sic! Raum für Kunst, Luzern CH (2014). Winner of the 2019 Prix de Rome, shortlisted for the 2023 Turner Prize.
rorypilgrim.com

elieli / Elisabeth Raymond (1991) is a multidisciplinary artist and choreographer. They graduated from SNDO, the School for New Dance Development at the Amsterdam University of the Arts, with a degree in choreography. Eli are navigating through a field of entanglement, ecology and technology. They are working through scores of listening, listening to the gentle pushes of bodies. Bodies as in landscapes, bodies as in matter, bodies as in beings. Recent exhibitions and performances include: 'SOM e.t', Konträr, Stockholm (2025) and 'Oceanic Feelings,' Fotografiska, Stockholm (2024). Eli live and work in Stockholm, Sweden.
elieli.se

Milady Renoir is a poetasse™, performer, and workshop facilitator since 2004, working with people full of stories to tell-write-shout. She also facilitates training sessions for professionals from cultural organizations, continuous education, and social justice collectives resisting state violence. She prefers poetry and the stage to unspoken words and misunderstandings, even though they are fertile ground for poetry. Milady writes for journals and podcasts on arts, humanities, and political analysis, fully dedicating herself to the reclaiming of rights for undocumented people. She contributes to radio programs, performs with her fifty-something grumpy body, and writes pleas, slams between two doubts and three urges, while keeping a sensitive thorax, a tight throat, and a raised fist.
miladyrenoir.org

Oscar Santillán (1980s) is an artist and founder of studio ANTIMUNDO, based between Amsterdam and Quito. He holds an MFA from Virginia Commonwealth University (USA) and has been a researcher at the Davis Center for AI (USA) and NIAS (NL). His work merges science, fiction, and non-human perspectives. Recent exhibitions include 'The Mountain Algorithms,' MacAlline Art Center, Beijing (2024), 'Plants & Planets,' Hortus Botanicus Leiden (2025). Santillán lives and works in Amsterdam and Quito.
antimundo.org.

Laurel Schwulst (1988) is a designer, artist, writer, educator, and technologist interested in ambient forms of design and literature, public works, and the poetic potential of the world wide web. Selected projects include: *Perfume Area*, a book of fragrance reviews (2015), *Flight Simulator*, a travel app (2019), and 'How to Build a Bird Kite,' an online tutorial and meditation with the New York Times (2021). Schwulst currently teaches at Princeton University and founded Fruitful School. She lives and works between New York City and Princeton, NJ.
laurelschwulst.com

Mindy Seu (1991) is an artist and technologist who graduated with distinction from Harvard's Graduate School of Design. She is now an Associate Professor in the Department of Design Media Arts at University of California, Los Angeles, and formerly taught at Rutgers University and Yale School of Art. Her practice focuses on technology-driven performance and publication, with an emphasis in revisionist internet history, techno-criticism, and citational practices. Seu's latest publication, the *Cyberfeminism Index*, is a pseudo-encyclopedic book that gathers three decades of online activism and net art. It was commissioned by Rhizome, awarded the Graham Foundation Grant, and went on an international book tour with eighty-nine performative readings across eighteen countries with sold out events at the New Museum (NYC), Whitechapel Gallery (London), Amant Foundation (Brooklyn), Lafayette Anticipations (Paris), among others. She is currently developing a new lecture performance called 'A Sexual History of the Internet,' set to tour in Fall 2025, along with an eponymous artist book published by Metalabel. Seu lives and works in New York City and Los Angeles.
mindyseu.com

Camila Sposati is a visual artist and researcher born in São Paulo, Brazil. She holds a Master's degree in Fine Arts from Goldsmiths College, London and currently lives in Vienna as a fellow of the Academy of Fine Arts PhD program. She published the book *Stone Theatre by Revolver* (Berlin, 2016). Her work investigates processes of transformation and energy, using methods that often come close to scientific research methodologies. She has transversely examined processes on a microscopic and global scale. In her work, Sposati juxtaposes material and historical processes in order to challenge the material in its official time and its significance. Her Phonosophia instruments address the reversibility of the role of object and subject, which questions who these agents are and what an 'object' is.
camilasposati.com

Christel Stalpaert is an activist and works, with different companions, at the Arts Department of Ghent University. She is Senior Full Professor and director of the research center S:PAM (Studies in Performing Arts and Media) and co-founder of the research network 'CoDa – Cultures of Dance.' She recently published Performance and Posthumanism (with van Baarle and Karreman, 2021) and is currently working on her book 'hyphenated thinking: performance (studies) activating ecological encounters.'

Corey Stover is an enrolled member of the Oglala Lakota Sioux Tribe from the Pine Ridge Reservation in South Dakota. He is the Vice President of the Medicine Root District Executive Board of Pine Ridge Reservation. Stover holds a Bachelors in Lakota Studies, with an emphasis in Indian Law. He is a powwow dancer and a traditional artist focusing on beadwork, currently pursuing an MBA in Sustainability with a focus on nonprofit management at Bard College.

Melita Stover Janis is an enrolled member of the Oglala Lakota Sioux Tribe from the Pine Ridge Reservation in South Dakota.

Carolyn F. Strauss (US/NL) is a curator, writer, and creative facilitator whose interests and experience traverse the fields of contemporary art, architecture, and emerging technologies, among others. As director of Slow Research Lab she has engaged a dynamic spectrum of thinkers and creative practitioners in local and international activities—exhibitions, performances, workshops, publications, and immersive study experiences—realized in collaboration with academic, institutional, nonprofit, and enterprise partners. She is the editor of *Slow Spatial Reader: Chronicles of Radical Affection* (2021) and co-editor of *Slow Reader: A Resource for Design Thinking and Practice* (2016), both published by Valiz. Since 2020, Carolyn is creator and host of the podcast *AI Murmurings* that speculates about (Slow) intersections of contemporary art and artificial intelligence. She is based in Amsterdam.
slowlab.net

Foluke Taylor is a therapist*writer, author, and co-founder of Protect Black Women. She is a British Association for Counselling and Psychotherapy accredited practitioner and currently a doctoral researcher at Goldsmiths College, University of London. Her research brings Black feminisms, creative writing, and abolitionist worldbuilding together to engage Black feminist poetics in an exploration of therapeutic possibility. Recent publications include: 'Lively up we self: A portal, some letters, and a black feminist chorus' (with Gail Lewis) in: *Black Women, Trauma and Therapy: Revolutionising therapeutic thought and practice* (PCCS Books London, 2025), *Unruly Therapeutic: Black Feminist Writings and Practices in Living Room* (W.W. Norton New York, London, 2023), 'Re-imagining the space and context for a therapeutic curriculum—a sketch' (with Robert Downes) in: *White Therapies + Black Identities* (PCCS Books, 2021), *Otherwise: Writing Unbearable Encounters Through the Register of Race* (LIRIC, 2021), *Black Paranormal: A Playlist in What is Normal: Psychotherapists Explore the Question* (Karnac Books, 2020).
foluketaylor.com

Alberto Isifin Tchama is one of the coordinators of La Voix des Sans Papiers in Brussels, a self-organized collective of undocumented people founded in 2014 that fights for the regularization of all undocumented individuals. Its members occupy several buildings in Brussels and across Belgium, turning them into spaces of struggle, socialization, and raising awareness about the violation of fundamental rights. In 2022, he co-published *Les Turbulents*, a comic book created collectively by sixteen people with Studio Baraka Grafika, exhibited at the Belgian Comic Strip Center in Brussels and supported by FRMK editions and Atelier du Toner.

Ovidiu Ţichindeleanu is a Romanian philosopher, translator, educator and culture theorist, writing on critical social theory, decolonial thought, international politics, and cultural history. Editor of the Romanian journal of contemporary art and critical theory IDEA arts + society, and collections coordinator at IDEA publishing house. Member of the artist-run cooperative The Experimental Research Station for Art and Life. Member of the Editorial Board l'Internationale Online, a confederation of sixteen museums and art institutions. Member of the Transnational Board of European Alternatives.

Rolando Vázquez Melken is Professor of Post/Decolonial Theories and Literatures, with a focus on the Global South at the Faculty of Humanities of the University of Amsterdam. Since 2010, he co-directs, with Walter Mignolo, the annual María Lugones Decolonial Summer School. He is advisor at the Jan van Eyck Academie in Maastricht, the Rijksakademie in Amsterdam and the TextielMuseum in Tilburg. He is author of *Vistas of Modernity: Decolonial Aesthesis and the End of the Contemporary* (Mondriaan Fund, 2020).

Evelyn Wan (1988) is an artist-scholar and dramaturg. She is Assistant Professor in Media, Arts, and Society at the Department of Media and Culture Studies at Utrecht University and resident dramaturg at If Time's Limited (Hong Kong). Her award-winning research reflects on historical and contemporary emerging technologies through the lens of decolonial media studies and performance studies. Recent works include research-creation project Archaeologies of AI (2018–) presented at soft/WALL/studs (Singapore, 2018), IMPAKT (Utrecht, 2024), and Hoxton Hall (London, 2024), and performance series Beyond the Shore (2023–) presented at Itoshima International Art Festival (Itoshima, 2023), Inter-Island Festival (Peng Chau, 2023), ICAS13 Conference-Festival (Java, 2024), and Hong Kong Arts Centre (Hong Kong Island, 2025). Wan lives and works in the Netherlands and Hong Kong.
evelynwan.com

Halidou Wuandaougo is one of the coordinators of La Voix des Sans Papiers in Brussels, a self-organized collective of undocumented people founded in 2014 that fights for the regularization of all undocumented individuals. Its members occupy several buildings in Brussels and across Belgium, turning them into spaces of struggle, socialization, and raising awareness about the violation of fundamental rights. In 2022, he co-published *Les Turbulents*, a comic book created collectively by sixteen people with Studio Baraka Grafika, exhibited at the Belgian Comic Strip Center in Brussels and supported by FRMK editions and Atelier du Toner.

Arkadi Zaides (1979) is an independent choreographer, curator, and researcher. He holds a Master's from AHK Academy of Theatre and Dance, Amsterdam, and has been a doctoral researcher in the Arts since 2021 at the University of Antwerp, Royal Conservatoire Antwerp (CORPoREAL research group), and Ghent University (S:PAM research unit). His performances and video installations have been presented worldwide. He has received multiple awards, including recognition from the Emile Zola Chair (IL) for his engagement in human rights issues.
arkadizaides.com

Joanne Zerdy has published on Scottish theatre and performance and co-edited, with Marlis Schweitzer, the anthology *Performing Objects and Theatrical Things* (2014). In the wake of her son Finlay's death, Joanne left academia to learn more about grief, permaculture design, and herbalism. She co-created Inviting Abundance with her partner Will Daddario to create offerings that weave together creative and embodied approaches to grief work, healing, and learning. Joanne teaches perinatal loss support trainings, facilitates a grief pen pal project, and co-teaches grief classes and workshops.

Martín Zícari is a writer, researcher, and performing arts producer. He studied at KU Leuven (PhD) and is currently Postdoctoral Research Coordinator at Ghent University. His work explores the intersections of memory, activism, and performance, focusing on affect and embodied resistance in Latin America. Recent publications include: *Afectos y violencias en la cultura latinoamericana* [affect and violence in Latin American cultures] (co-edited, Iberoamericana-Vervuert, 2022), *Affective Arrangements and Violence in Latin America* (co-edited, Journal of Latin American Cultural Studies, 2023) and *Oostende* (poetry collection, 2024).
martinzicari.com

Initiator, Graphic Design and Publisher

Slow Research Lab is a transdisciplinary research and curatorial platform that centers Slowness in contemporary theory and creative practice. Contributors to its programming include artists, ecologists, technologists, and activists whose experimental, sometimes speculative approaches to praxis challenge dominant systems or narratives, encouraging us to see the world through an expanded (Slow) spatial, relational, and temporal prism. Deeply committed to facilitating variable forms and scales of dialogue, as well as to embracing the unknown as a portal to unforeseen dimensions of knowledge, the platform aims to be a fertile, generative space both for charting new trajectories of creativity and for enlarging the boundaries of human consciousness.
slowlab.net

Haller Brun is an Amsterdam-based graphic design studio run by Sonja Haller and Pascal Brun. After graduating in Switzerland, they moved to the Netherlands where they established their own studio in 2011. They mainly work in the fields of art, design and architecture with a focus on editorial design. The work of Haller Brun is characterized by a combination of the Swiss tradition for precision and typography with Dutch directness and playfulness. It is rooted in a deep understanding of its content and based on an appropriate and strong concept. Their visual solutions are clear and effective and always refined and carefully crafted. Several of their projects have been honored with prestigious awards, including 'Best Book Design from all over the World', 'D&AD Awards' and 'European Design Awards'.
hallerbrun.eu

Valiz is an independent international publisher, addressing contemporary developments in art, design, architecture, and urban affairs. Their books provide critical reflection and interdisciplinary inspiration in a broad and imaginative way, often establishing a connection between cultural disciplines and socio-economic questions. Valiz is headed by Astrid Vorstermans and is based in Amsterdam (NL).
valiz.nl

COLOPHON

Editor
Carolyn F. Strauss

Authors
Paula Albuquerque, Kader Attia, Aïsta Bah, Scott Benesiinaabandan, Pacôme Béru, Cláudio Bueno, Derrais Carter, Raven Chacon, Joana Chicau, Guy Cools, Laura Coombs, Siobhán K. Cronin, Will Daddario, Edwidge Danticat, Thierno Dia, Mamadou Taslim Diallo, Henriette Essami-Khaullot, Silvia Federici, Mariana Fernández Mora, Ella Finer, Jem Finer, Mashinka Firunts Hakopian, Dakin Hart, Faïza Hirach, Candice Hopkins, Christine Hvidt, Carol R. Kallend, Theun Karelse, Danel Khojayeva, Suzanne Kite, Fran Kourouma, Jaron Lanier, Jason Edward Lewis, Pia Lindman, Gḷeb(s) Maiboroda, Pierre Marchand, Michael Marder, Nanako Nakajima, Florence Okoye, Marina Orlova, Jogi Panghaal, Moisés Patrício, Rory Pilgrim, Elisabeth (eli eli) Raymond, Milady Renoir, Oscar Santillán, Laurel Schwulst, Mindy Seu, Camila Sposati, Christel Stalpaert, Corey Stover, Melita Stover Janis, Foluke Taylor, Alberto Isifin Tchama, Ovidiu Ţichindeleanu, Rolando Vázquez Melken, Evelyn Wan, Halidou Wuandaougo, Arkadi Zaides, Joanne Zerdy, Martín Zícari

Project editor
Simone Wegman/Valiz

Copy-editing
Leo Reijnen

Proofreading
Erin Woshinsky

Index
Carolyn F. Strauss and Erin Woshinsky

Graphic design
Haller Brun, hallerbrun.eu

Typefaces
Lyon Text, ABC Diatype semi-mono

Paper inside
Munken Print White, 90 grs, 1.5

Paper cover
Natural Strongboard, 265 grs.

Printing and binding
Wilco Art Books, Amersfoort

Publisher
Valiz, Amsterdam, 2025
Astrid Vorstermans
www.valiz.nl
in collaboration with:
Slow Research Lab, Amsterdam
www.slowlab.net

International distribution
NL/LU: Centraal Boekhuis, www.centraal.boekhuis.nl
BE: Epo, www.epo.be
GB/IE: Central Books, www.centralbooks.com
Europe (excl GB/IE)/Asia: Idea Books, www.ideabooks.nl
Australia: Perimeter, www.perimeterdistribution.com
USA, Canada, Latin-America: D.A.P., www.artbook.com
Individual orders: www.valiz.nl; info@valiz.nl

This publication has been printed on FSC-certified paper by an FSC-certified printer. The FSC, Forest Stewardship Council promotes environmentally appropriate, socially beneficial, and economically viable management of the world's forests. fsc.org

This publication was made possible through the generous support of the Creative Industries Fund NL and the Cultuurfonds

creative industries fund NL

het cultuurfonds

ISBN 978-94-93246-46-1
Printed and bound in the EU, 2025